Stephen Morris has been a consistent fixture in New Order since 1980. The band's long career has included multiple world tours and headlining appearances at festivals, as well as a performance at the closing concert for the 2012 Olympics.

Outside of New Order, Morris has released albums and television soundtracks with his wife Gillian Gilbert under the name The Other Two, and has contributed in the studio and on tour to Bernard Sumner's project Bad Lieutenant. He is also well known for owning a collection of tanks, which he drives recklessly near his home. The first volume of his memoirs, *Record Play Pause*, was a *Sunday Times* bestseller.

FAST FORWARD

Confessions of a Post-Punk Percussionist

Volume II

STEPHEN MORRIS

CONSTABLE

CONSTABLE

First published in Great Britain in 2020 by Constable
This paperback edition published in 2021 by Constable

1 3 5 7 9 10 8 6 4 2

Copyright © Stephen Morris, 2020

The moral right of the author has been asserted.

A CIP catalogue record for this book
is available from the British Library.

ISBN: 978-1-47213-254-3

Typeset in Electra by Hewer Text UK Ltd, Edinburgh
Printed and bound in Great Britain by Clays Ltd, Elcograf S.p.A.

Papers used by Constable are from well-managed
forests and other responsible sources.

Constable
An imprint of
Little, Brown Book Group
Carmelite House
50 Victoria Embankment
London EC4Y 0DZ

An Hachette UK Company
www.hachette.co.uk

www.littlebrown.co.uk

To Mum, Dad, Amanda, Les, Flo and the Gilbert sisters

CONTENTS

PART 1:

REBOOT

I get on the 747 at JFK with the rest of my weary bandmates. Down the umbilical tunnel with its smell of aviation fuel, carrying passport, boarding pass and far too many bags.

Me and Rob start jostling our way towards the tail end, as far to the rear as we can go. The back of the bus, the place where childhood trips to Chester Zoo had once seemed such a lark.

See, it wasn't a dream

Past what might be the stairs to the exclusive and quite possibly mythical upper deck. The place with the promise of orgies. Up there a nightclub or at the very least a bar are rumoured to exist. Terry Mason, our approximation of a tour manager, claims to have seen it once, but it's a definite no-go area for the overloaded economy traveller.

We apologetically carry on pushing and shoving our way to the back of this flying charabanc. All the way down to the budget smokers' haven in the jumbo's rear end, where once the stylised illuminated cigarette is extinguished, we can spark up and cough and tipple the night away.

Seatbelt securely fastened at all times because you never know, and with our luck you certainly don't.

The screaming-engine dash down the runway. The lurch and tilt as the ground falls away

The red-eye to Heathrow.

Stuck in the middle row with the elbows of my fellow nicotine enthusiasts intruding on either side. The tiny metal ashtray half full of debris from my scratchy tangerine seat's previous fag-smoking, gum-chewing occupant. I don't care. I've just seen the sun go down on New York City.

Well, I think I've just caught a glimpse of something that looked like a Manhattan sunset through the Boeing's porthole, and that's something I never thought I'd see. I'm feeling romantic, so yeah, I don't care if it was actually only the reflection of the plane's navigation lights through the glass. I'm on my way home to my mum's Sunday special. Dried-up beef and watery gravy.

I forgo the dubious pleasure of renting the painful plastic stethoscope earphones. Tired and emotional, I'll take in the fake airline glamour and just sit here and smoke, wallow and wonder.

'Why does everything we touch turn to shit?'

Maybe I'm being a tad hard on myself there, I mean things hadn't been *that* bad, had they?

Only twenty-two. Still a young man really. I'd got myself into a fantastic post-punk band purely by my dubious ability to bang the drums in a convincing and regular manner. That band – Joy Division they were called – had gone on to make two fantastic – one might almost be forgiven for coming over all *NME* and using the old hack term 'seminal classic' – albums. Then, to use another popular cliché, 'poised on the brink of reaching the dizzying heights' of who knew what sort of success, our vocalist, lyricist and friend Ian had taken his own life.

There's more to it than that, obviously, but the bare bones are there.

That left the three of us – me (Stephen, but you can call me Steve), the drummer, Bernard Sumner, guitar and keys, and Peter Hook, known to all as Hooky, bass – along with Rob Gretton, our somewhat unorthodox manager, in a bit of a spot.

We now have more problems than we had when we began this transatlantic excursion and even less of an idea how to solve them. But we are stoic northern bastards, not the sort of folk to let a little thing like a tragedy of epic proportions dissuade us from following our haphazard path to rock greatness. Oh no!

Following Ian Curtis's suicide, we'd picked ourselves up, changed our name – well, the band's name – from Joy Division to New Order, and set out on a short tour of the east coast of America. Here we had been outsmarted by New York's wise guys, who had divested us of all our worldly goods. The greater proportion of our uninsured musical equipment had been heisted away overnight in a metaphorical puff of smoke. The last remnants of our former incarnation ripped from our grasp.

Ever get the feeling that someone's trying to tell you something? Like maybe think again, reconsider. You've had fair warning: turn back *now*. Abandon this life of darkened clubs, loud music and semi-professional late-night drinking and drug taking.

The trouble is, even though we are undeniably in the shit up to our necks, we are having such a fabulous time of it that we just laugh and wonder how much worse things can possibly get.

We have found ourselves doing the one thing we'd always dreamed of and we aren't going to give up that easily. We are awkward like that. Awkward and perverse. But better than that, we are *great*, we are exciting and, most of all, interesting to boot.

So, when this plane finally lands, more shit is going to happen.

Me and Bernard looking serious. Boston, September 1980

In the immediate aftermath of Ian's death, our biggest problem was the somewhat obvious question of what were we going to do about the, er – dare I mention it?

The singing.

A scant three or four weeks (if records are to be believed) after Ian's suicide – and still raw and numb with that rabbit-stuck-in-the-head-lights emptiness and uncertainty, that death tends to bring – the well-meaning idea arose that, like falling off a horse or bicycle, the best way to deal with the grief-struck was to remount the steed and carry on.

'It'll give them something to do. Take their minds off it,' says the well-meaning advocate, along with the old faithful, 'Life goes on.'

There is, of course, some sense in all of that but it never feels like it. Some sense and Factory Records – our artfully anarchic label – are not exactly cosy chums at the best of times.

Given the allure that tabloid tales of wild sex parties featuring popular rock vocalists could have, it is one of life's mysteries that the most difficult post to fill in the beat combo of the 1980s was that of lead singer.

I had discovered early on in my teenage attempts at starting a band that the guitarist position was *numero uno* in terms of attracting applicants, followed by various instrumentalists descending in popu-larity to bass player then drummer.

Saw players also could be hard to find, but it would always be the singers that were thinnest on the ground.

Perhaps it is the degree of exposure that's to blame. The feeling of nakedness. The musicians all have their instruments to hide behind, the singer is unprotected with only a microphone stand to deflect the gob and flying bottles of disgruntled punters. It seemed to me a little too raw and daunting.

There are no two ways about it. To the average guy, the idea of singing in public feels extremely uncomfortable.

The reality of my singing was much worse than that.

And then there was the business of having actual meaningful words to sing in the first place. The writing of music was for us, an intuitive thing, something that you just FELT, but words were some-thing that required a bit of thought. It made me appreciate just how lucky we had been knowing Ian and what we'd lost with him.

There was always another path we could take: forget the singing and lyric writing entirely.

Maybe we could become Factory's house band, a Mancunian version of Spector's Wrecking Crew? Most likely it was TV presenter and 'Factory supremo' Tony Wilson's idea that we should go into the studio with Kevin Hewick and have a go at being his backing band for the day.

Kevin was Factory's latest 'signing' (not exactly the best word to describe the relationship between the label's musicians and those in charge, but 'participant in a great experiment in social and artistic engineering motivated by a spirit of altruism and powered by praxis', although more accurate, is far too unwieldy, off-putting and undeniably pretentious).

There may have been a suspicion that Kevin was a candidate for the vacant singing spot. But we knew by then that no one from outside was going to be getting that job. Every time the idea of someone else as an Ian mk2 came up, I cringed. It was a terrible idea.

We'd gone into Graveyard Studios in Prestwich, with Factory's Martin Hannett producing as usual, to see what it felt like being a session band. The studio got its name due to its proximity to an actual graveyard. It wasn't as if we were going all-out goth: it was purely a coincidence that our future was being determined in a graveyard.

Our last attempt at working there had not ended well. Previously, it was Martin's drug intake that had caused the fuss. Stewart, the studio owner, was a bit nervy and not too keen on excessive amounts of ganja being smoked on the premises.

This was a big problem. An assault on Martin's personal freedom and liberty. Smoking pot was second nature, essential to the creative processes, and who the fuck did he think he was?

Stewart may have crossed swords with Martin before. Most studio managers in the north-west had at one time or another. A Mexican stand-off ensued with the usual northern banter.

'Fuck OFF.'

'No, you FUCK OFF.'

'No, YOU FUCK OFF.'

A spiral that ended with Martin downing tools and going home while Rob tried to negotiate some sort of cost reduction. Complete waste of a day.

Today, that was all in the past. Never to be spoken of again.

But being back at Graveyard still rankled Martin a little. Martin Hannett rankled easily.

Kevin Hewick was an easy-going sort of guy. He had good songs in a certain singer/songwritery style. They reminded me a bit of the stuff I'd done back in my folk-band days.

Kevin's songs were in a vein that Tony liked, but they weren't really us. So, we tried to make them sound like something that was.

I imagine the downside to being a session musician is that some of the time you are going to play on songs that you probably don't like that much, so you just do the best job you can. You're trying to please someone else at the end of the day. Your opinion doesn't really matter. At times this can be a good thing; playing music which, in the normal course of events, you wouldn't touch with a barge pole, can be an education. There's always something you can learn from someone else even if that thing is:

Don't ever do it again. Under any circumstances.

We did our best.

From the start it was obvious Martin wasn't that keen. There was an atmosphere of awkwardness, like a date going badly. No amount of grinning and bearing was going to resolve the feeling that we were clearly not cut out for this. Wrong time, wrong place would be my pathetic attempt at self-justification. The folky song 'Haystack' came out on Factory's European offshoot, Factory Benelux's cassette compilation called *From Brussels with Love*. It's actually pretty good. My impersonation of Hal Blaine is a bit lightweight though.

There was another song we did called 'A Piece of Fate', which somehow provoked both Martin and Bernard to flee the studio. Things had gone from awkward to difficult with Kevin's observation that our new name was reminiscent of the MC5/Stooges spin-off, 'The New Order'. This did not go down well. Bernard took umbrage at Kevin's comments and Martin just took umbrage and took off.

The version we did of 'Fate' wasn't that bad but as the recording seems to have been totally exorcised from musical history (no mean feat in this day and age), you will just have to trust me on that.

Our first attempt at collaboration had not been entirely successful, but by the end of it I was certain that we were never going to be anybody else's band.

And so it was that this slightly sorry episode raised the curtain, fired the starting pistol or whatever you want to call it, on what I like to think of as the New Order Singing Competition.

A game of three contestants, which, on the face of it, no one wanted to win.

Like the irresistible force and the immovable object, something would have to give. But just what that was still remained a mystery after our visit to the US.

Despite losing our gear, we'd picked up lots of inspiration of various kinds from our visit to New York City but nothing that directly helped resolve our situations vacant quandary.

1

GILLIAN

Gillian, Rotterdam 1980

October 1980.
Back home, weary with jet lag.

I had trouble getting out of bed before noon. We'd all suffered from this sophisticated new affliction. Bernard, always the worst of sufferers, claimed not to have slept for days. Meanwhile the restless managerial mind of Rob Gretton had been whirring away through the long, dark, sleepless nights.

I was rudely awoken by the sound of my mother shouting up the stairs, 'Stephen! It's for you! That man's on the phone again!'

I stumbled down, encouraged by the yappy dachshund nipping at my ankles, and into the kitchen, lit a No 6 just to annoy my mum, squeezed my way into the end of the seventies-style breakfast bar, and took the green plastic receiver from my disapproving parent.

'All right, Steve?'

It was, of course, Rob.

He began with the fateful words, 'I've been thinking . . .'

'. . . About the singing.'

'Oh, aye, and what have you thought?'

'Well, I wanted to ask you first, see how you felt about it.'

This sounded worrying.

'About what?'

'Well, I've been thinking . . . maybe we should get Gillian in.'

'What?!' Of all the things Rob could have said . . .

For my first thought was he was suggesting the introduction of a chanteuse.

'Yes, I think we should get Gillian in playing guitar so Barney can sing more.'

'What?! I don't know what to say.'

'I know she's your girlfriend and that . . .'

'Yes, there is that.' For it was true Gillian was my Girlfriend.

'. . . but that'll only be a problem if you ever split up with her,' he said. 'And anyway, I quite fancy her . . . so it won't be too much of a problem.'

He may have been joking about the last bit, although it didn't sound like it; I didn't see that one coming either.

Perhaps I was still asleep and it was one of those fevered jet-lag dreams.

Rob continued, 'Anyway, I think it's a fuckin' great idea. Let's ask Hooky and Barney what they think.'

'Er, right, OK, yes, that's probably the best thing to do.'

'I'll see what they're doing and call you back. You do think it's a good idea, don't you, Steve?'

'Er, I suppose so. Hadn't I best ask Gillian first, see if she's OK with the idea?'

'Oh yeah. Yeah, never thought of that.'

That was, as they say in Macclesfield (and probably everywhere else that has a bookies), a turn-up for the books.

But, thinking about it, the idea did make some sense, it would take some of the pressure off. It definitely made a lot more sense than having another singer, put it that way.

Just how to broach that question then.

I decided I'd play it safe with 'Rob wants to know if you'd like to be in the band.'

Some wimpy cop-out, pass-the-buck sort of line like that, randomly slipped into our evening's discourse at the Bull's Head.

'What's he want now?' asked my ever-inquisitive mother.

'Er, nothing,' my ever non-committal reply.

'You want to get out of your bed and do something. You'll get nowhere staying in your pit like that all day. Why don't you get up and go and do some work for your dad?'

'And why don't you read the *NME*?' my grumpy reply as I skulked back to wrestle with the duvet for another forty winks.

Although I no longer considered myself an employee of my father's tap and kitchen furniture empire, there was a widely held belief among the senior members of the Morris household that I was merely on some sort of sabbatical and that sooner or later I would retake my rightful place as a workshy member of the firm's salesforce.

In keeping with the wider-held traditions of Macclesfield, my long-suffering girlfriend Gillian had been working at Halle Models' lingerie mill as a machinist while continuing to sell children's clothes on her parents' Wythenshawe market stall at the weekend.

The Gilbert family had moved to Macclesfield from Whalley Range in 1964. Dad Leslie, mother Florence, and daughters Gillian, Julie and Kim entered 61 Gawsworth Road at the same time as I was in the early tentative throes of Beatlemania, just around the corner at number 122. I was so enthralled with Batman comics and Airfix glue at the time that I never noticed their arrival.

Les, who had been a merchant seaman, now worked in 'contruction' – an artist in the use of bricks and mortar. Florence was also a machinist; she knew her way round an overlocker, a skill much in demand in 1960s Macclesfield.

Gillian and her sisters were educated at shiny modern Broken Cross Primary. I meanwhile got my schooling done at Christ Church with its coke furnace and hymns.

Gillian's eleven-plus sent her to Tytherington Secondary Modern School, where her artistic inclinations soon earned her a promotion to Macclesfield High School for Girls. This was the female equivalent of King's School, the former place of higher learning of both Ian Curtis and myself. Though at the time I was ignorant of that fact.

Ian left with qualifications, in the form of O levels.

I got the boot at 14 for my fondness of illegal drugs.

It was while at high school that Gillian came across my sister Amanda and, eventually, me. Gillian's further education continued at Stockport College.

After finishing her HND in art and business studies at Stockport in September 1980 she was thinking about enrolling for another year's studies while filling in time at the mill.

On paper, Gillian was overqualified for the job of joining New Order. Five O levels and an A level – an A LEVEL! I might be wrong, but I don't think the band had a single A level between us.

Gillian Gilbert was a busy girl. She made me look uneducated and bone idle.

We'd been going out together for over two years, which made us an item of sorts, and Gillian had been to enough Joy Division gigs to get a pretty good idea of what she would be letting herself in for with Bernard and Hooky's Salford ways.

Our social interactions were either gig-based or, failing that, took place in the not-so-quiet corner of the pub next to the Space Invaders and the fruit machine, before adjourning back to chez Gilbert for a spot of supper and a clean-out of Gillian's pet hamster's cage. He went by the not uncommon name of Hammy. Which coincidentally had also been Ian's nickname at school.

That night, over a lager and lime, I did my best to be charming and asked how she might feel about Rob's brainwave.

As an ex-member of a short-lived punk band – the Inadequates – Gillian was keen on the idea. The allure of music played in dingy, sweaty clubs is strangely irresistible. She began planning ahead and thoughts turned to blowing the dust of her somewhat inaccurate SG copy.

'Wonder where I put that guitar?'

Rob called a band meeting in the top-floor flat overlooking the railway line in Chorlton that he shared with his partner Lesley.

Our warm-up chit-chat mostly revolved around the subject of who was still suffering the worst after-effects of the American trip and the anticipation of nice new shiny replacement gear. There's always a silver lining.

Before long, Rob began easing into the subject at hand like some Agatha Christie or Conan Doyle detective on the verge of cracking a vexing case.

'You're probably wondering why I've called you all here today. Well, I've been thinking . . . Steve, skin up!'

He continued, 'Er, where was I?' before the whistling kettle in the kitchen provided a more urgent distraction.

Returning with brews in hand, Rob started again, 'Oh, yes, like I was saying, I've been thinking and . . .'

Slowly, slowly, after a lot of skirting around the edges, joint rolling and tea brewing, Rob got around to making his case that perhaps someone could be brought into the band, not to sing, but to play guitar and keyboards instead.

He went about it mainly by smoking a lot more dope and trying to ac-cent-uate the positive benefits of this plan as much as possible.

'I reckon it'd be a good idea to get someone else in. That way you lot can concentrate on the, er, singing . . . if you could call it that. Hey, Hooky, have a go on this. It's good stuff. This'll sort your jet lag out.'

Peter Hook, never a fan of the smoking of weed, for once reluctantly acquiesced. For Rob was correct: it was indeed good gear, and an outbreak of mild hysteria was starting to take over.

'And I was, erm, thinking maybe, hmm, Gillian . . .'

Rob's suggestion was met with laughter and some incredulity.

'What, Steve's Gillian?'

'Yup, that's the one.'

More laughter from Bernard and Hooky at the sheer off-the-wallness of the idea, and at the astonishing suggestion of getting a female involved at all. We had only recently escaped the 1970s, remember.

It was obvious something needed to change. At the few gigs we'd done there'd been an awful lot of instrument juggling going on – with me occasionally swapping drums for keyboards, coupled with the fact that none of us could convincingly sing and play at the same time. Gillian's involvement could potentially solve a lot of problems.

I should perhaps explain a little about the average New Order band meeting. The purpose of these occasions was obviously to make some resolution, to reach a decision: to discuss and weigh up the options, then vote and produce some sort of agreement.

The trouble was that we weren't that good at making decisions. As time went on, we would get much worse.

Back then, youthfully indecisive, we would either agree with Rob or, at worst, say we'd think about it and then have another meeting, putting the thing off for as long as possible in the hope that it would either sort itself out or get forgotten about. If not, a show of hands would be the decider, with Rob having the casting vote in the event of a tie. An unlikely outcome now that we were three.

What Rob was suggesting was going to put me in a potentially tricky position. I had come to the conclusion that my opinion on this matter could be viewed as a 'conflict of interests' or, more accurately, 'Damned if you do, damned if you don't.' Maybe I was ducking the issue but I thought, in a futile attempt at remaining blameless, I would be better off remaining impartial and just letting Bernard, Hooky and Rob decide. My hedging of bets would become dangerously habitual.

By this time Rob's flat had become thick with the pungent fug of a homegrown haze. Stoned-ness was taking hold of everyone present.

'Well, she's your girlfriend, Steve, what do you think?' asked Rob, as he batted the ball back into my court.

Bastard.

I tried out a suggestion in what would become my normal fence-sitting manner.

'Well, why don't we give it a try? If it doesn't work, it doesn't work. I won't be very popular in the girlfriend department but at least we'd have had a go.'

The clincher from Rob and his usual last word on most things: 'Well, has anyone got any better ideas then?'

We all knew the only answer to that one.

No.

Motion carried, on a strictly trial basis of course.

Though I don't recall a specific time period being agreed. Strictly speaking, the trial period following my audition for Joy Division's earlier incarnation, Warsaw, in 1977 still hadn't officially expired.

Then there was the question of how the other girlfriends would take the news.

'Well, are you going to tell my Iris then? Eh, Rob?' asked Hooky.

'Oh yeah, and what are you going to tell Lesley, Rob?' was Bernard's considered response.

'I think Steve should tell them . . .'

The steaming kettle whistled again in the kitchen.

'Er, good point . . . cup of tea anyone?'

Think positive, I told myself. After a chain of negativity this could be a step in the right direction.

I began to fret about how best to formalise this proposal with Gillian's parents. For instance, was I supposed to have the man-to-man chat with her father outlining the band's prospects and asking permission for the use of his daughter's hands in unholy guitar racketry?

For better or worse, that sort of thing?

Fortunately Gillian's parents both had a fairly punk attitude to life and the bended-knee bit was never required.

To the casual observer, Gillian may appear the shy and retiring type.

Do not be deceived. I had seen her engage in disputes with bolshy cloakroom attendants that have turned distinctly nasty.

Take it from me, she can give as good as she gets. Asking her to check in her favourite Chinese blue satin jacket at Macclesfield's Krumbles nighterie was asking for trouble.

The poor cloakroom attendant was stunned by the emphatic rebuttal: 'No, you're not getting your hands on this! Sod off!'

You'd think she's been asked to remove a leg.

Not always the quiet wallflower you've been led to expect, our Gillian.

Gillian claimed to have met Yuri Gagarin. The first man in space. Wow. I had been an infant space enthusiast and the fascination still hadn't worn off. Her story was backed up by her mother.

The encounter had happened in Wythenshawe back in 1961. Which made Gillian a babe in arms at the time and, as for 'met', it was more like 'waved at from a distance'. Still, it was closer to space than I'd ever been.

In the Gilbert house on Gawsworth Road, surrounded by denim offcuts, well-worn sewing machines and mountains of thread, Gillian excavated her sister's genuine Bontempi organ from its under-the-stairs cupboard of neglect. Blowing off the dust, we coaxed it wheezing back to life and began to do some homework. Once I found the key widely held to be middle C we were in business.

I demonstrated what I thought the keyboard parts on 'Truth', 'In a Lonely Place' and 'Procession' were. My renditions were not met with entirely uncritical approval.

'Are you sure that's right? . . . That bit didn't sound right,' observed Gillian making notes in her pocket diary. 'Isn't it more like . . .?'

Well, I was doing my best.

Gillian put some new strings on her Inadequates guitar, which honestly didn't improve it, and we were set.

The first rehearsal we had together at Pinky's, our crumbling Salford rehearsal room, was another one of those cautious, eggshell-walking, first-date affairs. Despite knowing Gillian well, both Hooky and Bernard were uncharacteristically polite and tried to refrain from coarse language

'Pardon my French.'

And farting, even more of a challenge.

'Ooh, excuse me . . . Hooky, there's ladies present.'

A bit late-seventies sitcom, I know, but an icebreaker none the less.

Bernard dispensed guitar manicure advice.

'You'll have to cut your nails, you'll never be able to play guitar with nails like that.'

Gillian was naturally shy and understandably nervous. I felt like a go-between or translator, a bit uncomfortable.

What was I supposed to do? If it all went west . . .

It didn't, of course. Though it was certainly awkward at times.

Rob turned up later and good-naturedly took the piss out of Gillian and the rest of us for being coy. Rob was very even-handed in his piss-taking.

'You're a bunch of sexist fucking tossers. Sorry, Gillian.'

Gillian laughed. We all laughed. Laughter is infectious like that. Gillian laughed a lot.

We set about replacing our stolen equipment. I ended up with a Gretsch drum kit in walnut.

I didn't put a lot of thought into the purchase, if I'm honest. They didn't have anything in black. Not a popular colour, apparently. But it was there, now, ready to take away and there was a discount. They looked like drums and sounded a lot like drums when you hit them. And Charlie Watts played Gretsch. Sold!

I never really wholeheartedly took to my Gretsch drum kit. The walnut colouration reminded me too much of the kitchen furniture I used to sell for my father.

To satisfy my interest in producing weird electronic sounds – an obsession I'd first acquired in Joy Division – I got myself a Pearl Syncussion drum synthesiser to replace my purloined and greatly missed Simmons SDS4 synth.

Bernard had acquired a bargain but slightly imperfect Gibson 335 and a Yamaha amp while in New York, and Hooky was in the process of getting an elaborate bass rig custom made for him: an Alembic pre amp, a Roland pre amp, a delay and a Crown DC300 power amp plus Hooky's signature sound Electro Harmonix Clone Theory chorus pedal. The output of all this was channelled through two huge bass cabs. Like the cabs themselves Hooky's bass sound was huge.

We would all go round music shops with Rob and his chequebook, looking for keyboards to replace the ARP Omni string synthesiser.

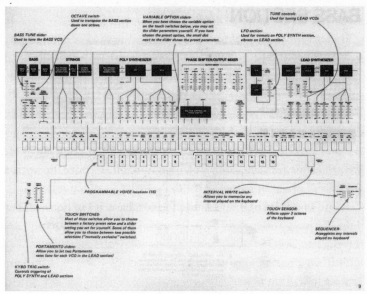

The Quadra attempts to explain itself – I love a good manual

We were after something that could reproduce the ethereal sound of our previous keyboard but with greater potential. Bernard decided the ARP Quadra was the business on the basis that it claimed to be four synths in one and that had to be a good thing, didn't it? More for your money.

For nearly two and a half grand, probably the most we'd ever spent on anything, it turned out to be not quite as versatile as the Quadra's name implied. But it did have that distinctive sound and a few other useful tricks. The main one being its claim to programmability. Not quite what you'd get away with today, but close enough for what we wanted in 1981. It was a machine with a memory. Along with the Doctor Rhythm drum machine this was our first tiny step towards some digital destiny.

New gear always leads to a burst of creativity and so it was with Bernard, Gillian and the Quadra (for it was Gillian who would end up being the

keyboard's keeper live). We replaced the kit-built Transcendent synthesiser we'd used in Joy Division with a Sequential Pro-One, which would
serve as Bernard's keyboard at very early New Order gigs.

Gillian was the right thing at the right time.

She'd never written songs before but that didn't matter. The three of us
could write music well enough: something we'd learned to do in Joy
Division by playing in a room together while Ian pulled words out of his
bag of notebooks. Rob's idea was Gillian would learn the same way we
had. In fact, it may have been an advantage that we didn't end up with
someone who could turn up and announce, 'Why don't we try an idea of
mine I've been working on?' Or even worse: 'I think it would be much
better if you played it this way instead of the way you always have.'

That would never have worked.

Somehow, a bit tentatively perhaps, Gillian fitted in. Rob added
her to the payroll and she joined us at the going rate of £62.50 a week.

She wrote down what she was meant to play in her little notebook,
Bernard dictating as though she was his personal secretary.

Gillian's first experience of the recording process and Martin
Hannett's unconventional production techniques was our re-
recording of 'Ceremony', starting what would become a New Order
habit of confusing the record-buying public.

There were now two versions of the same song: the first, recorded
as a three-piece in New York, in a green sleeve and the new Gillian
version in a white and blue sleeve. In true Factory style, sometimes
the records sleeve got jumbled so the cover isn't a good indicator as
to which version is actually inside.

Here's a tip for the confused: the New York version starts with just
bass and hi-hat, the second Gillian begins with bass, hi-hat and bass
drum. Trust me, it's simple really. I can usually tell the difference.
Well three out of five times.

We never re-recorded 'In a Lonely Place', though the two edits (well, more accurately, two different endings) would in time become yet another source of New Order confusion and fan dispute.

As well as Gillian's introduction to the fold, Rob's other big idea was that Factory should start – or should that be restart? – a club. At the time I naively assumed this would be just a follow-on from what Tony Wilson and Factory co-founder Alan Erasmus had done at Factory nights in the Russell Club in Hulme. A place for bands and local talent to play.

Lesson one: never assume anything.

In later years it would prove impossible to get anyone to own up to being the instigator of the project but, speaking for myself, I heard of it first from Rob.

The benefit of this 'club', Rob explained emphatically was, provided we were involved in some way, it would be a good way of getting money out of Factory. Rob always complained that it was impossible to get answers from Tony. Well, answers of a straight nature delivered in plain English.

Rob's problem with Tony stemmed from difficulty in knowing how many of our records Factory had actually sold. There were no reliable figures other than the ones scribbled on the back of Tony's hand in easily blurred red Pentel.

'Anarchy' and 'accountancy' were mutually exclusive. I suspect Tony would prefer the word oxymoronic. None of this was helped by the complicated mix of distributors Factory used.

I should stress here, before you get the wrong idea, that money was never a motivation for our doing anything. The idea that music could make us rich seemed ridiculous. That we could eke a living out of it at all was surprising enough.

Rob had a laissez-faire attitude to many things, but he was always good at keeping records. He liked to keep things organised and up to date.

In New Order, we continued the democratic arrangement we'd begun in Joy Division. The three of us plus Rob and now Gillian were a partnership. There seemed no reason to do anything differently. It was equal shares for all. We were all paid the same wage, and anything else would get split equally.

As an idea this is fine and dandy, very noble. I can't think of many other bands that would regard the drummer as an equal. Particularly when it comes to songwriting, but then splitting everything equally seemed like a fair way of doing things.

As long as everyone gets along and/or there's not a vast amount of money involved, the idea works fine.

Rob took what figures and records of sales he could elicit from Tony, added the receipts from Joy Division and New Order gigs, and enlisted the help of an accountant to formalise them. Make sure everything was above board. No monkey business of any kind. He always wanted to make sure that Debbie, as Ian's widow, got her fair share.

This accountant (who shall remain nameless) advised Rob that it would be absolutely fine for us carry on our monetary affairs on a cash basis: only declaring the amount of money we'd actually received instead of what might be coming down the theoretical misty pipe-line of Factory. Rob took this to be sensible advice. Accountancy being widely regarded as a sensible profession.

This temporarily got Rob off Tony and Alan's back. Now we'd got some proper accounts – official-looking blue-bound documents – we could see that New Order hadn't made any money at all.

It was true, for New Order hadn't really done anything by that time. You aren't really going to set the world on fire with the proceeds of one single, an ill-fated US tour and a handful of gigs, are you?

There must have been some cash floating around from somewhere though, Joy Division most likely. Shortly before we'd set off for New York I'd emptied my bank account and bought a Panasonic 'portable' VHS video recorder and camera, thinking I could start making movies of some kind.

Experimental and avant-garde was the genre I pretentiously envis-
aged my creations inhabiting.

'Wow.'

What's that I hear you say?

'Big deal.'

Now don't be like that, this was really something. The dawn of the
'video revolution' was upon us. VCRs weren't even called VCRs at the
time (the world wasn't quite ready for banal initialisms), they were
just plain 'video recorders'. They were still exclusive, rare items in
the 1980s. The coveted top prize on many a TV quiz show, such as
3,2,1, *Bullseye* or *The Generation Game*.

This was also at the height of the videotape format wars: Betamax,
VHS or Video 2000? The battle had been raging (as battles tend to do)
for about five years, but domestic video machines still hadn't really
caught on in a big way. They were extremely expensive. £500 was a
fortune. No wonder most sensible people would rent these luxuries.
My portable example was extremely large and very heavy, comprising
two huge boxes: a tuner and the actual recorder itself, along with a
ray-gun-shaped camera – like something out of *The Jetsons* – complete
with a charger for the machine's bulky batteries. I accepted its size as
a potential asset or guarantee of quality, as rose-tinted spec-wearing
early adopters do. I also thought carrying the thing might be a good
way to keep fit.

In truth, it was portable only in the sense that it had a handle to
pick it up with. Transportable would have been a more accurate
description and then only if you were an accomplished weightlifter.
It had a black fake-leather case and a shoulder strap barely strong
enough to heft its bulk. The battery fully charged would last for just
under half an hour. I would go out in my increasingly unreliable
Ford Cortina with Gillian on the lookout for interesting things to
film before the winking red light came on and the battery expired.

I'd inherited this interest in home movies from the unlikely source of my mother. When I was about six or seven years old she'd spotted a standard 8 mm cine camera and projector/screen combo going for a knockdown price at the local chemist's. That the camera was of Russian origin made it nearly as mysterious as where this new-found interest had come from in the first place.

My sister Amanda and I would be reluctant stars of Mum's mini movies. She would slice up strips of film with tailoring scissors and stick the bits together willy-nilly with the aid of Sellotape. A pioneering technique in the field of avant-garde Macclesfield cinema.

Once these masterpieces were completed – her editing sessions traditionally took place at the dead of night – Auntie Elsie and cousins Sue and Kath would be summoned and the back room of Gawsworth Road would be converted into a pop-up cinema. The dining-room chairs would be arranged in rows and the screen put up in front of the drawn curtains. The premiere of her work would then take place with myself the self-appointed musical director. I would crawl under the screen to the Pye record player and put a stack of 45s on the spindle: Little Eva, Chubby Checker and Elvis, usually in that order. I found it really exciting and weird; the way the music seemed to make my Mother's films seem much better. The bit I always liked best (apart from the end) was when she rewound the film and I would magically go backwards up the slide in the playground. It always got a laugh.

When we moved house my mother decided that home-movie making was a bit of a bind and the projector found its way into the micro annexe of my tiny bedroom known colloquially as the 'Fairy Cupboard'. There it lay, surrounded by an impressive pile of musical detritus until the day in 1980 when its services were once again required as part of the Joy Division ad hoc porn cinema for striking steel workers at Pinky's. An unfortunate affair best swept under the carpet. I realised there and then that I was not cut out for the job of projectionist at a dirty old man's cinema.

But video was going to be hugely important in the future, that seemed blindingly obvious to me. Nearly every science-fiction movie I'd seen featured video tech of some kind or another, and everybody seemed to communicate via TV screens, so it just seemed natural that real life would unfold the same way. Using it to record *Coronation Street* – something my mother found extremely impressive – was nowhere near advanced enough for me and, following her earlier example, I wanted to do something creative with the technology.

Jumping in feet first, with no idea about exactly what video production involved, I decided I was going to be a pioneer. I'd watched enough TV to know the camera was an obsessive liar, so getting it to twist the truth on my behalf would be simple enough. Surely anybody could do it.

It soon became obvious that with no easy way of editing these tapes together with Sellotape, my dreams of becoming Macclesfield's Stanley Kubrick were doomed to failure. Undeterred, I began carting this unfeasibly bulky item around to gigs, where I would try and pressgang someone – Dian Barton, Rob or Terry usually – into pointing the camera at the stage and pressing record. It was not met with much enthusiasm.

By anyone.

'What the fuck have you brought that thing for?'

'There's no room in the boot.'

Gillian would roll her eyes as if to say, 'You know what he's like . . .'

It was humoured as an eccentricity of mine. I soon collected a large collection of murky recordings, mostly with heavily distorted sound. If you squinted, you could just about make out someone who might be Bernard or possibly Hooky. But as to what song it was we were playing, that was anybody's guess. They all sounded like an overloaded concrete mixer.

I also began suffering with a bad back

The execution just needed a little bit of improvement, I just needed to do a bit more research. Maybe ask a professional.

Tony, being employed in the current-affairs side of TV, had installed a professional editing suite in the cellar of his home in Didsbury, a few streets away from Alan's flat on Palatine Road aka Factory HQ. So, in a continuation of the punk DIY spirit, Factory too was branching out into video.

In June 1980 Ikon – Factory's video department – was set up. A year or so later, I would spend many a dope-befuddled afternoon with Ikon's main man and Joy Division film-maker, Malcolm Whitehead, cooped up in the dark of Tony's basement learning how video editing actually worked. It was complicated and clunky. But the thought that this was going to be a big thing – an extension of music, the combination of sound *and* vision – was irresistible to me.

2

EARLY GIGS

Gillian's first gig: 25 October 1980 at the Squat in Manchester.

This was less than a month after the return from our American misadventure.

We were playing more or less the same set but with a lot more confidence. 'Procession' with Bernard singing and real drumming was a huge improvement on our earlier drum-machine version.

Bernard's singing had an honesty – he had a really good way of not trying too hard to actually sing that somehow worked.

Many of our early gigs teetered on the edge of falling apart. I kept slamming away trying to use energy to hold it together while Hooky and Bernard took the 'If you don't like it, fuck off!' tack, and concentrated on playing, lost in their own little worlds. Bernard frequently forgot the words and replaced them with ever-increasing improvised obscenities. Bathed in blue light Gillian, stage right at the Quadra, did her best to exude an air of quiet calm, with Hooky menacing the unsuspecting onlookers at the opposite side with his huge bass rig.

This was not a thing that I'd admit to back then, but I thought New Order were the bee's knees. The best thing ever. I might have started getting big ideas and all that, but all the same, that is what I truly believed. I kept my head down and drove. Well, I hit the drums as fast and furiously as I could.

As far as actual driving business went, things had taken an unfortunate turn. My wheels had let me down. The Olympic blue Ford Cortina, my then much-abused but now fondly remembered vehicle, was expiring. It coughed, wheezed and belched smoke in ways that no healthy vehicles should. The thought of my being carless was terrifying. Much like my driving.

Something would have to be done. I had places to go, people to see, gear to shift: all this hurly-burly needed regular reliable motorised transportation. We were practising twice a week in Salford and, given that the hours involved could stretch out, the train and bus timetable wasn't really a winner.

Giving the matter some thought I came up with three options to resolve this crisis.

I could resort to the slightly unreliable (but in the past tried and true) mithering method of scrounging the loan of my mother's motor. Unfortunately, she was all too aware of the state of the Cortina quietly rotting outside the front door and even the most tentative polite exploratory requests for possible aid were met with an emphatic refusal. 'The last time you borrowed it, you left it stinking of smoke and fag ends so you know what you can do . . . You can take a running jump!'

Or I could turn to Hooky for advice on the acquisition of a new vehicle in the cheap-as-chips category that was his area of expertise. That most of these motors, scavenged from scrapyards or the murkier pages of *Exchange and Mart*, seemed to be potential death traps did put a bit of a damper on that one. Plus, Hooky's use of phrases like 'just needs a new big end' or 'engine's knocking a bit' didn't exactly fill me with confidence. If he had mentioned dilithium crystals, protons and quantum mechanics, that I would have understood, but in the early 1980s nuts and bolts, engine oil and Earth-based practical mechanics were a complete mystery to me.

Or I could return to the original source of the Cortina. My father.

The Ford was still legally his. Every time I got pulled over by the bored feds in the early hours, the interrogation spiel ran thus

Flashing lights, pull over, wait while frantically hiding drugs.

Copper politely taps on window. 'Excuse me, sir, is this your vehicle?'

'No, officer, it's a company car owned by G. Clifford Morris Limited.'

Then the usual 'Where've you been? Where you going? Why have you got a pile of drums on the back seat?' line of questioning, culminating in the sternly delivered, 'If you don't want to get stopped again, I'd get that nearside brake light seen to if I were you. On your way.'

So maintaining the 'company car' deceit could have its rewards.

To execute the third option, though, I would have to resort to grovelling and at least suggest that there was a chance of the prodigal son returning to his employ. Perhaps on some sort of casual basis, let's say. I made an appointment to see my father and put forward my application for the non-existent post of part-time delivery man and errand runner. From the start, my dad knew where all this wheedling was headed. He'd seen me wheedle before and I think it amused him. He'd also seen the wreck of the Cortina mouldering outside so he knew all too well where the blatant lie was heading. Another blag from his firstborn.

Clifford was receptive to my proposition, subject of course to certain terms and conditions.

The business could afford another vehicle, which I could have occasional use of, provided it was cheap. Yes, there's always a catch. But the mouths of gift horses are best left unexplored.

And so it was that for just under £2000, a bloody king's ransom really, I waved a sad goodbye to the Cortina and found myself the part-time owner of an almost-new white Citroën G special saloon complete with starting handle. I did ask what was special about it.

'It may not be the fastest car on the road today, but nothing can touch it when it comes to stopping' was the salesman's pitch. In a few years' time, I would find out how true this claim was. But for now . . .

I was a laughing stock.

'What the fuck do you call that?'

'Fucking hell, Steve, that's not a car, it's a fucking eggbox with an engine.'

Hooky was right, for the interior of an eggbox would probably be more spacious and definitely more comfortable.

I wasn't actually sure where the engine was, now he came to mention it.

The front was my best guess, that was where all the rattling sounds came from at any rate.

I tried to improve its beige velour interior with mustard seat covers, a Christmas present from Gillian's parents. But using thick hairy twine to attach these ill-fitting bits of fabric just added to the ridicule. Gillian was embarrassed to be seen in it. She was not the only one. Only Rob could see any merit.

'It's not that bad, Hooky, at least it fucking moves.'

I kept my end of the bargain by doing the odd unpaid tap and leaflet delivery for my dad on rehearsal- and gig-free days.

Why didn't I save the loot I spent on the VCR for a rainy day event such as this? That is a question I asked myself at the time but, one way or another, money would always find a way to burn a hole in my pocket.

Beggars, as they say, cannot be choosers, but the sooner I jettisoned this cramped comedy car the better.

By the time the first few months of 1981 rolled around, we'd written a bunch of new songs, 'The Him', 'Senses', 'Death Rattle' (AKA 'Chosen Time') and 'Little Dead' ('Denial') all expanding our meagre set list.

Quite prolific really, but the music writing was a breeze compared to the struggle of the lyrics and the titles. Our morbid sense of humour led us to title each successive new composition with some reference to mortality.

The song-writing itself followed on in a similar way to Joy Division: starting with a foundation of bass and drums, recording, then jamming until we had two or three sections that worked together. Gillian took the role of an additional pair of hands for Bernard. He'd come up with a keyboard part that Gillian would play while he worked out some guitar bits or vice versa. Hooky and I, meanwhile, stuck to our respective comfort zones of drum and bassing. But sticking to what we knew wasn't going to help us move on from our past. If we were to do that some discomfort would be unavoidable. Some anguish. That nervy 'what the fuck am I supposed to be doing here?' thought never really went away. There was always the feeling that something was missing – the elephant no longer in the room.

Gillian felt it most, an outsider in our bloke-based world. She would get upset – always thinking if Ian hadn't actually died she wouldn't be doing any of this. Like maybe she was some kind of Jonah. My would-be nemesis the drum machine was also worried (if machines can worry). The beatbox that filled a gap of sorts in our brief three-piece days now only got called on to do its party piece on one song, 'Truth'. I reluctantly still played synth on that one. The rest of the time it remained impatiently waiting for love and new batteries, perched on the Quadra at the keyboard end of the room. It was mostly neglected when it came to the writing of new tunes, possibly thinking, 'My time will come' (if machines can think). And laughing to itself in sinister fashion (if machines can . . .).

By the end of March 1981 the Doctor Rhythm was popular again. Just as an experiment – I love a good experiment – we'd plugged a lead from its enigmatically labelled CSQ socket to a gate input on the Quadra, pressed play and the chattering synth and drum-machine rhythm pattern that would evolve into 'Everything's Gone Green' was born. The mechanical rhythm sounded fantastic. It was Kraftwerk on a tight budget.

The experimentation of 'Everything's Gone Green' was a turning point for us, a trip round a bend that left one bunch of problems behind us and eventually, in the passage of time, led to another lot of troubles. But hey, that was years away so let's wait till we get there, eh?

We'd returned from New York not exactly disco-dancing fools, but we'd heard a lot of interesting records in clubs and on New York radio. There was something very exciting about all the early hip-hop/rap stuff I'd heard in New York that reminded me of punk – the spirit and the energy but with a groove. That's what we had in 'Everything's Gone Green': energy and a groove. Something different.

Brilliant as 'Everything's Gone Green' sounded, it left me in a bit of a quandary. What exactly was I supposed to do on it? It sounded fantastic on its own. The gear we were using at rehearsals wasn't great and if I tried playing along to the drum machine, I soon went badly out of time, and I had to keep stopping and starting again. Hooky meanwhile continued to play more melodic riffs on the bass, something he was always fantastic at, as there was enough rhythm coming from elsewhere. In fact on EGG nearly all the melody comes from Hooky's bass guitar.

Having the acoustic drums coming in and out did turn out to be an interesting effect. But at the time I remember having a crisis of confidence. The drum machine's ability to stay in time with the synth it controlled, no matter what, began to annoy me: smug mechanical bastard! I resorted to hitting my (much quieter) drum synth in retaliation with a scowl.

Speculating over whether we could or should have done things differently in these early days is a pointless enterprise. It was all we had, all we knew, and crystal balls were thin on the ground. Today everyone is a critic and entitled to express their opinion on the minutiae of history, but rewriting the past and shedding tears while waist-deep in discarded dairy produce does nobody any real good.

The drives home after the first rehearsals were sometimes a little fraught. Taking what I thought of as my lucky late-evening route home on the A34, the sometimes too insecure Gillian would worry.

'I don't know if they like me or not.'

I would walk head first into the Gilbert trap with my ill-considered, 'That doesn't matter. *I* like you,' hoisting myself by my own petard

An indignant 'Oh, so *you* like me do you?' would be followed by an audible sigh and a tut as she tried unsuccessfully to sink back into the Citroën's tortuous pew.

My attempts to stop digging the hole I found myself in were futile. 'No, I didn't mean it like that, you know I didn't . . .'

By then it would be too late. We would continue in the awkward silence of 'you just can't win-ness' before my apology would finally be accepted somewhere around the Bollington turn-off.

I suppose the problem was Hooky and Bernard didn't know quite how to talk to Gillian. Yes, we all knew her pretty well by then but I think there was a suspicion that Gillian could turn out to be some sort of female spy or informer who would pass on incriminating information about some of the more 'dodgy' gig-based dalliances to those who must never know.

Gillian, even though she didn't approve, was not a snitch.

For Gillian practising at Pinky's was not without its perks or, more accurately, perk. Being a member of the sisterhood of machinists and overlockers meant she was entitled to access the normally locked perfumed cubicle in the otherwise rancid toilets. The ladies who worked downstairs, sewing God knows what, soon spotted her as one of their own and granted access to the special key they fiercely guarded from the unhygienic noisy boys that practised one floor up.

On hearing this Bernard became interested in how he himself might gain access to the privileged privy. The answer 'sex change and take up sewing' came as a disappointment to him.

At the early gigs, our set was usually eight songs long, just short of our entire repertoire. Eight songs was long enough, and 'leave 'em wanting more' is a grand showbiz adage.

Rob encouraged us to do more 'interesting' gigs, play unusual places: do what he called 'wacky stuff'. Our agent/promoters for most of these early shows were Kevin Millins and Colin Faver, who somewhat questionably called themselves Final Solution.

We'd met Kevin and Colin towards the end of Joy Division and they were keen to help out with our new incarnation. Kevin was always on the lookout for oddball gigs. The first of these was a proposed magical mystery coach-trip extravaganza to Bodiam Castle in Kent. A great idea that fell victim to the English weather – September's always a bit of a dicey time for an outdoor gig. A castle with a roof may have been a better bet. Kevin later tried rearranging it in a disused asylum just outside London, but the building was just too grim with an overpoweringly malign atmosphere. The sort of place that reeked of misery and sadness. Great as a horror film location, not really the place for a fun night out.

We also experimented with the idea of using quadraphonic sound. We'd used some of Pink Floyd's PA kit for Joy Division's final gigs and I knew the Floyd were big on the quadraphonic immersive sound experience. So it seemed like a good idea to push the boat out and hire the full Floyd experience (without the flying pigs). The inclusion of Martin Hannett as sound engineer for these performances was perhaps not such a stroke of genius. Let's just say Martin's stoned studio faffery did not translate well to a live environment. That there were only two of these shows (Roadmenders, Northampton, on 7 February 1981 and Heaven, our first big London gig, on the 9th) says it all: it was an interesting idea that didn't quite come off.

None of this gig playing was what you'd call 'proper' rock-band touring. None of the away-from-home-for-months-at-a-time road trips living in the back of a transit awash with booze and groupies.

Rob would turn up at the rehearsal rooms late afternoon with his briefcase and notebooks. He'd have a spliff, open a notebook and ask, 'Fancy playing Bristol a week on Friday?'

We never said no.

Pile the gear into a van and off we'd go with Terry, and our road crew Twinny and Dave Pils shifting and setting up the gear. The rest of us driving down squashed like sardines.

For the most part these were round-trip affairs with only the odd weary motorway-service pull-ins on the way back.

The rare occasions where we had an overnight stopover were a novelty for me and Gillian as we would have to pretend to be a married couple to reassure po-faced B & B proprietors that all was above board and there was no premarital hanky-panky involved in the slightest. Rob, Hooky and Bernard laughing gleefully at our obvious unease.

'And this is Mister and Missus Morris, isn't it, Steve?'

We played every show like we had something to prove. Mostly ignoring the audience, with Bernard turning into a Pernod-fuelled reluctant front person.

The arrival of Gillian stage right somehow prompted us to 'smarten ourselves up a bit', a favourite admonishment of smart Perry boy Rob Gretton.

The mostly Army & Navy look lost its appeal and something slightly classier snuck in. Hooky in particular had taken up the smart suit or at least tweedy blazer look, even wearing the occasional tie on stage. Proper shoes temporarily replaced the jackboots. Bernard stuck with smart button-up white T-shirts and the occasional tank top.

Gillian, new to the boards, immaculately made up her hair, always crimped to perfection, and wore various antique dresses purchased after long hours of perusing (I know, I was her co-peruser) in Macclesfield's Satins and Silks second-hand dress emporium. Until an argument with the shop's elderly, eccentric proprietress got her banned from the place.

Your narrator and fashion sense were still strangers to one another.

Perhaps to compensate I made up my mind that I was going to change the way I drummed. Change my 'musical' style somehow. The way I played the drums was something I'd never really thought about before. I just unconsciously did what I felt and hoped for the best.

In Joy Division I'd done a lot of busy tom-based riffs. That, I thought, should be the first thing to jettison. I aspired to take Jaki Leibzeit, the drummer from Can's advice, 'be minimal'. Easier said than done, like breaking any habit. Just as I was contemplating giving up the tribal tom-style drumming, other bands such as Adam and the Ants and Bow Wow Wow took it upon themselves to adopt it in the style of the 'Burundi beat' drum riff. 'It'll never catch on,' I seethed as they stormed up the charts.

Eventually it would turn out to be technology that changed what I played and the way I played it.

Movement, the first New Order album, still features quite a bit of Joy Division-type tom-heavy drumming ('Senses', 'Denial', 'Doubts Even Here', 'The Him' and 'ICB'), much of it masked by Martin's production. but by the second, *Power, Corruption & Lies*, I did manage to cut it down to one track, 'Murder'.

Changing what I played was a bit like giving up smoking: you know you should stop, but can't imagine a life without nicotine and disposable lighters. The ritual of the first-gasper-of-the-day rush. What could you possibly replace it with?

Maybe I should try and explore my new drum synth's potential?

Now, I wasn't the first person to have the synthesised drum idea. Kraftwerk had been doing it for years and Warren Cann from Ultravox was doing something similar.

I'd got my first drum synthesiser in 1978 – it felt like the future then, so it seemed a good idea to do more with it, now the eighties were finally here.

In time the gear that had been stolen in New York was recovered. It turned out that a gang, avaricious renegade musicians presumably, had been frequently targeting visiting British bands. They would tail the easily spotted hired U-haul truck back from gigs to the hotel where, once the coast was clear, they would help themselves to the van and its contents.

A detective who reminded me of Popeye Doyle took us to a huge warehouse where all of New York's recovered goods were stored awaiting reclamation. An Aladdin's cave piled high with booty. Every single nickable thing you could possibly imagine and some you probably couldn't. The week before, the detective boasted, they'd had John Lennon's boots in, but Yoko had wanted them back.

We sifted through this treasure trove and reclaimed whatever gear we knew was ours and some things we knew weren't but looked like they might be useful. I think we still owe the Stranglers a few bits and bobs.

My Joy Division drum synth mysteriously was one of the things that never turned up. I'd replaced it with the Syncussion, despite never having heard of one before. I liked the name though and I'd seen a photo in a magazine. It looked very scientific on its spindly metal stand. The fact it came with a nifty blue plastic shoulder bag sealed the deal. I'd always had this thing about portability. Being able to beat a speedy retreat from a disgruntled audience was always a priority.

My latest electronic gizmo, of course, worked in a completely different way to all the others I'd used up until then. I wasn't deterred. So long as it could produce wild and interesting noises – that was the main thing. It excelled at producing sci-fi sounds of ray guns and rockets along with an ample supply of clanging metallic noises.

I wanted sounds like that. Sounds that were weird and unnatural. If I wanted a natural drum sound, I could just hit a drum. The idea of a synthesiser to me has always been to make sounds that nobody has ever heard.

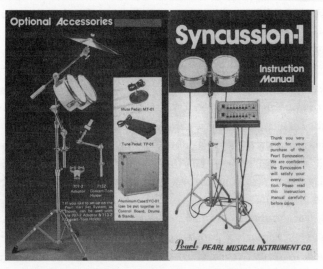

As well as a good manual, I also love optional accessories

I scoured music magazines for news of any more electronic innovations which might be useful to a technologically inclined drummer. One of these, which got great reviews, was made by pioneering British firm Simmons, so without reading all the details and small print with its frequent mention of that word Disco, I decided I had to have a Clap Trap.

The clue was in the name. The Clap Trap specialised in mimicking the sounds of, you guessed it, the hand clap (also used by Throbbing Gristle and the Human League apparently).

Following my purchase of the video recorder and my comedy car I was getting a bit of a reputation as a buyer of white elephants.

'Well, Steve, what have you bought now?' was the reaction to the machine's unveiling.

'Er, it's a Clap Trap.'

'And what does it do?'

'It makes clapping noises.'

'And why did you think that might be useful? We've all got hands, even Rob.'

'Well, I, er, um, thought . . .'

The device did not garner approval from my fellow musicians. They were immune to its charm and potential. The box would sit there clapping away to itself in what was, I finally had to admit, a particularly monotonous and annoying manner.

It could clap slowly or it could clap incredibly fast but . . . 'Steve, it's fucking useless.'

The Clap Trap did redeem itself in one unexpected fashion. Another band had begun to rent the room above ours. I forget their name. But they had a dedicated drummer who would vigorously practise on his own directly above my head. His violent thrashings would dislodge large chunks of the mildewed ceiling, which would rain down on my noggin.

He would drum for hours on end and, brilliant as his technique undoubtedly was, those in the room below could not hear themselves think while he worked.

Enter the Clap Trap, a machine which Bernard felt produced an equally annoying din. He proposed a contest of man versus machine.

We laid a PA speaker flat on its back pointing at the ceiling and turned the happy clapper on full blast, while the four of us decamped to the grim café round the corner for a brew and a butty.

On our return the monotonous automaton was still clapping away with the same robotic enthusiasm but the doubtless gifted tub-thumper above had realised he'd met his match and called it a day. We could resume our racket-making in peace.

I wonder what the Human League and Throbbing Gristle did with theirs.

3

IS THIS THE WAY?

Wondering when the next bit comes in

Less than a year after Ian's death we had a new name, a new member and about a dozen songs. A very productive period really. A transitional time. The New Order singing competition had all but resolved itself following my merciful early retirement, with Bernard taking on most of the vocalising, and Hooky still singing a couple of songs. All three of us engaged in the business of the writing of lyrics. Lyric writing, we seemed to think, was men's work.

I found two or three tins of Carlsberg Special Brew could be quite inspirational when it came to the composition of words. The deciphering of my scrawl the next morning, though, was a bit problematical. As to what these words were about or actually meant I had no recollection.

'ICB', 'Chosen Time', 'Procession', 'Cries and Whispers' mk2 and 'Mesh' mk2 were all products of my Carlsberg-fuelled scribblings. 'Sixth form drivel,' I remember was Julie Burchill's verdict on my lager-driven lyrics. A bit harsh, I thought. Still, she was qualified with words so should know drivel when she heard it. I wasn't going to argue with an expert.

We were new to the job, it did not come naturally to any of us. It had to be done, though, and nothing worth doing is ever easy.

That difficult first album.

By the time we started work on recording *Movement* in April 1981 we had all of the songs written and we were very good at playing them (most of the time). We even demo-ed the tracks before we went into Strawberry with Martin, so everyone had a good idea of how the songs would sound. But in retrospect, when I think of *Movement* it still feels like it's something awkward and not quite there yet.

Then there were problems with Martin. There were a couple of reasons for these.

Firstly, the old perennial: money! Specifically, money he felt he was owed by Factory. He was a director of Factory Records, but like everyone else involved had not seen any actual Factory accounts.

Had Martin done a standard production deal with Factory for a percentage instead of becoming a fully fledged director of the enterprise, he would, so he thought, have done much better out of *Unknown Pleasures* and *Closer*. Feeling hard done by is never conducive to a healthy working relationship. Martin had jumped ship from Rabid Records for what looked like a better deal with Factory and now that deal turned out to be not quite what he'd imagined. This problem predictably focused itself on Tony more than any of us.

Tied up with the financial gripes was the impending arrival of "The

Club', something that Martin as a director of Factory had strong negative feelings towards. What had a club to do with the making of records?
Surely a studio or at least some cutting edge gear would be a better
'investment'.

> SM (Stephen Morris): How did you get involved with, dare I
> say it, Factory Records?
> MH (Martin Hannett): Well after I invented it, I did some talent
> spotting – I got a talking head and a hitman and some groups.
> SM: This is your recipe for success?
> MH: Every time!
> MH on Factory dissatisfaction: As far as I was concerned it had
> a lot to do with my budgets which suddenly vanished down
> a hole in the ground called the Haçienda.

Secondly, there was his relationship with the band. Bernard and
Hooky had both been extremely unhappy with the end result of his
productions, and certainly his methods. Not that criticism was a
thing that bothered Martin too much.

On top of that there was the big dilemma of what he was supposed
to do with the band that used to be Joy Division but wasn't any more.
I got the feeling that he was unsure. At times, Martin didn't seem
convinced that our carrying on was really such a good idea.

Gillian had very little experience of Martin. We had re-recorded
'Ceremony' with her, which Martin had produced. But she had yet to
learn the full extent of Hannett's peculiar production practices.

Martin, in fact, turned out to be very pleasant towards Gillian. He
was polite and helpful towards her most of the time – that was
surprising. During the recording of 'Doubts Even Here' and
'Procession', with Bernard away for a few days holiday, Martin
suggested that Gillian should try doing some singing. The rest of us
had, so why should she be an exception?

With Bernard away, Martin came up with the idea that, to pep up the end of 'Doubts Even Here', Gillian should have a go at doing a spot of backing vocals.

The thorny problem of what exactly to sing was neatly solved by Rob's suggestion that we just nick a bit out of the Bible. It was out of copyright and God hadn't sued anyone lately, so a safe bet.

A bible was produced from who knows where and some extracts located at random by Rob. Gillian set about reading the selected verses. You wouldn't exactly call it singing but it sounded pretty good. Encouraged by this, Gillian then went on to do some proper backing vocals on 'Procession'. She did a better job than me anyway.

All was well until Bernard's return from his break. 'I don't like it. I've never imagined a woman singing on any of our songs.' was his considered response.

'No me neither, Barn' was Hooky's volte-face.

This was a bit of a blow to Gillian's confidence. To be fair, she had been reluctant in the first place and had only given in to Rob's persuasive nature.

To this day, the subject of Gillian's singing is one that might be described as touchy. Awkward, embarrassed silences and a general sense of discomfort from all concerned surround its mention, which is why, within New Order, it very rarely is.

As was par for the course, it was Martin's production on *Movement* that caused the most dissatisfaction. Compared to Joy Division there were a lot more electronics on the record. The Doctor Rhythm drum box makes it first appearance and the majority of tracks feature synthesisers – the sort of thing that would have suited Martin, you'd have thought. But no, the recording and mixing of *Movement* dragged on and on. It wasn't as if Martin hadn't heard the songs before. He'd done live sound for us at those gigs earlier that year – the ill-fated Pink Floyd quad sound experiment. Now back in the safer territory of the studio, he still struggled to get it right. As was to be expected it was the drummer who bore the brunt of it. On *Movement* Martin managed to reach some kind of zenith of drum-fuckery.

He had taken exception to my new walnut Gretsch kit. I couldn't really blame him. The walnut finish still troubled. Every single drum, he informed me, rattled and squeaked in a manner that displeased him greatly and was frankly hampering his efforts to achieve the sound he was hearing in his head.

'Sort it out, Steve,' he said with a grin and left me to it.

This sorting out involved totally stripping down everything to its constituent parts. A complete drum dissection – or more accurately autopsy. Every single drum head, hoop, nut, bolt, screw and washer was removed in the quest to find the source of Martin's troubling rattle. Many hours and several more reassemblies and strip-downs later, Martin found the source of his dismay.

This he judged to be the springs in every one of the drum's tuning bolts. The removal of every single one of these springs made Martin happy. Unfortunately, it also made the drums more or less impossible to tune from that day on. A small price to pay

A few years later I ended up giving the kit away to Shan – drummer with Stockholm Monsters. I've still got a box of almost forty springs that I forgot to give him. I come across them from time to time and shudder.

Maybe it was our collective lack of confidence that was to blame for Hannett's mood and the endless sessions. Despite knowing the songs well, the uncertainty never left; Martin didn't know what to do with us. Overdub followed overdub. Remix after remix. More sessions at Island and Marcus studios in London did little to improve things; Martin just got more and more belligerent; demanding more and more drugs before he would even consider starting work. In return Bernard and Hooky got more and more pissed off with him. Like an irresistible itch that begs to be scratched, things finally came to a head during the mixing of the 12-inch version of 'Everything's Gone Green' when Martin cleared off in a fit of pique and left Hooky and Bernard to finish the mix by themselves. It was the final session and the wee small hours so I had already knocked off for the night in a fit of boredom with the sniping.

Another bit of irony was that it would be 'Everything's Gone Green' that would be the first step in the direction that would later define New Order.

The song's title had arrived spontaneously as we were programming the rhythm track at Pinky's. After a few hours of button stabbing, synth chattering and drum bashing, I sat down on a rickety chair, rolled a joint and inhaled deeply. The weak sunlight was reflected off the glazing of the swimming baths opposite and diffused through the grease-smeared window of our room. Momentarily, the light seemed to me to take on a crystalline glow, giving the room an aquamarine haze.

'Everything's gone green,' I observed.

'That's good, let's call it that then,' said Bernard, who hadn't noticed my Condor moment.

Ultimately on *Movement* we ran out of studio time and patience. The problems with Martin and the general sense of uncertainty of a future without Ian – the singer-shaped hole – always meant it was going to be an uncomfortable experience. For me *Movement* is a difficult record to listen to without recalling the grief and insecurity we were feeling at the time.

It has had a lot of criticism over the years, much of it from the band. But the album's really not that bad.

Yes, there's a lot of things that we could have done differently. But that's where we were at that point: hesitant and very uncertain. From a production point of view it's a tiny bit like *Unknown Pleasures* in that the live versions of the songs had much more power, energy and conviction than Martin's production suggests.

Occasionally when I hear the odd track unannounced and unaware, in unfamiliar surroundings like a hipster boutique for instance, I am surprised at how good it sounds.

It is the sound of a band being thrown in at the deep end, treading water until we figured out how to swim.

We did our best. In hindsight – a thing which is of course completely useless – I think if we had waited a couple of months *Movement* could have been a completely different album. The next few songs we would write would really be the shape of things to come.

Movement FAC 50 might have been over but FAC 51 was lurking just around the corner along with another pile of trouble. Starting with Martin – already unhappy with Tony and Factory. The idea of Factory branching out into the leisure industry was finally a step too far for him. He turned to the law. Seeing his budgets and his bands disappearing into a void was too much.

A long, bitter and at times acrimonious wrangle between Martin and Tony, Rob and Alan ended with Martin's resignation. He launched a lawsuit to get Factory wound up. As a director he felt he was being unfairly prejudiced against.

Who'd have thought that just the idea of a club could cause so much discord?

Of course, if you look closely it wasn't so much the idea that was the problem. Factory owning or running a club made perfect sense. I couldn't argue with that, it was good idea. It was something that Manchester needed, a club for people like us. It was the scale of the enterprise that I didn't anticipate. A dancefloor, a stage and a bar are the three main prerequisites for a venue. How much could that cost? Not that much, surely. Maybe a few grand. Not much more.

If someone had said at the time: 'We are going to build a club the like of which the world has never seen. Not so much a club, more a grandiose experiment in cultural engineering and high art,' the chances are I still would still have said, 'Sounds great, why not!'

Now, had a man arrived one day with a large chain and a collection of heavy rocks and announced, 'Hi, I'm here to measure you up for

47

your own personal millstone,' like something out of a nightmarish twentieth-century version of *A Christmas Carol*, I might have got a bit twitchy and said, 'Hang on a mo'.'

But ignorance is bliss – everyone knows that. It is however no defence in a court of law – as many have discovered. We were about to embark on something Tony would refer to as: 'An experiment in popular art.'

But that was just up the road a-ways and around that bend. In the meantime, I was now sleeping well.

It slowly began to dawn on me that New Order was taking over my entire life. Driving Gillian home from gigs and rehearsals, getting lost occasionally and talking constantly about the band was something I'd grown used to with Ian.

But now the odd evenings off too would end up in some band-related blather or other. The subject of New Order was inescapable.

Which leads to another elephant-like question or is it more of a dilemma? The awkwardness of being a couple in music.

There is a wealth of opinion on this matter which says that, much like admitting women into the golf club or the freemasons, it is not a good idea. That it will not . . . nay, *it does not* work. Or if it briefly does, it always ends badly, very badly.

Being in a band is not an environment that encourages domestic bliss. Being a couple within a band is asking for trouble. I could understand the problem.

As a fan, I distrusted Yoko and John. Don't ask me why, for they did make some great out-there records together. I just didn't dig 'em at the time. It felt iffy somehow. The world view of the couple-in-rock thing really is best summed up with Spinal Tap's Janine and David: the cliché girlfriend who takes over and ruins the friendship of the two guys who've been chums since the pram.

'She's only in the band cos she's the drummer's bird' is demeaning but that's the way some saw Gillian, with me cast as some sort of chaperone or go-between with Gillian as some New Wave Trilby. To my shame, I felt in an awkward spot – a feeling I never really got used to.

I am by and large an easy-going, freewheelin' type of guy. But I have this problem with being told that I shouldn't do something. That it's a bad idea. I feel that I stubbornly have to ignore the advice, however well meant it might be.

No matter how it looked, and despite the aforementioned old-fashioned nonsensical opinions, the two of us were somehow going to have to make it work.

None of this was easy for Gillian. Apart from her obviously becoming the only female in what was formerly an all-male testosterone-driven preserve, there was the matter of what she was expected to do when it came to writing. As none of us knew precisely what that was, we couldn't exactly tell her. We'd learnt how to write by playing together and unconsciously understood how to do it. We just made it up as we went along. It was not something we understood or could even begin to explain to anyone. She too was thrown in at the deep end and expected to work it out for herself. In that respect the four of us were all in the same confused and uncertain boat.

There must have been some money flowing into Factory and trickling down to us, as we got an automotive bonus in the form of new cars for the road-legal among us.

I gladly returned my teeny-weeny Citroën to my father. Shamefully, I hadn't actually run that many errands for him.

Hooky and Bernard, recently transitioned from two wheels to four, each got matching black Alfa Romeo coupés. Sporty little numbers. I ended up with the 'group car': another bloody Citroën. This one a maroon Familiale with obligatory mustard-velour interior. It was a huge eight-seater estate car that handled like a canal barge. Very French – quirky, weirdly stylish but stubborn.

It was trouble from day one.

We hadn't got off the garage forecourt before the car caught fire. Acrid-smelling smoke came billowing out of the central air vents. A quick-thinking Gillian extinguished the blaze with a handy tin of coke.

'Yeah, it's a common fault that,' the salesman lied. 'They all do that. We'll sort it out when you next bring it in,' as though he didn't expect that visit would be too far in the future. It wasn't.

Maybe it was the brown syrupy residue from the fizzy fire extinguisher that offended the French motor's delicate sensibilities that got us off to such a bad start. Maybe it expected only *vin rouge*. But things only went downhill from there.

This Citroën would tire easily. It wasn't what anyone could call nippy and it didn't like to travel long distances. Not exactly plus points for a band in a hurry.

Stopping at the services on the way to a gig was asking for trouble. The Citroën would stubbornly refuse to start, giving not even a splutter. It would require a rest of several hours before it would even consider moving again. This resulted in it being abandoned en route to quite a few early New Order gigs.

Glastonbury 1981 was a classic Citroën disaster journey. This was an age devoid of mobile phones, so help could be a long walk and an even longer wait away.

We got stranded at Strensham services having made the mistake of stopping for a cup of tea and resting the French automobile. The Citroën had taken a dislike to the M5 and refused point blank to go any further. Each futile turn of the key produced only a tiny ping from some Gallic relay or other. It sounded more and more like a metallic '*non*' with every attempt.

Opening the bonnet and looking at the enigma of an engine did no good. It just looked back. Even Hooky, normally quite a man with motors, was stumped. Somehow we managed to hire another car and left the evil machine to wallow. We left the keys and the doors open in the desperate hope that someone would steal it.

This delay to our journey resulted in an unforeseen increase in the amount of alcohol consumed en route. It is fair to say that upon our arrival at Glastonbury's corrugated pyramid cowshed/stage Bernard was somewhat worse for wear. Inebriated or rat-arsed would be a better description.

In 1981 the amenities available at Worthy Farm were nothing compared to those of the twenty-first-century century weekend glamper. The pyramid was the ONLY stage and the fact that it was predominantly cowshed was barely concealed. What it lacked in facilities it more than made up for with the atmosphere and beauty of the location.

I doubt Bernard remembers much of that Glastonbury debut but luckily Tony and Malcolm were on hand to make some sort of visual documentary of the occasion. The storming set included Bernard taking a tumble and performing most of 'Procession' on his back.

Most of the audience were unimpressed by our performance and were impatient for the headliner – coincidentally my old faves Hawkwind – to take to the stage. The angry chanting of 'Hawkwind, Hawkwind' in the mostly silent gaps in our set did make me wonder what had happened to the old hippy mainstay of peace and love. Festival gigs are frequently chaotic and tense and unpredictable affairs, but this one was largely exacerbated by a temperamental four-wheeled machine.

The Familiale baffled many an AA man and the mechanics at the garage began to fear its inevitable return. I found the trick was to never turn off the engine, which made it quite an expensive vehicle to run.

It did have two good points: a radio-cassette player that worked and a huge futuristic ball-shaped ashtray that needed emptying only every couple of months or so. Say what you like about the French car industry but they got their priorities right with that one.

Why did we make such a misguided purchase? Tony and Alan both drove Peugeot estates and, despite his experiences in my tiny GSpecial, Rob thought this said something about the quality of French engineering. He would never consider getting a Peugeot though, in case we were accused of being copyists. So it had to be a Citroën for better or worse.

I suspect that the rest of the band, and particularly Gillian, thought that I was abusing or tinkering with the car in some way and that all its malfunctions were down to me. I felt like some kind of jinx. The same thing started to happen whenever synths or the drum machine went a bit awry. I began getting funny looks.

Glastonbury 1981 poster. I renew my acquaintance with Hawkwind.

4

TEMPTATION

Becoming frustrated with my lack of success in video production. I decided somewhat optimistically to branch out into home computers in the hope that somewhere in the wacky world of impractical computing lay a solution to the problems I was having with editing videotape and, more importantly, coming up with weird digital visual effects.

In hindsight the main flaw with most of my homemade video creations was that I tended to focus on static inanimate objects, something I could have done just as well with a polaroid or any sort of still camera really. But my ever-present gung-ho optimism told me that learning about things such as photography and lighting was so old-fashioned. Video was new and had its own rules, which I could happily make up as I went along.

'Watching paint dry' would have been a good title for most of the stuff I produced. It would have been more interesting too.

I was also building up a substantial collection of what I considered classic films taped off the TV and, of course, a selection of stuff in the 'video nasty' genre: *Texas Chainsaw Massacre*, *Spectre* and *Caligula* along with a pirate copy of *A Clockwork Orange* were particular faves. Oh, and everything I could find by John Waters, *Desperate Living* being essential viewing. These were sourced as a rule from the central hub of eighties entertainment – the dodgy corner-shop video-rental emporium.

I may have been kicked out of school with no qualifications. I may also have got the sack from a cushy job in a mill, and ended up in an even cushier job in my dad's business, and was presently looking at what my parents still thought as an uncertain future in the music business. But there was one thing of which I was certain: computers were going to be a big part of the future, particularly mine.

At the time, my old school was investing in a large computer building so turned it out they weren't so dumb after all. But why would anyone have to be taught about computers? I sniggered. I believed I knew all I needed to know.

You told them what to do and they went and did it.

Simple as that.

Massive tape reels would shuttle back and forth in the process, whirring, clicking and bleeping away. If they got a bit stroppy they could be defeated with a simple 'why?' input; anyone who'd ever watched Number Six trying to break out of the village in *The Prisoner* knew that one.

I figured I was a natural at the old computer game. So, just to get on the right side of them, I began giving them all my money. Well, the bit that was left over after the LPs, fags, booze and pot had been paid for.

At first, it was the Pong game (slo-mo table tennis with a square ball), then the relentless marching Space Invaders machine that'd replaced the pool table down the pub. I was easily led and soon became addicted and dazzled as all those zeros and ones took a fortune in loose change from me.

This one-way street of mindless joystick-jerking and button-stabbing fun, while educational in the ways of the slaughter of regimental aliens, was a dead loss in actually learning how to get one of these digital demons to do my bidding.

I would have to take the binary bull by the horns and show it who was boss.

In March 1981 I acquired my first computer. A Sinclair ZX81, bought by mail order and ready assembled. I really didn't trust myself with a soldering iron. I'd had enough trouble with the Airfix glue. The ZX81 was, according to its maker Clive Sinclair, the first of what would later become known as a 'home' computer.

Sir Clive did have a point; his machines were a commercial success and truly were many people's introduction to the world of byte manipulation.

Now that I was no longer transporting my drum kit home for the night, my tiny bedroom began to feel unusually spacious. This aberration didn't last long; very soon I was filling this void with what I thought would be the makings of my own digital laboratory.

Hearing the ding-dong of the doorbell followed by the inevitable bark of a small dog, I guessed the postman was in need of my attention. I hurried downstairs before my mother could beat me to it, relieved the postie of his parcel, which I confess was much smaller than I'd been expecting, and rushed my techno-treasure up the stairs away from prying eyes and yapping dogs.

I connected the flimsy seventy quid's worth of plastic and microchips to an old black-and-white telly I decided nobody would be watching any more, plugged a cassette recorder into the jack holes in the back and got ready to be blasted into the future.

Blast is probably not the right word for the Sinclair experience. The ZX81, with its minuscule 1K of memory, was torturously slow.

I began to pore over the manual, then spent hours tapping keys feeling immensely proud of myself when I got the 'tell me a joke' program to run successfully. It was of the evergreen 'knock-knock' variety with several seemingly random permutations.

The knock-knock novelty soon wore thin.

Surely it could do more than this? I headed for the local branch of Dixons, which had recently started selling software cassettes.

Loading games from a cassette tape was, I soon discovered, a frustrating process, ending in failure nine times out of ten, even when the programs loaded without an error message.

The monochrome snail's pace the games ran at was disappointing compared to the coloured fizz and the excitement delivered by the pub's new Pac-Man machine. Lacking the arcade joystick, the controls were much more difficult and the ZX81's monochrome sluggish alien hordes overwhelmed me every time. I doubt I ever got to level 2.

I did my best to persevere but I was young and impatient and therefore needed immediate gratification. What did I expect for seventy quid, after all? More than I'd got, obviously.

For guidance, I read more and more of the new glossy personal computing magazines that were beginning to take up large portions of WH Smith's shelf space.

It didn't take much reading to convince me that if I wanted to get anywhere with my digital daydreams, I would need something more powerful. I didn't know what that might be but I liked the sound of it.

I ended up spending even more cash (just under a grand – God knows where I got that sort of money) on a 16K Apple II Europlus and a proper floppy-disk drive (no more cassettes for me), and I began my career as a floppy-disk juggler.

As a brand Apple appealed to me. They seemed like a company founded by a bunch of teenage males living in a garage full of unpopular electronics projects. To me, that seemed a pretty idyllic existence. Their main rivals, Commodore with the PET and IBM with their PC, came across like a bunch of men in suits with an acronym fetish.

Along with the new computer, I'd got hold of a couple of add-on circuit boards that called themselves the 'Mountain Computer Music System'. Now this was more like it.

I now had something that could play *music*.

OK, it was very squeaky fairground-type music but it was a million times better than the mute ZX81. The Apple would do a passable imitation of an ailing church organ, an almost but not quite convincing jazz quartet and a fairly realistic clavichord sound with which it would perform some quaintly crap *Clockwork Orange*-type classical tunes. Not a single sound that would pass for a drum or a synth bass, but it was early days.

After a few weeks getting to know my way around the Apple, I eventually reached a stage where I could turn the thing off and on with confidence.

So I took it to a rehearsal.

We were still at Pinky's at the time. The familiar 'What the fucking hell have you got that for?' awaited.

Following my Clap Trap debacle this was the not altogether unexpected reaction it received. Even Gillian laughed in embarrassment. She had to put up with my tedious digital ramblings on an almost full-time basis.

The Apple's plaintive reedy rendition of 'Für Elise' failed to convince anyone that they were looking at the future of rock and roll, much less the future of music as we knew it. I had much the same feeling as I had grown used to in my earlier 'don't call us we'll call you' drumming auditions.

It was just a matter of time.

At early New Order gigs our equipment would often go wrong. Gillian's synth would misbehave and go out of tune. Bernard, suspecting it was Gillian's fault, would get annoyed, then angry. His guitar would bear the brunt of his fury.

It was spectacular and brilliant.

His stage patter was basically:

'Fuck off.'

'What a shithole.'

'Turn off that fucking light.'

'Turn down the bass drum.'

'TURN DOWN THE FUCKING BASS DRUM!'

'We're never playing here again, ever.'

Hooky just glared, occasionally with sympathy, before hitting a few heavily delayed and affected bass notes as punctuation in the gaps between songs.

My outlook was 'here we go again, keep playing and try to see the funny side', while Bernard got angrier and angrier with each malfunction.

I lived in dread of the inevitable post-gig autopsy/blame-apportioning ritual. I would drink as quickly as possible to cushion the slings and arrows or, more accurately, the carpet bombing.

The storm would swiftly abate with the arrival of one or two young ladies and normal service would resume.

'Hi, I'm Sandra.'

'That's a nice name. Are you from around here?'

'No, I'm from a fanzine. Why did you only play eight songs?'

'Would you like a drink?'

Thoughts of the night's disaster would dissolve as new possibilities presented themselves.

I believed that there had to be a way to make our gear more reliable. I felt that computers could do that. They could do anything, couldn't they?

I had to admit they did look fucking boring and my little rehearsal-room presentation of the Apple II had not exactly been inspirational, but by now Bernard was becoming very interested in using this new digital technology in music. Bernard has always had a great sense of curiosity about all things electrical, musical and otherwise.

Once while I was driving to a gig, his inquisitive nature got the better of him. He became curious about the combustibility of a drummer's hair. As the nearest available drummer, I became his unwitting victim.

'Can I just borrow your lighter for a sec, Rob?'

The next thing I knew there was an acrid smell and I felt an extremely unusual burning sensation on the back of my neck.

Feeling a bit bored, Bernard had set fire to my head at seventy miles an hour as a bit of an experiment. What happened was . . . my hair began to burn much faster than he imagined it would.

Luckily Rob managed to put the blaze out before it reached the top of my head.

'Fucking hell, Barney, what do think you're fucking doing?'

'Nothing. I just wanted to see what would happen.'

'You could've got us killed.'

'How was I to know it'd go up like that? It was like lighting a fucking candle. What do you put on it anyway? Petrol? I'd change yer hair gel, Steve.'

Yes, he's always been curious has Bernard. Always up for an experiment, but usually he confined them to either the rehearsal room or the recording studio.

No long after we'd finally completed *Movement*, Bernard made another innovative acquisition.

The sequencer had arrived.

The Powertran 1024 Note Composer.

Another kit-built box of tricks. This was assembled by Bernard with some help from a friend of Martin Hannett by the name of Martin Usher. This other Martin was a full-on boffin. An archetypical mad professor, he worked at Siemens. He knew his stuff! He had perfect pitch, could read circuit diagrams upside down and back to front, understood the potential of digital technology and was a professional programmer to boot.

To Martin Usher, the mighty Powertran 1024 Note Composer was some sort of clockwork toy. He modified the sequencer so that it could play in time with the drum machine and tripled its memory capacity. He was a bit like Q in the Bond films only with wilder hair.

I'd first seen Martin Usher, or at least his legs, at a King Crimson gig at the Free Trade Hall in March 1973. I didn't know who he was at the time. He was performing important electrical surgery on Robert Fripp's poorly mellotron throughout the entire show: just a pair of legs sticking out from underneath a keyboard for an hour. His contribution did not go unrewarded as he was introduced at the end of Crimson's set and received a round of applause for what Robert Fripp called 'a fine display of the art of mellotron tuning'.

The uninspiringly named 1024 Note Composer, which could only converse with the outside world in hexadecimal digits, would turn out to be a gateway to the future. And like all such portals, as I knew from my heavy dosage of sci-fi, it could lead to either ecstasy or misery depending on how you utilised its potential.

One thing was certain, though: it had not been designed to be used by a pissed-up live band playing sweaty gigs night after night.

It was a device capable of being extremely simple and baffling at the same time. Instead of simply instructing it to play song one, for instance, Gillian would have to dial in two hex numbers (the start and stop address of the pattern) by means of the eight knobs above and below the number display.

For the period in 1982 between *Movement* and *Power, Corruption & Lies*, Gillian would have to try figuring out what these numbers meant on a dimly lit stage while the rest of the band glared at her impatiently. Fortunately, if the numbers did get misdialled wrong the results could sometimes be surprisingly 'interesting' and could be fixed relatively painlessly.

Bernard would intervene, changing the numbers and consequently the pattern, and hit reset. This gave the impression that the little black box could improvise and was jamming along with the band in some way.

The ditties labelled 'New Fast' and 'New Slow'
later became 'The Village' and 'We All Stand'.

Whatever the drawbacks of the new technology when playing live, it meant that immediately after our disappointment with *Movement*, we were able to write 'Temptation' and 'Hurt'(the sequencer's debut), both fantastic experimental songs.

This pair of tunes were a mixture of jamming, primitive electro and a bit of mild psychedelia. They were both blithely euphoric-sounding tunes. That built on the blueprint of 'Everything's Gone Green' but pushed it further away from the widely perceived seriousness of our former selves. Had they been included on *Movement*, it would have been a very different-sounding record.

Martin Usher helped with the modification of a new drum machine to pal up with the sequencer. The Clef Master Rhythm was produced by a local company in Bramhall catering for the home organ enthusiast.

It was Martin Usher's synchronised pairing of this drum box and the Powertran sequencer that would be the engine of the next collection of New Order songs.

With the release of Joy Division's *Still* (a 'posthumous' collection of oddments including the recording of our last ever gig together) in October 1981, a month before *Movement* came out, I felt we had put a full stop on Joy Division. Our movement towards new technology in New Order was part of that break from the past. I began to think of Joy Division as some kind of unmanned rocket or satellite that continued to travel onwards alone through some kind of musical equivalent of darkest deep space awaiting discovery by the curious and passionate.

It didn't put paid to the questions. We got a reputation for a band that didn't do interviews. (The number-one question I still get asked in interviews is 'Why don't you do interviews?') At that time, it was mostly because we just got asked the same question over and over, like we were a band with blood on our hands being grilled by the music police.

'So why did he do it then?'

As though we'd never been asked before. As though we'd never asked ourselves that same question each and every day.

The way I felt about Ian began to change ever so slightly as time went on.

Suicide is selfish.

Towards the end of the recording of *Movement*, I raided my bank account once again to purchase another Simmons product, the SDS5 electronic drum kit.

People (optimistic drummers, mostly) said these things were going to revolutionise drumming forever. So always up for something a bit revolutionary myself, how could I resist? Even if I did think the things looked a bit naff. They were very popular with New Romantic bands – Spandau Ballet were keen early adopters – so maybe that was what put me off their appearance.

Today, if you're going to be an eighties covers band then a set of these hexagon-shaped drums shows you've done your research. Their sound is immortalised in the closing seconds of every episode of *EastEnders* on TV.

The other problem with the SDS5 apart from the gimmicky sci-fi shape of the pads was that the things were made of the same stuff as police riot shields. Although this made them undeniably durable, if not indestructible, it also made them difficult (and painful) to play.

So with the help of Dave Pils, my drum roadie, I ripped one to pieces, tore out its innards and transplanted the guts into a regular snare drum. Bingo. I ended up with a Frankensnare. Half real, half simulacra. A freak of nature. A real snare drum you could augment with an electronic sound. It was not entirely reliable, but on a good day it could do a convincing imitation of Bowie's *Low* drum sound. At the time, that was my main goal in life.

On a bad day it sounded like a machine gun with a bad case of hiccups. Despite its flakiness, I loved it, and that was how I got the drum sound that I used on 'Hurt' (more commonly known as Cramp) and 'Temptation' (and many more).

The beginning of the 1980s brought forth a resurgence of interest in one of my favourite teenage pastimes.

LSD.

Yes, friends, microdots were on sale again!

Pot and speed were the two staples of the working band – utility drugs for relaxation and stimulation as required. Not the entire band though, it has to be said. Most of us were completely clean living and some only clean living most of the time.

There was now a renewal of interest in the creative possibility of acid. In the past, my experiences of it had been either extremely enjoyable or very horrific but always very time-consuming. A trip could take a couple of days out of your life and, in a recording studio, time was precious.

The solution to this was surprisingly simple: micro-dosing, taking a tiny bit of acid each day, not enough to send you on a full-on psychedelic voyage, but enough to do ... something. Get you thinking outside the box, sharpen your concentration. Maybe this helped, maybe it didn't. It stopped things getting boring, put it that way. And it may have been partly responsible for how good 'Temptation' turned out.

The first couple of live versions of 'Temptation' were instrumental, but at Bradford University, in October 1981, Bernard did one of his first spontaneous live lyric improvisations. It was as brilliant as it was surprising, as if the words had been delivered by some uncanny alien force. Almost as if we were a lighting conductor or some kind of psychic channel.

I remember being really shocked (in a good way) at how great his words sounded. The 'up, down, turnaround' and the bit about eyes and 'never met anyone quite like you before' were there pretty much from the start. We managed to spin it out for nine minutes. It was so good I didn't want it to end.

There are some fantastic early live versions of 'Temptation' and 'Hurt' from around this time. I really like the one from the Peppermint Lounge in New York where we segued the two songs together. 'Hurt', being an instrumental at the time, was a bit awkward for Bernard, who had nothing to do for most of the song except switch the drum machine patterns, but his melodica blowing was ace.

The next single was always going to be 'Temptation' and 'Cramp' ('Hurt'). They were so good. We just wanted to get the songs out as soon as possible. The great thing about being on Factory was we could do this without the fuss and fretting of it fitting into a release schedule. We liked spontaneity or rushing in foolishly as it is commonly known.

This was also our first attempt at the record-producing game. Hooky and Bernard, I would say, found the experience liberating. Finally free of Martin's enigmatic ways, they could go about getting the sound they always felt we should have had.

If I'm honest, I wasn't keen on the idea of self-producing. I felt having a producer to act as peacekeeper/scapegoat would stop us arguing unproductively among ourselves. I was unsurprisingly but none the less democratically outvoted. As the main advocates of our new endeavour, Hooky and Bernard took a leading role. Having been the most unhappy with Martin's treatment in the past, I figured this was only fair.

So at the chilly wintery end of 1981 we trekked down to Advision studios in the shadow of London's Post Office Tower and set about the job of getting the songs down while they were still inspiring. It's interesting that on the track sheet Hooky has Rob aka 'Perfect Rob Gretton' down under the producer/musical director heading. This was probably something Rob insisted on. His major contribution to the record was the insertion of a snowball down Bernard's neck while he was recording the vocals for 'Temptation'. Yes, folks, that whoop was not a joyful exhortation. It was entirely ice-induced.

During the recording of 'Temptation', I got a bit annoyed that the drum sound didn't quite turn out the way I wanted. The slow modulation effect we stuck on the snare drum was undeniably weird and original but not in a particularly good way. The way the volume went up and down through the song sounded like a slightly indecisive drummer or a wandering microphone. Everyone else seemed to like it. We were new to the producing lark and we didn't really know as much as we thought we did.

I'd always spent a lot of time doing the drums with Martin and, painful as that could be at times, we had a way of working together. Bernard and Hooky had their own idea of how things ought to sound and didn't want to waste time while I pissed about with the Simmons triggering and other time-wasting nonsense.

Bernard mending the sequencer – aided and abetted by Gillian and Rob

Instead of just recording one long version for the 12-inch and editing it down for the 7-inch, we recorded two completely different versions of the track. This, we probably thought, was much more interesting than simply editing it down. Perhaps we felt that editing was somehow cheating. Most likely we simply didn't know how to do it.

For me, 'Temptation' is a turning-point record, a brilliant emotional rollercoaster of a song, but mostly utterly euphoric. That's why it's still great today. It's a great song despite its production not being our greatest effort.

The task of turning 'Cramp'/'Hurt' from an instrumental to something that might in a certain light pass for a song was a collaborative effort at lyric writing, though word stealing might be a more accurate description.

We'd bought a stack of books down to London and while Bernard was doing his guitar overdubs the rest of us trawled through the pages for lines that might work as lyrics.

'I am the boy you can enjoy' was filched from James Joyce, who had already nicked it from a panto – *Turko the Terrible*. 'I bet you hate this' was Bernard's sceptical addition to the cut-up phrases laid before him to sing. As was the ever-hopeful 'No more mistakes'. No idea where 'Give me give me give me' came from. Abba, possibly?

Two days later, after we had finished mixing, Bernard felt that the entire mix of 'Hurt' would sound better if it had a bit of reverb on it. This prospect horrified the studio engineers – they'd never heard such a ridiculous idea: putting the *entire* track through a reverb after it was all mixed and therefore technically finished? But to Bernard's credit it did improve things. Unfortunately we forgot to make a tape with the reverb on. We just cut the record with the effect on live and left it like that. Ever hopeful that someone else would take care of everything else.

Well, you learn from your mistakes and one of our first production errors was to take acid in the cutting room.

It wouldn't be the last.

The job of a producer has come to include many things over the years. In the early days of music production it was a more-or-less a strictly technical occupation. The 'act' was kept well away from the business end of the recording process and left to get on with the performance of the song while the producer saw to it that the best possible recording was made.

It was inevitable, though, that curious musicians would become interested in what was going on behind the glass window that separated them from the boffins in lab coats who twiddled the knobs on the red-hot mixing console. Just as inevitable was that the boffins themselves, being somewhat musically inclined, would want to come up with suggestions as to how the performance of the artistes might be improved. The natural development of this symbiosis was that the producer could at times be as important or occasionally more important than the musicians. Martin worked with us in a similar way. Legendary producers such as Phil Spector or Joe Meek ran the show and crafted a record both musically and sonically.

It was the realisation that the recording studio could be as much of a musical instrument as a guitar and some drums that interested me. Using studio effects to change and manipulate the sound ...

5

BAD TRIPS

The dystopia that Orwell had conceived in *Ninety Eighty-Four* (the book, not the year) felt like it was becoming a reality in the 1970s and early 1980s. Europe was being readied as a potential theatre for a 'limited' nuclear war and computers would obviously be involved in all this – evil computers that kept files on everyone and everything, huge machines controlled by governments who would naturally deny their existence.

There were many people I knew would go to great lengths to avoid giving away any information about themselves for fear that these electronic titans would then use it to spy on them in nefarious ways and control them with various despicable methods.

'Once yer in the system pal, that's it, they've fuckin' got ya' was the opinion widely held among Macclesfield's free thinkers and drinkers.

That most of the people I knew were pharmaceutically paranoid and also on the fiddle is the most likely explanation.

But we'd all read enough in the papers and seen enough episodes of *Tomorrow's World* and sci-fi flicks to know what was coming and that it wouldn't end well. (Although I can't actually remember one celluloid vision of the future that predicted a nation of zombies becoming terminally addicted to a fiendishly tricky game involving garishly coloured candy or fruit, much less cartoon avians with anger issues. Now that would have been a dystopia too far.)

Yet I wasn't scared. I continued my brave pursuit of how this computer power might be put to some sort of actual musical use. The best place to look, I guessed, would be the States, where former hippies were transforming themselves into the digital evangelists of tomorrow.

As luck would have it, November 1981 saw us set off on New Order's first proper US tour. This was Gillian's first exposure to the United States.

This got off to a slightly calamitous start when upon arriving at the Holiday Inn in Heathrow it was discovered that one of us had somehow forgotten to check their pockets for drugs and found, of all things, a bunch of microdots. Taking acid the night before getting on a plane for a long-haul flight to Los Angeles might not seem to be the brightest of ideas but, in the spirit of waste not want not, I did it anyway. Say what you like about budget airlines these days, but in 1981 Freddie Laker's sky train certainly knew how to make flying fun – particularly in economy. Turbulence had never been so enjoyable.

By the time the drugs finally wore off, we were renewing our acquaintance with Ruth Polsky, who was sunning herself by the pool at LA's notorious Tropicana motel. Previous guests included the Ramones, Alice Cooper, the Doors, the Stooges and a hoard of giant cockroaches. Bernard still has nightmares about the cockroaches.

Ruth was organising most of the gigs on the tour as well as facilitating free drinks and nights on the town. We also met up with her fellow East Coaster Michael H. Shamberg who was by now running Factory's New York 'office'. Michael would document our New York gig at the Ukrainian National Home in his film *Taras Shevchenko*.

Highlights of this tour were having to pull out my passport every time I wanted to buy a beer, and Terry and Dave underestimating the time it would take to drive a van from LA to San Francisco. This resulted in a good old 'who's going on last?' headline stand-off with Simple Minds. They finally relented and we ended up going on about one in the morning when Terry and the gear finally turned up. I think one or two people stayed up to see us.

The show at the I-Beam on Haight Street two nights later was a much better gig. We even got a good review from Greil Marcus.

On a sunny day off in California, we all took a Jack-and-the-Beanstalk-themed trip out to Palo Alto in Silicon Valley, the mecca for the digitally minded.

I knew all the big companies were located there and it was there, in this hotbed of tech, we ended up buying ourselves a thing called an alphaSyntauri.

This sci-fi-named object was a very early digital synth that, in conjunction with an Apple II computer, could produce any sound imaginable. This, we were told, was the hottest new thing in the digital synthesiser business, and digital meant better!

That it actually consisted of a bunch of floppy disks, circuit boards and keyboard that needed to be wired up to the Apple II before it would even think of making a sound didn't seem to faze us.

We were impressed by the sales pitch, although Rob and I were both a tad miffed on being told that our demo of the machine was taking place in a totally non-smoking environment.

Bloody Californian health freaks.

I spent the rest of the tour reading the alphaSyntauri's manuals and pretended that I understood what I'd been looking at.

Back at home, Bernard and Gillian and I would spend many late nights in the rehearsal room, scratching our heads and trying to make sense of all the gobbledegook.

It was a complicated, very slow and completely tedious process.

Pretending to understand what I'm reading

You would put in a series of numbers that represented the harmonic spectra of the sound you were hoping to make – I had no idea what those words actually meant, trusting mostly to luck – then leave it for about an hour while the computer worked out what it thought you were after.

Finally it would announce it was ready, then produce a parp or a squeak.

Compared to the instant gratification of twiddling a knob on an anologue synthesiser, the mathematical input the computer expected was as dull and boring as the sounds it eventually produced. It was as far from interactive as it was possible to get. Maybe we were doing something wrong?

We struggled with the thing for months, trying every conceivable permutation of number and harmonics, but could only coax out of the machine seemingly limitless variations on the theme of 'parp' and 'squeak'. Next to the powerful raw sounds that could be easily produced by the Quadra or the Pro-One, the alphaSyntauri seemed a weed with a futuristic-sounding name.

There was absolutely no way it could be used live in a sweaty club with an impatient crowd who had not come to be parped at.

Of course, as the alphaSyntauri's advocate-in-chief, I got the blame for its naffness. The suspicion was that I was jinxing it in some way.

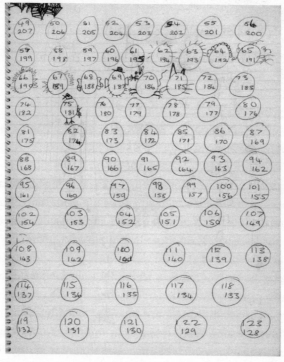

Sometimes I got the feeling that Gillian wasn't taking our exploration of Harmonic Spectra entirely seriously

Nobody could summon up the enthusiasm to discover what the problem might be, except Martin Usher, who had a few goes fiddling with the source code and just laughed inexplicably.

'Why on earth are you expecting a digital synthesiser to sound exactly the same as an analogue one anyway?' he asked.

My problem was I was always hoping to be cleverer than I was. I felt like I became a drummer mostly by pretending that I was one, and I expected that I'd be able to do pretty much the same thing with programming – just pick it up as I went along. To an extent I did, but most of it involved the sort of head-scratching work I'd run away from doing at school.

It wasn't really rock and roll, was it?

But had I ever *really* been a rock and roller?

I was an idiot: just an impatient young man who pissed about with electronic machines while reading odd books about science fiction, Aleister Crowley and sympathetic magic. I finally admitted to myself that perhaps I was barking up the wrong tree.

The alphaSyntauri got put back in its many boxes and was finally stuck under the bed.

Not long after our return from the States, the maroon band transportation vehicle decided it'd had enough of life in showbiz. Travelling back up the M1 from a gig with just me and Gillian aboard (by this time nobody else would risk travelling in the vehicle) the Citroën put on a fine display of what it did best, which was stopping. To avoid piling into the back of a line of traffic, it decided it would show it's surprising prowess in the emergency-braking department. Which was not exactly what its driver had intended or expected.

You know the slow-motion sensation you get in emergency situations: relief that the vehicle has managed to stop at all, then the few seconds of unnatural silence as a quick study of the rear-view mirror reveals the horror about to unfold from behind. Crump follows crump followed by yet another crump.

There's nothing quite like being the lead car in a thirteen-vehicle pile-up.

The now slightly shorter than it had once been triumph of the

French motor industry ended up being hauled on the back of a recovery vehicle, which dumped it at a garage somewhere in Birmingham.

'Looks like a roight off that, mate,' was the mechanic's assessment. It didn't look that bad to me. If you just ripped off several panels from the car's rear end it would have been right as rain in a Mad Max kind of way.

'You won't be gittin' howm in that heap.'

By the time we'd settled up for the tow, the pair of us were skint.

With a suitcase in each hand, I introduced Gillian to the ancient art of hitchhiking.

She wasn't keen on the idea but with no change for the phone we weren't in any position to beg for help.

So we made the best of it and trundled on as Gillian bemoaned my driving skills. 'I told you to slow down,' said in true Stan and Ollie 'another fine mess' fashion. She did have a point.

We got to Hilton Park services without too much difficulty, just as it was getting dark – then the rides dried up.

Finally we got a lift to Knutsford services where to our surprise and amazement we pulled up at exactly the same time as a Salford Van Hire truck containing our gear, Rob and Bernard. See, they'd rather squash into a hired Luton than risk another trip in the Familiale. The wonders of synchronicity.

We piled in, a tiny bit squashed, but we were saved.

Sadly, it was not the last we would see of the Citroën. It turned out to be a lengthy repair job, by the end of which Rob had passed his driving test and the car became his. It lasted a few months more before finally expiring outside Strawberry at four in the morning in a lake of green suspension fluid – the final act of a terminally depressed *voiture française*.

I resolved that in the future I would follow Martin Hannett's advice and only drive cars of Swedish manufacture.

'Good crashing car, the Volvo; acres of metal and heated seats' was Martin's channelling of Jeremy Clarkson.

6

DOES NOT COMPUTE: THE HAÇIENDA

Hang on, didn't you mention something about a club?

Whatever became of that idea then – that grand scheme of Rob's to raise money by extracting it from Factory and Tony's clutches?

Throughout all the aforementioned thrills and spills of songwriting, recording and gigging there had been the bubbling undercurrent referred to by all as 'The Club'.

Whenever it was mentioned I still had an image of somewhere small, dark and dingy, a smoky room with a stage at the end and a bar at one side. Say club to most people in eighties Britain and a similar image would enter their heads too.

That's what clubs were like in them days. Mostly.

During Rob's rehearsal visits he would ask, 'Do you want to know what's happening with the club?'

From the way that he said it, you could tell that what was coming next would probably not be good news.

From the first, it all sounded a bit odd. The location was to be in a building on Whitworth Street just around the corner from Joy Division's old rehearsal space at T. J. Davidson's. On my way down to Joy Division's Sunday rehearsals, I would wait at the traffic lights and look at one of the buildings.

International Marine, said the white and blue sign. Those two words fired my imagination and I was eight years old again watching puppet adventures on TV. International Marine conjured up an amalgamation of *Thunderbird*'s International Rescue and *Stingray*'s Marineville.

'Ever wonder what goes on in there?' I'd ask Ian. Underneath were the words 'Yacht Showroom'. 'How the fuck does that work then? A yacht showroom in Manchester?'

I imagined the building's interior as an enormous swimming pool in which a small fleet of vessels floated, awaiting inspection by seafaring types.

'How do they get them in there? I mean they can't sail 'em down Oxford Road, can they?'

I had no idea that boats could be transported by road or even that there might be a canal adjacent to the building. Back then, Manchester's waterways were another world. A refuge for unwanted prams and other household detritus. Maybe even the odd barge, but they weren't part of the city I knew.

The lights would change and we'd be up the stairs at T. J.'s revisiting last night's X-rated flick.

I'd never be in the market for a yacht, would I? So I guessed I'd never find out what went on inside International Marine's building.

'You know that place on the corner of Whitworth street?' Rob went on. 'The end near Central station, down from the Palace, across from the City Road boozer.'

'Is it near to where International Marine used to be?'

'Yeah, that's the place. It's going to be in there.'

Now I knew that yachts took up a lot of room – I'd been to the seaside a few times – especially if they were floating in the enormous purpose-built swimming pool of my imagination. So when Rob said 'in there' I guessed that he meant in a basement of the building or a nice cosy corner perhaps.

'Tony's speaking to Saville about designing it.'

'Well that'll never happen then, will it? Not in our lifetime.'

Occasional Factory director and designer Peter Saville's reputation for tardiness had become the stuff of legend and was a long-running band joke. It was not entirely undeserved.

Peter, possibly fearing the ribbing and grief he would get if the project were to be subject to lengthy delays or possibly because he had something better to do, passed the job on to an acquaintance of his, one Ben Kelly. Peter handed over the project with the buck-passing covering note that Ben had done similar things before and would be much better at it than he would.

I revised my mental image of this club. It was still dark and dingy but it looked like it had been furnished by Habitat – angular piny chairs, probably with elaborate ashtrays.

'So this Ben Kelly, he's done clubs before, has he?'

'Er, mm . . .' before moving on to other news. 'Well, apparently he's done Lulu's bathroom.'

Some of Rob's 'other news' could be a bit surprising, confusing or at the very least disquieting. Let's hit pause for a second and take a stroll down the potholed thoroughfare they call 'Memory Lane'.

Following Ian's death and Joy Division's ongoing success at record selling with its knock-on effects on the fortunes of Factory records, Tony felt like some sort of special reward was deserved, like a medal or a commemorative stamp or some-such. A carriage clock for example?

Possibly fearing the design and creation of such an item would have been too costly and time-consuming should Peter Saville become involved, Tony went for a more abstract form of reward for our labours – the corporate enticement of shares in the company. Now here's the thing – we interpreted this apparently symbolic gift as something that would, in the spirit of the three musketeers (and D'Artagnan) be ours. Rob on the other hand took a different view. As we were but simple musicians perhaps it would be best if he treated this intangible booty as solely his. Trouble was, and it would turn into trouble eventually, he never told us this at the time. What difference did it make? The shares were worth fuck all anyway. This was Manchester not Dallas and Rob was not JR Ewing.

What was the problem? Money was coming in from somewhere. The record-buying and gig-going public would be my guess. We weren't exactly rolling in the stuff but we certainly weren't starving either. I didn't give much thought to whether this coin had been earned by Joy Division or New Order. At the end of the day, it was all one and the same thing wasn't it? As long as Ian's widow Debbie got her fair share, it didn't seem to make much difference.

The crumbling rehearsal room by Broughton Baths in Salford seemed to be entering some terminal stage decay, almost as if it was beginning a process of self-demolition. Our half of the room (by the window through which light struggled to pass) was always untidy and ramshackle like a student squat. The other half, inhabited by A Certain Ratio, always had a more organised look about it. The dividing line was a curious-looking pillar – an indication of an ill-advised and poorly executed 'knock-through' at some point in the building's chequered history.

At the far end, beyond Donald's drum kit, was a small step that led to an open cupboard of gloom full of empty flight cases which in turn led to a mouldy, hellish version of Narnia. Mould was growing from each corner of the ceiling, and the pillar was the centre of a pentagram of cracks and fissures.

Probably best if we got out of Pinky's before the place came down upon our heads.

We put our foot on the property ladder and became owners of a single-storey stockroom, now surplus to the requirements of the North Western Gas Board. It was in a no-man's-land at the back of a row of shops on Sandy Bank Road in Cheetham Hill.

Rehearsal studio in Cheetham Hill ready for a nuclear winter

The building's principal advantages were a small car park, a large drive-in loading bay and easy access to Woolworths and a dizzying array of fast food. A mere stone's throw away lay a Spud-u-Like, the Jolly Roger chippy and the jewel in the crown, a KFC! Now this was living the high-calorie good life. It even possessed a sink with hot and cold running water!

Our Factory label mates could now have all that mouldering space at Pinky's to themselves while we moved into a swanky place of our very own.

Even the most imaginative estate agent would struggle to describe the building without including the word bunker. That is how I came to think of it; a good place to spend a nuclear winter. It was a long, low, squat building adjacent to a disused church, and a large abandoned graveyard extended right up to our back wall. As the building was lower than the cemetery, technically we were on the same level as the dead. Which did make the place feel creepy at times. Sometimes very creepy indeed.

The band tend to the graves on the other side of the wall

On the other side of the wall, the graves themselves were in an advanced state of decay, long neglected and overgrown, and most had been vandalised over the years. Many of the funereal monuments bore graffiti daubed on with a brush, much of it commemorating the Munich air disaster of 1958. 'Busby Babes Live On 58' was heavily featured alongside the ever popular moronic, racist glyph, the badly drawn swastika. It was a peculiar area only a few yards away from a busy street but somehow totally disconnected from it.

As this potential studio was discreetly concealed behind a row of shops, its privacy also made it a convenient place for the working girls to carry out a bit of business.

Returning through the little ginnel shortcut, hands full of baked potatoes, chicken and chips, I often stumbled (literally) across a bit of hastily improvised 'how's yer father'. Embarrassing for all concerned, as you can imagine. I would turn on my heels, beating a hasty retreat with a 'oops, er, very sorry' and go back the long way round past Woolies.

'Are they still there?' was Hooky and Bernard's overenthusiastic response to my shocking news.

'Let's just go and have a look ... best make sure she's, er, they've gone ...'

Despite the hookers and the decaying mortal remains, the building was a considerable improvement on our last place. New recruit Mike Cauldfield, Terry and Twinny had soundproofed the place and transformed it into something that looked a little bit like the bare bones of a recording studio.

Rob would later lay claim to having participated in the building's remodelling but according to Mike this only amounted to the partial painting, in pillar-box gloss red, of an old metal desk left by the previous occupants. Rob apparently fancied this as a possible place of work. There's nothing like having your own desk – besides being a good place to put the phone, it projects an aura of efficiency and reliability. Rob never completed this not particularly demanding task and the desk ended dumped in the loading bay.

'Don't chuck that desk out. I'm going to finish off painting it one day. It'll look fucking great when it's done.'

This became another of the many things Rob never got round to doing, like getting fit and taking up karate.

The building's downside was (like most recording studios) its lack of windows. Illumination came by means of that most modern of methods in the early 1980s: the track-mounted row of coloured spotlights.

Bernard is very particular about lighting. From the earliest gigs we did as New Order we employed a youthful gentleman by the name of Andrew Liddle to take charge of the lighting. He's still got the job today – remarkable considering how frequently he is admonished by Bernard from the stage. But Andy is *very* good at his job.

'Turn that fucking light out, Andy' became a staple of Bernard's stage banter. Another quip was 'Andy, what's that fucking cabbage doing on the back of the stage?'

At rehearsals, Gillian and I, usually first to arrive, would turn on a couple of lights – enough to read by. Hooky, next to arrive, would turn the rest on for the full Boots the Chemist harsh glare. Bernard would without fail turn up last, sit down and wince.

'Can you just turn a few of those blue lights off? They hurt my eyes.'

Then: 'Steve, can you turn off those green lights? They're giving me a headache.'

Until, with a tut, he'd get up and turn off the few remaining white bulbs off . . . then on again . . . then off again . . . and so on for the rest of time.

This happened whenever we rehearsed, regular as clockwork, and it still goes on today.

Maybe Bernard is nostalgic for the power cuts of the 1970s. More likely it's just a manifestation of his natural artistic temperament.

Part of the problem was the fact that the only natural light in the building came through a series of small rectangular skylights in the ceiling (until even these were blocked off following frequent break-ins). It was easy to lose track of time as we played. It was a functional space though not particularly inspiring, it has to be said. We invested in a new four-track reel-to-reel tape machine and a sixteen-channel TAC mixing desk, the secrets of which soon became Hooky's responsibility and area of expertise.

As a band, we were increasingly self-contained.

Entry was a complicated procedure. Pinky's had a single padlock attached with screws to its rotting door. Cheetham Hill, on the other hand, had a sophisticated alarm system. Gaining access involved nipping across the road to the phone box, ringing the alarm company, reciting an easily forgotten code along with a precise time of entry, then dashing back across the road, opening the reinforced steel door, and remembering exactly how to disable the alarm before the bell went off and the old bill arrived. The boys in blue were frequent visitors.

'What goes on in here then?' was always the initial line of enquiry.

'You a band then?'

'What you call yerselves?'

The build-up to the evergreen 'Never heard of ya!' punchline. Meanwhile, other major construction work was taking place down the road at 'The Club'. This continued fitfully and, it would eventually turn out, extremely expensively. I don't think any of us had been invited to see the goings-on at the place for some reason.

'It's just a building site, there's nothing to see really.'

Or 'Tony's got the keys.'

Distant alarm bells began ringing when Rob, in his regular news round-ups, came out with, 'There's a bit of a problem at the club. The fire brigade say the balcony needs rebuilding.'

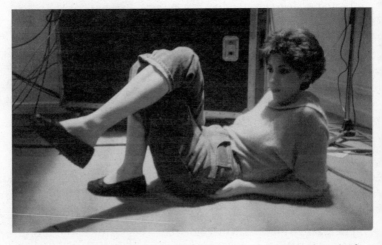

Gillian relaxing at Cheetham Hill. Looks quite nice inside, doesn't it?

I was having a very difficult job recalibrating my mental image of a dark little Habitat-furnished club to incorporate a *balcony*. But then I remembered that Images, one of the finest nightspots of my Macclesfield youth, used to have something that could be classed as a balcony. In reality, it was more an elevated platform than anything. Pissed-up punters would regularly injure themselves tumbling down the metal spiral staircase. So maybe it wasn't that bad. But still, it was the first time this B word had been mentioned.

'Any chance we could er ... have a butcher's, Rob? It'd be interesting.'

As a former Images regular I considered myself well placed to proffer advice on potential balcony difficulties.

Rob, slightly reluctantly: 'If you want.'

What was going on at the end of Whitworth Street was not a total mystery. Donald Johnson and Martin Moscrop from A Certain Ratio had seen the place. They'd even been inside with Tony.

'Have you seen the club? It's fucking mega, s'going to be ace,' was Donald's verdict.

That sounded encouraging but nothing beats seeing with your own eyes.

I arranged to meet up with Rob and Tony the next time we came through town on the way to rehearsals. Pulling up outside, I said to Gillian, 'I've always wanted to go inside this place, see if they've still got the enormous swimming pool – the one they used to keep the boats in.'

Gillian gave me one of her doubtful looks.

'All right, Rob.'

'Tony's just parking up, it's through here ...'

Rob ushered us through the door and into a cavernous space littered with construction debris. It was freezing.

'Wow, it's fucking huge. Is this where they kept the boats?'

'How did they get the water in?'

Rob, never a potential yacht owner, had no idea.

Tony Wilson appeared at the other end of the chasm.

'All right, darlings, what do you think?'

'It's fucking massive, Tone. Whereabouts were you thinking of having the club exactly, down in the basement?'

Tony did his seal-like laugh and spread his arms.

'No no, darling. This is the club! You're looking at it.'

The words 'does not compute' flashed somewhere inside my head as my jaw hit the cold concrete floor.

I'd been in smaller cathedrals.

'Ah, you had me going there for a minute, Tony. You're taking the piss, right?'

'No, he's not, Steve,' affirmed Rob. 'This is it.'

'What, all of it?'

'Yeah, come and have a look at the balcony up here. It's fantastic,' was Tony's encouragement.

Words failed me. My imaginary dingy nightspot vanished in a puff of recently rolled smoke.

'But it's fucking enormous, the heating bills must be phenomenal.'

'Look at the view from up here on the balcony. Isn't it great?'

My fear of heights kicked in so I took Tony's word for it.

'Any truly revolutionary act or idea has at some stage or other been unthinkable,' Tony said.

I was flabbergasted; surely this was some sort of dope-fuelled nightmare from which I would soon awaken?

If only.

It turned out, initially at least, that I was absolutely alone in having doubts about the club's viability.

Killjoy Steve!

Bernard and Hooky, who it has to be said had been in a lot more discotheques than me, initially thought the club was a great scheme.

Though with some reservations.

The main one being did anybody at Factory actually know what they were doing?

We thought we were partners in this enterprise and as such we wanted our input to be taken on board. Money was being spent and some of it was more than likely ours (Joy Division's or New Order's? Who would ever know?) so our curiosity was justified.

And so a grand tradition was established, one that later became known as the 'Haçienda crisis meeting' but was for now just called 'discussions about plans for the club'.

Tony and Alan had recruited Howard 'Ginger' Jones (no, not the singer with a penchant for half-naked men miming being in chains) to be the establishment's manager and Rob's friend Mike Pickering, recently returned from a spell living in the Netherlands, was in the frame as a DJ.

One of our ideas that came out of these brainstorming sessions was that it would be a really bright move to have the place open six or even seven days a week. It seemed daft that most clubs only opened at weekends. Think of all the extra profit they were missing out on by not doing this one simple thing, the fools!

My input in the good idea department was the club should have some screens or a few tellies (yes, I was still a video bore) like the clubs we had seen in New York.

The club was to be called 'The Haçienda' – Tony's idea, nicked from 'Formulary for a New Urbanism' by Ivan Chtcheglov, a Situationist fave of his. (By the way, if you happen to speak Spanish and are wondering why Haçienda has a cedilla when it normally doesn't, welcome to the world of Factory Records.) Young Ivan had in his time planned to blow up the Eiffel Tower and ended his days in 1998 in a mental institution, coincidentally just a year after the club finally closed its doors. But let's not get ahead of ourselves here and spoil the surprise.

31 May 1982.

The great and momentous day arrived. Three weeks after 'Temptation' came out and after many meetings, much delay and additional emergency expenditure, the club was opening its doors for the first time. Trouble was, just because those doors were open didn't necessarily guarantee access to those with ... let's just say a vested interest.

'Nah, mate, yer not coming in. Invitation or members only tonight, sorry bud.'

That was not the way I expected to be received on the opening night. Not that I was expecting the red-carpet treatment. It would have clashed with the décor.

It felt like another rerun of Warsaw's attempt to get to play the last night of the Electric Circus.

'OK,' I squeaked before conveying the bad news to Gillian.

'Don't they know who you are?' she enquired of me.

Bernard Manning's Dressing Room

That possibility had crossed my mind but I thought I'd allow the doorman to let a few more of his mates in before I brought it up.

'Look, there's Tony. Tony! Tony . . . Tony! TONY!'

Tony disappeared.

'I don't think he heard you.'

It was Gonnie Rietveld, in charge of the door for the evening, who finally came to our rescue.

'Welcome to your club,' she said and ushered us in to join the small crowd milling around on the other side of entrance. Those who weren't looking for a drink were just looking bemused.

'It's magnificent, but it's not what I expected' as Bosquet might have said.

For it looked nothing like anybody's idea of a club, or a music venue, or even a bar come to that, prompting the usual gestures of uncertainty:

'I don't know, what do you think?'

'Do you know where the cloakroom is?'

'Where is the actual dancefloor?'

If it did nothing else, it got people thinking.

That's quite an achievement in itself.

It was painted for the most part in pigeon blue with reflective safety bollards surrounding what may have been the dancefloor and yellow-and-black hazard stripes emblazoned on industrial steel pillars. The dancefloor was a slightly raised area just the right height to confuse the unwary or tipsy. It was an accident waiting to happen.

The Haçienda looked more like an art gallery than a nightclub. The main bar was at the far end of the huge ground-floor room and the stage seemed to be an afterthought: a black slit in the middle of the right-hand wall.

I asked Ben Kelly many times why this was and I still don't quite understand the answer.

The sound system was appalling, and the amount of daylight streaming through the glass roof did nothing for the ambience, which on the opening night gave the place the welcoming atmosphere and cosiness of a Sunday afternoon in a B&Q DIY superstore.

'There's still a fair bit needs doing,' said the supposed manager 'Ginger' Jones.

'The sound system is a bit shit,' understated the DJ Mike Pickering as someone else put 'Anarchy in the UK' on the decks. It sounded like somewhere in the distance Johnny Rotten was singing into a bag of rusty nails while gargling iron filings. In other words, to call the sound system 'a bit shit' was being extremely kind.

'You're not wrong there, Mike,' I concurred. 'You're not wrong there.'

What I did marvel at were the two large video screens suspended from the ceiling either side of the letterbox stage. On these club VJ Claude Bessy (hidden in his tiny side-stage bunker) projected clips and the output of the astronomically expensive Chromascope video synthesiser. 583 quid was an awful lot of money in those days. Unfortunately, his struggles to produce psychedelia for the 1980s were no match for the sun's rays streaming through the glass roof. They rendered his visual outpourings all but invisible to the naked eye.

I know it sounds unlikely – bright sunlight and Manchester not being exactly synonomous – so perhaps we could have been forgiven for not seeing that one coming too.

It was only one of the myriad items on what the modern property renovator would call a 'snagging list'. At the time, it was an 'enormous cock-up list'. Just a tiny bit more money would have to be spent.

How much money had been spent up to that point is open to question. The answer seems to be continually revised as the years go by, possibly to allow for inflation. But somewhere the wrong side of quarter of a million pounds sounds about right. So *a lot* of money.

Just for fun, we can do some 'How much would that actually be today?' type calculations. I reckon around two million. See if you can beat it!

Rob summed it up in 1982.

'The idea was considerably cheaper than it turned out; it did look absolutely brilliant, especially when it was empty.'

Which it was for a long time.

Fellow club owner Bernard Manning, the ironically booked seventies comedian doing the opening turn, gave his considered opinion.

'I've played some shitholes in my time but this is really something.'

That was a *bit* harsh, I thought.

What was the big idea behind the Haç again?

Simply to open a club for the likes of us.

A place where we could all go, and get in without having to wear smart clothes and a tie.

That hadn't worked out for me so far at the Haçienda, but I have got one of those faces.

Clubs at the time mostly fell into two categories: dives in dodgy dark basements designed for late-night drinking and fighting; or the Stringfellows type of dazzling *Saturday Night Fever* discotheque for the smartly dressed, tie-wearing man and the white stiletto-wearing female.

There were notable exceptions, mostly around musical clans (Pips, the Roxy, Wigan Casino, etc.), but nothing like the clubs we'd been to in New York. They were a mix of everything and everyone.

Like Joy Division looking forward to writing the next song, which would be better than the last, Tony wanted the next idea, the next project, to be grander and 'more Factory' than the last. Factory was never really just about records or communications, it was always about the future and what it could do there.

The Haç was like one of those 'wouldn't it be great if . . .' stoner discussions full of grand ideas, mad ideas. Yeah, the Haç was one of those. A mad idea.

The Haçienda felt to me a leap too far into the dark. An idea that could be sustained only as long as there was something coming in from outside to sustain it.

Aesthetically and ideologically, it was a work of genius.

Commercially, a return ticket on the *Titanic* would have been a better investment.

Ignorant of this, our collective all-for-one-and-one-for-all spirit of adventure could extend its life. But once you begin to rely on creative (or more aptly speculative or imaginative) accounting to make things look better, you're sunk.

For me, the worry was that we had bitten off more than we could chew or even comprehend entirely. A simple idea that had become grandiose and over-elaborate. But in the punk tradition of anarchy and fuck tomorrow, I stuck with it. For as long as we were all in the same boat there was some sort of security and democracy. Some strength in numbers. We were all in it together.

Tony could always convince us that, however bad it looked, there was really nothing to worry our little heads about.

We were, after all, still friends.

It was much more about doing something new, something that changed things, than turning a profit.

In the same way that I had with Ian and his illness, I still thought everything would be OK.

What naive optimists drummers are at times.

We all instinctively understood music. Tony, Alan and Rob didn't create any, but they knew a good song when they heard one.

FAC 51
THE HAÇIENDA

THE STATE OF PLAY AFTER TWO WEEKS AWARENESS.........................
APPEARED.

E.S.G. Bernard Manning, Cabaret Voltaire,Eric Random, Teardrop Explodes,
23 Skiddoo, Vic Godard & Subway Sect.

APPEARING.

		MEM.	GUESTS.
Tues. June 8th.	John Cooper Clarke & Group.	2.00.	3.50.
Fri June 11th.	James King & The Lone Wolves.	2.00.	3.50.
Tue. June 15th.	Orange Juice.	2.00.	3.50.
Sat June 19th.	Culture Club.	2.00.	3.50.
Tue. June 22nd.	Defunkt & Higsons.	2.00.	3.50.
Sat June 26th.	New Order. Free to Members. No Guests.		
Tue June 29th.	52nd Street & Swamp Children.	1.50.	2.50.
Sat.July 3rd.	Funkapolitan.	2.00.	3.50.
Fri July 9th.	A Certain Ratio.	2.00.	3.50.
Wed July 14th.	Echo & The Bunnymen.	2.00.	3.50.

OTHER LIVE DATES WILL BE INCLUDED SO WATCH M.E.N FOR DETAILS.
ON NIGHTS WHEN NO LIVE ACTS APPEAR, THE FOLLOWING ADMISSION PRICES
APPLY. MONDAY TO WEDNESDAY, MEMBERS FREE, GUESTS £1.00.
THURSDAY MEM. £1.00 GUESTS £1.50.FRIDAY MEM £1.50 GUESTS £2.50.
SATURDAY MEM £1.50 GUESTS £2.50.

FLIES IN THE OINTMENT...

It has become apparent since the opening of the Hacienda that the
sound system we have is not sufficient for the size of the building.
We are correcting this by adding to the system and perhaps treating
the roof with acoustic baffling.

IDEA'S BOX...

If you have any wonderful and bright idea's or complaints about the
club,write them down and hand them in at the reception or post them
to the club. This is your right!

VIDEOS..

We have had many requests for different videos, so we have decided to
ask you to submit your own tapes. If you bring your master piece to
the club, with your name, address and membership number written on
it, we will have a look at it and maybe show it. All your tapes will
be returned. The best tape we see each week will receive a free ticket
to the concert of their choice at the Hacienda,so don't delay, and
enter this exciting competition now!

CONT'D.

Flies in the ointment

But opening a club the size of the Haçienda wasn't the sort of
thing you could do intuitively and just make up as you went along.
Which is what we did. We were making costly mistake after costly
mistake in the execution of this social experiment. Who knew it
could get so convoluted, with so many people involved?

Our grand idea of opening every night was a complete failure.

Gig nights worked. Put on a band that people want to see and they'll turn up wherever it is – that much we knew from the Factory nights at the Russell Club. But the rest of the time when it was an infant-revolutionary-try-anything, club nights were hit-and-miss.

Mostly miss.

The music though, when you could hear it, was always great. The sound system was never perfect, but over time did get a lot better. That became Hooky's pet project. The DJs played stuff that wouldn't get played anywhere else and hot new bands wanted to play there.

So what if the Haçienda was losing money? At least it was losing it with style. So long as we were happily gigging and making music that people wanted to buy, all would be well.

The initial costs, if you're interested, were Contracts sum – i.e. doing the place up – £194,910, sound and lights a staggering £72,051 plus the rent came out at £300,602.23. I'm not sure where the 23p came from.

7

ALWAYS READ THE MANUAL

The house I shared with my parents and sister in Macclesfield became a more and more transitory space. I was arriving while they were departing and vice versa. Conversations with the rest of my family usually began with 'What time did you get in last night?' when they actually meant that morning. My post-sunrise arrival was now accepted as a matter of course.

I did my best to persuade the other residents to stay out of my bedroom in my absence, which of course aroused my mother's suspicion as to what mischief I might be getting up to in there. My room was by then becoming home to all manner of sensitive electronic equipment and gizmos connected together in the haphazard, ramshackle way that I went about connecting most things.

It didn't take long for the word to spread on my mother's grapevine.

'I don't know what he gets up to these days, since he's been in that band. He's got a ruddy computer, cameras and all sorts in there! It's like bloody Jodrell Bank.'

This disturbing news naturally piqued the interest of the wider reaches of the clan and before long I began receiving visitors. Auntie Elsie and Uncle John with my older cousins Kath and Sue in tow were the first to knock.

'Can we come in? We've come to see this famous computer thing you've got.'

It was a tight squeeze. I could only admit two room inspectors at a time for reasons of health and safety.

With my audience standing elbow to squashed elbow I turned on the ZX81 and after several abortive attempts at loading finally managed to get the 'Tell Me A Joke' program to run.

'Ooh look, Kath, it says "Knock Knock". Do I have to talk to it? Who's there?'

'No, Sue, you just press that key there.'

'Lettuce,' said ZX81.

'Oh, look. Lettuce who?' as Sue pressed the same key again. The computer responded with its regular punchline:

SYNTAX ERROR.

'Lettuce Syntax Error? No, I don't get it Stephen. Is it one of those weird jokes that you like?'

They left me to my own devices with an only mildly ironic 'It's marvellous what they can do these days, Stephen, it really is.'

They didn't ask to see any of my video creations either. Memories of my mother's home movie afternoon teas still lingered.

All of my time was spent either with the band or with Gillian, and in either situation the topics of conversation were very similar. Gigs, gear and songs mostly. Well, entirely.

It was New Order 24/7, there was no getting away from it.

This was the one thing that I hadn't anticipated when Gillian joined: thinking and talking about Rob, Hooky and Bernard became a full-time occupation.

I began spending more and more time at Gillian's house on Gawsworth Road, becoming in the process inevitably better acquainted with the rest of the Gilbert household.

Both Gillian's parents were younger than my mum and dad, and I found we had tobacco in common. My dad's four-cigar-a-night habit I considered more an affectation than a proper nicotine commitment.

Florence, Gillian's mother, was a full-time smoking professional but father Les staunchly stuck to the only-after-sunset regime.

As émigrés from Manchester, it's fair to say they found some of Macclesfield's ways a little peculiar.

Les had led an interesting life. Following his compulsory National Service in the Army Catering Corps, he'd run away to sea and joined the merchant marine to see the world. Broaden the mind with travel and ship scrubbing.

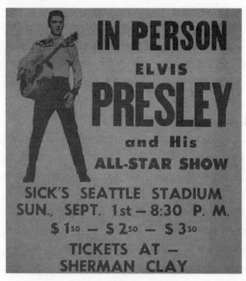

Worth jumping ship

Les's globetrotting came to abrupt end when seeking treatment for an ear infection he'd picked up in Japan. He unsuccessfully tried to find a doctor at the next port of call but, following a lengthy misunderstanding of the workings of the American medical system, Les found his ship had sailed, abandoning him in Seattle.

That this took place at exactly the same time as Elvis was in town playing at the rather unfortunately named Sick's stadium is one of life's curious coincidences. Who would pass on the chance to see the King? Sadly, though, the local feds got hold of him – Les that is, not Elvis – and finding his story suspicious, locked him up in the local jail, pending further investigation.

A shame really, for in another of life's curious coincidences one James Marshall Hendrix was also doing his best to get to see the King perform in Seattle. Jimi Hendrix and Les Gilbert – I'd have loved to have seen how that one worked out if they had gone into partnership. Hendrix and Gilbert, it's got a nice ring to it.

Following his spell in the glasshouse, Les was deported and told never to darken Uncle Sam's door again. Gillian worried that her father might still be on the FBI's records and that in time, she too would be pulled in and denied access to the so-called land of the free. Guilt by parental association. It can happen.

Les, now finding himself landlocked, took to building – life on the hod as it's known. In the process he learned the black art of JCB operation before finally becoming a sort of artisan whose speciality lay in the field of concrete construction and manipulation. With a bit of grit, sand, cement and water, anything was possible.

Concrete was his métier. There was nothing Les couldn't do with the stuff. His car was fixed with a dob of concrete on the back axle, and he once fashioned a fish tank from the material, a treat for his daughters Gillian, Julie and Kim. The fish, did not survive for very long in this alien and slightly toxic environment. But Les had done his best. If the fish didn't like it, it was entirely their fault.

So, Les was a doer who would turn his hand to any practical or entirely impractical task. This as well as working the market stall. He was also fond of the music of Tangerine Dream.

My first experience of Les the builder was his Gawsworth Road loft-conversion project. Gillian's minuscule bedroom was getting overrun with records, sewing machines and stock, in much the same way as my own room had once been full to the gunnels with vinyl, cymbals and drums.

Les's solution was to expand upwards. He would simply knock a hole in the ceiling and turn whatever was up there into a new living area for his eldest daughter. It'd be like having her own flat, he said.

This was in stark contrast to my own father who, although in possession of a theoretical knowledge of plumbing and building, was clueless when it came to the actual practical doing of things. That he left to someone else.

'Always get a professional,' was Clifford's advice.

He knew, for instance, that the most likely cure for a leaky tap was a new washer. But as to what this washer might look like and how its replacement might be put in place he was at a dead loss.

Les, on the other hand, was not averse to the random disassembly of things.

'Always turn off the stopcock first,' was Les's advice.

That said, he wasn't usually a safety-first kind of man. He had a cavalier disregard for building regulations and authority in general. When I asked if the council would be OK with his structural alterations to his home: 'You don't want to get involved in any of that bloody rubbish. Who's going to sodding tell 'em anyway?'

I could kind of see his point. But surely the people next door would cotton on that something was amiss with all the banging and timber deliveries? I kept that thought to myself.

Les, on hearing of mine and Gillian's latest news on the band and the Haçienda shenanigans, would offer advice based on his long experience as a man of the world.

'You know what you want to do with them silly sods? You want to tell 'em to sodding sod off! Give us a smoke, Flo.'

It didn't take him long to transform the loft into something vaguely habitable. A great deal of sawdust and offcuts of plaster board were generated in the act of this transformation, which never completely lost Les's hallmark of a perpetual work in progress. I'm not decrying Les's skills here, for he showed a great deal of imagination and did a much better job of hammering and sawing than I could ever do.

I would manhandle keyboards and amps up the rickety wooden steps to the new Gilbert penthouse and, as the sun and draught streamed through the Velux windows Les had inserted in the building's roof, we would read the manuals and try to figure out how they worked.

The computer, though, was never admitted to this realm. Despite my acquisition of a graphics card and a painting software package called Painter Power, which I thought might appeal to Gillian's arty nature, the computer left her cold.

'What's it for? I mean, what's the point of it? You can draw just as well on a bit of paper with some crayons.'

She didn't trust me and my endless digital ramblings. A bit of the good old Macclesfield scepticism I knew and loved had rubbed off.

'It'll never catch on.'

Gillian's distrust of the computer as a creative tool is one that has never gone away. To this day she will shy away from using one to create or record music. She gets all analogue purist and pines for the heady days of the Dolby-less cassette recorder. But as a means of sending cryptic notes and cute pictures of animals to people who she doesn't know from Adam, she finds it is an absolute godsend.

Compared to strumming a guitar and banging some drums and cymbals, programming the drum machine and the sequencer was something that required thought and patience. It was definitely not an instinctive or even intuitive process. It replaced Hannett's baffling method of drum recording as time wasting par excellence in the wider New Order vocabulary, i.e. that of the people who weren't actually doing the button pushing.

I may have said it before and, if I haven't, I'm pretty sure I'll be saying it again: programming is *not* a spectator sport. It is a one-man job requiring, as I was finding to my chagrin, patience.

Following on from 'Hurt', we got on a roll of writing ideas for tunes in the Cheetham Hill bunker, based around a sequenced bass line, with the drum machine doing a basic pulse that I would embellish with live drumming. Songs like 'Ultraviolence', 'We All Stand' and '5-8-6' were, like 'Temptation' and 'Hurt', usually live jams of indeterminate length or order. Sometimes brilliant, occasionally dire, depending on the level of 'inspiration' and equipment behaviour on the night in question.

The way it started to work and the shape of things to come in terms of programming a song went like this: Bernard would have an idea, then with the help of Gillian as his unwitting assistant or amanuensis, he would try and coax the sequencer to play something like the idea in his head. I would attempt to translate his boom-crack-boom-crack rhythmic description into something the Master Rhythm drum box might understand, more often than not getting it slightly wrong, sometimes in a deliberate attempt at improvement. Hooky would put the kettle on and leaf through this week's 2000 AD on his chair at the mixing-desk end of the room – symbolically the opposite end to that of programming. He would stick it out as long as he could, offering advice as to how things could be improved or, even better, sped up, before realising he was beat and either going home or suggesting we did something else instead. Hooky always believed in the more spontaneous method of riff composition, something he was always fantastic at. He would multitask at rehearsals, playing bass, working the desk and controlling the tape machine.

Once the sequence and drum machine had been programmed, we would jam around them until we had something that sounded like the basis of a song.

Rob would turn up sooner or later with his maroon Samsonite briefcase and notebook with offers of gigs. A couple of spliffs and the regular dose of even-handed piss-taking were the precursors to the unveiling of the briefcase's contents.

'Someone's been on about some gigs in Scandinavia. How do you feel about a trip to Sweden? I've always fancied trying a sauna.'

Or:

'Anybody fancy a trip to Italy? I keep getting mithered by this Italian bloke. Now I know the food's going to be a problem but . . .'

La Dolce Vita

Travel broadens the mind and we were nothing if not broad-minded.

The sunnier the destination the better, that goes without saying, but we were game for any place that we could get to play our eight-to-ten-song set to paying customers.

That was the whole point of writing new stuff, to see how it went down live.

26 June 1982.

The inevitable happens and yet another New Order tradition begins.

The Haçienda gig! No. 1.

A month on from the shambolic opening of the club we found ourselves doing the first of many shows at the place.

The hometown gig spectacular. It's Manchester: you've got to do something special.

In these early days of the New Order live experience we continued the practice handed down from Joy Division of not deciding which songs to play for a particular night's recital until the last possible minute. The hastily scribbled setlist would be doled out literally as we were stumbling on to the stage.

This one would be a tad different. In the pursuit of doing that special thing that Manchester craved, we did that most un-New-Order-like thing. We indulged in a smallish bit of forward planning.

'Let's do a segue.' But which songs? And in which order?

Hang on, Stephen. What is this segue thing exactly?

Glad you asked. Just in case you thought I was showing of my knowledge of musician-y words, it is the playing of a collection of songs without interruption – mixing smoothly from one to the next without pause – much like Jive bunny or Stars on 45, remember them? Sorry to remind you – let's continue . . .

The great advantage of deciding the set list minutes before playing was that it gave proceedings a sense of urgency, of spontaneity or, more accurately, gave us no time to ponder, to dither and um and ah about stuff. Just get on and do it, and leave the verdict till later.

The decision on which songs to segue shouldn't have been that difficult. We'd done 'Everything's Gone Green' and 'Temptation' or 'Hurt' and 'Temptation' mixed together, and both of those combinations worked. But this time we'd go further and add another song: the three-song jamboree. So, newcomer '5-8-6' got included on the short list.

Phew, that was simple ... but which order should we sequence them?

To me, it obviously had to be '5-8-6'–'Temptation'–'Everything's Gone Green'. But I'm pretty sure we tried every possible combination of those three songs before arriving back at the one we first thought of.

Still, not too painful.

Then a further elaboration or innovation (depending on which side your bread is buttered) presented itself.

'You know the video screens at the Haçienda? Well, wouldn't it be great if we did some video that would fit with what we were playing? They could show that on the screens!'

Or:

'Hey, Pandora, what's in the box?'

Whoever actually first came up with this idea is lost in the mists of time but there are two suspects: me or Bernard.

Whoever it was, I would have definitely pointed out to all concerned that it would be a bit of a long drawn-out process, a road full of pitfalls and convolution. I'm pedantic like that.

In short, it would be fucking boring to bring this simple idea to fruition.

But hey, it was a challenge and an interesting experiment, and we all love those don't we? I certainly do. There was also the little matter of the shortness of time available: a week or less to get everything done.

How times had changed when we used to write a song in a day.

First of all, we would need a recording of the track to cut this potential cinematic masterwork to.

So, following the rehearsal at Cheetham Hill where the foregoing was decided, Gillian, Bernard and I set to work.

As '5-8-6' was still kind of a jam, we figured if we did something that was more or less the right tempo, the right length and with the right beat that would be enough to edit some visuals to match.

We recorded twenty-two minutes of the drum and synth backing track to '5-8-6' with added delays and filtering in places where it got a bit boring. On its own it sounded pretty good but it was really just a template, not a proper finished track.

The next day the three of us – Bernard, Gillian and your humble narrator – shut ourselves in the dark basement of Tony's editing suite in Didsbury along with Ikon's Malcolm Whitehead plus a pile of cult shlock VHS tapes. Inspired by the William Burroughs method of cut-up, we began to set these to music.

There were bits of 2001, *Apocalypse Now!*, *Alligator* (a forgotten classic in the reptilian horror genre) and other bits of tenuous video stuff I'd shot or rented. It was, as predicted, very slow going.

Why had we recorded twenty-two minutes when there was no chance we could edit a video of that length from the snippets we'd got? Exuberance, I suppose. We gave up – with a yawn and a that'll have to do – after we'd managed to edit together about four minutes.

We were all quite pleased with the results.

The more eagle-eyed of you may notice that there was one person still missing from this bout of tedious Cecil B. DeMille-type activity: Hooky.

Why was this? To be honest, I think we all thought that it was going to be such a boring bit of work that he wouldn't really be into the idea anyway. Maybe I thought Bernard had told him what we were doing and Bernard thought that I had.

Either way, none of us thought we were doing something behind his back. Unfortunately, that was not the way Hooky saw it on being informed of our cinematic labours at the Haçienda soundcheck. He was extremely upset with what he felt was a slight on him by the rest of us.

New Order was the four of us doing stuff together at the same time, not three of us going off without him. He felt excluded. He was very unhappy about the whole thing.

With the benefit of hindsight (here we go again), he was probably right: we should have told him what we were doing, but I never thought it would be such a big deal. I was very surprised, embarrassed and a bit taken aback by his reaction.

We promised that we'd never ever do it again. Honest.

Over the years, the track now known as 'Video 5-8-6' or 'Prime 5-8-6' has become some sort of art thing rather than the musical accompaniment to a man being eaten by an alligator, which is always how I remember it.

Once we'd all apologised for our reckless thoughtlessness and repaired the damage that carelessness had caused, the gig at the Haçienda fell apart after the second or third song when the power went off.

After shoving another few grand in the metaphorical Haçienda electricity meter, we resumed our set and, despite the appalling sound that the layout of the place actively made worse, it all went swimmingly.

'Loved it, darlings,' gushed Tony afterwards, 'especially the alligator video!'

Gillian's mum Flo, on being introduced to TV's Mr Wilson for the first time, endeared herself to him with the words, 'I like you on the telly, Tony, but now that I've actually met you I can see why a lot of people don't.'

Gillian's father Les pointed at what he considered the still half-finished-looking architecture.

'What bunch of sodding cowboys did you get to do this for yer? They were having a laugh. You've been bloody robbed.'

8

A TECHNOLOGICAL INTERLUDE

There had to be an easier way to get this technology I'd been collecting to do something that was useful and hopefully not too divisive.

If computers could get a man to the moon then surely they could knock up something handy to a gigging band, no problem.

My computer programming skills, I figured, weren't quite there yet but I was certain if I persevered and read enough books on bytes, peeks and pokes, it would eventually come good. But as to how or when, I was still clueless.

The trouble with early 1980s music technology was it didn't have a great business model. How could it? No one could figure out exactly what it could do. Where the profit might lie.

An accountant would have just come straight out with 'Sure, it's a nifty idea, all right but will it sell? Who's going buy a box that sounds like a drummer? Not drummers, that's for sure. They never need plugging in. Once guys like Ringo cotton on to what we're up to, they'll be after us with blazing torches and pitchforks.'

But for a bright young lad keen on the inner workings of a Z80 microprocessor and eager to get ahead of the times, one smart idea could be a game changer. If you could just think it through.

At the start of the 1980s, something game-changing did actually come along and it fascinated me: the Roland TR-808. A drum machine that was incredibly easy to program. Even if its poorly translated manual was a bit impenetrable.

One look at the device and with a little imagination you could understand its inner workings.

Roland TR-808

OK, maybe not completely understand. But suffice to say that the 808 had a chain of flashing lights that moved from left to right in time to the beat. A constantly lit LED meant a sound would be triggered at that point – elegantly simple. Someone with no musical or rhythmical knowledge at all could come up with something cool in a matter of minutes.

It was intuitive and inclusive. In the same way that punk and new wave had opened a door for bands in the seventies, so the 808 unveiled a whole new world of possibilities. A whole new kind of music. Yet its sound was still in the grand tradition of the Wurlitzer organ and earlier Roland-type rhythm machines (like our Doctor Rhythm):

unrealistic and synthetic. I thought this was a good thing. If you want a real drum sound, just hit a real drum.

When it was first launched the 808 was not a great success and it wasn't seen as a great step forward. Mostly because it used analogue technology and in the eighties this was beginning to be thought of as old hat. But the TR-808 grooved in way that no soon-to-be extinct dinosaur should.

IT SEEMED TO BE ALIVE.

It invited you to press its coloured keys and twiddle its tiny dials. It wanted to play with you. It was a comic-book machine.

A work of art.

Eventually it would turn out to be the sound of the next generation. It launched whole new genres of music that, without its sound and accessibility, would never have existed.

Meanwhile, another musical marvel was waiting. One that would become the most important thing of all to me. Its origins lay in the ongoing struggle between record producers, engineers and the bane of their lives.

Drummers!

The recording of a drum kit is, as I had discovered with Martin Hannett, a fiddly, capricious and time-consuming process. The more drums that are involved the worse it gets. Microphones have to be positioned, drums have to be tuned, damped or removed. Squeaky pedals have to be de-squeaked. It could take hours, sometimes days to get a good sound.

Then there came the matter of getting the drummer to perform satisfactorily, possibly the hardest part of all.

By the time the hours of fruitless pounding spent searching for the perfect sound are declared over, the drummer probably hates the producer, the engineer and the rest of the band, who he holds responsible for his torment. That loathing is generally reciprocated by all concerned.

Surely there had to be a better way?

But better for who exactly?

Sometime around the end of the 1970s, rock perfectionists (of an occasional jazzy bent) Steely Dan were in New York embarking on the time-consuming process of making their seventh studio album, *Gaucho*.

At the core of Steely Dan was an American musical virtuoso duo, Walter Becker and Donald Fagan, who wanted only the very best session musicians in their quest for sonic and musical excellence. This, of course, meant they went through quite a few drummers in the process.

'Not quite what we are after. Sorry.'

Only the best will do. The shamed drummer skulks out of the studio swearing 'Never again!' as he spits on the unwelcome mat of the New York studio floor.

'Next!'

These were top-line session players, the crème de la crème – Hal Blaine, Bernard Purdie, Steve Gadd – all rhythmic royalty. None of your rubbish.

But Steely Dan they wanted more.

If only there was a machine that could be programmed to play a beat that actually sounded exactly the same as a really good drummer playing a real kick drum and a real snare drum. They didn't want any of the knicky-knacky-knoo ping sound for which analogue drum machines were known, reviled and in some cases loved? They wanted the real deal, no compromise. A human sound without the human drummer's frailties.

By chance, the engineer they were working with at the time, Roger Nichols, was some kind of computer whizz kid.

'Sure that's possible,' he allegedly said on hearing their frustration. 'I could do that, I just need a hundred and fifty thousand dollars.'

A nice round number.

In six weeks he wrote the code that gave birth to ... Wendell, the computerised session drummer that didn't waste time, tell bad jokes or smoke dope.

Meet Wendell

The fact that it could (allegedly) take up to twenty minutes to coax one simple snare beat out of the newborn Wendell was neither here nor there. A wheel had started to turn and a future was creeping into view. A future that looked none too bright for the jobbing snare basher. For Wendell's ace in the hole, the thing that set him apart from all other mechanical beat-makers of the day, was that he was a sampler too. That killer kick sound, which was the fruit of hours of search and toil, was there on a disk ready and waiting to be called to service in a matter of minutes.

Wendell was credited on the album and received a gold record for his 'work' on *Gaucho*. He never married, never felt the need to go solo and never took to strong drink or drugs.

Purely by coincidence, if you believe in that sort of thing, at more or less the same time another clever American, Roger Linn, was working on a similar idea: a drum machine that could sound exactly like a real drummer. A machine that would do as it was told and keep on doing it till you pulled the plug or pressed stop, whichever happened first. So realistic that if you closed your eyes you'd swear you were hearing a real gentleman or lady expertly banging real drums in a professional manner.

This would become known as the Linn LM-1 or more commonly the Linn-drum. It would change the studio recording of the rhythm section for well, I could say forever, but that's such a long time.

At around this very same time, I was still in Macclesfield at my parents' house, turning up at all hours, treating the place like a hotel, driving my parents to despair, sitting on my own drinking late-night Carlsberg Special Brew, etc. I like to think that success hasn't changed me. I was there one evening when I happened to turn on BBC Two just as *The Old Grey Whistle Test* was starting.

This particular edition didn't seem to me too promising – the run-of-the-mill Doobie Brothers-style fare – and truth be told I was only half watching.

Then on came a feature about Stevie Wonder in the studio.

The simple fact that my sister, Amanda, was a fan of Stevie's meant that I could never be (his early stuff was great, of course, and I loved 'Superstition', but the Temptations and Smokey Robinson would always be my Motown faves) so I still wasn't really paying that much attention. Something about the secret life of plants or something and . . .

There it was: the wooden-lined Linn drum machine with Stevie Wonder punching the buttons on its black and orange sloping front panel. I had never seen or heard anything like it.

Even on crappy TV speakers it sounded incredible. It sounded exactly like a man playing real drums in a posh studio would sound, without a tom-tom or cymbal stand in sight!

'That was funky,' I thought.

It was the same revelatory feeling I'd had seeing Kraftwerk playing drums with knitting needles on *Tomorrow's World* in 1975.

Not realising what a naturally talented and funky drummer Stevie was, I believed that all it would take was for me to acquire one of these marvellous devices and I too would be knocking out fat funky beats with my finger-tips and be the envy of all my friends.

And so I developed yet another case of misguided musical gear lust.

The rest of New Order were, like most people in 1981, unimpressed with the Roland 808.

Again like most people, they reckoned the Linn was a definite winner. But still ridiculously overpriced at four grand. For slightly more than half that price American synth manufacturers Oberheim had just released a rival machine, which they called the Oberheim DMX. This was in some respects even better than the Linn, and DMX sounded very scientific. Mysterious – I liked that.

So being a thrifty, club-financing band on a budget, this was the machine for us.

PART 2:

POWER UP

** WAIT - LOADING **

Eighties computing was not for the impatient

The music I listened to began to change as the 1980s progressed. For some reason the inspirational music from Germany that I'd always loved seemed to hit a dead end. I started to move away from my old staples of prog and rock albums and began an uneasy relationship with records that I would formerly have considered (possibly mistakenly) to be disco.

I began to see this as more of a commercial version of the hypnotic sequence-driven synthesised stuff that bands like Tangerine Dream and Kraftwerk had been doing for years.

I bought music by Giorgio Moroder, Sylvester and a stack of albums in that unholy category of 'various artists', all of which featured the words 'rap' or 'disco' emblazoned on their uninspiring covers, before eventually making my own cassette compilations of 12-inchers.

Unlike the usual single/album output, the 12-inch single seemed faceless. The people behind the music were anonymous – was it an actual band or just a track invented by a producer in a recording studio?

There were no in-depth reviews in the music papers, no sleeve notes, nothing. Tracking down a 12-inch was more like the Northern soul uber rare single quest than anything band-based.

On the way to gigs Bernard would play interesting tracks on the car cassette player, which I would then search for on vinyl only to be faced with a number of different versions of the same song. Sometimes I guessed the title or mix wrong and sometimes, even if I did get it right, the record was a long-sold-out limited-run pressing.

The record collector in me loved all this investigating and hunting, but I found the facelessness of it disappointing. Even when there was a picture on the sleeve, the artwork was, at best, crap.

It was always albums by bands that I identified with. I suspected the credits, lyric sheets and sleeve notes gave clues to the personalities involved in the music's creation. Made you imagine a connection with those involved in the record.

At the end of the day the thing was that none of this really mattered. As long as the music made you feel something.

I was listening to these tracks on a hi-fi in a tiny bedroom in a nice house on a suburban street in Macclesfield. The same way I listened to everything. Although this was very satisfying for nearly everything rock, psych, country, punk and prog, it was not the environment that the 12-inch extended dance mix was designed for.

In my bedroom some of them just seemed to go on and on. Unnecessarily repeating the same bit over and over the experience was somehow lacking something. It was a bit like listening to a film soundtrack without having seen the movie.

What was lacking, of course, was the correct environment.

The place where this music was designed to flourish.

The same track heard on a proper full-on sound system in a flashing-light, vibe-filled club turned into something else completely. It revealed itself as something that only made sense when played extremely loud and in the company of other people – preferably lots of other people. The words didn't matter. It was all about a mood that took you to another place if you let it.

And to let it, you had to feel it shake your bones. The place to do that was not in your bedroom. Certainly not in the house you shared with older more sensitive types.

I began to see the point of something that I had previously dismissed. Most of the time while driving to gigs we would listen to tape compilations we'd made and somehow the monotony of the motorway and the sense of anticipation worked with the music.

'This one's good, Barney. What's it called?' Rob would ask.

'No idea. I think it's Italian or maybe German.'

One particularly intriguing single was Afrika Bambaataa's 'Planet Rock'. Intriguing because I'd first guessed it was an unlikely new Kraftwerk collaboration. Wrong again, Stephen, for this was another New York experiment taking elements of 'Trans-Europe Express' and twisting it into something else, similar to what Grandmaster Flash had done with 'Another One Bites the Dust' on 'Wheels of Steel'.

More than that, 'Planet Rock' sounded fantastic and the production was brilliant. It turned out to be the work of Arthur Baker.

9

POWER, CORRUPTION & LIES

Even though I was still wary of not having an outside producer, after *Movement* and the parting of the ways with Martin, we became much more in control of our own sound and new influences crept in. We'd not done that bad a job of producing with 'Temptation'. Yes, we'd made a few mistakes but who doesn't fuck up the first time? Chalk it up to experience.

Our next attempt at the job was slightly more troublesome.

A John Peel session usually involved a trip down to the BBC's studios in Maida Vale, London, and a session with one of their house engineers and producers. A session for John Peel was an opportunity for bands to try out new unrecorded songs and to experiment. For many listeners to Peel's show, it was often the first time that new up-and-coming groups – names familiar from gig reviews in the music press – had the opportunity to reach a wider audience. This was New Order's second go.

This time we arranged for some special kind of dispensation from the BBC and were allowed to produce it on our own up north at Cheadle Hulme's Revolution Studios.

We spent two days on four songs and did a pretty good job all things considered. But the actual process was what you might call fraught. An argument and a grumpy storming-out at the end of day one put a bit of a pall on things. Let's call it musical differences and move on.

We'd kissed and made up (not literally) by lunchtime the following day. But the upset only went to confirm my fears that self-production might not be the best way to go about things.

But who could we get to produce us? Someone whose records we all liked and who we would all get on with.

Arthur Baker's name came up more than once. But who the hell was he and how could we get in touch with him? He wasn't in the *Yellow Pages* under 'Hot American Producer'. There was no Google, so instead we did what we usually did.

We asked Rob and Rob asked Tony and Tony asked someone else who asked ... but, for the time being, nothing concrete came of it. Arthur Baker was just a name that kept on appearing on a growing number of records in my collection.

Whenever we were down in London working or playing, we'd usually meet up with our friend and gig promoter Kevin Millins for a night out.

Kevin would take us out to various London hotspots – nights at Heaven were a favourite. Unlike the Haçienda, the sound system in the club was fantastic and the music and 'atmosphere' made for many a fun-filled night – followed by a hazy morning after.

It was here that the music of Sylvester and Patrick Cowley made perfect sense. I don't think the term Hi-NRG was around at the time. It was just called Gay Disco, but it was the energy of the tracks, the way the bass drove and the synths sparkled, that got me.

Cowley's extended version of Donna Summer's 'I Feel Love' is still one of the best remixes of anything by anyone. If you don't get excited by that track playing loud in a club there is something seriously wrong with you. The extra-long mix was a very difficult record to get hold of, and I think I only had a cassette of it at the time.

It would be great to hire a producer who could do something like that.

There was something standing in our way, though. Something that I know is hard to believe.

* * *

Over time, New Order had got themselves a reputation as being a bunch of awkward bastards. If you don't go along with things that are expected of you. this can happen. It is often a good thing.

And we *were* awkward bastards. Wilful too. We would always try to play a different set every night. Not that easy at the very first gigs when our set was generally eight songs long, only one or two fewer than the sum total all our songs.

'Play that new one,' Rob would suggest. 'I like that one.' And so, even though we were unsure of how it went and had no proper lyrics, we'd give it a go. This might mean that we didn't play a song we were expected to play, so that furthered our reputation as contrary souls.

Word got about.

It was around this time when there was a bit of a shift in the people who came to see us. In the very early days our audience seemed to consist largely of Joy Division fans come to pay their respects. Generally, these adopted the look they thought typified Ian Curtis (this they assumed from photographs of Ian and Joy Division): short hair and grey raincoats. They didn't smile much. They were mostly men.

They had a look that said, 'Sorry for your loss' and 'Why did he do it?' Their number dwindled when Gillian joined the band, with a few diehards finally giving up the ghost after hearing 'Everything's Gone Green'.

'It's a shame really but they're not . . .'

'How dare they have fun in their grief and misery?'

I enjoyed annoying these people as a matter of principle.

Not signing autographs was another principle of ours. What do you want my autograph for? What does it mean?

Our attitude to music journalists irked, too. Some of them were OK but generally we distrusted them and didn't like the idea of doing interviews.

It's no surprise we were thought a tad awkward.

Then there was the matter of encores. That was something that would get us into trouble time and again.

'It's a cliché,' I thought. 'Corny showbiz shit.'

Despite warming to disco, there were some areas of the entertainment profession I regarded with as much glee as a week in purgatory or an eyeful of red-hot needles.

If we particularly enjoyed the gig we might do an extra song or, perversely, if the audience were a little bit grumpy and we'd gone down like a lead balloon we might do another just to further aggravate the spectators.

Unpredictable, that was us.

The idea that you went to see a band, they played a few songs, they stopped, you clapped and shouted a bit, then they came back on and played a few more songs – the same night after night after night – was phoney as fuck. It was showbiz and we weren't showbiz. We had no interest whatsoever in anything to do with it. Showbiz was corny. It was also *old*.

Still, promoters and club owners expected you to do the expected, to play the game. They wanted you to do an encore to stop the audience turning nasty, and the audience could sometimes feel short-changed by our short-set, encore/no-encore policy. There could be complaints. There could be violence. Or there could be the odd riot.

So it's possible – just possible – that there may have been those in the music business who weren't that keen to work with us and who viewed us with suspicion.

Many of our live tribulations were down to equipment malfunctions. We were using modified kit-built tech and we were writing more and more songs using it. '586' was followed by 'Ultraviolence', 'We All Stand' and 'The Village'. The drawback was that customised Clef Master Rhythm drum machine/Powertran 1024 sequencer combo could really only play one pattern at a time, and that was it. There was no way of easily chaining patterns together to make one longer sequence. If we wanted to carry on down this road and expand the potential we would need MORE GEAR! An upgrade! Equipment of a let's say more professional persuasion.

We would visit various synthesiser emporiums and explore the latest cutting-edge gear on offer (at the right price, of course). Not wanting a repeat of the alphaSyntauri saga, we took our by now battered Pro-One with us so that after the salesman's spiel we could plug it in and ask, 'Can it make a sound like this?'

Usually it couldn't so we would move on to something else, before drawing up a shortlist and driving a hard bargain.

Now, through our recent post-Movement gear acquisitions – we were proud owners of a DMX digital drum machine, Moog Source mono synth and the Prophet 5 polyphonic synthesiser complete with a polyphonic sequencer – we could with a little ingenuity and a lot of patience play much more complex patterns. These patterns could in turn be chained together into an entire song arrangement.

That would be funny wouldn't it?

Just imagine, if we connected them all together.

Walk on.

Press a button.

Leave the gear to play a song all on its own.

While we piss off back to the booze in the dressing room and chortle to ourselves.

An invisible band!

It'd be a laugh, and we liked nothing better than a good laugh. We'd be doing an encore and not doing one at the same time.

We'd already had a bit of practice at this: encores consisting of extended jams around 'Everything's Gone Green' would end with us leaving the stage while the drum machine and synth continued playing. While Terry struggled in the dark to find the button that made the synth chatter stop, applauded or booed by the crowd.

It could go either way.

Creating this automatic song would also be an exercise in learning how all this new equipment worked or didn't. That too could also go either way, as we soon found out.

The final piece of hi-tech gear we acquired (and the most expensive) at the time was the Emulator. This battleship-grey and blue wedge-shaped keyboard was one of the first polyphonic keyboard samplers.

Any sound you could make could be recorded and played back with the pitch controlled by the keyboard. A machine of Martin Hannett's dreams.

The thing arrived at Cheetham Hill and after running through a few of the incredibly lifelike floppy-disk sounds that came in the box – barking dogs and motorbikes mostly – we decided to find out how good this piece of computer-based hardware was at doing our bidding. After all the struggles we'd had with the alphaSyntauri and its unconvincing parping, the Emulator turned out to be simplicity itself. Within a few minutes, we'd sampled our first fart.

Had you been there, I'm sure you'd have done the same.

In laddish glee, we fell about laughing hysterically. Samples of the inevitable puerile swearing phrases like 'Fuck off' and 'You twat' soon followed. The Emulator was a winner on so many levels. It opened up a world of creative possibilities.

Gillian was not too impressed.

But the Emu was cool, every band wanted one, and within weeks it was seen on *Top of the Pops* – a barking-dog novelty record raced up the charts.

To learn what the actual potential of all this new equipment was we set about writing a tune, as much another experiment as anything. It was inspired by the always inspirational Donna Summer's 'Our Love', Shep Pettibone's remix of Sharon Redd's 'Beat The Street' and very loosely based on the arrangement of 'Dirty Talk' by Klein and MBO. We had a cup of tea and got straight to work. It took quite a while.

The weak spot with all this new gear was how all this digital information got stored. Turn off the power and the poly-sequencer and Emulator's memories would empty. Amnesia would strike. In order to forestall this potential disaster the Prophet had a microcassette

Willing the Emulator to work

(just like a tiny dictaphone tape) and the Emulator boasted a 5-inch floppy drive, to keep its contents safe. This would, at least in theory, avoid the unhappy calamity of hours of work disappearing into the ether. The Oberheim DMX drum machine was on the face of it a bit smarter. It had a backed-up memory. Turn the power off, switch it back on, and your work of genius would still be lurking inside.

This was all well and good. Theoretically foolproof in fact, but that depended on the fool in question.

I'd programmed the patterns for the song that would become 'Blue Monday' and put them in an order that satisfied Bernard and Hooky. It had taken long enough to get this far, so wouldn't it be a good idea to make an additional copy as well as having the automatic DMX backup? Good idea, I thought, so out came the nearest cassette recorder and the data was dumped.

Quite literally.

'SEQ EMPTY,' the DMX said when I pressed play. All my work, not just on this one song but everything else I'd done, weeks of work, was vaporised with what was supposed to be a reassuring beep.

No problem, hadn't I just made a tape back-up? Simple: rewind the tape and press play, and all would be tickety-boo again.

'BAD DATA,' the bastard box said.

'YOU TWAT,' was my reply.

I reached for a drumstick with which to teach the machine a Basil Fawlty-type lesson, while Bernard and Hooky fell about laughing at my dismay.

'You daft twat, you'll have to do it all again now.'

As if I didn't already know that.

Of course, after loads more work, they would insist, 'No, it was better before.'

There is a version of the story which has me bumbling about the rehearsal room like some stoned Frank Spencer before tripping over the mains lead, pulling the plug out and wiping the lot, with the band looking on in sitcom horror.

A bit of dramatic licence there, I believe. But the upshot is the same.

My new digital drum buddy and I hadn't got off to the best of starts. But on the plus side, it was a breeze to program and, once I'd got the hang of it, very enjoyable.

If I ever forgot how the drum fills were supposed to go I only had to listen to the remix of 'Beat the Street' to remind myself.

Unlike the poly-sequencer, which was Gillian and Bernard's personal source of torment.

To say programming the sequencer was difficult is a bit of an understatement. It required keeping a very accurate count of the number of times the step key had been pressed. We're talking hundreds here at least. Get it wrong and the results were usually disastrous, meaning you had to start again from the very beginning, or occasionally they could be unexpectedly brilliant, as was the case with the out-of-time top-line sequence on 'Blue Monday'.

The anatomy of the slightly forgetful DMX

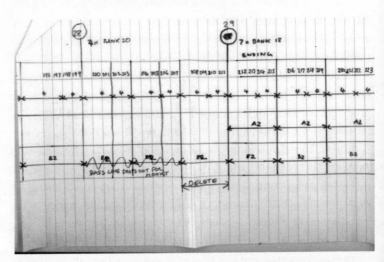

Gillian's Blue Monday Scroll (excerpt)

In the winter of 1982 we returned to London and Pink Floyd's Britannia Row studio, where Joy Division had recorded *Closer*, to begin work on the second New Order album. It was our first entirely self-produced album and the start of a long and happy relationship with Mike Johnson, who had done some assistant engineering on *Closer*.

Mike was very fastidious and methodical. He was level-headed, which we often weren't. He was also very good at keeping track of what had been done and what still needed to be done. Supervised by Hooky, Mike became the designated driver.

He was a bit straight though; Rob in particular took the piss out of him mercilessly. For his part, Mike took it well and fitted in easily.

Hooky immediately ensconced himself in the control room at the mixing desk next to Mike, thus staking his claim at the top of the production hierarchy. He was keen to learn and refused to budge, like he was trying to set a studio control-room endurance record.

Producing a record that involves any degree of programming is a bit like warfare: brief periods of intense excitement, when some actual physical playing takes place, followed by long periods of inactivity and boredom. Hooky wanted to be on the front line.

Hooky and Mike would do their best to keep track of what we were doing, while in the recreation room Bernard, Gillian and I programmed away on the sequencer and drum machine – counting button pushes, losing count and starting again.

To make certain we didn't have a repeat of my alleged *Some Mothers Do 'Ave 'Em* incident back at the rehearsal room, we backed up everything and Gillian plotted every click on the sequencer on to an ever-expanding scroll of paper. It was Gillian's own version of the Bayeux Tapestry. It would eventually take up the entire length of Pink Floyd's full-sized snooker table.

The interpretation of this digital score required a bit of imagination. Instead of musical notation, which none of us really understood, we invented our own language of numbers and crosses so we had some sort of visual reference as to what was supposed to be going on inside the machine's mind.

We worked hard, very hard, and took what we were doing seriously. It was a very creative period, as Gillian's introduction to the band had been followed by the addition of the sequencer and the DMX. This was like having another two musicians: one playing a synthesiser and the other doing a very good imitation of a very good, if occasionally forgetful, drummer.

For me and Hooky, these additions meant our playing had to adapt. Hooky had already started playing more melodic parts on a six-string Shergold in Joy Division so I guess he refined that to fit round the sequencer, playing more like a lead guitarist and less like a traditional bass player.

Me, I reached a similar accommodation with the DMX by coming up with riffs that would fit around it. I began playing more sparsely, as doing anything else sounded cluttered. I began doing riffs that came and went instead of playing all the way through. It wasn't easy, but it was interesting and we were all learning as we went along.

There was a lot of reading in the control room and the stack of paperbacks and copies of 2000 AD on Hooky's side of the mixing desk soon began to pile up. It was a blurb on a paperback copy of Animal Farm that gave us the title Power, Corruption & Lies.

For me, making the album was a peculiar experience. Compared to previous album sessions, I was doing a lot of work but, it seemed to me, not much of it involved the actual hitting of drums.

Even though there are only two tracks on the album where the drum parts are entirely artificial, I still felt like I was short-changing myself somehow. I felt like a sellout, a cheat – that I should be playing more. The main reason I felt that was because of the way I'd done things in the past with Martin. I used to spend hours and hours doing take after take, seeking Hannett's idea of perfection.

Now I was playing an entire drum kit, just like I did live, doing only two or three takes. It all seemed a little bit *too* easy that at times I almost missed Martin's tortuous jigsaw method of recording.

Almost.

There were plenty of other opportunities to feel pain as I struggled to keep the new digital boxes functioning, studying nonsensical manuals in attempts to diagnose whether it was the machine or the operator that was at fault. It was usually fifty–fifty.

Equipment malfunctions were regular occurrences. The polysequencer would act up and the veteran Quadra was showing signs of road weariness. Luckily just around the corner from Britannia Row lay the Synthesiser Service Centre, run by synth menders extraordinaire Ron and Don. They were often reparing and modifying our equipment performing many updates and improvements to the (still occasionally forgetful) Oberheim machine.

Despite the odd bout of amnesia, the new drum machine sounded fantastic, especially on the track that became 'Blue Monday'. The title came from *Breakfast of Champions* – I was working my way through Kurt Vonnegut's books at the time. 'Goodbye Blue Monday', the book's alternate title, was the slogan for the Robo Magic washing machine. Its technological advance promised to improve the lot of the American housewife. I empathised with that. Wasn't that what we were doing?

We were writing, editing, adding to the idea that had been formed in the rehearsal room, adapting the song all the time. 'Blue Monday' turned into an epic, a titanic struggle between man and machine. It changed again as the human parts were added over the top, especially Hooky's brilliant spaghetti-western bass part.

Rob, as usual, was with us throughout the recording and loved it.

'It's hot this one,' he'd say. 'Fuckin' mega.'

'Turn it up.'

'Louder!'

So we did.

I don't think any of us we were completely convinced by Rob's extreme enthusiasm for the track.

Rob taking care of business

That it would be a single, though, was obvious. There was no way a track that long was going to fit on the album for a start.

In a further attempt to keep the track completely automated, I'd plugged a speech synthesiser card into the Apple and tried teaching it to, well not sing exactly, more rhythmically vocalise. Something like a rapping Dalek, I thought. The results were not entirely popular with my comrades and got 'accidentally' erased.

So it goes, as Kurt himself also says.

There were quite a few nights off, especially early on. Always the way of things when working in a studio.

Our domestic arrangements for these sessions were similar to the recording of *Closer*. We all lived together in a rented flat, this time a bijou residence on Basil Street behind Harrods in Knightsbridge, a change from the usual hotel situation. It was Gillian's first real experience of living with the band for an extended period in a confined environment. On returning to the flat late Hooky usually went straight to bed, the rest of us hung about smoking, drinking and talking shit.

Gillian, though, after spending the day writing her poly-sequencer sheets now found herself getting requests for late-night snack creation.

'Er, Gillian do you fancy making us a butty or a bit of toast? Have you got any pitta bread? I love pitta bread . . . with lots of butter,' from Rob as he took up sole residence on the sofa, spreading out his weary bulk and making himself comfortable while Bernard adjusted the lighting to his personal satisfaction. We would then settle down to watch fuzzy videos of 2001 or *Caligula* for the umpteenth time.

'And a bit of cheese . . . Or bacon . . . Lots of butter! Pleeeeeeeese. Go on . . .'

It didn't take long for this playful misogynist piss-taking straight from a seventies sitcom to wear thin. The response would either be 'Fuck off, Rob, make your own toast' or the occasional manufacture that trading standards and food hygiene would condemn: bits of scrap rescued from the bin, mouldy pitta bread and cheese, and rancid butter were all stuck under the grill in the vain hope this might discourage further requests for room service.

'Skin up, Steve.' It was my turn to attend to Rob's needs. 'And don't forget to buy some Jaffa Cakes tomorrow.'

An inevitable consequence of studio boredom was that Rob's gambling obsession would get out of hand. We'd recently done a gig in Athens and the Greek promoter Patros Moustakas had taken an interest in distributing our records in Greece. Patros was a bit of a wheeler dealer, a bit of a lad. He also shared Rob's interest in ridiculous wagers.

Patros was in London for a bit so to be sociable he came down to the studio and, in an attempt to butter us up, took us all out for a meal.

This, as you would expect, involved a fair bit of drinking and on completion of the dessert portion, Rob expressed a characteristic interest in a cigarette. Patros unveiled his challenge. He pulled out a fag and a freshly minted five-pound note.

'OK Rob, I bet you this five-pound note.'

'Fiver? You're on – what's the bet?'

The wager was that Patros would place the note on the back of Rob's hand and Patros would put a lit cigarette on it.

If the fag burned a hole in the cash, Rob was the winner.

Now you may ask yourself quite why a fiver with a hole burned in it was such a great prize? I know I did.

But Rob liked a bet, however outlandish.

'Go on then. No cheating, mind.'

'No cheating, Rob, you just hold the fiver nice and tight.'

Patros stubbed his Dunhill on the note for maybe five or ten seconds – at least until there was the unmistakable smell of burning flesh. Rob only winced slightly.

'Go on, Rob!' cheered Hooky.

Gillian squealed.

'Just check the note now, Mr Rob.'

Rob did as he was told and was disappointed. He discovered the fiver was not even faintly singed – unlike his hand, which now sported a large angry blister.

'I'd get some Savlon on that, Rob, quick,' advised Hooky.

'You're a lucky Greek bastard, Patros!' Our manager felt he had been diddled. 'Double or quits,' which was fast becoming the Gretton catchphrase of the moment.

If he was surprised at this, Patros did a very good job of hiding it. I don't think he had ever had the chance to pull this ruse twice with the same victim.

'OK, let's try the other hand . . .'

'I'll beat ya this time, ya twat.'

The note was placed on Rob's unscorched hand and . . . the same thing happened again.

Burning flesh and unsinged fiver, for as Chief Engineer Scott was fond of saying, 'Ye cannae change the laws of physics.'

A two-nil victory to Greece. Bernard, tipsy and suspecting it was open season for the branding of managers, grabbed a cig off me and tried to stub it out on Rob's forehead, but it was a bridge to far for all concerned.

Rob carried the stigmata of this pointless wager for the rest of his life. Isn't alcohol a wonderful anaesthetic?

Being a couple in a band was a bit of an odd existence, made only odder during recording.

For a start, there was never any privacy. Bernard, Hooky and Rob were always there, either squashed in the control room while we were working or listening back to something, or sprawled in the recreation room when it wasn't being used as an extension of the studio.

The only escape was when we volunteered for (or got press-ganged into) the mundane domestic activity of shopping. Besides newspapers and dodgy magazines, we seemed to go through an inordinate amount of pitta bread and butter.

Being cooped up for hours at a time listening to the same thing over and over and over, it's really easy to lose focus, and getting out into the real world of groceries, bookshops and chemists was a chance to get back down to earth.

Hovering around the make-up counter in Boots the Chemist while Gillian fussed over the right shade of eyeliner was a peculiar antidote to the stresses of producing an album.

On a whim and spotting some prank potential, we bought a magnificent stuffed rat from a taxidermist's, which went under the witty name of Get Stuffed, on the Essex Road. The objective was to play a jape on Bernard. So thoughts of the band were never that far away, even if they were just to exploit Bernard's profound dislike of the rodent population.

For the most part I enjoyed the fact that as a couple Gillian and I were regarded as a single entity, and our adventures away from the all-lads-togetherness of the studio were a good way of avoiding the attention of 'The Authors'. There were two of them who were frequent visitors to the studio. One was Mark Johnson, who was writing a book about Joy Division. He would mither and pry and ask stupid questions, always at the worst possible moment.

The other was Michael Butterworth, Dave Britton's partner from House on the Borderland Manchester bookshop where I spent a lot of my time back in my happy school-avoiding days. Mike was just hanging around spectating and writing 'something observational'. He was also living with us at the Basil Street flat for a time – you couldn't get much more fly-on-the-wall than that.

Mark and Mike could be a welcome distraction at times. But then I couldn't see why other people would want to write a book about us. Much less two books.

To me, *Power, Corruption & Lies* is the first 'proper' New Order album, one that breaks away from what we'd done with Joy Division and heads somewhere completely different. We'd worked together and produced a record that was entirely our own.

Instead of just recording songs that we had already written and knew well, we would write and rewrite parts in the studio as we went along. The tracks that we had been playing for a while with our old gear – '5-8-6', 'We All Stand', 'Ultraviolence' and a very rough version of 'The Village' – ended up getting adapted and reworked as we got the hang of the new equipment. There was no automation on the desk in Britannia Row – I'm not sure if it had even been invented then – so mixing would involve everybody working buttons and faders on the mixing desk in real time as the mix went down.

'Murder' is one of my favourite tracks from the session, for obvious reasons. Not that I have any interest in premeditated or even random slayings, it's more that the track mixes lots of frantic drums with samples from various favourite VHS cassettes.

Bernard had decided that he wanted to write the bulk of the lyrics himself. He said it was difficult for him to sing words when he didn't actually know what they meant or what they were about. The rest of us still chipped in odd words and lines here and there when needed, but I quite fancied the idea of doing a track that used cut-up dialogue for a change.

I still came away from *Power, Corruption & Lies* with the suspicion that I might have been the turkey that voted for Christmas.

I loved the technology and found all it could do exciting – the fact that within it lay the potential to change everything, not just in music but everywhere. We would talk about this all the time, the five of us. Tomorrow's world, the world around the corner. A world of nukes. An automatic world run by robots. I remembered my early drummer friend's advice, that synthesisers were things to be watched and handled with care. Hadn't I just gone and embraced the whole field of electrically derived music?

What if he was right? What if I'd just talked my way out of a job? I could see the possibility of a future where being a drummer would be about as much use as a highly skilled Latin-speaking dodo trainer.

What increased my apprehension in this was the fact that the DMX was an absolute breeze to program.

Hell, even a cat could come up with a red-hot beat just by trotting across the Oberheim's buttons.

I fretted . . .

I imagined the producer of twenty-first century saying, 'Drummers?

Remember them? All that time and messing about they took? All that coaxing just to get a simple four-on-the-floor beat out of the bastards?'

'BEEP BEEP!' the glowing future DMX responded gleefully. The smug git.

I saw myself like a mouse in a maze following the Pac-Man trail of digital novelty that led ultimately to one place and one place only: an inevitable looming grey steel door emblazoned upon which was a sign with big red letters that said:

'DRUMMER SCRAPHEAP . . . Please enter quietly!'

I would fall through the door and onto a pile of my former percussive pals, some still gibbering forlornly about the time they once met Steve Gadd at a drum clinic.

I pretty much felt the same way I imagined the dinosaurs must have done when first spying an unusual fiery ball in the sky. 'But that couldn't actually happen, could it? I mean not really?'

I have to admit that there were times I feared it very easily could.

The one thing that troubled me the most, though, was not that the DMX would take my place. I'd heard the beep and seen the 'PATTERN EMPTY' and 'BAD DATA' messages more than enough times by then to know its flaws and weaknesses. A stoned, semicomatose drummer with a broken arm could still produce something that resembled a beat that could move your feet. A drum machine in a bad mood . . . would produce zilch. It would need care and maintenance to restore its precision, constant supervision to keep it performing.

All I needed was booze, drugs and a packet of number No 6.

So, no, it was not the drum machine that troubled my dreams and turned them into dystopian nightmares.

My thoughts had moved on to the Emulator. Or rather the idea of where all this sampling and digitised sound might one day lead: 'Trouble Brewing'.

For much as some feared that photography was theft of the soul, I could see that something similar was ultimately going to occur with sampling and music.

The Emulator could steal a groove.

Not just a sound that had been worked on for hours or days, but a whole rhythmic or melodic phrase that could have taken months of work could be regurgitated at will. At the press of a button. In a matter of seconds.

The Emulator was a source of inspiration and wonder. Just before we ventured south to Britannia Row, Rob brought Peter Saville down to the Cheetham Hill bunker to see what we were up to.

'They've got this keyboard that can make any sound you like. Show him, Steve.'

So I did my Emulator demo, loading in a few motorbike noises and barking dogs. The barking dog preset and the one labelled 'Erotic-sounds' were very popular. Peter lit up a Dunhill and casually inspected my box of discs.

'Stephen, what are these for?'

I explained that they stored the Emulator's sounds. He pulled a disk out of its paper sleeve.

'Oh, I see. Would it be all right if I borrowed one?'

I had no idea what he thought he was going to do with the thing so humoured him.

'Yeah fine, Pete. I've got loads.'

And that was how the idea for the sleeve of 'Blue Monday' came to be. I never got the disk back.

Maybe I was overthinking it. But the world I'd imagined, where technology was a friend to all, was turning out to be a little wide of the mark. The future's always wildly unpredictable, that's why prophecy is such a mug's game and the bookies always win.

I mean who would have suspected that the company behind the Emulator would in 1987 come up with a device that combined drum machine and sampler; the sp1200. That device really was something revolutionary. Here was Wendell's grandchild. It became the 80's hip-hop vinyl sampler of choice. Obscure Jazz records were grist for its cut-up mill. Digital technology would change the world starting with the drums.

We'd taken the first tiny steps with digitising sound back in Joy Division with Martin's AMS, not knowing that the equipment we were using would eventually transform the way that music was written, recorded, distributed and listened to. Record companies, too, were blissfully ignorant of the ramifications and the existential threat ahead.

In the early eighties, they were still struggling to come to terms with home taping. They were being a bit short-sighted and couldn't see where this 'digital thing' might end up. The industry thought it had solved this 'problem' with the introduction of the CD in 1982, the year before *Power, Corruption & Lies* came out.

'You've never heard it so good,' they said.

'Indestructible,' they said, as they covered the silver disc with jam. Happily ignoring the fact that the cases the discs came in fell apart a bit too easily. That's assuming you could get the fiendishly difficult plastic wrapping off them in the first place.

Wrong on both counts, as it turned out.

For even then there was no way this particular genie was ever going back in the bottle. I repurchased my vinyl on CD along with everyone else as major record company CEOs happily kept expense-account-lunching away, oblivious to the monster under the table.

In New Order, we were young and foolish, and, we thought, scientific. With an eye on the pros we mixed the PCL recordings down on to digital.

Once it's digitised it'll last forever, I thought to myself. I'd read the future-tech mags and this belief was widely held at the time. Much like the guy who on playing Pong on his Atari for the first time thought, 'It doesn't get any better than this!'

I was wrong. We all were.

Firstly, the technology would improve and secondly far from being permanent the digital tapes would degenerate a lot faster than anyone expected. Twenty years is nowhere near forever; by the time the twenty-first century rolled around most of these digital tapes were unplayable.

Luckily we also made safety copies on to old-fashioned, half-inch analogue tape, which although prone to some physical decay could be fairly easily resuscitated by sticking it in a warm environment for a bit. It turns out that's what airing cupboards are for, well I never.

A worn-out analogue tape could always produce some semblance of sound. Its digital cousin would either remain silent or spew out an unpleasant harsh chatter. Generally, a bit of both. The sort of din that can't even be passed off as avant-garde Musique Concret.

If you're going to be an early adopter, don't put all your eggs into one basket. That's my advice, for what it's worth.

As is the usual course of events in the making of an album, what began as a bit of a leisurely stroll ended as a frantic, manic, round-the-clock race against time. The mad dash to the finish line.

In the normal course of events we could always buy more studio time. But in this case we had our first tour of Australia booked and that would not budge. We packed up all our gear, drove back to Manchester, and then drove straight back down again to get a plane from Heathrow bound for Sydney.

Rob was keen that we played the newly finished 'Blue Monday' live at the earliest opportunity.

'Can't be done, Rob. It's impossible. We'll never be able to play that one live,' was Bernard's reaction. Hooky, I think, hedged his bets.

I took it as a bit of a challenge. It prompted the old response that if I'm told by someone else something can't be done, I have to try and do it.

We arrived in Bondi Beach in the middle of the night and the next day found ourselves a tiny rehearsal room to try and do the seemingly impossible.

Hampered by the jet lag and general lack of sleep for the past three weeks, we struggled. But after a hesitant start it turned out to be not too difficult to translate the studio sequences into a workable live version so long as the gear held up.

In an attempt to mitigate against any disastrous equipment failures, we'd taken Mike Johnson from Britannia Row and electronics genius Martin Usher from Manchester with us to the southern hemisphere.

Martin turned out to have a curiously talismanic effect, in some reversal of what's known as the Pauli effect. As long as Martin was in the same room as any piece of digital paraphernalia, it worked faultlessly. Soon as he left, calamity struck. Every time.

There was one slight problem. For in our reconstruction of 'Blue Monday' into a live entity, there had been a bit of 'who plays what?' juggling. Hooky, whose bass parts came and went throughout the song, ended up claiming my syndrum parts to fill his gaps and I, as the one who apparently had the most faith in technology, ended up as the Emulator wrangler.

'It's only fair, Steve.'

I took the point manfully but reluctantly.

My trouble – and it was a petty and egotistical one, I see now – was that I had thought with Gillian's arrival my keyboard 'playing' days would be over. I'd always felt awkward and uncomfortable tickling the ivories at the best of times, never mind keeping track of floppy disks, inserting, loading and pressing keys while keeping my fingers mostly crossed. The thing I most distrusted became my responsibility.

If I felt uneasy as a keyboard player, I sympathised with Bernard who probably felt just as uncomfortable in coming to terms with being a singer.

'Blue Monday' went on to become a massive worldwide hit.

I think it was the sangria-soaked tourists in Spanish holiday discos who first spotted its potential as some sort of dance anthem. After Rob, of course, for his estimation of the track's hotness proved correct and surpassed even his expectations.

We'd made what would become a dance classic and not one of us could cut a rug to save our lives. Rob would boast that he'd been a great Northern Soul dancer in his day and he could very briefly do a fair approximation of an ex-Wigan Casino jockey when the mood took him. I could do a self-conscious embarrassed shuffle but what is drumming if not dancing sitting down? And that I could do pretty well.

'Blue Monday' even gained the attention of one of its inspirations: Kraftwerk. Possibly not noticing that the choir sound bore an uncanny resemblance to a track of theirs, they were so impressed by the record that I got a phone call from Düsseldorf seeking detailed information on just how the song's bass drum sound had been made. I did my best to oblige, but I got the distinct feeling that they weren't too convinced by my explanation, which was basically 'buy an Oberheim DMX'. I think they wanted something a bit more technically precise so I put them onto Mike Johnson, who put them onto Britannia Row, after which they probably gave up, suspecting that we were taking the piss.

Peter Saville's floppy-inspired die-cut sleeve was a work of genius, as was his colour-coded Henri Fantin-Latour floral update. Peter was going through his die-cut phase (early copies of OMD's first album had even more holes) which would continue until someone said enough was enough. The legend that Factory lost money on every copy of 'Blue Monday' is a great myth, but sadly not true. Myths rarely are. If Factory actually lost 5p on every copy sold, as the story goes, they would have gone bust in a matter of months. Nobody is that daft, not even me. (Apparently by the end of 31 May 1983 Blue Monday had sold 230,340 copies and had made £113,477.78 fact fans! It took a long time to discover that.)

Another 'Blue Monday' legend is that it is the bestselling 12-inch of all time. An accolade indeed, but it's open to question. Don't let that spoil a good story though. Let's just say it almost certainly is the bestselling 12-inch of all time and always will be, and move on.

10

TIRED AND EMOTIONAL

You could be forgiven for getting the impression that Gillian and myself had some sort of placid, docile trouble-free relationship. The sort of lovey-dovey idyllic romance that only other people ever seem to have. A misty-eyed romance much like those portrayed in the books published by Mills and Boon. My mother, an avid fan, had a closet piled high with these slushy tales of idealised love.

Was it really like that?

No, of course not. It never is.

Have you ever known someone for more than a few months without at the very least having a minor disagreement or tiff, or argument that finally descends into a blazing row over the bill after that not-so-romantic meal for two? Gone without speaking to each other for days before the utter stupidity of the situation begins to dawn?

I've already told you that I consider myself an easy-going, free-wheelin' sort of guy. I'm not sure either you or I believed it, though. In the mirror, I frequently see an obsequious drip, easily led, manipulated or just plain pushed around. One of the many reasons I avoid looking in mirrors.

At times I can turn into a monster. You may laugh at the thought, but it is not a pretty sight. A vile petulant, screaming, ranting fiend. We've all been there, done that.

Haven't we?

It is most often Gillian who gets to see the monster. You know, you always hurt the one you love, probably because they have the misfortune to be always handy, always there, to see you at your absolute worst.

I can put up with a lot, take an emotional battering in my stride, absorb it all like a sponge, see the funny side of it all. It's an essential skill necessary to survival in a band. But all these minor psychological injuries build and build before finally manifesting themselves as paranoia, depression or, if you're lucky, just a stand-up screaming rant. An event that one day all involved will look back on with a kind of sentimental pining, when a session reminiscing on the glory days of youthful folly scrapes the dirt and unearths the remains of the half-forgotten trauma.

'Hey, do you remember that time when I went berserk?'

'What *was* that all about? You were *really horrible*, an utter bastard! I hated you.'

Something that was really nothing.

But in the pressurised, rarefied, artificial reality that is a youthful band on tour or confined in the recording studio, these things can feel like nothing less than the end of the world.

Alcohol or drugs are usually a catalyst to these emotional eruptions but mostly it's exhaustion – running on empty.

'Tired and emotional', the heading these outbursts get filed under, fits the bill most of the time.

Take the first Australian jaunt, for example.

The first thing Rob did on arriving in the heat of Sydney was to run into the sea at Bondi Beach in the middle of the night, leaving me standing in the sand trying to make sense of the large and numerous signs that said 'NO THONGS'.

What the fuck was a thong?

I should have asked our promoters and guides, Vivian Lees and Ken West, but didn't want to display my Pommy ignorance.

We took to regular drinking in the local subterranean beachfront boozer, the curiously named Fondue Here situated conveniently just in staggering distance of the Cosmopolitan motor lodge, our Sydney residence. We had followed the flickering neon arrow in the direction indicated, down some well-worn steps, and entered the dank booze cavern.

One of the things that first struck me about the place was its desperate mirror ball. So encrusted with years of nicotine strata and general grime was this dancehall totem that it no longer sparkled, not even a tiny twinkle. Instead of reflecting, it absorbed whatever rays fell upon it and kept them, never to be seen again, like some ballroom black hole.

This contributed much to the overall vampiric surfing disco ambience of the place. As if the idea of eating molten cheese on a sun-soaked beach wasn't odd enough.

Fondue Here was an establishment popular with the local fluorescence-adorned, warpainted and tanned Fosters-swilling local wave boarders.

Bernard, wishing to buck the tinned lager-drinking trend, took to ordering a sweet sherry, possibly to calm an upset tummy, a malady to which he was occasionally prone. Usually after a night on the Pernod.

However upon placing his dainty sherry glass on the screen of a tabletop Galaxian machine, he was alarmed to notice unusual activity in the depths of his beverage. Living at the bottom of his glass was some form of almost microscopic life. They may have been sea monkeys but my money was on Australian surfer fleas of some kind. No doubt the hardy, alcohol-dwelling sort, preparing to do a hang ten in the sherry.

Bernard, alarmed and visibly shaken by this beverage pollution, made a hasty exit to the relative safety of his bed, retching as he made his way up the stairs to the street. The rest of us continued with the canned swill until dawn, then headed back to the Cosmo to watch a video – *2001* or accidentally recorded episodes of *Minder* most likely – on the portable VHS I'd lugged over to Australia with me.

Living the dream.

I attempt a remake of *Picnic at Hanging Rock*.

The thing is, as long as there was a bit of onward momentum, the anticipation of the next gig/town or excitement of some other sort to look forward to, things would mostly be ok. It was all there in the itinerary that regulated life. A security blanket of sorts. The ravages of exhaustion could be temporarily dodged by means of chemistry.

It is when that regulated existence is coming to an end that the wheels have a tendency to come off. The return to 'normality'. Back to a time when trips to Marks & Sparks replace the soundcheck, and the news at ten and late-night films are a poor stand-in for the excitement of a gig. Exhausted, but with boredom beckoning.

This depressurisation gives rise to some rock-and-roll equivalent of the bends, the phenomenon dreaded by the normally fearless devotees of scuba diving.

One such occasion was the long flight home.

The return that brought the onset of the peril. It was a mighty long way from Australia to the UK.

So to break up the tedium of this aerial marathon, the wise and sensible thing to do was break the journey at some point. You know, pull off at the motorway services to stretch the old legs, as it were.

This got billed in the now ripped and dog-eared itinerary as a brief stopover in Bangkok, which in 1982 was a very different place to the one it is today. I mean, I hope it is. I've never been back.

Eighties Australia had seemed a lot like mid-seventies England, but to a lad from Macclesfield, Thailand was like nowhere I'd ever been. A hot sticky, alien world. A disorientating and crazy city. At the airport signs like 'Persons with Beatle haircut not admitted' and 'No defacing or insulting of the Buddha image' amused and confused my inner Macclesfieldness. Then, after doing a bit of tricky time-zone mathematics, I realised we would be stuck there for between eight and ten hours.

'Who wants to stay here at a fuckin' airport for ten hours?' asked Oz, our sound engineer.

There were few takers.

'I fancy a Chinese,' said Rob.

Now a Thai would have been a much better bet, but this was the 1980s and the two cuisines were easily confused. The 'How about a nice Thai?' from me got nowhere.

Rob was adamant.

'I want a fuckin' Chinese!'

So it was with a sense of deep foreboding and recalling the immortal words of Willard from *Apocalypse Now!*, 'Never get out of the boat . . . Unless you were going all the way,' we left the monotonous, drab safety of the airport terminal and set off for the heart of darkness, or the nearest Chinese food palace.

Piling into a waiting cab: me, Gillian, Rob and Dave.

'All right, mate? Know any good Chinese places?' Rob's opening gambit to our driver was both insulting and optimistic in equal measure.

It was the middle of the afternoon.

'No Chinese. Most restaurant closed now, but I know good place.'

A doubtful Dave enquired, 'Sure you don't fancy a Thai, Rob? Thai food's really nice.'

'Nah, I want a fucking Chinese.'

Rob Gretton, it has to be said, was very fond of Chinese cuisine. His favourite eatery in Manchester and possibly the entire world was the Kwok Man, a restaurant renowned at the time as the only place in town to serve beer after midnight.

So we began a lengthy taxi journey across paddy fields and dank fetid swamps, the sticky air permeated with the odours of raw sewage and burning rubber.

Finally, after about an hour of bumping and swerving, we arrived in a bustling car-fume-filled, horn-honking, tattered-poster-bedecked metropolis. It may or may not have been Bangkok city centre.

The urban geography of the place just seemed crazy, no pattern to it at all. Bikes were duelling with motorised rickshaws as we pulled into a side street with angry taxis blaring at our rear. The driver pointed to a smoked-glass-fronted place up some concrete steps in what looked like a small shopping arcade closed for the season.

'This best place – Chinese and Thai.'

'How much? Got any cash, Steve?'

Gillian gave me one of her doubtful 'what the hell are we doing here?' looks as I thrust a wad of freshly exchanged baht over to Mr Gretton.

The restaurant was deserted but the air-conditioned chill was welcoming. Its décor was mostly muted brown – can you mute brown? – with the odd golden Buddha and mounted willow-pattern crockery framing what looked like a Ming-style vase.

Finally, someone emerged from the back.

'You still serving food? Manger?' as Rob made the internationally understood hand-to-mouth gesture of a hungry Mancunian.

Our waitress looked unsure of Rob's intentions, disappearing through a doorway before reappearing in the company of an elder gent with rolled-up sleeves and a bow tie. He nodded and ushered us to the familiar large lazy-Susan-type circular table. We were the only customers.

Rob got straight to business.

'You do beer? Tsing Tao?

'Singha, yes, how many?'

'Let's have six to be going on with!' holding up the requisite number of fingers.

The real trouble commenced with the arrival of the first course of liquid refreshment.

These were very large brown bottles of quite strong beer refreshingly chilled and easily consumed on totally empty stomachs.

Stomachs that would mostly stay that way, if you ignored the fluid input.

Gillian, peering up from the menu, gave me a more amplified version of the 'what exactly are we doing here?' look.

I attempted reassurance.

'What you havin' then?'

'I don't know, has anyone got a menu in English?'

We hadn't and neither did the maître d'. So we got another round and Rob resorted to ordering food by a system of numerology, the idea being that a number 27 in the Kwok Man would be more or less the same on the other side of the world. Rice was easily managed by pointing at a bowl and some chopsticks and doing some exaggerated munching.

We had many hours to kill. We didn't eat much but drank plenty.

Now is probably a good time to mention Gillian's appearance.

Gillian is much given over to altering the appearance and particularly the colour of her locks. On the afternoon in question, her look was sort of auburn that veered towards vermillion in the sunlight. She was also wearing a very short leather skirt. It would later emerge that this was not the normal attire for a late lunch in Bangkok.

But when she got dressed that morning I doubt she anticipated spending a large portion of the day getting seriously boozed up in an unfamiliar Asian country.

Some rice, one hot and sour soup and many, many beers later, things got a little leery.

It was becoming evident that our by now loud and rowdy behaviour was, despite our being the entire clientele, becoming unwelcome with the management and we were overstaying our welcome.

We would have to venture into whatever it was that lurked on the other side of the smoked-glass windows.

Reluctantly, we stumbled out into the retina-burning light of the bustling narrow street.

'Did you leave him a tip?'

'Now where the fuck are we?'

Roasting in the humid heat, dodging pedestrians and bicycles in a bleary attempt at getting our bearings, it soon became very evident that Gillian was attracting a great deal of attention from the locals.

My 'What you fucking looking at, mate?' didn't help matters, for whichever way you looked we were outnumbered by the gawping curious who were becoming more curious by the minute.

Gillian's red hair and short skirt aroused and enraged many of the locals both male and female. Who would have known that scarlet tresses could provoke such alarm and fury in the Thai community?

Pissed and disorientated, I began to get annoyed and angry but, not knowing who it was I was supposed to get annoyed at, I took the easy way out and decided that everyone except me must be to blame for this state of affairs.

Had I been thinking logically, it would have been obvious that it was Rob's mania for hot and sour that had landed me in this particular soup. But for some inexplicable reason, I decided that the principal architect of my misfortune must be Gillian – the person who was by now the uncomfortable centre of the untoward vocal attention we were getting from the populace. Perversely, it was she who had to be most blameworthy.

I fell into an alcohol-fuelled jealous rage.

As we shuffled our way drunkenly down the narrow street, the pointing and shouting in Gillian's direction only increased, as did the level of her discomfort.

Realising that the threat of the offended locals was increasing with each step we did that most British of things: we crossed over the lane and retreated in the opposite direction. Dave by now had taken Gillian's arm and was attempting to diffuse much of the locals' curiosity.

'Fahk off, mate!' while I fumed quietly to myself.

It was then that Rob spotted something in a shop window.

'Hey, I fancy the look of that suit. I need a new suit, me, let's nip in here and see how much they want for it. Bet it's dirt cheap, gonna be a fuckin' bargain, bound to be.'

Getting off the footpath and away from the enraged onlookers seemed like a bright idea so we piled into the tiny shop after Rob.

Racks of clothes of all types, colours and sizes lined the walls of the claustrophobic establishment, by now full to bursting point with our arrival.

'Hey! Ask how much he wants for that suit in the window while I have a look for a nice shirt.'

While Rob thumbed through the racks, Dave did his best.

'Hey, mate, how much for that . . .' At which point the gent behind the counter became very agitated, pointing at Rob and shaking his head, muttering what sounded like, 'No, no, no – no ticket! You have ticket?'

'He says you need a ticket, Rob.'

'A ticket? It's a clothes shop, not a fucking bus!'

At which point Dave, the most sober and by now the only sensible member of the party, spied some large grey industrial machinery on the other side of a beaded curtain.

'HOW MUCH FOR THE SUIT, MATE?' shouted Rob, pointing in the direction of the window.

'No ticket!'

At which point a penny dropped in the mind of Dave Pils.

'Oi Rob, I don't think it's a clothes shop . . . It's a fahkin' dry cleaners, a laundry.'

Meanwhile, in a quiet corner of the establishment, the dials spinning in my head came to an abrupt stop on three lemons. I had completed my transformation from a simply pissed Jekyll into the enraged Mr 'fuckin' bastard' Hyde, and began berating Gillian in no uncertain terms.

'It's all your fault this! All this. All your fucking fault. I've had a fucking nuff!'

What exactly Gillian had done to cause this is simple to answer. Nothing.

I'd just snapped.

I just couldn't comprehend what was going on, none of it made any sense to me – it was a waking nightmare. How had I entered this pit of hell? And who had brought me here?

The pressure cooker blew.

After spending the past three months overindulging in the never-ending burning of countless two-ended candles, the cooped-up living in a studio and a flat, then going straight on tour, all in the close proximity to the same closed circle, came spilling out of me in a torrent of pointless rage. My befuddled brain had found the person responsible for all my imagined suffering, and it was none other than my very own girlfriend.

'Why? What've I done?' she asked in an attempt to diffuse my childish tantrum.

'You know what you've done!' my haughty response.

'What?'

That this argument was insane is beyond question, but once you begin to get a crazy idea, it can be very hard to back down. So instead you double down. Logic flies out the window and the bird of paranoia flies in. Insanity reigns supreme.

'All right then, how much for just the shirt?' as Rob pulled a hanger from the rack.

'No TICKET!' wailed the till keeper.

'Rob, we've got to go. It's a fucking cleaners!'

'What? Go on, you can sell us this one.'

'No, it's a cleaners!'

While I continued my spiteful tirade.

'That's it. You know what you've done!'

'I've not done anything!'

It's hardly surprising that the Englishman abroad is viewed with so much distrust and fear by so many.

Realising that I couldn't actually think of a single thing that Gillian had done to bring about this predicament meant nothing. I'd think of something eventually, I surely would.

My booze-induced machismo still refused to back down and instead turned on to the old childish tactic of couple bust-ups the world over.

The silent treatment.

From the tumbling out of the laundry on to the street, through the cab ride back to the airport and the ensuing umpteen-hour flight back to the supposed sanity of the UK, my sole exchanges with Gillian consisted of spiteful glares and the odd petulant grunt.

I refused to sit next to her.

The rest of our party, usually quick to pounce and take the piss out of any apparent tiff between the two of us, were for once alarmed at my incoherent ravings.

Rob and Dave became Gillian's knights in shining armour, which only made things worse.

They must be in on it too! The bastards. I'd long suspected as much.

As my behaviour became more obnoxious with each passing hour, the more confused and upset Gillian became.

What a fucking stupid, moody bastard I was. Looking back now it was shameful and unforgivable behaviour. Whatever I have said about the tour–recording–tour turmoil, there are no excuses. That you always hurt the one you love is no justification. How she ever came to forgive me I'll never know.

I'd like to say it never happened again . . . but honestly?

Life is never like that, is it? We make the same mistakes again and again.

There are always catalysts for this. Exhaustion and alcohol.

And drugs.

But mostly, it's boredom that's behind the wheel.

As rock-and-roll tales of torment and woe go this is probably not up there with the greats. No one ran amok with a firearm while in the throes of a three-day coke and smack bender. No televisions were hurled from top-storey windows and no policemen were called. No, just a nice if largely liquid Chinese meal and a slightly comedic visit to the dry cleaner's. How could this be the stuff of nightmares in anybody's book?

Therein lies the awful truth of the main peril of the touring band.

These things are very much like the many demises of teatime TV cartoon antihero Wile E. Coyote:

The frantic pursuit of the imaginary feast
Culminating in
The frantic gravity-defying windmilling of the legs in thin air
The loss of focus on reality
The insidious ripening sense of self-entitlement
The over-inflation of the ego already fit to burst
The loss of perspective that concludes with the inability to
    laugh at the desperate situation

Bit pretentious that
Let's call it sense of humour failure
The Princess and the Pea effect
When the tiniest of disruptions brings forth a meltdown of
cataclysmic proportions
The search for someone to blame but not me
Then with a sickening inevitability ...
The crash.

11

THE PLEASURES OF LIVE TV

Top of the Pops: damned if you do, damned if you don't

Despite a decade of habitual viewing, *Top of the Pops* steadfastly maintained its ranking as the show I most loved to hate. Despite this loathing, I'd secretly been planning for the big day when my own appearance on the BBC's flagship chart show would upset the youthful nation's TV applecart in the same way as Bowie's 'Starman' or even Alice Cooper's 'School's Out' had back in the 1970s of my youth.

'Fucking miming's shit though!' was the band's general reaction on being alerted to the possibility that the nation's favourite weekly chart round-up might have lowered its standards: it seemed likely that it was going to be forced to bow before the weight of popular opinion and ask us to appear.

Miming!

We'd never do that, we had principles. If and when we appeared, we would play live, we wouldn't pretend, we wouldn't act, we would keep it real.

I thought *TOTP* was fake, phoney as fuck – a belief which does miss several points but scores highly in the noble aspiration game.

We would only consider lowering ourselves to appearing on this sham of a show if we could perform on our own terms and thus bring about the downfall of the establishment overnight.

Daft as it seems now, at the time I honestly believed that, even as I became dimly aware of the shotgun that was pointing at my shoes, preparing to fire.

I was a serious individual with unshakeable conviction.

'They don't want us to do it because we will show up all the other acts as miming buffoons!'

Expose the fakes!

The viewing public would no longer be duped by this sinister conspiracy perpetrated on them by the establishment's media tool. (Even though they weren't duped: everyone already knew about the miming.)

We would show them!

There had been a time, not long after Ian's death, when the video of Joy Division's 'Love Will Tear Us Apart' had almost made it on to the airwaves, only to be defeated by striking television technicians.

We were almost on when 'Ceremony' first came out, but the Beeb would not entertain the notion of us turning up and playing live.

They were obviously afraid of where it all might lead, of what teatime TV anarchy might ensue:

Keep Music Live, Man!

And so at long last the great day arrived and we were finally to be accepted on to the closely guarded symbol of the pop establishment and allowed to perform on our own terms: we could be denied no longer. The dawn of the revolution was surely upon us.

It ended up being an event that epitomised New Order's sense of perversity.

Our first top-ten smash was a single of un-single duration (although it must be pointed out that we went to a lot of trouble editing and programming a special short version that would fit within *TOTP*'s time constraints – see, we do compromise).

And that song is something which I am on record as saying wasn't actually a song, being partially mechanised, but nevertheless, we would perform that partially mechanised not-song absolutely live.

The not-song that Bernard had once declared would be impossible to play live at all.

The not-song that mostly played itself.

And still I cocked it up.

All I really had to do, apart from press play and tap the odd key or two on the Emulator, was to load two or three floppy disks in the correct sequence into the Emulator's clunky drives.

Easy. But in the glare of the studio lights in front of the audience of shoulder-padded fruggers, I couldn't even manage that. So in awe was I of the glamour of the situation, I fed the floppies in the wrong order. Instead of the mighty thunderclap I and the rest of the band were expecting, out came a wimpy choir going 'ahh' instead.

I could blame the machinery, but for once that worked without a hitch. No, it was definitely me. Human error. It did make me smile though, even now I laugh at myself being such a glum oaf.

I got the Moog solo bit right, but it was no consolation. It made it worse if anything.

On reflection I think I missed the point, that *TOTP* was meant to be a bit of a laugh. The thing didn't require the serious amount of angst that we had put into it.

It was not a great visual experience. ('It was great TV, darling,' was the catchphrase that Tony would frequently trot out to justify our thankfully infrequent duff live TV appearances).

You couldn't even say it made great radio, despite the best efforts of the BBC. I mean, they did try the best they could to make it work. To sound good.

For, as it turned out, the BBC was only slightly less keen on the idea than we were.

'It'd be great if more people came on and actually played live' were presenter Richard Skinner's words of encouragement.

Not everyone involved was quite so enamoured of us. I remember one of the BBC's cameramen, used to more animated jitterbugging pop stars, muttering to someone up in the gallery, 'We've got our work cut out with this lot. They don't move a fucking muscle, none of them. I've seen more life in a cemetery.'

We stuck out like the proverbial sore thumb, saved only by our apparent indifference to the whole thing.

Deprived of all the hard work and layers of production that had gone into the construction of the record, 'Blue Monday' came across as the dampest of squibs.

'Well, I don't think much of this lot, do you, mother?'

'Oh no, turn it over, father. There's a Karl Marx programme on the other side. That Groucho's funny, in't he? Funnier than this lot anyway.'

'Bloody miserable sods.'

I may be being cynical. It's possible that a few unjaded viewers 'got' the point of what we were trying to do, and thought, 'What the fuck – this is brilliant!' And went out and bought the record and became fans for life. That was what we hoped would happen anyway.

Our hopes were dashed. We did make history of sorts. We became the first band to have a single plummet down the charts after appearing on the show. I suspected some TV light entertainment conspiracy was to blame for this, or the unreliable gear – it certainly wasn't my fault, was it?

The height of our equipment unreliability was reached shortly before we began recording our next album.

We'd been asked by the BBC to take part in a *totally* live TV extravaganza they were doing on 25 August 1984. 'Totally live', no miming, yes, this was right up our street. We'd learned many things since our infamous *TOTP* 'Blue Monday' experience a year earlier. Sadly we'd forgotten most of them by then.

We'd played a show at the St Austell Coliseum on the 23rd, where Bernard was struck with a flash of inspiration.

'Let's do something special for this *Rock Around the Clock* thing.'

New song 'The Perfect Kiss' was sounding great live so Bernard suggested we should do a mega-mix of this and 'Blue Monday', join the two together in a segue.

Simple eh? Why not? It'd never failed to be a winner in the past, had it? This idea gained traction as the gear was being loaded on to the truck after the St Austell gig.

I, being ever optimistic, reckoned it would take no more than one or two hours max to achieve this feat of programming magic.

Before the truck set off for London, Terry had unloaded the spare DMX, Prophet 5, sequencer and an amp, and politely asked the hotel receptionist if it was OK to use the seafront lounge for a spot of synthesising/programming. Terry and Hooky then set off with the rest of the gear on a leisurely drive to the big city.

The next day Gillian and I set about connecting up this mini set-up on the small stage normally used by the local cabaret trio to entertain the residents as they indulged in their luxury afternoon teas of scones, strawberry jam and clotted cream.

Suffice to say my estimate of the complexity of the task was woefully short of the mark. Alcohol-induced optimism may have been to blame.

It took all fucking day.

I have never claimed to be the world's greatest in the field of time-and-motion studies, but this one took the biscuit.

The problem I always find is my failure to factor in the amount of pissing around that will be required. Mostly originating from Bernard's creative indecision.

'How about if we tried it the other way round?'

Then many hours later, just as an end is in sight, 'No, it was better how it was before.'

Just a mirage.

All this was enacted before a growing audience of mums and dads and their beach-crazy children.

'Mummy. what's that man doing? Why is he making that horrible noise?'

Until the old chestnut, 'Can I have a go, mister?' put in its inevitable appearance.

Gillian, Bernard and myself did our best as children's entertainers while Rob sought comfort in Stella Artois from the newly arrived Cornish barman. We did our best tweaking, arranging and rearranging until long past teatime, when we eventually had something that fulfilled Bernard's vision.

Having learned much over the past year, I saved the DMX to cassette and Gillian saved the elaborate and lengthy sequence data on to two micro tapes (always make a backup, kids).

'Let's just make sure it loads, OK, just to make absolutely sure.'

Gillian did the magic button presses on the sequencer and, like a charm, the patterns began to play. Mission accomplished.

We didn't particularly fancy a late-night trek to London, so my already faulty time-and-motion services were called on once more. Hadn't anybody learned anything?

'How long do you reckon it'll take to get to London, Steve?'

'Ooh, only a few hours, I should think. It's not that far. It'll be quiet anyway.'

'Don't have to be there till twelve anyway,' chipped in Rob. 'Loads of time.'

Except it was a lovely sunny Bank Holiday weekend!

Everyman and his wife, the kids and the dog had taken to the roads with their caravans in traffic-stopping convoys.

The hour upon hour of stop-start driving got us to the BBC literally with just minutes to spare. We were feeling ever so slightly frazzled.

No problem, though. Hooky and the crew will have it all set up and under control. All we would have to do was swan in, stick the tapes in, press load and play, and all would be off. Soon the entire country would appreciate the fruits of our long hours of button pressing.

The sequencer, though, had other ideas. It flashed all of its lights at once – its own sweet way of saying BAD DATA (or, more accurately, YOU'RE FUCKED).

No problem. Gillian pulled out the backup, stuck it in the slot, pressed load and, guess what?

We were fucked.

Bernard, already in a mood from the drive and the extremely harsh lighting of the studio, erupted.

'We spent all that fucking time for fucking nothing. Well, what we going to fucking play now then? Fucking shit.'

The floor manager called 'Ten minutes!'

'Fucking bastard shit. Fucking cunt.'

I had to admit that all our hours of button pressing and entertaining bucket-and-spade-carrying children and their weary parents might have been better spent but it was no consolation.

Hooky and I hastily concocted a short setlist – none of which Bernard felt like playing – and went for it.

Into the breach.

You could cut the tension in the room with a knife.

'Whose fucking idea was this?' Throughout the short performance Bernard became increasingly incandescent.

'If he says fuck one more time, I'm pulling the plug,' the director squealed to Ozzy, who was doing his best to sort out the sound from the chaos.

It was both fantastic and hideous. Watching it back, it is gloriously chaotic. The TV viewers must have looked on in horror, gripped as the spectacle unfolded. There is no other word. It was spectacular!

Why the thing worked fine in a cosy Cornish tearoom but not in the BBC's Portland Place studios I still can't explain to this day. God knows I've tried.

Needless to say from that fateful day forward the Prophet sequencer's days were numbered. There was this hot new thing called MIDI coming out that was today's future.

The answer to my prayers. Some of the more tedious ones anyway. MIDI is an acronym for Musical Instrument Digital Interface and basically what this meant was that every synthesiser manufacturer agreed upon a standardised digital format. This would allow synthesisers and other musical devices to communicate with each other regardless of make or model.

One of the limitations of the Emulator was that it had to be controlled by its keyboard. Wouldn't it be great if it could be hooked up to the drum machine, or maybe some drum pads, and played like a drum kit? I tried hooking it up the computer, but I think you can guess what happened.

MIDI was a tantalising word that had been around since 1981. It had been a hot topic in electronics and music magazines for years, although I do have to admit that reading articles, mostly written by boffins, about its potential didn't exactly help me understand how it was supposed to work in practice. I just employed what they call magical thinking and chalked it up as the stuff of dreams.

As soon as we'd finished recording our next album, we set about programming everything into this fancy new system. For me, this was the stuff that dreams are made of. Ohh, all those manuals I could read at bedtime.

'Big deal, Stephen, have another line and tell us some more unwholesome stories of the good old days.'

Oh, all right then.

12

STATE OF CONFUSION

Hip-hop pioneers keeping it real with knitwear

Following our first troubled foray to the East Coast in 1980, we became frequent visitors to the land of the free and the home of the brave.

These outings were usually chaperoned by our American friends Michael Shamberg and Ruth Polsky. Thanks largely to Tony's plans to establish a Factory outpost in the States, our exposure to the actual workings of the American music industry – the biz of the big US labels – had by and large been successfully avoided.

America's hotel's bars and clubs, though, those we had pretty well covered. Yes, we had that angle down pat.

Despite what might be seen as our apathy to American mega success we'd gained some kind of momentum. This was due in no small part to our music getting frequent plays on a thing known in America as 'College Radio'.

There really is no equivalent in the UK. We'd had commercial radio since the early seventies, of course, but to me that seemed to be just a copy of the BBC with adverts and more jingles. The music, for the most part, stuck to the same narrow chart-playlist format.

College radio in America is a completely different fish kettle: a number of largely independent stations playing diverse and interesting tracks to satisfy the eclectic tastes of a mainly young student audience.

Whatever success New Order had in America in its early days had its origins in airplays on these stations.

'Blue Monday' got picked up by club DJs and came to the attention of one of the East Coast's hot up-and-coming producers: the aforementioned Arthur Baker.

When the idea of doing something with Arthur had first come up a year earlier, nothing had come of it, but it turned out he seemed to like our records.

We of course liked his records too, but the thing was that they were all we knew of Arthur. We still had no idea how he liked to work, his taste in music and so forth.

In the twenty-first-century, a couple of clicks is all it takes – the entire history of a life is laid bare before your very eyes. Likes, dislikes, the odd video, even a selfie or two, it's all there, whether you like it or not. It's very hard to erase, so I'm told. So, today it's easy to get a rough idea of who a person is or at least how they present themselves.

Not so in January 1983. All we knew were the records Arthur had made and the rumour that a UK jazz-funk band called Freeez were keen on working with him.

That was the sum total of our less than encyclopaedic knowledge of Arthur Baker. As to what Arthur really thought of us was anybody's guess.

One of Michael Shamberg's great skills was what is known today as networking. Michael was a great socialiser and before you could say, 'Arthur who?' Michael had met up with Arthur. A 'collaboration' of some sort was finally arranged.

We would go to New York and record a track with Arthur. For some reason, possibly because we had such an admiration of Arthur's work, there was a bit of a bullish optimism about what exactly this might involve.

Optimism, or was it simply blind faith?

'What gear will we be taking with us?' my whiny, ever-pedantic self enquired of my fellows.

'We won't need any gear. We'll be in a studio, they'll have loads of stuff.'

'Well, hadn't we better, you know, come up with an idea for a tune or something?'

'No, it'll be fine, he's a producer, he'll have loads of ideas.'

'Maybe a bass line or something?'

'No, don't worry, it'll be fine.'

I was dubious. It's my factory setting, and another of my many flaws, but just occasionally I sense correctly that there is impending doom.

'Confusion' was an apt title, because that's what the collaboration largely seemed to consist of.

Arthur, for his part, thought we as hardworking musicians and songwriters would have a ton of brilliant demo ideas ready to go and, of course, we thought exactly the same of him.

In my head – never the most reliable of places – I had this image of Arthur as some skinny young hip dude, a beatbox-owning, Nike-wearing nerd, probably with an interest in skateboarding and a large collection of baseball caps.

The reality turned out to be somewhat different, although he probably does own a baseball cap.

In the flesh, Arthur was a great big bear of a man. A wild and woolly long-haired, bearded gent. Someone who looked like they would be more at home in the company of an outlaw biker gang than body popping on a street corner around an oversized ghetto blaster.

It takes all sorts and as a rule appearances can be deceptive. Especially those first ones – common knowledge by now, that one.

Arthur was no exception.

Meeting Arthur for the first time, I suspect, reassured Hooky as much as it confounded my hip-hop expectations.

Arthur clearly had rock credentials and had no problem with guitars; that box got ticked fairly quickly. Arthur was clearly confident, a man who knew what he was doing, which did little to dispel my anxiety as to what exactly he expected we would be doing . . .

We'd been writing songs together since 1977 but this would turn out to be the first time we'd be involved in an on-the-spot 'songwriting collaboration'.

'So you guys, you got some ideas right? I wanna hear them.'

Like naughty schoolchildren who'd forgotten to do their homework, we coughed, giggled and shuffled.

'Er now, we thought that, er, perhaps you might . . .'

Arthur stuck us in detention at Fred Zarr's little demo studio in Brooklyn for a couple of days to work on our own, while he finished off working on his Freeez track.

We were trapped in a studio with a load of keyboards we'd never seen before and couldn't really understand. I took to comfort reading the manuals as we fiddled and waited for inspiration to strike.

Which of course it never did, so we pissed about some more and floundered instead.

We filled reel upon reel of tape . . . with total rubbish, aimless jams that went nowhere with only the odd slightly interesting or amusing sound, some doodles, the odd not quite riff. Nothing like the demo of a hit that Arthur might have been expecting. It was definitely something Fred Zarr had never witnessed before.

I'm pretty sure Arthur never listened to all of the 'ideas'. Nobody who valued his sanity could. The sound of a road drill would have been more suggestive of a tune.

On the face of it we were doomed. We knew how to write songs in our own particular way but this wasn't how we were used to working, that was the problem. Nothing brings on writer's block quicker than being stuck in a room and told to write.

We spent the rest of the week with Arthur – in New York's Unique studios, the birthplace of rap and hip-hop, so I'm told.

Here, against all the odds, we rescued victory from the jaws of defeat and actually came up with something everybody kind of liked.

It was a song built around a rhythm from Arthur's TR-808 drum machine with only one spare two-bar pattern to work with.

All Arthur's work was in the rhythm box and was not to be disturbed.

One of the disadvantages of the 808 was its lack of the somewhat unreliable tape dump that made life with the DMX so interesting. On the 808, if you wanted to archive your work it would have to be carefully transcribed on to graph paper in a series of noughts and crosses. That never let you down.

Or you could just try and remember it. That let you down every time.

Sometimes being limited to just two bars can be a good thing. It would stop me getting over-elaborate and force me to just stick to the basics, which despite my 'poor workman blaming his tools' type whingeing, is what I did. Most of the beat variations were created on the desk during Arthur's mix-down.

During the course of this at times uneasy session, Gillian got to sing, an anomaly that got passed because a) someone else was doing the production and b) everyone, even me, was having a crack at it.

I vented my spleen when I realised that actual real-world drumming was going to be surplus to requirements by getting violent with a grand piano and doing random backward cymbal and snare-drum overdubs.

Hooky played bass – the end bits – while Bernard came up with all the synth bits, and also played bass.

Everyone – yes everyone – did bits of lyric writing and so they all lived happily ever . . .

Only joking. Happy musicians? Never.

It was a nervous bit of tightrope walking aided and abetted by the introduction Arthur's keyboard wiz John Robie.

John was keen to make us all aware of his brilliance. He impressed both Bernard and Hooky with his over-the-top New York man-of-the-worldness, which cancelled out most of our mistrust of the 'muso-shit' he came out with.

John knew about keys and musical rules like what notes went where. Things that, being a drummer, I'd always tended to ignore.

The fact that we managed to get the bare bones of another idea down as well is pretty remarkable.

At the time, it was only a very rough-sketchy doodle, but it got substantially rewritten and later turned into 'Thieves Like Us'. Arthur came up with the title. He'd seen it sprayed on a wall on his way to the studio.

He was keen on knowing what things were called.

This was a peculiar novelty to us. Most of our creations were known as 'the new one', 'the new new one', 'the new synthy one' or something equally abstract until the last possible minute.

Coming up with a title first? What madness. You'll be wanting a title that fitted the lyrical content next. Oh hang on, hadn't we just broken that tradition as well?

In the end, despite the rocky start, we didn't do too badly.

Working with someone new and getting to see the way other people worked and went about making music – it made you think. We had a way of doing things that suited us. We would turn up to rehearsals at Cheetham Hill, talk about the weather and the *NME*, then go through a few songs or jam for a bit. Stop. Have a brew, listen back to the reels of jamming and see if anything stood out.

If it did, we'd work it out and play around it some more to see if it went anywhere. Sometimes it did, sometimes it didn't. Like panning for gold, we would occasionally find a nugget. The hard part was turning the nugget into something else, ideally another song.

The trick was to keep doing it.

Like everything in life, repetition was the key to success and the occasional bout of futility. Looking back now it might seem as though we were musically naive. We would do things that just sounded good to us even if they weren't musically correct mostly because we didn't know what the musically correct thing was. We weren't into music theory – I certainly wasn't. But working with a sequencer involved learning about the nuts and bolts of notes and especially timing. The difference between a quaver and a crotchet for example or that C,F and G sounded good but C sharp did not. We stayed well away from sharps and flats; they were too complicated. Too much like Jazz man. Bernard just had a very good ear for the things that worked best musically.

We never analysed what we did or even talked that much about music and why we did what we did. We just got on with playing it. We worked at it, Bernard especially, for with the burden of lead singer comes many responsibilities – so I'm told. But working with Arthur we'd been put on the spot.

Stuck in a room and told to write a song: we were out of our comfort zone. I didn't like to say to Hooky and Bernard, 'I told you we should have come here with something we'd already prepared earlier,' but I did anyway. A lesson every young person should have learned from watching Valerie Singleton on *Blue Peter* as a child.

We toured the US yet again that summer of 1983 – you couldn't keep us away from the place. In July, we shot our first proper video in New York at the Paradise Garage and at the Fun House, following a marathon late-night drive from a gig in Trenton New Jersey.

Charles Sturridge, a Granada friend of Tony's whose claim to fame was directing a TV version of Evelyn Waugh's *Brideshead Revisited*, was the man in charge, with Michael Shamberg producing.

The idea of doing a video that actually featured the band I thought was a bit corny. Everybody did it.

But the band must appear in its own videos is one of the commandments of rock and roll and a promotion basic, apparently.

So the idea for the 'Confusion' video was it would show the life of a young female hip-hop devotee working in a pizza shop, Arthur working in a recording studio and us working (I use the term very loosely) on the stage at the Paradise Garage.

This triumvirate would then converge on the Hell's Kitchen electro club known as the Fun House. Home to the city's finest exponents of break-dance. If you'd told me then that this back-breaking windmilling form of self-expression would one day be an Olympic event like Judo I may well have scoffed, but if you'd been there to see it in the Fun House, it wasn't that big a leap.

This was the place that Arthur used as a testbed for his mixes. He would get DJ Jelly Bean to play the tape and, through the glass in the booth, observe the crowd reaction in a kind of voyeuristic product evaluation.

The identity of the originator of this idea escapes me. But it's a fair guess that it was cooked up between Tony, Arthur, Michael Shamberg and Charles Sturridge.

The video does a pretty good job of capturing the atmosphere of the late-night/early-morning Fun House electro crowd, which was the main point of the exercise. Pizza girl and her crew are totally natural. As for the band's part in all this, it was definitely not Oscar-winning stuff.

I think it's fair to say that had this been an acting competition, none of us would have come away with any prizes. As for myself, I would have deservedly finished last, somewhere behind the Fun House's metal detector.

Thing was, I couldn't help feeling like a gatecrasher at some fabulous party. I was intruding no matter how much I felt that this scene was fantastic and exciting. It belonged to somebody else, someone whose life I couldn't completely understand.

The music, yes that I got; the clothes, yes kind of got that too; even the crazy dancing – just pogoing carried to some more elaborate and athletic extremes.

It was another iteration of whatever sense of frustration led me into punk/new wave in the first place. We'd taken up drums, guitars and singing, and now it was drum machines, synths and rapping. The same but different.

The head-spinning thing did look cool, though. The sort of thing that pissed at a party in Macclesfield caused many a show-off hipster in a tracksuit serious back injuries. I thought I looked pretty good in the Nike tracky myself.

13

THE PRODUCERS

Ever had one of those days?

I confess that looking back on my life in the early eighties, I find it slightly weird or at least a tiny bit peculiar that, throughout the early years of New Order, Gillian and I were still living separately – with our respective parents.

Not very rock and roll, that.

Especially as everyone else we knew and worked with had a place of their own.

Mind you it wasn't as if I was spending much time at the parental gaff. I was away for weeks at a time, and my family and I had become almost total strangers to each other. Conversation was limited to short phone calls mostly along the lines of:

'I'll be getting in late on Wednesday. Can you leave the key in the coal shed?'

'Oh, you've lost yours again have you?'

I was never an entirely trustworthy son.

It wasn't as if we hadn't tried to find a place of our own.

It was more the fact that we seemed drawn to places of structural instability for some reason – probably because they all seemed such bargains. We'd go and see houses with character, 'express our interest', and end up getting knocked back on a mortgage.

We were seen as a bad risk: the alleged collapsibility of these places, combined with the fact that both of us were musicians and therefore an iffy credit prospect didn't exactly help either.

'So you're musicians? What do you play – piano, violin, cello?'

'No, I play the drums, we're in a band,' as if that mitigated my choice of instrument.

'Oh, you're in a band, eh? What's the name of your band then?'

'Er, New Order.'

'Never heard of yer,' was the usual precursor to the letter of refusal.

Everyone else had a partner with a 'proper' job, unconnected with music at least. Banks and building societies in the 1980s seemed to like that.

It suggested stability, reliability. These were payers who would not fly by night. Lenders and landlords didn't like insecure professions such as unpopular musician.

I supposed we could have lied and said we were a pair of lion tamers. That's a nice, steady, risk-free occupation.

But deception rarely ends well. It usually gets too complicated and unravels. A tangled web. Much easier to tell the truth. Honesty is always the best policy. So I'm told.

Eventually we found a place that wasn't in such a perilous state of disrepair, jumped the hoops correctly and, in the summer of 1983, I finally made a dishonest woman of Gillian Gilbert. The pair of us moved into an end-terrace cottage next to the canal on Hurdsfield Road in Macclesfield.

It had a shady garden pond populated by newts, a coal cellar and an upstairs room with a very weird, spooky atmosphere. Nobody ever liked being in there for very long. I soon filled it with records and books.

It turned out that my dad was very familiar with the area. As a child he'd attended the Ebenezer Sunday School just across the road. Also the family next door but one's son had been a primary-school friend of Ian; Ian's parents lived a short distance away. He'd gone to the primary school round the corner. More coincidences. It was a very small world after all.

My mother didn't take my departure terribly well. I think she suspected, or hoped, some calamity was just around the corner. Either Gillian would kick me out and I'd return to the fold, or more likely the house would turn out to be a dud and come crashing down around our ears.

My mum still thrived on bad news and general misfortune.

Gillian and I settled down to our life of unwedded bliss and, though I didn't realise it at the time, I was about to become a ham-fisted exponent of the do-it-yourself home-improvement brigade. Our motto is 'No job too big; every job half finished'. Probably sounds better in Latin.

Gillian had plans for the property. She set up a darkroom in the cellar for her photography and enlisted her father Les to the post of restoration builder/demolition expert.

In less than a week the nice seventies-themed cottage had been transformed into a nice late forties-themed bombsite.

I worried that my mum's prediction of doom was about to come to pass.

We really couldn't have managed our lives without the help of Gillian's mum and dad. They took over minding the house while we spent more of our time away gigging or working in the studio.

I remember back in 1983, sometime in the run-up to Christmas: when keeping up the custom of festive cheer, I had taken the well-trodden path to the offie down the road in search of a bottle of plonk and some more cans.

The off-licence's proprietor was well on the way to becoming my new best mate. He called out, 'Hey Marc, Marc, he's here again, that fella in the band I was telling you about! Now what can I get you, sir?'

Playing Pac-Man on the Apple II with Gillian's sister Julie

'Four tins of Boddies and a bottle of that Malbec, please.'

'Coming right up, young sir. I've got our Sylvia's eldest lad Marcus stopping with us for a bit. Ooh, he's ever so keen to meet you. Loves his pop music he does. Is that all right? Marc, Marc! He's in here!'

A surly youth stuck his head through the beaded curtain that led to the inner sanctum at the back of the shop.

'I was only telling him the other day about you being in a band. He loves all that sort of stuff. Don't you?'

'You that bloke out of New Order?' said the youngster.

'Er, yes that's me,' I said fumbling for a fiver and some coins.

'Yer band's all right, I suppose,' he said with a scowl

Marc, I suspected, was after a job at the *NME*.

'Thank you,' I replied. It's always best to be polite.

'Mm, but there's no way you'll ever be as good as Joy Division will you?' His put-down was delivered with an emphatic sneer, the kind only an angry young twat can pull off.

There was no answer to that one.

So I left and spent the rest of the night stewing and coming up with witty ripostes. It was pointless, of course.

I'd been a smart alec and an angry young twat once. What had happened to him?

In some folks' eyes, New Order would always pale by comparison to what we once were. The great attraction of the US and other far-flung places was that Joy Division didn't mean quite so much. Not then, at any rate.

It wasn't that I'd forgotten about Ian and our former incarnation or tried to deny his existence. We still played the odd Joy Division song every now and then, at soundchecks mostly. He was always there, somewhere. It wasn't as if we would ask ourselves, 'I wonder what Ian would have thought of this song?' That would have been pointless. But there was no escaping the fact that without him we wouldn't be doing any of this.

The 'what if?' question never really leaves, it's always lurking somewhere.

I just hated to be reminded of my massive failing.

With the exception of 'Confusion' we had self-produced everything since *Movement*. One album and a single doesn't seem much to shout about. But we were keen and fast learners.

Fellow Factory artistes A Certain Ratio too were starting to get into production. We'd all picked up much in the process of making records. In theory, there were multiple record producers at Factory's disposal. All that studio experience, just waiting to be put to good use in the expansion and diversification of the Factory catalogue, helping new groups get on.

There is more than a bit of irony in the fact that Martin, the man who was supposed to shape the sound of Factory's records, ended up attempting to wind up the label, while simultaneously none of the bands on that label wanted to work with him and ended up doing the producing themselves.

We all got co-opted into record production. First, Hooky with Stockholm Monsters, then Bernard and Donald Johnson from A Certain Ratio became a top production team working with 52nd Street, Section 25, Paul Haig and Marcel King. Bernard and Donald produced some really great records. Marcel King's 'Reach for Love' was Factory's or any label's finest single. It really should have been a top-ten smash hit.

It wasn't long before Gillian and I got roped in.

Through New Order's various trips to America, we'd become very friendly with Michael Shamberg and his partner Miranda.

Miranda was a dancer, artist and musician, and had played in various early NYC new wave bands, including one with a pre-Sonic Youth Kim Gordon. She'd also allegedly gone to a dance class with a pre-Madonna Madonna.

Miranda was in a duo with Carter Burwell called Thick Pigeon. They had made a few demos and Michael asked Tony if they could do an album for Factory – a lot of Factory acts, you may notice, were friends of friends of Tony's.

I am not suggesting that had anything to do with nepotism. Perish the thought! As if.

The way the division of labour went within New Order when it came to production jobs seemed to be:

Hooky: rocky,raw and punky.

Bernard: dancy and melodic.

Me and Gillian : anything a bit weird that we can't quite think what to do with but we've got to do *something* with.

Let's call them misfits. Misfits who could also benefit from a spot of drumming.

I think that's all our boxes ticked.

This was when I became more acutely aware that we were perceived as a single entity, the binary, non-specified 'other two', 'the rest of . . .' or just plain 'them two'. We were a pair, rather than two individuals. It's something that sometimes happens in bands. Particularly if they happen to be a couple.

We were the two in the back row. The quiet ones. I'd accepted this was the case within New Order so I shouldn't really have been surprised to see the opinion spreading further afield.

In all likelihood, Hooky and Bernard were otherwise engaged production-wise so, out of options, Tony asked 'the other two' if we, as friends of Miranda and with time on our hands, would like to produce Thick Pigeon's album.

'An album?' was my response. 'A whole album?'

Which I followed up with what would become my normal question when asked to do this sort of thing. In fact, with anything involving Tony:

'What's the budget?'

I wasn't asking 'What's in it for us?' I was just trying to appear efficient. It was more a case of how much studio time are Factory going to invest in the making of this record?

It's always good to know these things in advance. To know where you stand. Made you seem professional, like you knew what you were actually doing.

I never ever got a straight answer from Tony.

So from day one we were over-budget and out of time.

I'd been spending money, buying bits and bobs of musical gear and electronic gizmos for my own personal use. That makes them sound a bit like drugs, which in some respects they were. These were things that I knew wouldn't get past the New Order's 'waste of money screening test': a Sony F1 digital audio recorder; a Roland TR-808 drum machine; and a couple of small synths.

These I kept hidden in the cellar at Hurdsfield Road, which in time became a musty makeshift studio.

It was with this small set-up, plus the borrowed New Order Emulator, that we ended up making Thick Pigeon's *Too Crazy Cowboys* album. I learned one or two things in the process, not least that Carter Burwell is some kind of genius. Musically (he's now a world-class, double Oscar-nominated film-score composer) and otherwise.

As a first production job, an entire album was a bit of a mammoth task, but we got it done, had some fun – Gillian and her sister Kim did some signing – and I don't think it turned out that badly. We were all still friends at the end of it and that's generally a good sign.

Our other production assignments were a bit smaller: EPs or singles with 52nd Street, Red Turns To . . . and Life. These were much simpler propositions. But I did get the feeling that the expectations were that, as producers, someone from New Order would make whoever it was we were working with sound a bit like New Order The idea that something would rub off was never going to happen. The problem was, I wanted to do things that I wouldn't normally do in New Order; try new things.

The one I had the most fun doing, Can't Afford by 52nd Street, was possibly the most New Ordery. If you look for it on YouTube you can see me in the studio looking awkward; don't blink or you'll miss it.

Hooky relished being a producer so much he tapped Rob up for a loan and bought himself into a recording studio: Cargo studios in Rochdale of all places, scene of Joy Division's first Factory recording with Martin Hannett, which he rechristened Suite 16.

All of this extracurricular activity gave us insights into a world outside of New Order, and in the process I finally got to learn a bit more about film making.

Channel 4 had come up with the idea of getting bands to make short films on anything they fancied. I think that XTC, the Banshees, the Specials, and Echo and the Bunnymen also ended up doing it. Oh and us.

The series was called *Play at Home* and our contribution was hard-hitting no-holds-barred Alan Whicker-style exposé of the inner workings of Factory and the Haçienda.

It was, of course, none of those things. Still, some interesting and often amusing insights into what was going on in Factory at the time did surface in the interviews we did.

Larry Cassidy from Section 25 was fantastic, expressing what was then a widespread feeling among bands on the label. That of neglect.

Tony, being a broadcaster, was great, despite being naked in the bath with Gillian.

Unsurprisingly I wasn't much cop at interviewing. My most memorable contribution was when I was shot by Hannett, my old nemesis. Who at the time was embroiled in his legal campaign to destroy Factory.

The program was also an opportunity to have a go at film editing. Gillian, Rob and I went down to London and, in a small darkened editing suite near the Westway in Notting Hill, we got to put the film together.

As it was all shot on 16-mm film, it was much more like editing analogue tape than the convoluted videotape editing sessions I'd done with Malcolm in Tony's cellar. Basically it involved cutting the film into individual shots , spooling them off, then sticking the bits together with fancy splicing tape (not actual Sellotape, my mother's preferred medium). It was something I found I really enjoyed.

Just as New Order and other bands were exploring the possibilities of samplers, synths and sequencers, other new groups were writing great songs without any technological assistance.

In Manchester, the Smiths were the hottest new band in town.

'Have you heard the Smiths, Steve? They're fucking great!' and they were.

Everyone I knew loved them, and like it or not we became viewed as Mancunian rivals. Two bands living in the same town, how could they not be? It's amazing what people think.

There were two musical poles in my life the 1980s. On one hand there were the Smiths, Echo and the Bunnymen and Lloyd Cole; and at the other end of the spectrum there was all the early electro stuff and hip-hop 12-inchers. We were doing something that was a bit of both but not the same as either. We all had different tastes, but none of us particularly wanted to sound like anybody else.

Gillian liked the Smiths and Lloyd Cole while I preferred the scratching and beatbox stylings of New York rappers.We both loved Prince. I have to admit now that these days I find it is the guitar songs rather than the rapping and scratching that have dated the least.

There are many other things that the 1980s will be remembered for: shoulder pads, big hair, Lycra, Shakin' Stevens, New Romantics, rampant unemployment, Ronald Reagan and Margaret Fucking Thatcher. But for me it is the Sony Walkman – originally known as the Stowaway – that epitomises the decade.

A Sony Walkman that's seen better days

Masaru Ibuka's pet project launched a flood of spin-offs and boosted the fortunes of the world's cassette makers in the days prior to the uncorking of the digital music genie.

A gloriously simple idea, as all the best ones are.

In an accelerating world, why waste time sitting down at home just to listen to and appreciate music?

The Walkman allowed for time that would be otherwise wasted, on the bus, on the train or just plain on the street, to be livened up by your personal selection of sounds delivered in top-notch hissy hi-fi sound. Global tranquillity was unsettled with the arrival of the sound of a million hi-hat parts spilling forth from the Walkman's brightly coloured foam ear comforters.

Alone with the music, insulated from the mundanities of life, just digging the beat, feeling the groove to the exclusion of all else.

Except for the straight-looking fucker opening and shutting his mouth like some demented goldfish, gesticulating animatedly in your direction . . . just as the chorus is about to hit. The good bit!

'EXCUSE ME, EXCUSE ME . . . EXCUSE ME!'

'WHAAAAAT . . .' as the itchy foam gets impatiently tugged from the shell-like.

'Would you mind turning that . . . thing . . . down. I'd prefer if you kept your music to yourself. I can't think with that racket going on. If you'd be so kind . . . Thank you.'

That happened a lot.

I found the foamy ear-pieces itchy and the sense of dislocation from the outside world disorientating at times.

Listening to music was something I'd always believed should be shared and to turn it into a solitary pursuit seemed to me a bit selfish and elitist.

But I needn't have worried. The Walkman had that base covered in another unforeseen area.

For with the introduction of the snappily titled TCS-300 R, every man, woman and child could morph into a mobile location recording facility. The pocket-sized studio was born.

Despite the 'no recording' small print which featured on the back of many concert tickets, it was a breeze to conceal the stereo-recording Walkman in one pocket and a stash of AA batteries and blank cassettes in the other. Slip into the venue, have a couple of pints and when the main act took to the stage, press record and play and hope that the couple standing nearby would eventually give their ongoing vocal disagreement a rest.

The night's performance could be captured for posterity to be relived again and again and, of course, be shared with others who for one reason or another had been unable to attend the night's extravaganza.

We recorded all our gigs on Sonys, listening back for any moments of lyrical or musical 'improvisation' that might be worth including in a definitive version of a song at some later date. The post-gig analysis. Slow-motion songwriting. The Sony became an essential part of how we worked.

For fans of a wayward band like New Order this was interesting, particularly to those who were keen collectors, like myself.

New unrecorded and generally untitled songs would get their first airings live and over time the evolution of these songs could be traced. To the obsessive collector of music this was the stuff of dreams. By swapping tapes with the like-minded, many different versions of a band's work could be collected, compared and contrasted.

In strictly commercial terms this was lunacy. Technically these things were bootlegs. Call me misty-eyed or even stupid, but I didn't see that making a cassette of a gig was stealing the bread from my table.

Art versus commerce, the tricky tightrope.

We weren't that interested in commercial success as long as we could carry on doing what we wanted.

Neither were we interested in the idea that what we did was art of any kind. That was a poncey, pretentious, highfalutin idea, something to mock and take the piss out of.

'Artist . . . you? Piss artist more like!'

But maybe we were.

It's OK to say that when you're old and grey, looking back at it all with occasionally rose-tinted specs.

We were creating something. Maybe that's all art is, after all. Maybe those C90s made on the ubiquitous Sony are in fact artefacts that should be held in high regard, instead of stuck unlabelled and neglected in a drawer, which is my customary practice.

14

LOW-LIFE

'He's very quiet and thoughtful,' says Barney a bit sarcastically about Steven. 'But when he does talk he waffles on and on. He gibbers a lot and it's very hard to understand what he's on about.'

And Gillian?

'She's also very quiet,' says Peter. 'Like Princess Di.'

'She's easy to get on with,' adds Barney. 'She doesn't nag you like most women do.'

An inciteful interview, possibly for *Smash Hits* in 1984. They could've spelt my name right.

I often think of making a film out of all the video-cassette footage that I shot around this time. Maybe some kind of documentary based on New Order's first German tour at the start of 1984, with a working title of 'Why don't you ever play "Blue Monday"?' with someone like Matt Berry doing the narrating.

According to the internet, which never lies, we played 'Blue Monday' every single night on that tour. Isn't it peculiar the tricks that memory plays ... I could've sworn we stuck to our guns and bloody-mindedly refused point blank to play our smash hit at all. Ever. Just to annoy people.

We'd just come up with a brand-new tune, which we eventually called 'Face Up' and to us, as it was brand new, it was exciting and fresh and we supposed that other people might find it so too. They didn't. Most audiences wanted to hear stuff they knew, not the unfamiliar 'Face Up' or the tom-laden instrumental jam that went by the name of 'Skullcrusher' (one of Hooky's). We got mostly a bemused reaction best summed up as 'What the Fuck is zis Shit?'

Here is an interview, allegedly for a German TV show, gamely conducted in the dressing room by Monica – a very nice female German TV journalist – while New Order lounge about getting pissed and behaving badly. Rob is engrossed in a copy of *Playboy* and Gillian's reactions vary from mortified to just embarrassed.

We have just played the Metropol in Berlin, where we felt our performance had unfairly received what the press like to call a 'mixed response'.

I HEARD YOU DID LOVE WILL TEAR US APART AT THE SOUNDCHECK HERE TONIGHT

AND YOU DIDN'T WANT TO DO BLUE MONDAY AT ALL

I HEARD BEFORE, ONLY THE PROMOTERS PERSUADED YOU TO DO IT!!

IT MEANS WE STILL KNOW HOW TO PLAY IT

WHAT DOES THAT MEAN?..

THEY'RE LIKE "PLAY BLUE MONDAY" NO,NO,NO

OH NO!! HE'S AT IT AGAIN

OH YEAH GOD IT WAS HELL

WE JUST HAD TO DO IT!

THAT'S WHY WE WOULDN'T PLAY IT TONIGHT

THAT'S WHY WE DIDN'T PLAY IT TONIGHT!!

WE STAND UP AGAINST THE PROMOTERS!

HOOKY IS DOING A BIT OF LEG PULLING HERE.........

AS IS BERNARD......

REALISING SHE IS BEING FITTED WITH WOOLLEN SPECTACLES

THE PROMOTER SCUMEK SABOTTKA JOINS THE PARTY

SCUMEK!!! HOW MUCH DID YOU LOSE TONIGHT

ROB ASKS HELPFULLY—YET MORE PISS-TAKING!!!

BASICALLY, WE'D LIKE TO OFFER OUR COMMISERATIONS ON BEHALF OF OUR AUDIENCE

?....

WHAT DO YOU WANT US TO DO?

WANT US TO BE A POP GROUP?

WHAT'S A POP GROUP?

WE WERE IN THE SAME HOTEL AS NENA

SHE WAS PLAYING TO 6,000 PEOPLE

AND WE WERE PLAYING TO 60

99 RED BALLOONS, REMEMBER THAT ONE ??

All of which pretty much sums up our pissed-up, couldn't-give-a-fuck attitude. The same one that we'd always had. That punk ethos – not that we were actual punks. Not really.

But I think what you get from this excerpt is that there was an expectation from some that we should be moderating our behaviour, playing the game that was expected of us.

We were an outsider group who happened to make music that appealed to a much broader audience than just the weird or the peculiar. You make a record that turns out to be popular so you must exploit that success, promote yourself, do the decent thing to please your newfound and seemingly impatient audience.

A well-meant piece of advice.

This is what you ought to be doing.

Since the dawn of time – well since the invention of the gramophone then, if you're being picky – there had been a belief that America was the cock of the walk. Certainly in show business.

British bands would heed the call of their ancestors and set sail to 'break America'. For rock-and-roll mythology dictated that was where the *big* money was, the audience more receptive. If you could make it there you could make it anywhere. This tradition also equated money with success. Who can blame it?

It could be a long, gruelling road and, like the settlers in *Wagon Train*, not everybody made it through in one piece, if they did at all.

By 1984, we had toured the States three times – not extensively by the standards of most other bands of the time, but we weren't most bands were we? But neither New Order or Factory had a relationship with a label in the country. A company that could distribute and maybe even market our records in the States. Factory at the time was handled mainly by Michael in New York and for a while Rough Trade on the West Coast.

Tony, Rob and New Order met up with a gentleman by the name of Tom Atencio, a veteran of the LA record industry.

Everyone got on very well with Tom and, like fellow Americans Michael and Ruth in New York, he became another good friend, eventually assuming the position of New Order's American manager, a title that Rob always disputed. Rob and Tom would dispute many things.

Tom knew many people in the US music game; he was a great networker. Tom said he got what we were about, he understood where we and Factory were coming from. He set up meetings between Tony and David Geffen and nearly every other CEO of America's record industry. BIG SHOTS. People who suspected that Factory were some Marxist splinter group, probably best avoided.

Tony Wilson found he liked America. Like me, as a fan of seventies American bands, he found meeting record company veterans from that era a pleasure, people such as Lenny Waronker, David Geffen and Mo Ostin – names picked up from poring over the credits on the back of old vinyl albums from the golden age.

As he told Gillian in 1983: 'You should've seen me in New York with Bob Krasnow of Elektra. I had no clothes on cos I'd got caught in a thunderstorm.

'So I had no clothes on, I had my trousers, but I'd taken my shirt off. They ushered us into this room with William Lombard of CBS, ex-CBS, in their suits and stuff and they were very shocked. And they ordered us a limo to go home cos it was pouring down with rain. So when I got to the door afterwards about eight o'clock at night, Bob Krasnow said, "Listen, I know about your principles, but please take the limo for tonight."

'And I was on my way to the limo anyway, y'know. GREAT!

'I said "Listen, as Trotsky once said, 'While we fight to change life, let us not forget the reasons for living.'"'

In the end, it was Rob and Mo Ostin from Warner Brothers who finalised the US deal. Despite already having a publishing deal with Warners. We weren't interested in signing with them directly. Not cool, too corporate. We wanted something that had a bit of Indie-ness, a reflection of Factory's quirky charm. Like us off the beaten track.

I liked the *idea* of Warners, though. I totted up all the records in my collection and a high percentage of them were Warner-related product: John Cale, Zappa, Beefheart, Ry Cooder, the Dead, Sinatra, Van Dyke Parks, Alice Cooper, Wild Man Fischer, Joni Mitchell – even *Whistle Test* stalwarts Little Feat at a pinch. That must mean something, I thought, and that something I took to be that they must be an OK bunch of boys and girls.

A lot of their music was by what I in my teens considered freaky bands. So I figured that some in the company must be bit less *biz* than others.

The solution to being on Warners while still being independent from them was neatly solved with the discovery that Quincy Jones – who had his own label, a semi autonomous Warner offshoot, Qwest, much like Sinatra's Reprise had been – was keen. How did that sound?

Quincy Jones had heard of us?

The term legend is one that gets a bit overused these days but sometimes it doesn't go far enough to describe what an incredibly great musician and thoroughly decent human being Quincy Jones is. I know that sounds like an awards speech but it's true. To be on Quincy's label was an offer you couldn't refuse, it was perfect. You couldn't get much cooler than that.

It wasn't entirely about being cool and hip though.

Most pressing of all was the club continuing to need steady injections of cash, usually large, and occasionally the proceeds of the odd benefit gigs to keep it afloat.

The club was meant to be a place where people like us could go any time they wanted to do whatever they wanted, so you could eat, see a band or just hang about downstairs in the Gay Traitor bar and drink the cheapest beer in town, just about any night of the week. 'The Haçienda Must Be Built', as the Situationist slogan went; they also say (in the movie *Field of Dreams*) 'Build it and they will come.'

And that was the trouble. They didn't, not at first. Not for a long time.

During the week the place was a huge, cold, empty style cathedral.

We'd pop in for a drink after we finished rehearsing at Cheetham Hill, and more often than not it was empty. Just us, the bar staff and the odd couple of diehard Factory aficionados watching the tumbleweed blow across the empty dancefloor. We would sit cold and dejected under the balcony and glumly asked ourselves why this was. What the fuck had we done?

Factory operated on a set of principles that might have bordered on anarchy, but as long as we stuck to what we knew and understood – making music – all would be well. A bit of diversification, a bit of dabbling in other things such as video, worked fine.

But the club was different.

Months after it opened, nobody seemed to know or understand what they were doing but, as long as it continued to be underwritten in what everyone presumed to be a tax dodge by New Order, what did it matter? You could write a book, you could make a film about how crazy all this was, but it still wouldn't be as crazy as the real thing. Something would have to change. Compromises would have to be made.

Change is a good thing, a natural thing. Evolution its unavoidable. Embrace change!

Stay still and you die. You can't be a Luddite all your life – something I knew only too well.

But again, that was music. We understood that. The club was something else. Making it up as you go along is fine in music and art, but this was a much, much more expensive and grandiose affair. A murky world of business of which we understood next to nothing.

Following on from the pattern established in the making of *Power, Corruption & Lies*, we rented a house in Bayswater (the first in a series of odd west London accommodations) and went into Jam, the former Decca studio near Finsbury Park. Not exactly within spitting distance of Bayswater but there's nothing like a hungover commute through Regent's Park to get the creative juices flowing is there? In Jam we commenced the recording and writing of New Order's third album. We had five songs written more or less and one of these already recorded.

We'd written an instrumental track for a film that ID magazine were commissioning. 'Elegia' took its inspiration from Ennio Morricone's score for the duel scene in Leone's classic western *For a Few Dollars More*. You can't go wrong with a bit of Morricone. The film never got made and so we ended up with a fifteen-minute imaginary soundtrack to cut down for our next album. An instrumental that, as a kind of antidote to 'Blue Monday', had no conventional drums and a waltzy rhythm. The story that the track was dedicated to Ian is another myth, although I'm sure he did like a good western. Don't know where he stood on waltzes though.

The album's title was inspired by a quote from Soho legend Jeffrey Bernard: 'I'm one of the few people who live what's called the Low Life.'

We nicked it from a documentary on Mr Bernard, who impressed with his prodigious consumption of booze and general attitude to life. We made one concession, one step up the ladder of change, on *Low-life*.

It was the first New Order album to include a single, in this case 'The Perfect Kiss'. I kind of half justified this to myself because the real version of 'The Perfect Kiss' was such a lengthy majestic epic of a song – our most complicated and articulate programming to date – that the curtailed version on the LP was really just a trailer for the actual thing, the full-length feature of the 12-inch version.

I'd programmed myself out of a job on this one but as a consolation I got to play musical frogs on the track, a first for me and possibly all mankind.

The other thing that might seem to be a concession to the US label, if you overthink it, was the inclusion of a sort of slice of Americana in the western anti-war song 'Love Vigilantes'. It came from Bernard's idea to do a 'shit-kicking ye-haw' kind of tune, partly inspired by 'Ruby, Don't Take Your Love to Town', a song we all loved. 'Love Vigilantes' is a great song, and like all the best songs it's also very simple, but Bernard's lyrics and guitar and Hooky's bass make it fantastic. One of my favourites.

With *Low-life* I think we grew up and became a 'proper' band. Not necessarily polished, because that's not necessarily good. We wrote great songs and we played them with conviction, which usually is.

Everybody knew what they were doing and even if we didn't realise it at the time, we were somewhere near the top of our game. The gear, too, was constantly being updated. By the time we started making *Low-life*, Gillian's by then battered Quadra was reaching the end of its days. Its replacement was a thing called a Voyetra 8 – basically a sturdily made box with a skinny, uninspiring keyboard that always reminded me of an ironing board for some reason. Fiendishly complicated to program but with a fantastic sound, it became our main synthesiser for the next few years.

Following the pattern of *Power, Corruption & Lies*, three of the eight tracks on the album had entirely electronic drum parts ('The Perfect Kiss', 'Sub-culture' and 'Elegia'), which despite my earlier insecurities was something I was happy with. I began to view sampling and programming as diversification, something to enjoy; I no longer lived in fear of the drummer scrapheap.

Following 'Blue Monday', we had released two standalone singles both with my robot pal providing the beats – 'Confusion' and 'Thieves Like Us'. The upshot of this was that live I was increasingly flitting about from the drums to the Emulator and back again, standing awkwardly at the keyboard with my fingers crossed hoping the disks would load OK.

I was still very uncomfortable with the Emulator; it never seemed an entirely trustworthy instrument. It would always let you down at the worst possible moment.

Much like Basil Fawlty I did like violently thrashing it with a lump hammer or piece of scaffolding. Sometimes it would refuse to load its disks and frequently refuse to start up at all. I discovered that this was remedied by brute force. A short sharp shock administered to the correct place on its rear panel was all it took for normal service to be resumed.

This turned out to be a common fault. Many bands were now using these wonders live and word got about. I began getting phone calls from desperate roadies wanting to know exactly how and where the blow should be administered to coax the reluctant sampler into behaving. I was always happy to help. I liked to think of it as an evolution of the old whack-a-mole arcade game.

Doing a deal with a major label in America meant one or two changes.

These were never demands like, 'You *must* do this or else . . .'

They were more insidious than that, broached with phrases like, 'Don't you think it'd be a good idea if . . . you put a picture of the band on the sleeve . . . or at least the title . . . or maybe included the single? It would really help the guys in promo out a lot.'

So we compromised, ever so slightly I thought, nothing too rash or over the top. Peter Saville's concept, he explained, was that of 'de-mystification'.

The band were on the sleeve but not in the way you would expect. The complete reverse in fact: the drummer on the front and the singer buried on the inside. No title, but the name of the band was there if you tilted your head ninety degrees and focused hard enough. But there was the single 'The Perfect Kiss', a truncated version maybe, but it was there. The unit-shifting 'single on the album' gimmick we'd hated so much. Not completely selling out, was it?

Nobody really complained, if they even noticed in the first place. I noticed and put it down to necessity. Maybe people even liked it?

Low-life may or may not have been a conscious effort to break America, to sell the band to a mainstream audience, to break out of the college radio indie category we so easily slotted into. One of the key words here is promo, short for, you guessed it, promotion.

It was one of the bigger disagreements I had with Tony – and I wasn't the only one.

Factory put out some truly fantastic records. Not all of them were great, but most were: brilliant music, lovingly produced and elegantly packaged.

The bands put their all into making those records. But other than the few reviews in the music press and possibly the odd radio play, there was no way of the wider world being aware that they even existed. I could see the political correctness in this. In an ideal world surely that would be enough.

But this isn't an ideal world, and definitely not a level playing field. Other labels paid for adverts in the press and employed people specifically to bring their records to the attention of people who mattered, such as journalists and DJs. In some cases it mutated into the scandal that became known as payola but let's not muddy the waters, eh.

To some people, Factory's esoteric policy was highly appealing. The vinyl addict, rarity-hunting music snob in me loved the idea. That this brilliant band I had discovered was something only I knew about, my own personal property, made me feel self-satisfied and smug.

But the side of me that was helping musicians make these records also shared their disappointment that most people remained oblivious to their existence. I began to feel that this was very unfair.

The subject came up when Tony paid us a visit during the recording of *Low-life*. I asked if it was a waste going to the time and trouble of making great records only to watch them sink without a trace? Why bother making them in the first place if this was as far as it went? Chuck it out and hope for the best. Shouldn't Factory start playing the promo game a tiny bit, like everybody else seemed to do?

Tony was ideologically conflicted on the idea of promotion. He'd had a brainwave for the huge Hollywood billboard ad for *Closer* after all.

But the idea that Factory should pay someone else to plug records offended him. It was a step too far. 'But surely,' I reasoned, 'if everyone is doing it, should we be doing it too? Just to see if it works. Maybe sell a few more records?'

'Hypocrisy!' you rightly cry. Well, Tony certainly did. He accused the two of us, for Gillian agreed, of being 'money-minded'.

What had begun as a stoned debate about the ethics of making and disseminating music had somehow been turned into me asking for a pay rise.

Which was the last thing on my mind.

Tony scoffed. Rob scoffed along with him. But twelve months later things would change. The scoffing stopped.

15

ALL ABOARD FOR AMERICA

See, I do have legs – and no, I'm not wearing stockings

Tony, despite making out that the pursuit of money was ideologically vulgar, always maintained that one day we'd all be living in Beverly Hills sipping cocktails while the sun set in the Pacific.

I'd always thought the idea was ridiculous, and it filled me with dread. But now here we were: going for it Big Time!

Well, doing a fourteen-date US tour anyway. It was our biggest ever

and most overindulgent affair. In the course of this, we were introduced to various major record-label activities, all of which were based
around the premise: how the mainstream corporate labels went
about turning music into money.

The first of these initiations was 'The 'Meet the Staff in Burbank
Afternoon', where four hours of nonstop press and radio interviews
were punctuated by various Warner and Qwest employees appearing
in doorways, seemingly at random, saying stuff like: 'Hi, I'm Shelly
from marketing, great to meet you guys. *Lurve* your album,' while
vigorously shaking hands and/or air kissing.

The conveyer belt of interviews then culminated in . . .

'The Grand Surprise Album Playback Party'.

We were ushered into a room filled with every member of staff
whose hands had been shaken earlier but whose names had now
been forgotten. Meanwhile *Low-life* was played over and over on an
infinite loop. Factory was never like this.

I joined Rob in the corner in which he had taken up residence
with a big bag of grass.

'Fuckin' shit this.' He meant the surprise shindig, not the grass.

Eventually surprise guest of honour Quincy Jones himself turned
up and gave a bit of a speech before he joined me, Gillian and Rob in
the discreet corner and was his very charming self, whilst politely
refraining from indulging himself.

Tom Atencio engaged the more senior members of the Warner
organisation in sincere banter, hoping they wouldn't cotton on to
Rob's dope corner, while Bernard, Hooky and Terry were making the
most of the situation by sizing up the female promo staff. Bernard,
though, was flagging. He'd done the most interviews and was getting
a bit jaded by the whole thing.

But we all kept smiling like troupers.

It turned out that this was some sort of a toe-dip to usher in the
introduction of another record-company promo phenomenon. That

of the after-show 'Meet and Greet', or 'Grip and Grin' as it is sometimes known. At the end of every show on this tour, a small paddock was constructed – usually within easy reach of the dressing room – and into this enclosure would be herded a selection of lucky people such as radio competition winners, local record-shop owners or just general local big shots out for a night on the tiles. The band would be unwillingly enticed out with the promise of free drink or drugs, and the meeting and greeting would commence.

These proceedings would be handled by Ruth Polsky. Ruth's people skills were astounding. You don't get to manage New York's hippest clubs without a good grasp of them. One of her greater skills was the ability to persuade the unwilling to do the unthinkable without them even noticing.

I was taken by the novelty of the thing. The people were always enthusiastic, polite and nice but after about three or four of these soirées, it began to feel a bit like doing another gig after the gig and before the going out for the night to a club or a proper party.

A bit like the semi-compulsory encore, which we also found ourselves going along with after complaints from the record company about the odd riot resulting from our refusal to conform and go back on to play another song. Sorry Boston.

Riots were bad for business. The record company weren't keen on riots. Bernard got a telling-off.

But surely bad behaviour from bands on US tours was only to be expected, if not encouraged. This was rock and roll, after all, but only up to a point. So after a couple of extra-large post-gig vodkas, I would go and shake hands, sign my name and say hello to the 'lucky' winners and others who had a desire to get close to the band. Like Albert and the lion at the Blackpool menagerie. It could be a lot of fun – a great way to meet new, interesting and attractive people – and for Hooky and Terry this was the principal attraction. So long as they didn't bite.

The main question Gillian and I got asked, apart from the obvious 'Which one are you?' was 'Where's Burn-ard?'

I'm not complaining. We were young and it was all a lot more enjoyable than the average night out in Macclesfield.

I made the most of it, as you would.

Perhaps, compromising wasn't all that bad; having my face on the cover of *Low-life* certainly increased my popularity. It was no guarantee of widespread acceptance though. For despite my mugshot featuring on posters and tour passes, I still found I had one of those faces and was frequently barred entry to the gig by the overzealous US security staff.

The actual getting to the gigs themselves was at times a bit of an ordeal. The conventional wisdom of conducting an American tour would be to travel by bus. A sedate form of transportation providing you weren't attempting to emulate the acid-crazed merry pranksters of yore.

The road crew did this, but the band and their manager shunned the idea of claustrophobic sleep and snail-pace travel in the tour bus. For us it was the highway in the sky.

We would check out late and dash to the airport in two hired Lincoln Town Cars. A huge Detroit barge of a vehicle, with characteristic wallowing US suspension. Optimistically labelled a limousine, they were not really designed to be driven at speed and in comfort. It was one or the other. Never both. Bernard and Hooky in one, me, Gillian and Rob in the other.

The airport was often located by following the contrails of planes that looked like they might be about to land. A map, perhaps, would have been better, but it was usually the first thing to get thrown out of the hire-car window.

We'd then dump the cars, dash through the metal detectors and X-ray machines, hoping nothing incriminating was still in our possession – there usually was, but miraculously it never got spotted.

Jog to the gate, grabbing a hotdog-extra-mustard and a carton of milk on the way, jostle and bump all the way to very back of the now final-calling aircraft (usually an ancient 727) and buckle up next to the engines. After the howl and cacophony of take-off, I'd settle back to smoke my way to the next airport. We'd de-plane and collect the next brace of creaking Lincoln Town Cars – Hooky and Bernard's would make for the hotel for a snooze, ours went straight to the gig, again usually found more by luck than judgement, for the soundcheck. Then gig, then meet and greet, then club, then the hotel in the early hours. Then repeat.

Days off were usually spent in bed, catching up on sleep.

It was during one of these fitful bouts of half-sleep and crazed dreams that I realised the fire engine I was dreaming of was in fact the beige button-press telephone ringing angrily next to my head.

Shit, was there a gig tonight that I'd completely forgotten about?

'H'llo,' I slurred.

'Hi, Stevie?' said an American voice. Maybe it was a phone interview or something.

'Uh-uh,' I grunted.

'Hi Stevie, I'm calling about the show.'

'Uh-uh,' trying to find something to drink.

'OK, Stevie, just a couple of questions . . .' At this point my caller began taking very rapidly about things which made little or no sense. Maybe I was still asleep? I really hoped so.

'Sorry, didn't quite catch that.'

I was waiting for the firmer ground of 'So why don't you do interviews?' or 'Tell me about Ian Curtis.'

The man repeated his urgently garbled message but, it seemed to me, with even more emphasis on the garble.

'No, you've lost me there,' was the best I could manage. A doubtful tone entered the caller's phone manner.

'You *are* Stevie Morris, right?'

At last, something that I could understand.

'Yup, that's right, that's me all right.'

'Well, it's about the . . .' The nonsense resumed once more.

'Sorry, I don't know what you're on about, are you sure you've got . . .'

Getting a little impatient: 'You're Stevie Morris . . .'

'Yes, we've already established that, that is my name.'

'You sure?'

If there was one thing I was certain of it was the name my parents gave me.

'Yup, sure.'

'You a musician right?'

'Yup, right again.' Where was this leading?

'Stevie Wonder?'

Well, I like to think I'm a bit special, but nobody had actually called me by that particular nickname before.

'You *are* Stevland Morris, yeah?' he asked.

'Yeah, Stephen,' I replied.

'NO! Not Stephen, STEVLAND!'

'Er, no I'm not . . .'

There was a shriek that might have sounded a bit like 'fuckin' time waster' but I can't be certain.

An angry click and the line went dead.

'Who was that?' mumbled Gillian.

'Dunno. They were after Stevie Wonder,' as though it happened all the time.

And that is how I found out that the great Stevie Wonder and I share a very similar name. As well as an interest in bleeding-edge new musical technology.

I wondered if he was ever mistaken for me, then thought better-of it.

* * *

Another US-inspired innovation was Rob's adoption of the mantra of the Colonel; Parker that is, not Sanders. Henceforth he repeatedly declared he would be 'Taking Care Of Business.' This became his new catchphrase.

He would arrive at rehearsals, put down his briefcase and note-book and loudly announce to the room:

'Hey Barny, know what I've been doing? . . . I'll tell you what I've been doing . . . T.C.B, know what that stands for? No, well, I'll fucking tell ya, Taking Care of Fucking Business.'

He would get unusually boisterous while making these wild claims. Surely that was T.C.F.B? but no one pressed the point.

There was also a further addition to the touring regime. This was the semi-compulsory all-night hotel-room party. After the gig, after the meet and greet and after the free drinks at the local club, whoever was left standing would retire to some unfortunate volunteer's hotel room. Usually, Rob's where, after over-ordering room service, we'd demolish the contents of the minibar and whatever alcohol had been salvaged from the dressing room. Then smoke, sniff and talk shit over the soundtrack provided by an oversized ghetto blaster – one always seemed to materialise from somewhere – as the sun came up through the crack in the bedroom curtains. It was what was expected of a rock band on tour. So what else could we do?

Well, in America I could always watch TV instead. All those chan-nels to flick through; if I searched really hard I could always find one still showing reruns of *Sgt Bilko* or *The Beverly Hillbillies* from 1965. But in the eighties the hot new thing was music television. America had invented MTV – non-stop music videos. I won't say 'It was the future' because you're getting fed up of me saying that and anyway it wasn't. But done well, a music video could be a thing of beauty. Most of them, though, were incredibly boring. For every interesting video there were a dozen generic shit ones. It was mostly AOR or 'rawk', and there was a distinct lack of rap, funk and soul. The station seemed to have a preference for spandex and mascara-wearing white boys with long fluffy hair. About twenty minutes was all I could stand before returning to *The Clampetts*.

But the music video idea was something I still had ambitions for. I'd knocked a couple of what would now be called 'scratch videos' with Malcolm in Tony's cellar. These were mostly based on whatever clumsy pixelated graphics I could coax out of my computer. There had been one for the early version of '5-8-6' and later a slightly over-militaristic 'Blue Monday' video. I blame Malcolm for that: he got a bit carried away with the psychedelic tanks and Harriers when I wasn't looking. Much as I liked the concept of the music video, the idea of making some sort of MTV-friendly pout fest where we mimed to the track and did a bit of cringy acting was never going to happen, was it? I know we'd given it a shot with 'Confusion' but Official Band policy was anti-miming and our acting abilities were already established as virtually non-existent. Could we not just make an interesting film instead? Something cinematic.

Talking Heads had recently made a full-on proper concert movie *Stop Making Sense*, which Michael Shamberg was constantly raving about.

'Beautiful, really beautiful. You've got to see it,' he raved artistically.

This was not a small-screen affair but the full cinematic popcorn-munching extravaganza. I checked the Macclesfield Express but it was still *Ghostbusters* on at the Majestic.

Oh well, maybe next time I'm in London?

Meanwhile I had taped a film off the telly that I thought was fantastic: the allegedly true story of a man who had a chance meeting with Howard Hughes, a very interesting but slightly peculiar chap. The archetypal eccentric millionaire. This film was called *Melvin and Howard* and I thought it was very well made and brilliantly shot. As we were having a late-night movie-critique telephone debate, I mentioned this to Michael.

'*Melvin and Howard*? Howard Hughes you say? No, never heard of it.'

'You should watch it,' I said, 'it is really good. Very well made.'

Now, truth be told, I'd watched the tape a couple of times but always stopped before it got to the credits. Timed recordings frequently missed them off anyway – you were lucky if you got any sort of ending half the time. So, I had no idea who the director might be, but I suspected he or she must be very good.

Michael rang again. The director of *Stop Making Sense* was going to be in New York, and we needed a video for the *Low-life* single, 'The Perfect Kiss'. Michael was going to set up a meeting.

'Great,' I said. 'Have you seen *Melvin and Howard* yet?'

'Melvin and who? What's the director called?'

'Hang on, I'll tell you . . .'

I rummaged through the untidy and mostly unlabelled pile of VHS tapes stacked like a bizarre Jenga game in progress. I stuck in tape after tape until I found the one with the film on and hit fast forward, then rewind, then fast forward again.

'Hang on, here it is, really, really good film. You've got to see it . . . here we go. Da, da, da, da, da. Yup.' Pause. 'Directed by someone called Jonathan Demme.'

Who, it turned out, was, of course, the very same director of *Stop Making Sense* who Michael was proposing to meet. It was a spooky coincidence, or synchronicity, as omens were called in the eighties.

'He must be good.'

Michael knew the band's feelings on miming and the idea of doing something like *Stop Making Sense* – a live performance video – seemed like a perfect solution.

I say video, at over ten minutes long and shot on 35 mm with Cocteau veteran Henri Alekan as cinematographer and Jonathan Demme directing. 'The Perfect Kiss' was more an art short than anything MTV would ever be interested in showing. Shot at the end of March 1985, it's also a snapshot of where we were at the time. Both physically and psychologically.

Hooky – becoming more of a leather-jacketed rock god – vents his spleen on the bass and bashes the fuck out of my (far too fragile for purpose) Simmons 'suitcase' synthesised drum kit. Bernard – still singing with his eyes closed most of the time – is now definitely a singer. He's got passion in his singing and his playing. He still nearly cracks up in the first minute but manages to contain his laughter. Gillian, immaculate and beautifully cool and controlled (apparently), coaxes her all-new MIDI-sequenced Voyetra 8 synthesisers and Yamaha drum machine to stay on their best behaviour.

Me? I'm looking shifty behind the Emulator playing musical frogs, for fuck's sake, wishing I hadn't had that last line of speed and hoping nobody notices that I'm actually there in the first place.

Jonathan was a bit dismayed when he found the song contained no actual real drumming but had frogs instead.

It's the Cheetham Hill rehearsal room frozen in time and looking its best for once.

We must have had a tidy-up. Road crew members (without whom where would we be? etc., etc.) Slim and a very youthful Andy Robinson make cameos as disinterested onlookers.

It's a filmed performance. The sort of thing you watch at the cinema while enjoying a choc ice. It's meant to be seen on a screen thirty feet tall, so the sense of in-your-face claustrophobia is almost unbearable.

It was visually stunning, but the sound mixing – which was our responsibility (the band and Mike Johnson's) – was slightly more difficult. We were trying to make a live recording sound as good as the album version, which had been painstakingly edited together over a period of weeks. This and getting the film and the tape to sync together was not as easy as it first seemed. Still, we got there learning much along the way. Not least that Jonathan Demme was a lovely, patient and above all enthusiastic guy. He thought 'Love Vigilantes' from *Low-life* was so good he wanted to make another film based around that song, too. Thus beginning a trail of great New Order film ideas that went approximately nowhere.

I'm not sure that 'The Perfect Kiss' was shown that much, if at all, on MTV at the time. It was probably too long. But it did get shown in cinemas as a trailer, just after the adverts for the Indian restaurant. You know, the one tagged as being 'Only 100 yards from this theatre.'

Not long now

16

COR BLIMEY, IT'S THE TAXMAN

This story is riven with ups and downs.

Not occasional mild little bumps but wild swings from the giddy heights of something almost sublime to the 'uh-oh, we're really fucked here' depths of panic and woe.

As usual, it's when things seem to be ticking along calmly that the unforeseen calamity descends.

From a cloudless sky a thunderbolt strikes.

There's an old story that gets retold over and over again, a mainstay in the annals of showbiz and music. It's the tale of how the optimism of God knows how many anarchic entrepreneurs gets crushed in the dirt by the unwarranted intrusion of 'The Man'.

The bureaucracy, the faceless people in the offices upstairs. Those whose sole raison d'être is the rooting out of shady goings-on in the affairs of buccaneering free-spirited types such as ourselves.

The party poopers and bringers of woe.

The spoilers of fun.

Like so many who'd come before us, we found ourselves being investigated by the taxman. The Beatles had got a song out of him. So had the Kinks, kind of. In the seventies, many fled the country to escape his wrath. My teenage self viewed these refugees with suspicion. They called themselves tax exiles.

The up-and-coming band must have looked easy meat. Wide-eyed and ignorant types. Every rock biography contains some story of financial misfortune or other. These usually portray the musicians as hapless victims of some kind of evil Svengali-type manipulator who makes off with the cash, leaving the poor dumb artists bereft.

That sad old yarn unfortunately doesn't work here. We didn't need any outside help.

No one was ripping us off. We all believed we knew exactly what we were doing. We may have been naive in some respects but we weren't totally stupid.

But we weren't trying to rip off anyone else either.

We were men and women of principle. We did honestly want to bring about change, to make the world a better place. How altruistic that sounds, but it was the truth. We were not in it for a fast buck. Or even a slow one.

Surely, some mistake must have been made. That's the first reaction of every wrongly suspected tax felon and I was no exception.

We were getting a very reasonable wage and the benefit of a 'company car', even though Gillian's was a dainty little Fiat 126. But New Order were not hoarding vast sums of money in offshore accounts. Rob hadn't been funnelling cash to mysterious numbered accounts in Luxembourg or Switzerland.

No, surely there was a mix-up. Maybe it was a routine thing. I guessed the Inland Revenue must send these bureaucratic notices of investigation out to every band at some time. Possibly the odd light entertainer or jockey too.

Once the Revenue's investigative brains realised what honest, well-meaning folk we were, we'd get a nice letter of apology and that would be it.

'Sorry to have troubled you, sir.'

Problem solved. Just like that.

*   *   *

It turned out that this was not how these things pan out. The ladies and gentlemen of the Inland Revenue were tenacious and once they got an idea, however tenuous, that there might be a whiff of fraud or some sort of dodginess, they wouldn't let it lie.

Looking back on it now, it all seems a bit ridiculous. Today huge conglomerates can get away with all sorts of racy fiscal behaviour, always seeming to stay one step ahead of the taxman. That's cutbacks for you, or friends in government.

Today, it seems, the customs and excise investigation department is no longer the fearsome force it once was.

In the 1980s, however, the Revenue's investigation department was a fighting-fit unit of zealous men and women schooled in the more inquisitive methods of Torquemada.

They smelled something fishy and suspected we were hiding the truth, and sooner or later they were going to find out what it was.

Again, in this day and age you would think that we could have enlisted the help of some sort of professional. A specialist. A lawyer or maybe an accountant of some kind. Somebody accustomed to dealing with these things.

But we had done no wrong so there was nothing to fear, was there? The truth will out. All we had to do was have a nice cosy chat over tea and biscuits and everything would be hunky-dory.

We were summoned to the Manchester Tax Office on Bridge Street to explain our alleged fiscal misdemeanours.

It was like being up before the school headmaster again or the secret police. We faced the tried-and-tested two-man approach: Mr Nice, the younger, known as Tillmanns and Mr Nasty, a dour Scot, name of Munro. I felt like I was becoming some sort of magnet for humourless highlanders. God knows what karmic debt I had built up in some previous life.

From the start, we were considered guilty until proven innocent.

The early advice that Rob's accountants had given: that we could proceed on a cash basis – something along the lines that if we hadn't received the money we didn't have to mention it – was ridiculous, they said. Definitely dubious. It sounded like the fiscal equivalent of the 'a big boy did it and ran away' dodge.

We were hardened tax evaders trying to pull the wool over the eyes of Her Majesty's finest revenue officers.

'How can you say you've made no money when you've opened a bloody big nightclub?'

That, I have to admit, was a good question. One for which the 'A big bunch of anarchists did it experimentally and ran away' defence was hardly suitable. There was no way that one was going to wash.

'Mr Gretton, a popular band like yourselves must make some money from, say, the sale of T-shirts with the band's name on them? How much would that be, do you think?'

'Er, we don't do T-shirts.'

'Think they're a shit idea – cornball.' Yes, all right, we had done some badges but we would never stoop so low as to sanction a T-shirt!

'Oh, come on, I wasn't born yesterday. As a matter fact, it was only yesterday I saw a young man walking about this town wearing a T-shirt with the name of your band on the front. And you're telling me that's nothing to do with you, are you?'

'Er, no, we don't make any money from T-shirts, we don't do 'em.'

'There's this bloke does some of them but we won't take his money – fucking cornball.'

We and the taxmen all laughed at how ridiculous and unlikely this nonetheless completely truthful statement sounded.

I think Mr Munro had suspicions that Gillian was secretly sewing together the garments in her Gawsworth Road garret. I also suspect that he was labouring under the mistaken belief that Rob pressed and distributed the records himself from his Chorlton flat.

'How many records have you actually sold then, Mr Gretton?'

Now here the answer 'How long is a piece of string?' although accurate, would not have done us any favours.

So Rob took a deep breath and tried to explain our peculiar business relationship with Factory Records to the incredulous tax inspectors. Their brows furrowed.

'So, you're saying that you've sold, say, umpteen thousand records. You can't be sure because you've not had the money?'

Which was pretty much what we had been saying.

'Not my problem, Mr Gretton. That's not how it works. Say your name is Mr Heinz. You make beans and you sell ten thousand tins of those beans. That's what you've sold, right? You've made that money and you pay tax on that money. Right?'

'But records aren't the same as beans!' I helpfully tried to point out.

'No difference as far as I'm concerned. You sold it, you get the money, you pay the tax, simple.'

He did make tax law sound completely simple and straightforward. But the taxman might as well have come from a different planet to us.

On ours, different laws applied.

Our protestations that we didn't work like that fell on deaf ears. Rob's explanation that an accountant had definitely assured him that it would be perfectly OK to only declare the cash the band had actually received as a result of its labours was met with incredulity and disdain.

'I don't know who gave you that advice, Mr Gretton, but that advice is incorrect as far as I am concerned.'

Ignorance is no excuse.

The tax inspectors didn't believe Rob, and they didn't believe us. What they did believe was that we were part of a much bigger shady enterprise whose sinister tentacles stretched far and wide, and involved at the very least Joy Division.

'Explain to me again, Mr Gretton, what is this Joy Division?'

Rob did his best.

'So it's basically yourselves under another name?'

'No, it fucking isn't!'

And Factory, the Haçienda, Tony Wilson and probably every independent label in the entire country – we were in cahoots with them all.

'And you yourself, Mr Gretton. It says here you manage both this Joy Division and New Order as well as being a director and shareholder of what is now Factory Recordings. The company you claim is responsible for this ponderosa discotheque; another company in which I believe you are also a shareholder. And who is this Tony Wilson character anyway, Mr Gretton?' Mr Munro added for good measure.

Put like that it did look a little bit iffy.

A pretty bad day . . .

'We shall be looking into expanding our enquiry.'

. . . just got worse.

'But we've done nothing wrong, you just don't get it, do you?'

No, they didn't.

We were, at least in theory, musicians and despite history showing time and time again that musicians were sensitive artistic types who had and continue to have a very poor understanding of Keynesian economic principles, monetarism and the workings of the Inland Revenue, ignorance was no excuse. There was no mitigation, we were still in trouble. Most likely we wouldn't go to jail, but very large fines could be imposed.

We could be looking at a substantial bill, something in the region of three-quarters of a million was Mr Munro's gleeful estimate.

Incredulous at the unfairness of it all, we eventually did what we should have done in the first place. We got another accountant and a music-business lawyer to fight our corner.

What I thought might have been the opening of a can of worms turned out instead to be the opening of a shipping crate of various flavours of canned invertebrates.

The affair dragged on and on for years. Meetings with accountants and lawyers became regular activities. We became embroiled in something that none of us ever could have imagined. One aspect of which was the discovery that the metaphorical carriage clock – remember that? OK, the Factory shares that Tony had awarded us as a productivity bonus – were not ours, but according to Rob, in fact his. This was puzzling and surprising. We thought that he had been looking after them for us, but as Rob pointed out they were fucking worthless and what would we want them for anyway, we'd only lose them. He had a point but it was a troublesome niggle. The sort of thing some people call 'a bone of contention'.

Back in the days when the struggle to get a soundcheck at Rafters was the biggest emotional turmoil and battle of wills we'd had to face. The idea that one day we'd be arguing over shares and director-ships would have seemed ludicrous. The suggestion that we'd be sat in a room of bureaucrats wrangling over how many copies of *Unknown Pleasures* we'd sold . . . ridiculous! It'd never happen A popular liter-ary term for this situation would be a nightmare of Kafkaesque proportions.

'You never know when you're well off,' as Auntie Elsie used to say. How true that was.

I took to comfort drinking.

'So, that nightclub of yours then, the Haçienda, int'it? What's that about then? Int'it not just a bit of a tax dodge like?' the former man at the pub, now working in the off-licence down the road, would ask with a chuckle as I made my regular purchase of a bottle of vodka and a carton of orange juice. Was he in cahoots with the taxman too?

Vowing never to shop there again, I would bite my lip with a smile (not easy) before scuttling off home to drown my sorrows.

Our fifty–fifty deal with Factory meant that supposedly half the cost of the establishment and running of the Haçienda had, one way or another, come from us. Of this not inconsiderable sum, the taxman wanted his share. How were we expected to pay tax on money that we hadn't received in the first place? How could we pay what we hadn't got? Had never, in actual fact, ever had? For the loot had gone straight from Factory directly to the club instead of taking the more circuitous route of passing our front door first.

'It is contended that the payments to Fact 51 Ltd (sic) were wholly or partly for non-business purposes, that there is a lack of commercial reality over the arrangements behind these payments and the return received for the payments, that the payments clearly represent capital expenditure and were for the purposes of the trade of Fact 51 Ltd, not for the profession of New Order.'

Arguments were batted back and forth between accountant, lawyer and taxman for years. Then, as is traditional in the world of financial wrangling in all its many forms, a compromise was reached.

Eventually it boiled down to this: the taxman was prepared to accept that the money that Factory had paid into the Haçienda on New Order's behalf could be classed as 'promotional expenditure'. Meaning that we would be exempt from paying tax on that amount. This was, of course, good news and a relief.

But the flip side of this was that, as it was an 'expense', we could never see it again. The cash that we had earned but had never seen was spent. The boat had sailed, left the former yacht showroom, never to return.

We had effectively waved goodbye to that for good, for better or for worse. Theoretically it could never be repaid as it was not a loan. Rob's idea of the club as a way of getting our money out of Factory and Tony's clutches had ended up being a one-way street leading to a cul-de-sac.

It could have been worse.

'What you never have you never miss,' was another of Auntie Elsie's popular sayings. 'You live and learn,' that's another of her conciliatory homilies.

Actually it was worse. The taxman reckoned we also owed him a couple of hundred grand as a penalty for our 'mistake', which he kindly agreed we could pay in instalments, what used to be called easy terms or the never-never.

But despite this monumental financial fuck-up, we were all still friends, still a gang. There was no bitterness or sense of recrimination. Well, not that much. We'd fucked up yet again, that's all. It all fitted in with my bleakly humorous outlook on life. Which grew bleaker and less humorous with each passing day.

Despite all these shenanigans, both Rob and Tony still insisted that it would all sort itself out in the end. There would be some clever way of fixing it, there's always a way. It wasn't anybody fault. No one was really to blame for the mess and stress. Just one of those things.

Except, of course, the taxman, who was a bastard anyway – that goes without saying.

Our new expensive lawyer advised that in future it might be better if we changed the way we conducted our business.

And so instead of the partnership that had been established at the beginning of Joy Division in the spirit of fairness and democracy, we became a limited company with the five of us having equal shares.

This all seemed a bit of legal gobbledegook, but if a lawyer tells you something is worth doing, there must be a good reason. So Gainwest Ltd was born.

As we were now a corporate entity, of sorts, I wondered if I would have to start reading the *Financial Times* as well as *Melody Maker* and the *NME*.

Rob felt he'd been made a fool of. He'd been duped by an idiot number cruncher. Nobody makes a fool of Rob Gretton and gets away with it.

He vowed to hunt down and find the accountant who sold him the dud advice if it was the last thing he ever did. Rob would take care of business.

PART 3:

OUT OF MEMORY

Tony over-orders room service

As a teenage sci-fi fan I became mesmerised by the idea of entropy.

The word got bandied about to cover all sorts of plot holes in much the same way that quantum physics can be conjured up today up as an explanation of the most implausible anomalies in pretty much everything. Like it was magic or something.

Well, you never know.

This is probably over-simplistic but a definition of entropy might be: an absence of order or predictability; a decay from the ordered into disorder or chaos. It can be used to describe the heat death of the universe and so forth.

Hang on a minute, Steve, I've seen *The Lion King*. Why don't you just say 'Hakuna Matata, the great circle of life', it would be much simpler.

You make a good point, but what I'm trying to explain is that things, everything really – but in this case the bands of my teenage years – start out simple and well ordered, but then they get increasingly more sophisticated and accomplished until they reach a state of over-complication or chaos.

What my *NME*-reading self began to notice is that bands become more convoluted in all aspects of their being, picking up quirks and affectations from their forebears, peers and heroes along the way, until they reach some kind of critical mass and the whole edifice collapses or implodes. This is then followed by a period of reflection or, worse, solo albums. Then amnesia and/or the tax reminders kick in and the cycle is restarted with a few amendments or caveats, such as:

'I'll only do it so long as I don't have to travel with the rest of the bastards.'

And the great circle is joined once more.

17

ENTROPY IN ACTION

In keeping with the previously mentioned if somewhat tenuous laws of physics, the new songs we were writing were becoming more elaborate. This was largely down to the newly acquired MIDI gear that allowed easier programming and greater musical sophistication and convolution. It could still take some time to accomplish this. But it was possible to do things which almost sounded like an entire fifteen-piece band or orchestra.

The majority of this work took place in the confines of the recording studio. It replaced the rehearsal room as the place where, driven by Bernard, many of New Order's future songs would start life. MIDI, in case you were wondering, was the musical acronym of the 1980s – a buzzword, a must have. It stood for Musical Instrument Digital Interface. It made the programming of music much easier and at the same time much more complicated. I loved it.

In the early eighties, when much of this stuff was bright, shiny and new, the drummer was temporarily displaced from the recording studio by someone who handled 'drum programming'. These chaps, for they were as a rule male, were normally keyboard whizz kids given to the wearing of baggy linen pants held up by oversized comedy braces; their eyesight was enhanced by the wearing of large plastic-framed goggle glasses. They also rolled up their sleeves a lot to show that they did an awful lot of work. They looked a bit like the city traders of the era. Like most right-minded eighties folk they had a keen interest in shoulder pads.

They had fancy names. Like Tarquin.

These guys may have been musical genii, they may have had perfectly good rhythm sense and they knew their gear like a true-blue nerd would. But, and it's only my humble opinion, they had no soul. Instead they programmed beats that would be impossible for a two-legged, two-handed human to play, and they called it progress. They liked their crunchy digital snare drums to be the loudest thing in any song.

Like some defector from the Brotherhood of the Skin bashers, I did much of the drum programming myself and sometimes fell into the same trap. Things got a bit too clever-clever for their own good. The simple groove went out of style.

In a 'normal 1980s studio' situation you would have a producer and his chum the programmer doing all this tedious work. While the rest of the band gasped in amazement at the technical wizardry on display. Before retiring to the pub out of boredom. But in New Order it would be all of us doing the producing and more or less everyone doing the programming. You can see how this might lead to frustration and eventually a little bit of resentment. I felt it myself at times and I was doing a lot of it. Hooky wanted to play his bass, something he did extremely well in his own inimitable style, while Gillian and I were a couple of boring dimwits – a symbiotic entity, the knitting club, clogging up the system with our faffing. I suspect that Hooky felt Bernard was spending far too much time coming up with convoluted sequenced keyboard ideas when he could be rocking alongside him with his foot on the monitors in the time-honoured pose.

'Hello Cleveland!'

Just a minute, Steve. Aren't you the guy who thought Hawkwind were boss? What would Lemmy say about all this?

You make another good point. Thing was, I did sympathise with

Macclesfield, 1981. As seen from Gillian's garret. If you can see the hills, it's going to rain. If you can't, it's already raining. *(Author's collection)*

Gillian and Bernard see a ship in the harbour. I'm not a great sailor myself – more of a sinker if anything – although I can swim when absolutely necessary … *(Author's collection)*

Me, Terry and Hooky eating crisps noisily. Oh, the simple pleasures. Europe, 1982. *(Author's collection)*

Kilkenny, April 1983. Our first tour of Ireland, shortly after our *TOTP* 'debut'. They still talk about this gig – well, they do in Kilkenny. *(Dec Hickey)*

Me attempting to look cool. Kilkenny, 24 April 1983
(Author's collection)

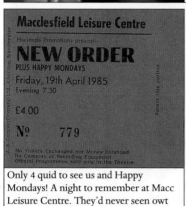

Only 4 quid to see us and Happy Mondays! A night to remember at Macc Leisure Centre. They'd never seen owt like it! *(Author's collection)*

In a Lonely Place. Bernard and the melodica at the Haçienda, June 1982. *(Author's collection)*

Michael H. Shamberg and Tom Atencio apologise for the hotel booking mix-up. *(Donald Christie)*

As well as being the producer of many of New Order's videos and Factory's man in New York, Michael was a filmmaker in his own right. He was also our occasional chauffeur. I can remember Michael driving our minibus back from a club just as dawn was breaking.

Although he was an excellent navigator, Michael would often have trouble distinguishing the road from the pavement.

What's wrong with this picture?
(Author's collection)

The charming Tom Atencio charming Gillian.
(Author's collection)

The Factory Xmas Blue Monday Awards presentation. That tree was shedding badly.
(Author's collection)

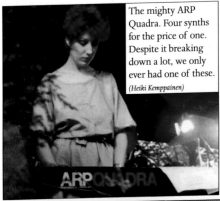

The mighty ARP Quadra. Four synths for the price of one. Despite it breaking down a lot, we only ever had one of these. *(Heiki Kemppainen)*

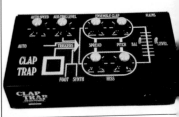

The Clap Trap, a self-deprecatingly named device. High on stamina; low on versatility. If you need a machine that claps, then this is the one for you. A bargain at £86. *(Author's collection)*

The Pearl Syncussion drum synthesiser received much abuse, mostly from its owner. It wasn't easy to play and fiddle with those sliders at the same time. *(Author's collection)*

The AlphaSyntauri. The manual to keyboard ratio is a bit of a giveaway. How did I miss it? *(Author's collection)*

The 1024 Composer. I know it doesn't appear inspiring, but it was. Another Bernard-built Powertran product. *(Nick Wilson)*

The Emulator. Awkward and temperamental. It could also be used as a very expensive whoopee cushion. *(Shayne Jordan)*

The Clef Master Rhythm. A great sounding drum machine made in Bramhall. The inclusion of the brush switch gives a clue to its target market. *(Author's collection)*

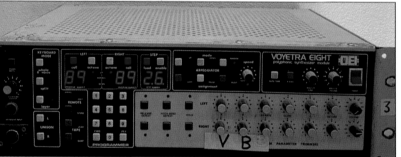

The Voyetra 8 as seen in 'The Perfect Kiss' video. A synthesiser with well hidden depths. It was years ahead of its time and is probably best described as 'not particularly intuitive'. *(Author's collection)*

The Prophet poly-sequencer. Now this one really does look uninspiring. Programming it was more like Morse code than music. *(Author's collection)*

The DMX drum machine. I always found the record and erase buttons a little too close together for comfort. *(Author's collection)*

Smoking in the sun. I burn easily so never take off my coat. Italy, 1982. *(Author's collection)*

Dear mum, Dad, Sam, Polly,

Having a really good time. Hope you are all well! It is really 'hot' here, and Stephen is already burnt after going in the sun for only 1 hour (well nearly!) We have been staying here for about 4 days and it is a bit like 'Blackpool' with 'sharks'.

TOGRAPHY PTY. LTD. – SYDNEY – TEL. 389 8310

Gillian's guide to eighties Australia: 'Blackpool with sharks'. *(Author's collection)*

Are we having fun? Another storming party. The Gilbert sisters: Gillian, Julie and Kim. Spot the difference. *(Author's collection)*

Opening night at the Haçienda. A bemused bunch of drinkers. Proper pint pots, though. *(Ben Kelly)*

Bernard, Hooky, Oz, Rob, Ruth, Dave and Tony join the cult of Mickey. Disneyland, 1983. *(Andrew Liddle)*

ate of the Nation': John Robie doing more
its than are strictly necessary. LA, 1986.
(thor's collection)

And action! Gillian at 'The Perfect Kiss' video
shoot. *(Michael Shamberg)*

urn the fucking light off, Andy!' Dallas, 1989.
drew Liddle)

Me videoing crucified moles. Swettenham,
1981. *(Author's collection)*

illian's hook-a-duck stall doing a brisk trade.
thor's collection)

A pre-acid house Haçienda dancefloor. A place where you had to dance to keep warm, or keep your coat on. *(Andrew Liddle)*

Bernard, Terry, Andy R, Andy L and Dave Pils waiting for the bus. *(Andrew Liddle)*

The RAT, a souvenir of *Power, Corruption & Lies*. Who'd have thought that something so cute could strike such terror in the dark of a Kensington flat … *(Author's collection)*

A hive of activity. The Other Two hard at work in the early nineties. Gillian spots a sheep. *(Author's collection)*

Hooky and I do appreciate the sound of a well-thrashed, amped-up guitar song, I really do.

But to me New Order worked best when we had a balance, when we mixed the two things up together. Instead of strictly sticking to one thing or another. And anyway Hooky would get to play bass on the track no matter what. He could always manage to come up with something extraordinary and brilliant.

Brotherhood, despite its title, felt like a disunited and fragmented record to make. It seems odd to think of it now but we began writing it less than six months after we'd finished *Low-life*.

It began on our first trip to Japan in May 1985 with Tony in tow, for cultural and video supervision reasons. I'd read Mishima's books and enough Zen stuff to work out that it might be a little bit different to life in Manchester. But nothing prepared me for the feeling of being on another planet. An indecipherable alphabet, an impenetrable language, all added to the otherworldliness of it all.

To top it off, we were welcomed like we were pop stars. Young female fans jumping up and down in excitement. That had never happened before.

Perhaps because of the *Low-life* sleeve, it was assumed I was some sort of heartthrob material – the singer perhaps?

'Stefen, Stefen, autograph please!' the schoolgirls squealed. It was like a crazy topsy-turvy dream. Bernard and Hooky found this highly amusing.

My inability to relax, the way I stressed and freaked at the tiniest bit of interest, was a constant entertainment to them.

Gillian, though, was not amused and for a very good reason. The idea that a female could be in a band and be anything other than a glossy figurehead or backing singer seemed incomprehensible to the mainstream Japanese music fan of the early eighties. Gillian was blatantly ignored and overlooked.

Like she was not actually there at all.

If she was not a singer what was she doing there?

In the many interviews we did together, when she was asked anything it was usually preceded with 'Are you somebody's wife?' as if that excused her presence.

All communication had to be conducted through the typically over-polite Japanese lady interpreters whose translations would frequently border on the surreal. The journalists would appear unhappy when they realised that they were only going to get to talk to Gillian, Rob and me (despite the album cover), and not Bernard and Hooky. Rob would get annoyed and confrontational.

'Why don't you ask Gillian any questions?'

Which just seemed to confuse and annoy the journalists, who out of politeness would treat the question as a joke.

Rob would ask the interpreters if this blatant sexism was just something to do with us or a more widespread cultural thing.

The translators kept their reserve but after Rob's persistent and sympathetic questioning finally admitted that it was just the way things were in Japan. This attitude was the norm, as was a kind of distrust of foreigners. I've been back to the country a number of times since then and this attitude is thankfully no longer around. Back then in the eighties, it was a culture shock to find that such an advanced country harboured some pretty nasty old-fashioned prejudices.

Maybe it was the complete lack of drugs or the weakness of the alcohol in the hotel bar, but the place seemed bizarre in many respects, including the work schedule that had been helpfully prepared for us.

We were there to play four gigs. Not too taxing you would think. But one of those gigs was to be filmed , which it turned out meant we would be editing and mixing the soundtrack. We would also be in our Japanese label Nippon Columbia's state-of-the-art studio to record and mix two new tracks ('State of the Nation' and 'As It Is When It Was') when we weren't conducting press and radio interviews. The detailed schedule allowed something like two hours' sleep a day. That's a work ethic for you!

The first gig in Tokyo's Koseinenkin Kaikan was yet another episode of cultural confusion. I wasn't exactly expecting that we would receive some kind of tumultuous reception, but the polite and delicate applause that followed each of our renditions did seem a bit on the tame side. Lukewarm, you might say. A bit annoying as we'd come all that way, after all.

After the last number we returned, slightly puzzled, to the dressing room.

'What the fuck was that about?'

'Weird audience or what?'

Tony, who had been supervising the videotaping of the show, stuck his head round the door and asked if we were going to go back on. To which we unanimously replied:

'No, fuck 'em.'

But after about fifteen minutes of deliberation we thought better of our original decision and felt that a traditional fuck-the-bastards, crowd-displeasing rendition of the Velvet Underground's 'Sister Ray' was called for.

So we went back on, passing a number of panicking concert-hall staff in the process. Our return to the stage was met with a much more enthusiastic response from the crowd, the majority of whom had been obediently filing out of the hall. They now flooded back and their demeanour transformed from politeness to wild exuberance. A bit of a friendly stage invasion then descended into a full-on riot! Police with batons at the ready were called, which only inflamed the situation further.

It was brilliant!

This was not a feeling that was shared by the Japanese promoter who was politely furious with our completely irrational behaviour. This was not done, and our spontaneous action was considered highly dishonourable. For it transpired that some particularly unruly crowd behaviour at a gig a few years earlier had resulted in a tragic death. Since then Japanese concertgoers were kept penned in their seats by ushers and enthusiastic responses to the band's performance in any form were strictly discouraged. We didn't know any of this and I daresay the promoter was equally unaware of our unconventional encore policy. The upshot was we had upset the applecart and generally made ourselves unpopular in certain circles of the Japanese music biz. The audience, though, thought it was fantastic.

No request tonight; free drinks instead

18

A ROCKET SHIP EXPLODES

Pretty in Pink world premiere ticket

28 January 1986.

The day after Gillian's twenty-fifth birthday and to date our only gig in Belfast, we were in the air again. Heading west. Leaving our troubles behind.

If there is one inevitability about the relentless life of a touring band, it is that sooner or later, one way or another, your health begins to suffer.

Stress even the healthiest body enough and eventually the weak spots will begin to show. A good night's sleep can fix most things, but not for long. Not if the cracks are too deep and the damage more serious.

As you've probably already noticed yourself. We've all done it. Taken it a bit too far, ended up in an 'uninhibited' state. Done things that we wouldn't have done in the normal course of events and paid the price.

Only a few weeks earlier, just before Christmas 1985, I'd gone tumbling over the edge. To be fair 1985 had been a bit of a busy year. 54 gigs in 10 countries not to forget the commencement of the tax inquisition; what pros we were becoming.

The trouble began, as most things did, with Rob Gretton.

Rob could not, for the life of him, understand why The Cure were so popular in France and we weren't. The fact that we played the country very rarely and even then only in Paris may have had something to do with it. Rob suspected it might be part of a wider conspiracy.

So to set things straight we went on a slightly more expansive tour of Europe. We embarked on what the itinerary called 'The New Order Christmas Shopping Tour'. With Quando Quango supporting.

The first French date was in Paris at the Eldorado on the 10 December, where we played Joy Division classic 'Atmosphere' and Bernard introduced a new tune, 'State of the Nation', as a 'song about prostitutes with big tits'. Something I had not previously known or suspected.

As a reward we were treated to a slap-up dinner by Michel Duval of Factory Benelux. Our man in Europe.

Michel had founded the Factory offshoot and its associate label Les Disques du Crépuscule with Annik Honoré in 1980. They operated largely independently of Tony while sticking to Factory's aesthetic. Like most things Factory, it was an odd and frequently brilliant relationship. In the twenty-first century, James Nice continues to maintain the FBN/Crépuscule heritage.

The night's gastronomic venue was the Brasserie Bofinger, a beautiful belle époque-style restaurant, all dark wood, mirrors and stained glass. As Michel was footing the bill, we were determined to get our money's worth. We took the entire road crew and, overcome by post-gig gluttony, unwisely over-ordered. I found myself landed with an unfeasibly large tower of fruits de mer. Lobster, oysters, crabs, shrimps, whelks, cockles and things in shells that had no name. This crustacean autopsy was conducted with a selection of implements that ranged from things that looked like large nutcrackers and oddly shaped knives to various-sized tiny metal toothpicks. All of this oceanic debris I devoured with careless gusto and washed down with a few bottles of something or other. The night gets a little hazy after that. It may have been the food and wine. It may have been the dubious yellow powder we had picked up on our way to Paris.

Somehow the bill got paid and we staggered on to the crew's tour bus and back to the hotel for a nightcap, spliff and bed.

A few brief hours of fevered sleep later and I was jolted awake by a burning stomach. I found myself lying in a pool of sweat with an urgent and insistent need to visit the bathroom. Fifteen minutes later, the same thing happened again. The trip from bed to bog turned into a seemingly never-ending cycle of dwindling energy and increasing pain and nausea. I watched the day dawn through the crack in the curtains, begging for an end to the torment and maybe just five minutes of something that felt like sleep. I felt like the blood had been drained from my body and replaced with molten lead. I couldn't stand up for long and resorted to crawling to the bathroom on my hands and knees. There's a painting by William Blake of Nebuchadnezzar crawling on the ground. I knew it best from the cover of Atomic Rooster's album, *Death Walks Behind You*, which was how it felt. That was me to a T. A lot skinnier and without the beard but apart from that . . .

Death felt like he was gaining fast.

William Blake's *Nebuchadnezzar*

Gillian awoke with a sleepy 'What time is it?'

Now too weak to even crawl, I collapsed in a heap on the itchy hotel-room carpet and groaned, 'Ill!' and puked again.

Gillian tutted. A bit unsympathetically, I thought.

The next three days were back-to-back gigs and, as everybody knows, the show must go on.

Likewise the bedroom lights, which seared my eyes that were still doing their best to remain closed.

'You don't look well,' was Gillian's analysis.

But being a trouper I managed to get dressed in haphazard slow motion, stuff whatever was lying on the floor into a bag and, on the second or third attempt, stagger dragging two suitcases out into the dazzling corridor.

I stumbled into Bernard.

'Fucking hell, Steve, you look a bit shit.'

'I know. I've told him,' said Gillian, as though I hadn't noticed.

Bernard giggled. 'You look like Rock fucking Hudson.' Comparing me to a Hollywood heart-throb might have sounded like a compliment, but he had recently died of Aids.

I collapsed on to the bags and groaned weakly.

I really couldn't move and felt like I'd been hit by a runaway steamroller.

'Go back to bed for a bit, you might feel a bit better,' was Doctor Bernard's sympathetic advice.

It must have been bad for Bernard was not normally given to such displays of sympathy.

I felt the reaper's dry hand on my shoulder.

'Wwwooooaghkayyyy.' I resumed crawling.

'I think we'd better call a doctor . . .'

Rob summoned a French physician and I was inspected and prodded while Rob and Gillian looked on. The medico eyed me with suspicion. I was whiter than the sheets I was lying on.

'He has eaten poison. Rest . . . don't move.'

'He's got a gig to do. Can't you just give him something?' Rob asked like I was a pit pony gone lame.

The doctor shrugged and shook his head. 'Non. Rest. Don't move, absolutment.'

He did some scribbling on a piece of paper. Rob, expecting a miracle-cure prescription, brightened.

'My bill.'

Rob got his wallet out. 'Er, does this include service?' He tried to work out what a GP's tip might be.

'Have a cig, Steve, you'll feel better, go on. I'll have one.'

'Uurgh.'

Lunchtime had been and gone and the hotel were keen to see the back of us. We were already late and the next gig was in Rennes, a four-hour drive away. The cig didn't help.

But on the show must go.

I wondered if Abba had been inspired to write 'Super Trouper' by a similar experience.

Our transportation for this tour de France was Rob's recently acquired Audi Quattro – a production version of Ingolstadt's fastest rally car. 'Vorsprung Durch Technik' built for speed not comfort. I was bundled into the back seat, wedged between the door, Gillian and Rob, a case on my knee and a plastic bag and bottle of water to deal with any unwanted eruptions. With Hooky at the wheel, the nightmare terror drive commenced.

The Quattro had a top speed of 135 mph. Hooky seemed to think that was the *only* speed it was capable of. There was much heavy braking accompanied by lurching, screaming, groaning and 'spillage' from the back seat.

The end was surely near, I thought, wondering if I had ever made a will or not. What a way to go. I closed my eyes and hoped when it came the end would be mercifully quick. The turbulent tossing and turning through the grey-green drizzle-soaked French countryside was relentless, though the threat of a violent death in a high-speed collision did manage to take my mind off my interior maelstrom.

I managed to do the gig (well, most of it – Simon Topping of Quando Quango did a bit of standing in at the start) and by 'Temptation', despite feeling incredibly weak, I began to remember where I was and why I was there. The healing power of drumming. Don't ever underestimate its restorative powers.

I slowly began to recover. But Rob was coming down with something else far more serious.

For a few weeks prior to the tour, Rob's behaviour had been much more manic than usual. His 'taking care of fucking business' catch-phrase, delivered in ever more bullish tones, was beginning to get on everyone's nerves but we just grinned.

'I'm a bit hyper,' he would say, which was a substantial understatement for he became progressively more and more bolshy and full of himself than he normally was.

Still, odd activity in bands is nothing unusual. Craziness is expected and if anything it's normality that seems a bit weird (and this was 1985, remember). So it's easy to put a bit of unusual behaviour down as just part of the job.

In Paris, I was lucky, though it didn't feel like it at the time. A few dodgy oysters and whelks are rarely fatal and easily diagnosed. It's simple enough to name the guilty party.

Sometimes, though, it's something else. An actual genuinely serious physical condition, which the lifestyle is masking. Rob was acting like he was going crazy. He would launch into long 'I am the greatest!' rants that made even the indisputably great Muhammad Ali seem like a shy and retiring wallflower.

We were used to late nights, groggily getting by on a few hours' fevered sleep, but these days Rob refused to be roused. Hooky would shout, bang on his door and ring his room non-stop in a reversal of the normal musician/manager behaviour.

A mumbled 'Fuck off!' being the usual response.

He could not be moved. The upshot of this meant that we were always late in leaving the hotel, and every journey with the by-then hyperactive Rob turned into another high-velocity race to the sound check.

In order to escape this turbulence, Gillian and I took to travelling sedately with the crew in the comparative safety of the tour bus, leaving Bernard and Hooky to struggle with the transportation of the management.

By Christmas it was clear to everyone that something was seriously wrong with Rob: he had gone from being extremely hyper to full-on off-the-scale scary maniac.

Clear to everyone except Rob.

He refused to accept that there was anything even slightly amiss in his demeanour. Being by then totally deranged, he resented even the mere suggestion that maybe, just maybe, he should perhaps really see a doctor.

Rob was incredibly strong-willed. Perhaps that's why he was such a good manager. Like it or not, and Rob did not like it one bit, it took a lot more than simple persuasion to get him to hospital to get help.

I'd always thought Rob indestructible and to discover that he was not was sobering, disturbing and upsetting. We tried to make a joke of it as staunch northern bastards do, but it wasn't funny.

'Oh, he's gone off his chump, lost his marbles, had a breakdown' isn't exactly sympathetic stuff, is it? As with Ian, we didn't know the full story. It would take some time before we did.

And so here I was, 35,000 feet over the Atlantic, leaving all that behind. Off on a simple, gig-free jaunt.

Easy. What could possibly go wrong that hadn't already?

We were off to the movies. To the famous Mann's Chinese Theatre in Hollywood, the one with celebrity hands enshrined in the concrete pavement outside. I knew it best from the words Ray Davies penned about it on the sadly underrated Kinks track 'Celluloid Heroes'.

Pretty in Pink is a harmless enough title for anything. Written by the then hot film-maker John Hughes, it was a teen flick – I guess you'd say that was John's oeuvre. The thing that made his name was stuff like *Sixteen Candles* and *The Breakfast Club*.

Pretty in Pink was getting its grand gala theatrical premiere at the prestigious Chinese Theatre and, as contributors to the film's soundtrack, we had received official-looking invitations to attend.

Not wanting to miss out – chances were this was going to be a once in a lifetime thing – and encouraged by Tom Atencio, who'd organised the affair, we jumped at the chance. Why not? Like I said, what could possibly . . .?

Well, the fact that we were off the leash, as it were, left to our own devices. Rob was in hospital. He'd missed the Irish tour, which we had bungled our way through regardless, the band and Terry reprising our old Joy Division roles as a tag-team pretend management.

Now hospitalised, Rob was missing out on a trip to LA.

At some point in our 747's journey a terrible thing happened. One of those horrific moments that in time gets frozen into the collective consciousness.

A rocket exploded on take-off.

On live TV the Space Shuttle *Challenger* went from proud symbol of America's technological mastery to crazy chaotic heaven-bound fireball.

While a nation looked on in shock.

Oblivious to all this, I glugged down more business-class vodka and dreamed of lines of coke to come. Gillian sighed and fidgeted, and ordered four more bottles for herself.

'FOUR! Are you sure that's wise?' I asked, in my best John Le Mesurier voice.

'They're only small,' she explained as I winced.

It was not a good omen.

For the film's soundtrack, we'd written a song called 'Shellshock' with John Robie, remember him? We'd first met in New York while doing 'Confusion' with Arthur. He had played keyboards on Electro classics 'Planet Rock' and 'Play at Your Own Risk', and written and produced 'One More Shot' under the name C-Bank. All these songs were among my 12-inch compilation cassette favourites at the time.

Robie, as we'd discovered during the making of 'Confusion', was a self-confessed prodigy, a musical genius, a keyboard wizard, and a compulsive flirt. He was 'one of the guys', if the guys were from NYC. 'Too full of himself', if the lads were from Macclesfield. He could get on your nerves if you were overexposed.

It's a New York thing. I expect.

The year before Robie had remixed 'Sub-culture' from *Low-life*, possibly as part of the ongoing Qwest 'break the band in the US' campaign. So when the request for a track for the new John Hughes movie came from Tom Atencio, John Robie's name was put forward as producer. Bernard had worked on the 'Sub-culture' remix with him and had enjoyed the experience a great deal, so Robie got his vote and he got the producing gig.

It is widely acknowledged that cocaine may kill you, but you're more likely to bore everyone else to death before it does. It will turn you into a self-obsessed, monstrous, gurning, yakking idiot.

Yes, friends, coke was a big influence on some of us at that time. Clean-living Hooky continued his long-observed abstinence. Even so it's all over 'Shellshock'. You don't even have to listen that hard. The hyperactive bass drum is a dead giveaway – another side-effect of this very moreish chemical confection. Before Rob's hospitalisation, he had taken moreish to extreme levels. It turns out you can have too much of a good – and by that I mean very bad – thing. Rob later acknowledged that the evil dust had been the cause of some of his calamity and he wisely never touched the stuff again.

During the cocaine-addled writing and recording of 'Shellshock' in Stockport's Yellow 2, an incident occurred. 'A good-natured prank.' For many years Bernard and Hooky had taken to amusing themselves with these japes. They usually involved a certain amount of schadenfreude or mild sadism as such practical jokes tend to do. This one was no exception.

The food had arrived in the upstairs kitchen area and Robie, fresh from squeezing more simultaneous notes than humanly possible from a keyboard, appeared to take his place at the dining table. Hooky spotted an opportunity for a bit of slapstick fun. He pulled away Robie's chair just as he was about to sit.

The producer took a tumble and fell on his arse. We all laughed, as slapstick japery dictated we should do. John was not amused in the slightest. Pride dented, he tried to half-heartedly laugh it off but he was furious inside. You could tell.

'C'mon, can't you take a joke?'

Things got fractious for a while but following the after-dinner line, normality was restored and Robie continued to regale us with his tales of sex and music while we got on with making the song.

Now the film was finished and we'd all been invited to the slap-up Hollywood gala premiere. Hooray.

Our plane arrived at LAX and it was immediately obvious that something was very wrong. The airport seemed almost deathly quiet, the expected bustle at immigration was replaced with a solemn silence.

The reason was evident once we got outside to the impractically long black limo that had been sent to collect us. The flag outside the airport was at half-mast and on the limo's flickering TV screen, the Space Shuttle exploded again and again.

'Fucking hell, that's bad.'

A quick pitstop for a few lines at the Sunset Marquis hotel and we were off to the flicks. It was a red-carpet-arrival do. The assembled celebrity actors and musicians paraded for the flashing cameras. A lensmen collared me and asked if I knew which of the guys were the band New Order.

'That's them over there,' I said, pointing with sincerity in a random direction. Some lucky passers-by got their fifteen seconds of bulb-popping stardom while Gillian and I skulked unnoticed into the theatre.

It was at the shindig afterwards when things went awry.

The celebrity gala buffet affair. An MTV-interviewing, air-kissing delirium. Molly Ringwald looked abandoned. I failed to notice Dweezil Zappa, Frank's son, who also had a part in the film. Fee Waybill thrust his microphone into willing interviewees' gobs. It was a feeding frenzy.

Robie felt that the time was right for him to extract his revenge on Hooky for the aforementioned chair-pulling jape.

As was somehow fitting, John went for traditional Hollywood slapstick for his riposte. The good old pie in the face, only it was more of a fairy-cake canapé than the full-on Mack Sennett custard job.

As the pie's victim, it was Hooky's turn to be unamused, his pride severely and very publicly dented. He went to the gents for a wipedown and a think.

It was here, allegedly, that our bass player first fell prey to the influence of the evil white dust. Emerging from the restroom with a newfound confidence, a smiling Hooky returned and repaid Robie's caking with a Glasgow kiss: a full on headbutt. An asymmetrical response, you might say.

It wasn't funny.

See how these things can escalate and get out of hand? How easily wars start?

Back at the hotel, we were up all night with Tom Atencio in crisis mode, trying to patch things up.

I explained to Tom about Rob's absence. We'd been trying to keep it quiet, but his non-appearance at the film's launch was a bit of a giveaway. Everywhere we went, Rob went too. Rob made sure things like the *Pretty in Pink* nutting fiasco didn't happen. We couldn't be left on our own for more than five minutes without some bloody disaster erupting from nowhere.

'If you had a brain between you,' he would say, 'you'd be dangerous.'

There must have been some diplomatic smoothing from

somewhere. Because for the next couple of days we were booked in Village Recorder Studio D with Robie to do an extended version of 'State of the Nation'. During the course of which I ended up in the backroom with the local dealer, taking part in some kind of marathon snort-off. The winner of which got to munch on some genuine Colombian coca leaf for dessert. It was an insane gurnathon. Neither I nor the dealer could converse in any meaningful way – he just chomped and gurned while I grinned and twitched. My friend, a fellow percussionist himself, had some top-secret information that he wished to share with me. He struggled hard to make a coherent sentence that would frame this hush-hush info.

'I been working ... on ... idea ... will revolu, rev, rev-rev ... change ... drumming ... forever.'

I was rapt.

'You got drum ... machine ...? Right ... all these hot guys ... they got fuckin' drum mmmmmaaacch-box yeah? Well, I got something they ain't got. *You* ain't got! Nofuckn'body ggggot! ... I got what you fucking need, man! What the world fuckin needs!'

I was all ears. I had to be. I too had lost the power of speech.

He chopped himself a nerve-steadying triumphant line ... And resumed gurning.

'Yeah, don't tell no one, or you're a dead man ... I've invented ... A BAG! Man! A fuckin' bag for your fuckin' drum machine ... You ain't got one of those sssss'suckers, do ya?'

Further spluttering enquiries on my part as to how this boon of a bag would differ from say any other common or garden item of luggage were met with fury from my former best friend. He felt he'd told me more than he should have and attempted to make me swear an oath of secrecy upon pain of 'DDDDDEAAATH'.

Is this how it ends? I thought. Not for the first time.

Somehow I managed to blurt the old Morris escape line: 'Er sorry mate, got to nip to the loo. Back in a mo.'

Before realising the door was barred. The bastards had locked me in with this lunatic.

I was disgusted with myself.

This was the nadir. Hooky would soon be taking Rob's vacant place at the snowy trough of ego nourishment and things would never be the same.

What the fuck were we thinking? Cocaine really is the most pointless recreational drug going. As an anaesthetic, it's OK. For transforming a shy individual into a gurning incomprehensible monster convinced he's the bees knees, it's fabulous. But mostly it's a vacuous complete and utter waste of time. Not that knowing this would have stopped me at the time.

The Space Shuttle didn't fly for another three years.

I should have followed it's example.

I began to feel like some kind of drug-cocooned Cinderella. Wishing that I'd never actually gone to the ball. Never found the hidden invite.

I was, as you've probably noticed, obsessed with musical technology. We were always looking at ways to increase the potential and reliability of our gear – provided it didn't cost the earth. At one point we seriously considered rationalising and upgrading our setup to something more 'cutting edge' – a Fairlight – an all in one digital synthesiser, sequencer and sampler, by then ubiquitous in sophisticated music circles. It was really a whole recording studio in a box. First seen on BBC's *Tomorrow's World* in 1979, by the early eighties the Fairlight was the acme, the ultimate digital musical tool. All the greats had one Kate Bush, Trevor Horn, Todd Rundgren, and its sound was all over the decade's biggest hits. Martin Hannett always wanted a Fairlight and he reckoned he'd have got it too if it hadn't been for that meddling club.

The box of tricks was loaned for a week. Bernard and Hooky were allowed to play with the thing while Gillian and I were kept well away in case we broke it. The Fairlight had been refined since its introduction in 1979 but its price hadn't. You could have opened another club for that kind of money – almost. So it went back to the shop with the 'Thanks but no thanks' tag. It had, however, given Bernard an idea: an interesting rhythmic bass and top-line sequence which eventually evolved into a song, 'Bizarre Love Triangle'. I think Bernard had that Sunday-paper-inspired title even before the song was half finished.

Looking back, *Brotherhood* feels like it was all done in a bit of a rush. In America Warners were keen for a speedy follow-up, and we were writing, recording and rehearsing at a rate which today seems impossible.

The way we wrote had evolved. Instead of being able to finish a song in a day or two at the most, in a burst of creativity as we had in Joy Division, now it was a bit like war. Brief periods of intense excitement when we came up with an idea were followed by hours of inactivity (for some) while manuals were read and the parts were programmed, sampled, edited and recorded.

Somehow the record ended up a bit disjointed and awkward, the idea that we were doing a half-acoustic and half-electronic record seemed a bit contrived, a bit forced. We had 'Weirdo', 'Broken Promise', 'As It Is When It Was', 'BLT' and prospective single 'State of the Nation' finished. The rest of the album was written entirely in the studio, which was increasingly becoming the norm.

We began work on the 1 April 1986 at Jam again, before moving to U2's studio in Dublin on the 18 May, then finally ending up at Amazon in Kirkby until the end of June.

Maybe it was all the flitting about that made the writing and recording feel disjointed. Maybe it was the background chatter of the ongoing mither from the taxman and Rob being occasionally AWOL. But to me the record sounds a little bit too dense. There were too many ideas that democratically got shoehorned on to the tracks; they don't really come across properly in the finished mixes and should have been ditched. A bit of an over-egged pudding. Maybe we should have had a producer. Oops, there I go again.

That said 'Bizarre Love Triangle' became New Order's greatest miss. An absolutely perfect pop record if ever there was one. It had a brilliant video, again produced by Michael Shamberg and always sounded fantastic live – I'm particularly proud of my Emulator playing on that one. Today it's up there with everyone's favourites, but in 1986 it was a damp squib. A thing that baffles me to this day. I think one review called it 'the work of idiot savants'. I'm still not sure what they meant.

Despite our occasional reluctance we were becoming dab hands at promotion – doing photoshoots and interviews in the hope that someone would see us on the cover of *Melody Maker* and rush out and buy our record. Just because we went along with it all didn't mean we had stopped being awkward bastards. Mellowed slightly maybe, but you never lose the knack to frustrate.

Music journalists still churned out the inevitable 'Why don't you do interviews?' question to add to the clichéd 'band risen from the ashes of Joy Division' theme and the 'why did he kill himself?' query. Many were told to fuck off.

And then there were the painful photo sessions. I still haven't got the hang of being snapped. For the *NME* these photos were mostly taken by Kevin Cummins. The ex-Negatives drummer was by now a photographer of repute and even renown. A necessity for the successful snapper was his assistant, someone who in the pre-digital age of photography would keep track of the various reels of exposed film and load the cameras. Her name was Rebecca Boulton. It still is. Rebecca was one of a growing number of young people who could see some appeal, some attraction even, in attending the Haçienda on a regular basis.

We expressed our gratitude.

Rob knew Kevin from match days at Maine Road. Rob, by then out of hospital and firmly on the wagon, would come to the photo session to proffer style advice, discuss City's form and generally take the piss. Rob took a shine to Rebecca straight away. I think he liked her efficiency and organisational abilities, or it could have been the way that she eventually relented and made him a nice cup of tea after refusing several earlier requests with a polite 'Fuck off, Rob.'

Either way, I got the feeling that seeing fellow City fan Kevin had an assistant set Rob thinking that he too could do with some extra help in the 'office'.

Rebecca was persuaded by Rob to defect from Kevin, to give up photography for a career in managerial assistance. It would turn out to be a smart move by Rob.

One thing I find very curious is that in all the books and films that document New Order and Factory, in particular, it's always the females involved that get ignored, neglected or completely overlooked. Lesley, Rob's partner, worked for a long time at Factory's Palatine Road office, as did Lindsay Reade, Tina Simmons and Tracey Donnelly. They all performed the thankless and frequently very difficult task of instilling order in the day-to-day chaos that was Factory. The most thankless task of all being arguing with Tony about the practicalities and viability of some of the label's activities. Most of which were conceived by Tony in the first place.

'Bloody women,' he'd say, like a child being denied a toy.

19

TOUCHED BY SUBSTANCE

To celebrate the passing of a decade since the legendary Sex Pistols' gig in Manchester 1976, Factory staged a citywide event called the Festival of the Tenth Summer. Ten events culminating in a festival at the G-Mex centre. I remember the day vividly for it was yet another occasion when the old Morris gift of invisibility turned out to be still active. The usual dialog – 'Hi, I'm with the band.'

'What band is that then?' for there were many acts on the bill that day.

'Er New Order?'

'What's yer name then?'

'Stephen Morris.'

The stage-door guardian consulted his many sheets of paper and frowned.

'Nah mate, yer not on the list.'

At precisely the same moment as my not-quite-namesake, the singer from the Smiths breezed past unchallenged.

'No, I think there's been a mix-up or something . . .'

'My name's Steven Morrisey.'

'Oh yeah, there you are, very sorry mate, in ya go.'

The ignominy!!!!

The whole festival got filmed and recorded and then forgotten about which was a shame. It was a good do – us, the Smiths, the Fall plus many many others. Maybe it'll surface on YouTube one day, you never know.

Tragedy returned again in 1986. In September Ruth Polsky died, run down by a runaway cab outside the Limelight club in New York. Ruth had worked on every US tour we'd ever done. She'd even worked on the aborted Joy Division tour and was at the time forward planning the next. Ruth understood New Order. She knew we would rather do 'interesting' gigs than the biggest payers, that hotels always had to have a swimming pool for Hooky and electric sliding doors for Rob. Much of the fun of the American tour went with her. Her death was a shock, a waste, a stark reminder of the fragility of life and you'd hope maybe a wake-up call. Well, three out of four's not bad.

As the taxman and his investigations continued to grind grimly on, our newfound and reliable accountant was drawing some not entirely welcome conclusions. In a nutshell, Factory owed us a lot of money. Not counting the controversial and not insubstantial amount spent setting up the Haçienda, the club required funding on a regular and usually urgent basis. New Order on the other hand could wait.

Nothing wrong with that, just another club-related pickle that I hoped would sooner or later sort itself out. Even though I didn't look it, I was still optimistic. I then had what I thought was a bright idea and unlike most of my wheezes it was a pretty sensible one: why not do an album that would cost very little to make? (There are lots of other claimants to ownership of this idea because it really was so fucking obvious, so let's just say that, most likely, it was not entirely down to me.) We had done all these singles that weren't available on albums. Why not stick them all together on one record – my hated and reviled singles compilation album? Maybe we could call it NOW *That's What I Call New Order*?

That way, maybe Factory could start to make enough to balance the books. Major labels do this sort of thing all the time as a way of

maximising their return on the back catalogue. They are always looking for new angles through which they can further exploit what they
(and you) already own. Now, the record-collecting fanboy snob in me
cries 'Rip-off' reflexively at the idea.

But pretentious prejudices aside, it did seem like the idea had the
potential to get around a home-grown problem. The 'cash flow crisis'.

Tom Atencio and Warners/Qwest loved the idea; it's a tried and
tested showbiz maximiser. There was one small caveat. One fly to
stick in the hair gel. They felt the thing would have a lot more oomph,
razzle-dazzle, have more of a raison d'être, if it were to include something new – a new smasheroo hit single, perhaps? That would be just
great. Help the guys and girls in marketing and promo out
enormously.

Now the idea that anyone could just conjure up a hit record from
thin air, just like that, struck me as ridiculous. What did it mean
exactly? What constituted a hit? To me 90 per cent of commercially
successful music was diabolical rubbish. It certainly was in the 1980s.
Some of it was fantastic, of course, but who really knows what people
love or hate? All we could do was come up with a good New Order
song and hope for the best. There's no accounting for taste.

Since moving into our little terraced cottage, my hi-fi had taken up
residence in the living room next to the TV. There really wasn't
anywhere else to put it. The major side effect of this was I had to
share my musical passions with the rest of the household; Gillian's
sisters and her parents Les and Flo were frequent visitors.

It probably won't shock you that much to discover they were not
particularly keen on listening to Van der Graaf Generator, Neu! or
Faust. I could get away with a bit of West Coast or Gram Parsons and
the odd Sugar Hill or Electro track, but generally there were
complaints, funny looks and tuts of displeasure. If I ever wanted the
house to myself anything by Can would do the trick.

I had to *share my turntable.* This meant listening to a lot of Lloyd Cole and old Motown (I'm not averse to a bit of Motown, but there is a limit). Gillian, however, had two items that found universal approval: Malcolm McLaren's 'Madam Butterfly' and an album by a band called The Pet Shop Boys. These were loved by all the family, they got played a lot, a lot more than Peter Hammill's latest anyway. These two Gilbert gems had one name in common; Stephen Hague.

It turned out Tom had been talking with Malcolm about his next project and the name of fellow American Stephen Hague came up. He had produced and co-written 'Madam Butterfly' and was McLaren's recommendation for a prospective producer. Everyone seemed to like what Stephen had done with this modern take on Puccini and the Pet Shop Boys, and despite the 'Do we really need a producer?' misgivings, he got the job. He booked some studio time for the end of May.

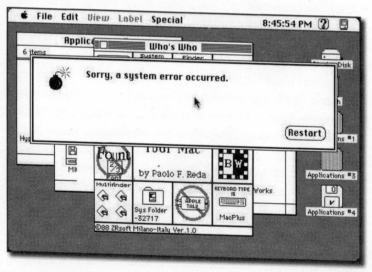

The ever apologetic Mac – I lived in fear of its chimes of doom

I'd bought my first Macintosh (a reasonably priced second-hand Mac Plus) computer towards the end of 1986 and installed it in the musty cellar at Hurdsfield Road. I set about discovering what the stylish little crash-prone box of tricks could do for a forward-thinking drummer. Compared to my former computing machines it was a breeze; I would stay down in the cellar for hours, merrily clicking away, entranced by the machine's cartoony graphics, its monochrome glow.

Once a week without fail my digital reverie would be disturbed by someone banging on the front door above.

It turned out Gillian had acquired a mystery admirer. A young man who would make a weekly pilgrimage to the house! God knows how he found out where she lived. He would arrive bearing gifts for her – knick-knacks, a plant, some old coins, quirky things. Trouble was she was never around when he called, so he just got me instead. The booby prize, out of breath from running up the cellar stairs and annoyed at being disturbed. The mystery man would blush, sheepishly thrust his gift into my hand, mumble apologetically something about missing her again and then bugger off.

Gillian, I think, liked the idea of this secret admirer. The weird plant that was part of her haul took up pride of place in the living room, where it steadfastly refused to wither. A reminder of my rival.

Strange, that I never got any stalkers, fans or admirers. The closest I got was the Jehovah's Witnesses. I was still a weird cult devotee, and would keep the evangelists talking on the doorstep for as long as possible until they grew weary and realised that as a convert I was a dead loss. I had a large collection of *The Watchtower* back issues mouldering in a corner of the cellar.

I loved my Mac. It really was a joy to use compared to the old Apple IIe, which was now slowly getting buried in a pile of quasi-religious pamphlets. Eager to acquire more Apple-related paraphernalia, I became acquainted with Ian Jackson, who worked at a company called Fairhurst Instruments just outside Macclesfield. Fairhurst were setting themselves up as Apple dealers/repairers. Ian was full of advice and free (demos or substantially discounted) software demos. Through him, I managed to get a copy of a program called 'M' developed by a company called Intelligent Music. It called itself 'an interactive musical composition tool'; I immediately liked the sound of that. I mean who wouldn't? It does sound impressive, doesn't it?

Interaction is such a clever word. I mean isn't that what music is all about? People listening to each other. Computers, though, aren't the best listeners.

M worked as a kind of semi-random riff generator. Jan Hammer ended up using it a lot composing the music for *Miami Vice*, so they say. Most of my interactions with M tended to be of the avant garde variety, mostly devoid of anything that might be mistaken for melody, or even rhythm, but with a lot of patient persistence the odd catchy snippet could be coaxed. The emphasis being on the word odd.

Obviously I'd kept the Mac well away from the Cheetham Hill rehearsal room fearing a repeat of my earlier Apple II/alphaSyntauri debacle. The 'What have you bought another piece of shit for?' scenario.

But as something that might possibly be a germ of a seed of an idea for a hit single, I foolheartedly and over-optimistically suspected the introduction of a semi-random riff generator might be a winner. The clock was ticking and no one wanted a repeat of what had happened on 'Confusion'. The end of May was fast approaching and, before you knew it, we would be in Advision Studios in London with Stephen Hague. Where it was hoped a new track could be conjured.

Bernard and Hooky were aware that computers generally and Macs specifically were creeping into music production. A friend of ours in Chicago had tried unsuccessfully to impress with the Mac's potential benefits and uses, but his demo machine just chimed and crashed and chimed and crashed. It didn't exactly inspire confidence. We had a Yamaha sequencer that, despite looking boringly like a portable typewriter, worked perfectly well. In fact, following the previous year's upgrade, we'd gone Yamaha crazy (we had two RX11 drum machines, two QX1 sequencers, a huge DX5 keyboard synth and a TX816 rack of eight synths). I think we were hoping for a discount on a motorbike.

After our early gear hiccups and technical malfunctions, the Japanese reputation for boring reliability at a reasonable price won us over. 'So why would we want to start using anything as risky as another computer hobby heap of shit?' was my expected reaction to the reintroduction of a personal computer. Still, we'd only got about a riff-and-a-half into our single search so surely it was worth a shot?

I dragged the Mac down to Cheetham Hill and set it up on a flight case while Bernard yet again fiddled with the lights. There wasn't a great deal of interest in it but, finally, during a pause in the jamming, we gave it a chance to shine. I'd like to say it was a great success and everyone was won over. But nothing ever really works like that. It was a bit slow at first but Bernard stuck with it and eventually could possibly see that there could be something in it that might actually be useful. After much randomising and 'Interaction', M finally came up with a pattern that was acceptable as a bit of a synth-bass riff that might lead somewhere. So, with the not-quite-a-riff safely copied on to the QX1 sequencer and two-and-a-half ideas in the bank, we called it a day and watched the gear get loaded up.

The Mac was off on its first session. It was not alone, for on arriving at Advision (by a strange quirk of fate the same place where we'd previously recorded 'Temptation'), I felt myself vindicated by discovering that Stephen Hague's set-up was based around an SP12 drum machine, my drum kit surplus to requirements, the now ubiquitous Emulator, a Roland synth and a newish-looking Macintosh SE30. I took an immediate liking to Stephen Hague and began 'borrowing' software off him. His Digital Performer sequencer was the first 'loan'. It wasn't actual theft, as such.

Who am I trying to kid? Of course it was. But in those early naive hurly-burly days of digital pioneering what was a little software piracy between friends?

We played Stephen our small riff collection and a couple of New York cassette club tracks as a direction and came up with a plan: he thought the first one-and-a-half riffs had the makings of one song; the second idea also had some potential and might be the makings of another.

Stephen's plan was that we would work out a rough arrangement of the two ideas: verse–chorus–verse–chorus–break–chorus maybe? That usually worked. Add some rough chords and then instead of Bernard adding more musical parts and overdubs, he would do his vocal parts, and *then* we would add any extra bits that worked around the words, build the track that way. Not the way we usually did things but there was some sense in it, particularly after the *Brotherhood* over-dubbing. Together with Stephen, Bernard worked out the guide parts on the computer, which then got recorded on to a Sony 3324 digital multitrack machine.

This approach naturally impacted on Bernard the most as he was inclined to leave the singing and lyrics until the last possible moment. This time, as soon as he'd come up with a vocal melody, he found himself prisoner in the top-floor flat we'd rented near Paddington, forced to write words. We only had one key to the flat and didn't trust him with it.

Although, as we'd discovered with 'Confusion', pointing a gun at somebody's head and saying 'Write or die!' is not generally conducive to creativity, it can sometimes work. While we left Bernard alone in the flat, the rest of us went to the studio and carried on working on drum samples and rhythm. We returned around midnight to find the flat bereft of food and drink and a well-fed Bernard still wrestling with words.

So me, Hooky, Gillian and Rob – until he felt asleep – tried to help, coming up with random words and the odd line to fill Bernard's blanks. By dawn we had the bulk of the lyrics. We were all particularly proud of the 'they're all taking drugs with me line.

The next morning, we headed back to the studio again, while Bernard had a lie-in, to be greeted by Stephen's 'Where are the words?' enquiry. 'They should have been done yesterday.'

Surprisingly the track came together pretty quickly. And despite our reluctance to follow Stephen's sensible advice that we dispense with the 'drugs' lyric, his insistence on sticking to a timetable paid off. We moved on to the second idea and repeated the process. By that time Hooky had found a title in a book (on the US Civil War, I think) and the first song was now called 'True Faith'. That the second song, '1963', turned out as well as it did was incredible. Stephen felt we had two potential singles, but having a unique B-side seemed more important to us in those days.

Collaborating with other people could be a rewarding experience. Despite the shenanigans with Arthur and John Robie, we'd picked up a few things about which key suited Bernard's voice, and from Stephen we got a few song construction tips and an introduction to the world of chord inversions. I began to realise that no matter how long you work at something there will always be something you don't know.

Just to further complicate things, with *Substance* we went into Yellow 2 in Stockport and recorded new versions of 'Temptation' (the original sounded a bit dated to us at that time) and 'Confusion' (to change the song into a better key for Bernard's voice). Then, as if things weren't complicated enough, some tracks got edited down and a couple of the names got jumbled up.

Substance became New Order's bestselling album. OK, technically it's not a *proper* album, more of a singles compilation. I'll quietly ignore that fact, but we'd somehow achieved what we'd set out to do: we'd written a hit. Michael made another absolutely fantastic video for 'True Faith', directed and choreographed by Philippe Decouflé, another Shamberg discovery.

Featuring bouncing elves, a choreographed punch-up and a turtle lady doing sign language, the video really stood out at the time. It was totally surreal and completely unlike anything else I'd ever seen. In fact it was so good it won a Brit award. Almost without trying, we had three aces: a great single, a great video and an absolutely brilliant album. And all because Factory owed us a fortune.

Who'd have thought it? All because of the Haçienda's voracious appetite.

Well, not entirely. The album also fitted nicely with America's 'keep them coming' release cycle.

Another US tour, with the Bunnymen and Gene Loves Jezebel, followed the established pattern of ever-increasing overindulgent behaviour. That was the lure of the US: with each visit the venues got bigger, the rider got bigger and, for Hooky and Terry, the number of accommodating young ladies also increased exponentially.

In 1987, after prolonged over-exposure to America and its small-screen entertainment, and its MTV obsession with all things AOR (an eighties acronym for Album Orientated Rock) generally and bands like Bon Jovi, Motley Crue, Journey and Whitesnake in particular, we found ourselves with yet another single that required a video.

'Touched By the Hand of God' was the result of a fevered night's work in a small studio (Pluto) in Manchester for the soundtrack of Beth B's movie *Salvation!* Arthur Baker had done a mix of the song that tidied up and improved on what we'd hurriedly done in a few late-night hours and in the process moved it into potential single territory. A single then in search of a video. The idea was blindingly simple.

'Fuck it, let's do an MTV piss-take.'

Following some kind of semi-established tradition of using interesting new film directors to make our videos, Michael Shamberg met up with Kathryn Bigelow who had recently made the excellent vampire film *Near Dark*. Kathryn liked our idea of the bouffant soft-metal spoof but wanted to add a bit of story around which the piss-take could be framed. I believe the technical term is subplot.

But subplots aside the end result required us dressing up as sub-metal leather-clad glam rockers with flowing locks. It was as if we'd gone on *Stars in Their Eyes* and expressed a hidden desire to be eighties glam rock staples, Poison.

Of the four of us, Hooky looked the least transformed. The making of the video was, despite a bit of self-conscious embarrassment, a hoot and the end result ticked all the right spoof MTV boxes. The only problem with the end product was that quite a few people didn't get that it *was* an actual piss-take and thought that New Order actually were a sub-glam metal band gone synth pop who dressed like that 24/7. It's good to confuse an audience sometimes. But you can have too much of a good thing.

Purely by chance, around exactly the same time as the making of the 'Touched' video, we had been approached by CBS records to explore the possibility of abandoning Factory and signing with them instead. Potentially huge sums were being offered and rather than just say no out of hand, Rob did the polite thing and arranged a meeting with them at their Soho Square HQ in London so they could see the bloodshot whites of our eyes as we refused. The date of this meeting was the day after our heavy-metal film shoot and so, just for a laugh, I rolled up in the full spiky bewigged, leather and chain heavy-metal drag. I do like a laugh.

There may also have been a bet involved.

Suitably titillated, we sat down in the CBS boardroom and listened to the pitch along the lines of what a great company CBS was and what a great future they could offer us ... All very interesting but there were strings. There are always strings. These days they call them terms and conditions.

At some point we had a break for a CBS-sponsored sandwich and as Argent's synthesiser emporium was just across Charing Cross Road, I was unable to resist the temptation to pop in and have a nosy at some new drum machines and synthesisers. I was still dressed in the 'Touched' glam-metal gear and as I waited for the lights to change at the pelican crossing near Centre Point, I felt a firm hand grasp my shoulder. I turned and was somewhat stunned to find myself facing two of London's finest coppers.

'Excuse me, sir, we've noticed that you have been behaving in a suspicious manner and we'd like you to come with us, if you don't mind.'

Now as a former member of the Tufty club, I'd crossed many roads in my life and I didn't think I'd done anything more or less suspicious this time around. What they actually meant was "Allo, 'allo, 'allo, likely looking lad 'ere and no mistake. Give him a pull and we're bound to come up with something.'

'Do you mind coming with us, sir, and emptying your pockets for us so we can give you a quick search.'

I didn't like the sound of that one bit.

This was not good, for although I couldn't be 100 per cent certain, there was a very high probability that in at least one of the metal-chained biker jacket's pockets would be something that the filth would find very interesting indeed. Oh fuck, I could see what was coming, the inevitable, 'Oh dear, oh dear, oh dear, what do we have here?'

Brain racing for a get-out, the best I could come up with was a meek and typically wimpy squeak. 'Er, I've just been making a video. I don't normally dress like this, officer.'

It didn't wash with the boys in blue

'Very interesting, sir, now if you'd like to step this way off the main road to somewhere quieter, where you can allow us to conduct a search of your person.'

Oh fuck, I've had it here, was my exact thought. Now, I'm not the sort of person who likes to come out with the indignant 'Don't you know who I am?' line. Experience has taught me the answer to that question was usually an emphatic 'No, sonny, I fucking don't!'

So I desperately stuck to my guns.

'No, honest, I've been making a video, I'm in a band . . .'

'Oh yes, sir. Just step round this corner, if you don't mind.'

I was totally fucked. I was dragged round the corner into Falconberg Court, with the two officers of the law holding an arm apiece, to face my certain doom.

As we turned the corner into the side street – and I know this is uncanny and unbelievable, but it's true – there in the road was . . .

A camera crew, big 35-mm camera, sound guy, the lot. Talk about coincidences, but there it was: someone making an actual fucking video.

'Yeah, there they are over there, look!' I said waving to the cameraman, who surprisingly waved back. 'Do you want me to ask if you can be in the shot too?' I asked my captors with newfound confidence. Not fancying their fifteen minutes of fame, the bobbies backed down with a somewhat deflated, 'No, thank you, sir, on your way.'

I mean what are the chances of that. It was almost enough to make me believe in divine intervention. My heart was racing with a mixture of adrenalin anxiety and relief as I got back to the boardroom. There I discovered that the jacket's contents were, as I feared, largely of the class A variety. There was a lot to be said for my normal look of dressing like a Nike-wearing geography teacher. It was back to an inconspicuous life for me. I was not cut out for the flamboyant life.

The CBS deal was, with the best will in the world, never likely to get anywhere. But it was nice to see what the 'big boys' thought we were worth. Like getting that antique clock that's been in the family for generations valued on *Antiques Roadshow*. It's always nice to feel wanted. Feel valued.

We'd taken a lawyer with us, though, just to make sure we didn't foolishly sign our lives away for five magic beans. The other thing was that, by talking to CBS, we were also sending a 'don't take us for granted' message to Tony.

Feeling confused by the glam-metal piss-take of 'Touched', the suggestion came from America that maybe, just maybe, we should think about doing an updated mix of 'Blue Monday' and maybe in the process perhaps shorten it a little?

An instinctive 'fuck off' from us was averted by the mention of Quincy's name as the prospective remixer. That was different. You don't say no to Quincy Jones.

One thing Rob could very easily say no to was the request by a soft drinks company to use 'Blue Monday' in a worldwide TV advert – Sunkist for their 'Drink in the Sun' ad campaign.

The ad company were a tenacious lot and not keen on taking no for an answer kept upping their offer, insisting on a face-to-face meeting. We were to be in Advision (again) with Mike Johnson updating 'Blue Monday' for Quincy to remix.

Bernard wanted to redo the drums and try some more synths. So Rob arranged to meet the Sunkist people at the studio so he could say no to their faces. There's nothing like the personal touch when it comes to rejection is there?

Unfortunately Rob had not turned up at the studio by the time the soft-drinks salesmen arrived. Now you don't get to work in advertising without mastering the subtle art of persuasion. The lady in charge was an old hand at being both charming and persuasive. Hooky and Bernard took an executive decision and decided to take over negotiations for themselves. Hearing that the offer involved the princely sum of £100,000, our newly deputised management team agreed it was an excellent idea – anything to help sell more fizz. Sunkist, however, wanted the lyrics changing to something more, well, Sunkisty. Bernard got a bit reluctant at this point, but being constantly reminded of the dosh on offer by means of an improvised DIY cardboard cheque. He swallowed his pride and agreed to extol the virtues of the beverage in song.

'Sunkist is the one,' Bernard sang between fits of giggles. The giggles came to abrupt end when Rob turned up. By then the adpeople were long gone.

'You daft bastards, what did I tell you?'

'You told us not to agree to anything, Rob,' was the naughty boys' sheepish answer.

'And what did you fuckin' do?'

'We agreed to everything, Rob . . . for a hundred grand.'

'Fuckin' idiots. If you had a fuckin' brain between you, you'd be dangerous.'

Oh, how we laughed. There was never really any chance that the ad would actually happen.

After Bernard finished improving the drum sounds, I further improved the song with samples of the sound of cash registers, Japanese girls and US gameshow hosts. I was especially fond of the phrase 'Oh no, they're going at it again! Ker-chiiiing.'

Meanwhile back at the Haçienda . . .

The folly continued.

There was a bit of a wait and a lot of financial drainage before something that worked eventually turned up. And that's putting it mildly.

There was so much flailing about, going to urgent business meetings, discussing important stuff like should we sell burgers or pancakes, Purdey's or Tizer? Why was the new cooperative system of management failing? Why was the sound so bad? Could we have another twenty grand, please – just until the end of next week?

All this urgent business became run-of-the-mill.

Eventually those in charge, having finally run out of friends of friends to employ and madcap schemes to concoct, came to the stark realisation that things could not carry on as they were.

What was needed was an expert.

Someone who actually had a bit of experience in the club-running business. Someone who had maybe done this sort of thing before.

A ridiculous idea, I know, but we were getting desperate.

Enter Paul Mason, who'd been successfully running Rock City in Nottingham. I think it was Alan Erasmus who found him. All the practical solutions were usually down to Alan.

The two Pauls, Paul Mason and Paul Cons (who was behind the famous Flesh gay night at the Haç), made changes – not always popular changes, it has to be said, but effective. They succeeded where other attempts at cooperative management and many other various wacky schemes hadn't. Paul Mason managed to balance the books and in eighteen months the place was breaking even, maybe even making a bit of a profit.

This was, of course, fantastic and the crisis meetings became fewer and slightly more jolly affairs. The thing for me was trying to work out how long the place would have to carry on making a profit before it would begin to recoup the accumulated losses.

A brief bit of scribbling on the back of a fag packet said, 'A very long time indeed.'

Paul, though, could do no wrong.

He was a golden boy. He liked a challenge, did Paul. He was very good as his job.

Gradually things began to change at the club, things began to happen – good things, the kind of things that actually worked!!!! The place was becoming popular with some unlikely folk.

Now I may have mentioned that Gillian was not an only child. She was one of three, a trio of Gilberts. Their names were Gillian (obviously), Julie and Kim. Now what I've probably neglected to mention is that this trinity whilst not actual triplets do bear an uncanny resemblance to each other. To the uninitiated or just uninformed this could be a great source of confusion and alarm.

Of the three it was Kim who was the most given to nights on the town frequenting hotspots or discotheques of this parish. She had been a regular at Macclefield's Silklands Suite prior to its untimely demolition. Now that Silklands was a car park or more accurately a patch of waste ground it was time for Kim and her friends to seek pastures new.

Imagine my surprise when upon attempting to gain admission to the former yacht showroom on Whitworth street, for me never an easy job at the best of times, I discovered my powers of invisibility seemed to have infected Gillian.

After a brief period of queuing, I did the usual 'Steve and Gillian from New Order, we're on the list, honest.'

And was met with 'You're all right mate, not her! She's the second one tonight.'

Kim, realising that there was some mileage to be had from her role as Gillian's stunt double, had taken to using her uncanny likeness as a means to gain free admission for her and her chums.

This would become a regular occurrence; somehow, Kim always managed to get there first. I have no idea how she did it.

Despite or maybe because of this newfound popularity, proceedings were ticking along relatively smoothly. Until yet another Gretton phone call delivered troubling news. Paul Mason was thinking of leaving. He was looking for something else to challenge him now the club was doing 'OK'.

I should say that this is something that Paul has subsequently denied, but nonetheless that was how it was put to me and the rest of New Order.

The idea came up that Factory should expand what Tony called its 'leisure division'. But another club? No one would buy into that madness again. Maybe something a bit smaller in scale – how about a bar?

Factory felt they were much more savvy, well Tony did, and began looking at places in an area that was ripe for redevelopment. Today it is home to the myriad bars, clubs and eateries known collectively as the Northern Quarter. Then it was just Oldham Street, home to decaying sweatshops and handy for the odd pet supplies store.

The bar would keep Paul occupied with a new challenge while the club was, so I was told, virtually running itself. I was sceptical, but I didn't much fancy the idea of losing Paul's expertise and returning to the chaos of the recent past.

'Well, because Steve's the most reluctant he can be company secretary or something' wasn't really the solution I had in mind but, thanks to my whinging and moaning, I became embroiled in what would become Dry Bar, an ironic name that Bernard came up with.

'The only kind of bar Factory will ever be any good at running.'

The knowledge that admission to Dry would never be a problem did nothing to ease my misgivings.

The project would eventually do for bars what the Haçienda did for clubs, complete with very similar worries, woes and ramifications. I was described as a non-executive observer, which sounds about right. Rob would regularly call me up with progress reports on the fortunes of the Bar.

'Just been speaking to Paul Mason,' Rob would say. 'S'doin' all right, Dry. That's good innit? Makes for a fuckin' change, eh?'

I had to agree with Rob that it was indeed good news and I felt reassured until one day, a few months later, there was another slightly different telephone update from Rob.

Surprise!

'Er, you know how I said that Dry was doing all right, well, turns out it wasn't.'

With an uncanny inevitability it turned out that, on closer inspection of the books, the bar had instead of making money actually been losing around £7000 a month and was now £210,000 in the red.

To be fair, unlike the club I did have a few free drinks in Dry, but I don't think it was anywhere near £1750 a week's worth.

20

THE LOTUS EATERS

In bands, much like in life, things change. They always do – they have to. They call it evolution. Nothing ever stands still. Expectations alter and affectations and disaffections develop. These get absorbed and accepted by all involved. It's sometimes known as 'anything for an easy life'. Though that is very rarely the eventual outcome.

Again as in life, when there are clear demarcations of roles this seems to happen less, everyone knows their place and tends to stick to it, more or less.

As long as everyone agrees to the accepted hierarchy.

Theoretically, at the top there was Rob along with Tony representing the record label as Situationist/anarchist social experiment.

For them an easy life meant keeping the musicians happy. With musicians (and arty types generally) this is virtually impossible as they are naturally unhappy and tend to fall into melancholy unless distracted by sex, drugs, flattery and expensive toys.

As long as the men at the top maintain a semblance of authority (is this turning in to a rewrite of *Animal Farm*?) those below are content. Safe in the knowledge that if it all goes wrong, the blame lies higher up. An air of competence is also handy too if you can manage it.

I can roll my eyes and hiss, 'Fucking Wilson,' secure in the belief that no one gives a toss what I think anyway.

It is the ancient division of the thinkers and the doers.

Trouble starts when the doers start thinking and, heaven forbid, the thinkers start doing.

As things stood Gillian and I were obviously at the lower end of this hierarchy.

Me, because I would do whatever with the occasional bare minimum of fuss. I occasionally managed a half-hearted tantrum just to keep up appearances. Mostly this would take the form of a petulant childish shrug, usually accompanied by a very weary 'whatever'.

Gillian, because she was seen as a woman in a man's world, was viewed as an apprentice at best, and a hysterical girl at worst. Easily placated with a 'Never mind, dear, cheer up.'

It really was that misogynistic at times.

Bernard's al fresco guitar solo

Having eventually decided or been persuaded to make a new album, the next question to be haggled over was where?

Everyone was bored of London. Nobody wanted to record in Manchester either. Too many distractions and intrusions of the wrong sort. Not that there were any studios in Manchester or the north-west deemed suitable for our purposes. The eighties chart-topping production team Stock, Aitkin and Waterman were rumoured to have a studio in town, possibly off Deansgate, but it was in constant use churning out hits. No time for the likes of us. How about a residential studio instead of the usual hiring a flat/hotel complication? We would be killing two birds with one stone and doubtless saving a ton of money as well.

So after trawling through trade mags and talking to people who knew about these things, we drew up a shortlist of two.

Mediterranean Studios, located in San Juan on the ever so hedonistic island of Ibiza – dripping with distractions of the right sort.

Or Real World Studios, Peter Gabriel's almost completed hi-tech studio outside the slightly less hedonistic town of Bath – suitable distractions could be found if you know where to look. I mean who doesn't like the odd bucket of home-brewed cider.

Hooky and Terry were dispatched to inspect the facilities of the Ibizan contender. Rob and myself got the Real World surveying task. I don't think this was decided by tossing a coin.

Real World, although still being built at the time, was unbelievable. All the hi-tech gear you could possibly need in a beautifully converted mill in the sleepy village of Box. The accommodation was in another beautifully converted and restored building adjacent to the main studio. The only slight drawback being it was also adjacent (very adjacent) to the main London to Bristol railway line. To those keen on the now neglected hobby of trainspotting, this could be seen as a boon. To others more concerned with a restful night's sleep, undisturbed by the roar of a passing locomotive, it could pose a problem. A small price to pay, I thought, and enthused accordingly.

Hooky and Terry were, on their return, even more enthused. The verdict being, 'I don't care how beautiful it is or how much fucking gear it's got. It's not got a swimming pool, has it?'

I tried to argue that Real World did have a lovely duck pond and swans and rowing boats. But no matter how you dressed it up, no, Real World definitely did not have a swimming pool.

The decision was easily made; we loaded all our gear on to a truck and shipped it all 1500 miles south to the Balearics. We were clearly on to a money-saver from the get-go.

Then there was the old topic of production.

'Why do we need a producer?' Bernard and Hooky questioned.

I, in my tedious pedantic way, felt we did. I still thought it diverted tension and gave everyone a common enemy or friend.

When this was followed up with 'All right then, who?' I always said, 'Why don't we ask Brian Eno?'

Eno's ideas on music and production intrigued me. I'd been a fan ever since Roxy Music. I also fancied the idea of making decisions with the aid of fancy playing cards; now that would save fussing time.

Possibly to indulge me, Rob or Tom Atencio would phone somebody who would phone somebody else who would phone Eno's people. Who said they would call back.

Later I would ask, 'What's happening with Eno?'

'He's not got back to us yet, but he will definitely – next week, probably.'

Or, 'He's just finishing off something, then they'll let us know when he's available.'

Nothing ever came of it. Maybe we were getting a bit of a bad reputation or something. I don't know. Over the years, we tried a few times to get him to help out in some capacity.

I did speak to Eno on the phone once.

I said, 'Hello Brian, it's Steve. I've always been a fan of yours ever since . . .'

He said, 'Can I speak to Bernard?'

Oh well. Never meet your heroes.

So, here we were once again, self-producing, which, despite my moaning, was something we were actually very good at, with Mike Johnson, as usual, doing the engineering and organising.

We had one-and-a-half songs actually written and about ten ideas of one sort or another. Some on tape and some ideas as sequences – on floppy disks for the now widely accepted Mac.

Eventually Tony would come to call *Technique* the most expensive holiday we ever had. He was probably about right. But hey, we could all find new and exciting ways to waste vast amounts of cash.

Shortly before we left for Mediterranean Studios there was an episode of Channel 4's *The Comic Strip Presents* . . . called 'The Funseekers'. Shot on Ibiza, mostly in the hotspots of San Antonio, it was a comedy send-up of a Club 18–30 teenage piss-up holiday.' The Funseekers, along with an earlier episode – 'A Fistful of Travellers Cheques' – the Spanish package holiday 'reimagined' as a spaghetti western, were essential New Order video viewing at the time. These hilarious films would turn into a great source of inspiration for the making of *Technique*. The rest of the inspiration would come from the island's exploding club scene, combined with my old hippy favourite, acid, and other more modern recreational drugs. The place was awash with ecstasy, dope and, of course, cheap coke.

The recording studio was along a rough dirt track, off a potholed death trap of a road, up a hill and in the middle of nowhere.

It was a beautiful setting evoking memories of Pink Floyd's *More*, the soundtrack to a film of an earlier generation's hedonistic life on the island.

Mediterranean Studios was at that time owned by the drummer

from Judas Priest and long overdue a makeover. The gear broke down a lot. The air conditioning didn't work, the control room was a haven for mosquitoes and the room with the best drum sound a paradise for lizards.

The reptiles would terrify me, scurrying across the ceiling above my head as I went to work. Never been a fan of anything that can walk on a ceiling.

But the studio did have a swimming pool, Hooky had been right on that. Best of all, it had a twenty-four-hour bar. Fancy not mentioning that!

The barman Herman couldn't speak much English and my Spanish was equally slight. But he was on my wavelength. I could tell from his first 'You won extasis, si? The best, muy bueno' that he was a likeminded spirit. His permanent grin was a dead giveaway. After a couple of Herman's pills any communication difficulties we might have had evaporated.

Along with the ecstasy *Technique* was our first album to involve substantial use of Macs and samplers. By then we had two Macs, my Mac plus and an SE, along with an Emulator 2 and a number of Akai samplers. Mike Johnson had invested in a Greengate DS:3 sampler, which ran on the old Apple II.

This was cutting-edge stuff in a less than cutting-edge environment. The two ageing MCI twenty-four-track tape machines had seen better days and the electricity was not exactly consistent. But the biggest hazard came from Bernard's overzealous use of mosquito-repellent spray, large quantities of which found their way into the delicate innards of the computers, forming a sticky residue that gummed up the odd hard drive.

We had Andy Robinson along again to help out. Andy was at the time a mostly logical soul but he quickly became seduced by the island's recreational activities. It was a bit like the lotus eaters bit in Homer's *Odyssey* only with pills instead of flowers.

There were, I think it's fair to say, plenty of distractions during the Ibizan phase of making *Technique*. But I also have to say that I think they were all positive distractions. Sun, sand, sea, an exciting and developing all-night/all-day club scene all made for a backdrop that crept into the writing and out to the sound of the record.

There's a space and mood in *Technique* that isn't there on *Brotherhood* and a lot of that is down to where our heads were at the time. It almost felt at times that we weren't making a record at all; there was little tension and no one was fretting about not getting on the record, getting by the pool or to the beach being a much higher priority.

The general impression seems to be that we didn't get that much done in Ibiza. Maybe that's true, but what we did get done had something intangibly good about it. Myself being the most sun-fearing member of the outfit, I got plenty of drumming and programming done, despite the fear of gravity-defying geckos.

'You don't need us for anything today do you? I was thinking of going to the beach for a bit. There's plenty of drums still need doing aren't there, Steve . . .? I don't think the hi-hat on the new one's quite right . . . anyway, see you later.' As Hooky and Andy breezed off for more Ambre Solaire.

With the two Macs – one running Intelligent Music's Upbeat for drum programming and the other Passport's Master Tracks Pro for arranging – I would translate live drum takes into MIDI notes and use that to retrigger drum hits on the Akai samplers. In this way, I could edit and fix up the 'real' drums in the same way as the programmed stuff. It was fiddly and obviously not much fun to watch or to do if I'm honest. But I really didn't mind that much being abandoned by the others going for a trip to the seaside.

I was not entirely a sun-fearing wallflower. There were more than a few nights, which occasionally spilled into days, spent sampling the local cultural highlights. Pacha, Ku Club and Amnesia were the main ones, particularly Amnesia. The idea of an open-air club seemed to me a bit weird, but the first time I was there I didn't even notice it was without a roof until the sun started streaming in. By which time I was, of course, completely addled.

Music and MDMA were the things for these nights out. I'd first come across E in New York in the early eighties, where it seemed to offer a much milder and generally more pleasant experience than acid.

By the late eighties, it seemed to have evolved slightly with a few unpredicatable variants (like 2C-P). What seemed to happen was that for the first couple of hours very little seemed to be going on, giving rise to the highly dangeous suspicion that the stuff was duff or at least very weak. Then suddenly, sometimes *very* suddenly, a slight feeling of anxiety gave way to a tidal wave of sighing and gasping for breath, an uneasiness that threatened to overwhelm.

The 'I've got to sit down, I feel a bit weird, I'll be all right in a mo' sense of panic, which sometimes felt like it would never go away, then faded, and a fuzzy glow like a warm bath would descend and everything was OK. More than OK, it was tremendous! The music sounded fantastic!

'Just a glass of water, please,' and we were off.

This ritual would be the preamble to many a night at the Haçienda too for a lot of people.

Like the clubs in Ibiza, the Haçienda was a large enough space for an E'ed up crowd entranced by house. The size and the layout of the club suddenly began to make sense. It was as if the place had been years ahead of its time and finally the real world had caught up.

At one point, our studio became a Club 18–30 tourist holiday high-light, like visiting pearl factories and ancient monuments or the sangria-fuelled banana-boat riding. The prospect of seeing a real live rock band in their natural habitat became a popular attraction for some of Ibiza's fun-seekers.

I think it was Thursday night which became barbecue-by-the-pool night. Terry had somehow struck up a relationship with a local lady tour rep who in turn had taken to inviting a selection of San Antonio's latest intake of youthful holidaymakers up to the studio. We ended up with a lot of lobster tanned visitors getting inebriated then copiously vomiting in undesignated containers.

'What do you do in the band then, mate?'

'I'm the plumber,' was my stock reply as they staggered off in search of a basin or handy bucket.

The pool-side bedlam of these coach parties soon became a bit too intrusive and we had to put a stop to that particular cultural diversion. Not an entirely popular decision.

We got back to the more sedate evening activities of hire-car wrecking and thievery of the island's road signage – most of which was now lying in a clattering pile in front of the living-room TV. The arrival of Bez and an entourage of Happy Mondays from Manchester only added to the fevered climate of chaos that began to envelop the sessions.

It was during one balmy and unusually peaceful evening, sitting by the pool watching the sun slowly set on the green hills on the opposite side of the valley, that Rob casually announced to Gillian and myself his plans for the future. He would, he said, be taking more of a back seat from the management of New Order as most of his time in the future would most likely be dedicated to the shepherding of Bernard and Johnny Marr's forthcoming project. I was slightly taken aback. Had I been completely sober, I would have been completely taken aback.

Perhaps I should rewind a bit here.

Ever since the earliest days of New Order and his victory in the New Order Singing Contest, Bernard had never been entirely comfortable with his prize.

From time to time, once a year on average, Bernard would point out to us that he had never wanted to be the singer. This was true, for none of us had really wanted to sing except for Ian. Bernard claimed he felt his role was merely that of something akin to a spare tyre awaiting the band's arrival at some musical Kwik-Fit where his burden would be relieved. A fresh singer would be installed and all would be tickety-boo once more.

Bernard's role within New Order had obviously grown since the simpler days of Warsaw. From guitarist and song arranging, he'd then added synth building, then keyboarding, continuing with singing, lyric writing, sequencer programming ... the list goes on. Bernard was doing a lot, there was no denying that. We were all doing a lot more than we had, back in the halcyon days of Warsaw. We had evolved. We would all try and help with lyric ideas when asked, but on the whole Bernard seemed happiest – perhaps that's not the best choice of word – when he was in the studio working or supervising. Some people are just like that.

Usually Bernard's misgivings at his musical lot in life seemed to fade after a day or so and normal service would be resumed. The underlying causes, though, didn't disappear and the disquiet rumbled away in the background. There was no escape from the feeling that for a long time we'd had to keep on doing what we were doing to provide money for Factory to spend on the Haçienda and then Dry. What once had been funny and anarchic was now becoming a source of anger and resentment.

The thing was, Bernard was very, very good at what he did. All of it. He is unique. We all were. Maybe that was the trouble.

The Smiths had split in summer of 1987 and Johnny Marr found himself in Los Angeles at the same time as us. New Order and the Smiths both used the same PA company (Oz PA) and Eddie, the monitor engineer, brought Johnny along to the gig to meet us. It was here, after the show, that the idea of Bernard doing something with Johnny first arose as a way of throwing off the oppression he felt existed within New Order. Johnny was interested in learning about synths and Bernard was just the man to explain their intricacies.

Hooky's distrust of synths, sequencers and now computers continued to grow. We'd never needed them in Joy Division so I suppose he felt why did we need them now? This was what frustrated him, they were a distraction and Bernard was the figurehead of this superfluous faff.

Polarisation starts here.

Us two, the quiet, waffling drummer and his even quieter girlfriend, were stranded in the middle of no-man's-land. A place where you can see both sides but are constantly caught up in the crossfire. My take, for what it's worth, is a good song is a good song no matter if it's written on a kazoo or a computer.

We all knew that Bernard was keen on doing something outside of New Order. That was no surprise. Rob's new management arrangements, now that was something else.

Rob continued describing his vision for his future.

He said he was training up Rebecca Boulton to take over the day-to-day running of New Order. A simple task, apparently, while he dedicated the larger proportion of his brain power to the more complicated task of launching Bernard and Johnny's new project to stardom.

There's no two ways about it, I felt jilted, surplus to requirements.

Bernard's desire for some sort of artistic freedom was one thing. It ticked a box on the rock-and-roll normality bucket list, but hey . . . Rob, however, had got us into the Factory–Haçienda mess and now it looked like he was jumping ship.

'So that's it then? You've had a better offer and you're fucking off?' I wasn't angry or annoyed at Rob's news, just a bit disappointed. Despite all our problems, he was still a friend like Tony and Alan, and even though at times I disagreed with everything he said or did, I couldn't be mad at him for very long.

Eventually Rob's plans fizzled out when Bernard and Johnny took what became Electronic elsewhere for management. I doubt very much that they had ever been remotely aware of Rob's plan at the time.

All good things come to an end and, fast running out of hire cars to write off, road signs to steal, Es to neck, overcomplicated sampling to do and even unnecessary hi-hat parts to invent. After two months we sadly said a hungover farewell to our musical Club 18–30 and made our way to the sleepy duck ponds of Bath. There, we would take the skimpy ideas we'd got down in Ibiza and turn them into something that sounded like an album.

Real World Studios

Unfortunately Bath was a little bit too close to London and its many distractions. It wasn't long before I found myself the designated driver to club nights at Heaven c/o Kevin Millins. Throughout the country acid house was taking hold, at warehouse raves full of fluorescent smiley shirts, strobes and loved-up dayglo people. It was becoming a national phenomenon. What the tabloids call a craze.

Ecstasy, along with the hypnotic music, the scene's driving force, was a very warm, cuddly, touchy-feely experience. With acid, getting touched or touching things was not normally a pleasant experience, but E was very tactile. Everyone felt connected to everything, part of a great sweaty dancing tribe, hands up trying to touch the lasers, lost in strobing, flickering clouds of smoke.

There were times I believed I could actually dance – and I was not the only one who suffered from this delusion.

Grown men who in the normal course of events would be hard pressed to muster a half-hearted shuffle found themselves frugging with dayglo gusto. Hands held aloft while blowing a whistle.

'Can you feel it . . .'

It was really something extraordinary. Then out into the cold dawn with ringing ears and, God knows how, taking the Volvo-shaped carriage back to Bath before we turned into pumpkins.

It was odd to find that the scene had gone from Manchester to Ibiza to London, like it was following us around, like everything was a part of the same greater thing. It was like a global movement – an interconnected sigh. 'All right, matey?'

I imagined it felt like 1966 down the UFO club, like living the sixties trippy thing all over again. It really did feel like a second summer of love. It became the biggest youth movement since my early teenage hippie dreams.

In what may well have been another subconscious attempt to revisit the sixties I rediscovered my childhood passion for badly gluing and painting plastic models. As there really wasn't any more drumming that could be shoehorned on to the Ibizan tracks, in my time off from Emulator programming I began constructing an Airfix Sunderland flying boat. This I combined with an attempt to manufacture a sort of healthy homebrew version of Ecstacy by combining nutmeg with oil of sassafras. Now I know this is hard to believe but I'd read in some rave journal that this was the nearest natural equivalent to the chemical formula of MDMA. These raw ingredients being readily available from Bath's many new-age crystal supply stores. I decided to give it a go. The homebrew E was a dead loss (it just gave me a headache and there's nothing worse than a nutmeg hangover) but the flying boat turned out pretty well considering I had overdosed on nutmeg whilst programming holiday destinations on 'Mr Disco'.

It may surprise you to discover we actually got a lot of work done at Bath, most of the vocals and a lot of the music, but not so much that it clouded the relaxed summer holiday atmosphere that being on Ibiza gave the record. By that time we had been in the studio for the best part of three months and, beginning to have difficulty telling wood from tree, we enlisted the help of Alan Meyers (a Tom Atencio recommendation) on the final mixing.

The Real World sessions ended with a huge acid-house party in the studio. Coachloads of Haçienda-goers and DJs were bussed down from Manchester and mingled with locals at the free champagne bar. It was an absolute frenzy. The best party I think I'd ever been to. The studio was filled with smoke and flickering strobes. Someone tried walking up the wall, semi-naked bodies were strewn across the lawn and in the topiary, and there was one insane axeman but no real actual violence at all . . . amazingly the police never showed.

It was totally crazy and pretty much summed up what the making of the record had been. And only a few grand's worth of damage. Peter Gabriel was very understanding. I wondered what his end-of-album parties must have been like.

There's some Super 8 footage of it somewhere, shot by Richard Heslop. It never made it into the 'Fine Time' video or anywhere else. Thank goodness.

In a continuation of the album's off-the-wall-ness Tony approached

Victor Kiam (Remington razors, remember him?) to make a TV ad for *Technique*, which sadly never happened.

Technique didn't really contain any mega hit singles but it's got a unifying atmosphere, something that's hard to define; let's call it a 'vibe'. It sounds like a great album should. But maybe I am a bit biased.

It may have been the last time that tracks were recorded with us all playing together at the same time.

Like night follows day, after finishing the album we set off on yet another US tour – the longest yet.

A tour of two halves.

Bernard only agreed to embark upon such an obviously arduous enterprise because Marc Geiger, our agent, promised him a two-week holiday in the middle. Thus making it seem like two short tours instead of one marathon. Bernard was a little concerned by the amount of flying the tour required.

'With so many flights, we're bound to have at least one fatal plane crash.'

Which does beg the question: how many aviation mishaps would be required to finish off an entire band? For history dictates that one usually does the trick. Not wishing to be overly pedantic, I let that one slide.

The first half was with Throwing Muses. The second with Public Image Ltd and the Sugarcubes. As is naturally the way of the world of touring, the latter was harder and more gruelling and naturally more hedonistic than the first.

As a bit of a punk hangover, I was still slightly in awe of John Lydon and probably only managed a sheepish 'How do?' for the entire tour. Hooky got on with him famously, of course. Naturally I got on really well with Bruce Smith, PIL's drummer.

More or less halfway through the second leg, the years of Pernod supping took their toll and Bernard ended up hospitalised, resulting in a cancelled gig in Detroit. By this time the band's rider stipulated that beer, vodka, tequila, Pernod, champagne and asti spumante should be supplied in ever increasing quantities, frequently consumed in the same glass in a signature cocktail commonly known as a headache. Considering the scale of alcohol consumption and extracurricular antics that took place, it could easily have been a great deal worse. Although we were sick of the sight of each other at the end of the ordeal, we were still on speaking terms. Just.

There were times on that tour when, overtired and emotional, we came close to killing each other. According to Mike Pickering, who was there for some of it, our overindulgent behaviour put even Led Zeppelin to shame. No one got arrested but it certainly came close a couple of times. How no one spotted that huge leaking bag of MDMA going through the airport X-ray, I'll never know. Quite possibly, even Nero and Caligula would have blushed. I was so used to it by then that the excesses just seemed routine.

Rob lost the gig money more than once, leaving his maroon Samsonite briefcase filled with cash in somebody else's room after a late-night drinks-and-waffle party.

The next morning, hungover, he could never remember exactly whose room might have been the venue for the previous night's antics.

Luckily a quick scan of the room-service bill usually gave the game away. Our manager was a sucker for a three a.m. toast and jumbo king prawn feast. By a simple process of elimination the bag and its contents were soon recovered.

What went on during the US *Technique* tour has inspired a lot of creative typing over the years, some of it possibly quite confused because of the level of intoxication. I'm fairly sure that in one book I'm playing the synth and Gillian's the drummer.

Despite our excesses, the tour made money. Let's say (and this, of course, is a wild approximation, so don't sue me) around a million English pounds. Where did it go?

For a pattern seemed to have been established over the years that we'd begun to think of America as a kind of piggy bank. We would go there, tour like crazy, make some money, then come home and watch it vanish.

I began to have nightmares that I was on a hamster wheel, a spinning turbine that generated cash. This flurry of banknotes would be nightly hoovered up by a yellow and black striped vacuum cleaner, which swelled and expanded to bursting point. Before exploding in a puff of white powdery smoke. I took up reading Freud.

On our return to Manchester, Rob announced that Tony wanted to hold an urgent and important meeting about the future of the Haçienda and the more recently troublesome Dry Bar. Oh aye, I thought, here we go again. The nightmare was becoming a reality.

So important was this meeting that its venue was to be the grand and opulent Manchester Town Hall. This was probably because Factory's recently acquired office on Charles Street was still being remodelled by Ben Kelly. Tony invited along a gaggle of impressive accountants and business advisors to add kudos and impart facts: men with folders containing figures, and figures never lie. A business you could rely on, numbers. Big rooms and a bevy of suits were becoming a standard fixture of Factory meetings at that time. No more handshakes in the snug at the boozer.

Gillian and I trooped off to Manchester Town Hall to sit round yet another oversized boardroom table with Hooky and Bernard to hear what Tony and the business brains had to say.

Which basically was this:

Factory's big mistake ('There was only one?' you ask) with the Haçienda had been not to buy the building. They'd bought the Dry Bar building and though it was still early days for that venture, and despite the fact it was losing money, at least they had the bricks and mortar to fall back on.

Now finally there was a chance to fix that one big mistake of the club.

'Yes, kids, a once-in-a-lifetime opportunity, this magnificent property can be all yours. Just think about it. But don't dawdle, chances like this don't happen every day. It's not going to last forever.'

The building's owners wanted to sell the property and after some secretive negotiations it had been discovered that it could be had for the apparently not unreasonable price of . . . can you guess? . . .

One million English pounds.

More or less the same amount that we had just made out of the US tour.

Now I may have been somewhat jaded myself at this point in time, and possibly could have missed a point or two, but to me this seemed like a bit too much of a coincidence. I felt like we were being stitched up and getting coerced into sticking yet another huge chunk of cash into the Haçienda.

The four of us and Rob adjourned to another room to discuss this further and I expressed my misgivings on the affair. Surely Bernard, one of Factory's biggest critics, wasn't going to fall for this?

New Order remained a democracy, though, and a show of hands had me and Gillian outvoted three to two. This would become the way most votes on the Haçienda's latter days ended up.

Maybe I was being a little paranoid. But then, being involved with it was a total nightmare. None of us were businessmen. None of us had ever wanted to be businessmen. Yet here we all were sitting at a table with people who were supposed to be experts, giving us advice that we barely understood.

Every time I went for a night out at the Haç (assuming I could get in), I just found myself overwhelmed by anxiety. Did the walls need repainting? Why was the rubber matting coming unglued? And most of all, why did the ladies loos flood so frequently? And with such dire consequences? I was usually driving so couldn't get intoxicated to the point where I became oblivious. These things spoiled the night out for me and my attendances gradually became few and far between.

What made me uncomfortable was the nagging feeling that we might be mortgaging our future somehow.

In many ways it was a reflection of Rob's attitude to gambling: keep on betting until you win or go bust. That bothered me.

21

GOING SOLO

One of the inevitabilities in the life of any popular music combo, it seems, is that sooner or later – as a rule of thumb, after at least a couple of albums – one member of the combo, usually the lead singer or front person, will express a desire to flex their musical muscle, expand their sonic horizons and with them their ego. Yes, they will announce triumphantly that they are taking a break from the strait-jacket of the band situation, which is holding them back somehow, and embark on the naturally self-indulgent path of the solo project. They are bored and need a change of scenery.

In doing so they hope to prove to the world and, more important-ly, to the other members of the group that they are the bee's knees, the top banana, etc., without whom the other moptops are naught but lackeys basking in reflected glory.

There is also usually but not always a little tell-tale frosting of white powder around the edges of these proceedings. If not, then there will be some ego massage or a newfound interest in the mysteries of the occult or some other whizz-bang hocus-pocus planet-saving philosophy.

Maybe I'm being a teeny bit cynical, but that's showbiz. That's how it goes. I'm not talking about New Order specifically here, it's just some general rock-band behaviour that I've noticed over the years. Sometimes it works, Phil Collins and Sting; sometimes it doesn't Freddie Mercury or Mick Jagger.

Myself? I've never harboured any ambitions towards becoming a solo artist. I may have daydreamed a bit while strumming a tennis racket in front of a mirror back in 1972, but seriously, no. Not for me.

But this is the way it seems that many bands manage to lose their way, their momentum.

In 1989, Bernard would go on to do Electronic with Johnny Marr and Hooky would do his own project, Revenge, seemingly just because 'if Bernard's doing it I'm doing it too'. Not wanting to miss out.

The idea of a solo drummer seemed to me a little ridiculous. I remembered Buddy Rich, Cozy Powell and Sandy Nelson and shuddered.

Gillian too didn't feel the pent-up need to go it alone as a solo keyboardist. What else could we do? I recalled sixties *Opportunity Knocks* winners' Steven Smith and father, the organ and drum duo, and my blood ran cold.

We would become a pair of expert thumb twiddlers.

We'd already had a little bit of practice by then and were getting quite accomplished in the art of waiting around.

Patiently.

Things are never ever totally straightforward. For good or ill the hand of fate is always swatting at your heels. Fate or serendipity, one of the two. They're easily confused.

At some point during the second half of the *Technique* sessions (the ones at Real World in Box when stuff was actually getting done), we were visited by a man from the BBC. John Chapman was the producer for a series that the BBC had just commissioned. The programme was to be called *Making Out*, a comedy drama set around Manchester and written by Debbie Horsfield.

I liked John, he wasn't a conventional TV luvvie. He wanted to know if New Order would be interested in writing music for the series.

The series centred around the lives of a group of women working at an electronics factory in Dukinfield. The cast included Margi Clarke, who we had once backed on a version of Kraftwerk's 'Neon Lights' at a gig at Eric's in Liverpool way back when, along with Keith Allen. In his persona of Jerry Arkwright, 'northern industrial gay', Keith had supported us at a miners' benefit in 1984. Dressed in jockstrap and miner's helmet, he was almost pushed offstage by Terry, who assumed he was a stage invader or at least some kind of party pooper.

What John wanted was for New Order to provide some theme music as well as to write incidental bits for the entire series of eight episodes. Simple enough. We were nearly at the end of recording and had completed instrumental versions of all the songs, so we let him have a listen.

The idea was that we could just edit these up into convenient sections, slot them in as needed, and that would be it.

The project sounded very interesting; it was something new and different for us.

We all agreed to John's proposal and while Alan Meyerson continued mixing, Hooky and I set to work converting a small room in Real World into an annexe studio where we could do this experiment in sound-tracking.

It goes without saying that the job turned out to be a bit more complicated than I expected – but the technical challenges of synchronising a video player, a computer and a tape machine together would turn out to be the easy bit.

At that time, working in the world of New Order was a process with no real deadlines.

The world of scoring music for pictures, I soon discovered, didn't quite work like that. Things were expected to be turned around according to a tight production schedule.

John and the episode's director would come up to the 'studio', go through the programme with us, explaining where they wanted music to go and describing roughly what they thought it should sound like.

Then leave us to it with a parting, 'See you in a couple of days.'

A little stunned at their request for such swift and immediate action, I entered panic mode and began running around like a headless chicken.

Things then began to get a bit more chaotic.

We finished mixing *Technique* and Bernard and Hooky drifted off to their solo sojourns, leaving Gillian and me to it. We moved the gear we needed into our attic in Macclesfield, turned it into another studio and began a kind of musical production line.

The first two episodes were totally haphazard seat-of-the-pants experiences. We learned very quickly. We had to. It settled down to a two-week cycle for each episode. This sounds plenty of time, but compared to New Order's typical schedule it felt uncomfortably tight.

We'd had a little bit of a taster of tight movie deadlines in 1987, when New Order had contributed music to the film *Salvation!* That had been done in less than a week with 'Touched by the Hand of God' written in a frantic last-minute all-night session. In six days we'd come up with a few instrumental pieces that we hoped would somehow fit with the film.

'It would be really great if you could, y'know, do a song,' Beth said on the final evening. She had been angling for this all week, but we kept putting her off. Hoping she'd forget about the idea.

'Oh, OK,' we relented. 'When would you need it for?'

'Well,' she said, 'my plane leaves at eight in the morning so say by six thirty a.m.'

Bernard popped out to the Haçienda for a breather, returning with Bez from Happy Mondays and some 'inspiration', and we set to it. Hooky had a synth bass idea that was the starting point, Gillian had a synth melody, I had some samples and a chattering Emulator line, and Bernard did the rest.

It's amazing what you can do at the very, very last minute when you put your mind to it.

That was for one film and there were four of us (although by 1988 just getting the four of us together in the same room for one hour was difficult enough).

Doing a series of *Making Out* would be like doing the same thing on a regular basis. But as the idea was to edit tracks we'd already completed for *Technique*, it didn't seem like it would be too much work for the two of us to do on our own. Yet another example of my temporal over optimism. The soundtrack quickly took over our lives.

It soon became obvious that the tracks we'd recorded for *Technique* would be insufficient for an entire series. So the production line expanded from editing to re-recording and remixing and eventually to writing brand new stuff as well.

This was something we'd never thought of doing outside the band. But it had to be done and, once I put my jittery apprehension back in its box, I found the whole thing exciting and satisfying.

The fact that there was no time to agonise on whether something might be absolutely the right thing or not was strangely liberating. We began coming up with ideas all the time; lots of little musical sketches. These we would use to fill the scenes where none of the *Technique* tunes worked.

While we were discovering the joys of writing music for television our bandmates were off pursuing their other extra-curricular band projects.

Bernard and Johnny Marr had already got themselves another manager and Hooky had also dispensed with Rob's management services for Revenge – a very Hooky name, active and impulsive – but had stuck with Factory as his new band's label.

Rob was still managing Gillian and me but in all honesty we didn't take up a great deal of time and effort.

I was sorting out the logistics of what had to be done for the television project myself. It just seemed easier that way. I would speak to Rob about once a week and he'd pay us the occasional visit to see what we were up to and how it was all going. Then, in a 'if you can't beat 'em join 'em' moment, he too decided he was launching a solo project.

After claiming that Mike Pickering had been giving him saxophone lessons, Rob decided that blowing was too much like hard work and so decided to start his own label, Rob's Records, instead.

You know you've got problems when even your manager's gone off to do his own thing. I think Rob was feeling a bit miffed that Hooky and Bernard had gone elsewhere. Rob's miffedness didn't last long, and he still had great taste in music. His label put out some great records. He would always blame Neil Tennant for coming up with the name.

Since the *Technique* tour it felt like everyone else had cleared off on holiday and left us at home to do the dirty laundry and the washing-up. This sense of abandonment, combined with an acute awareness of time passing, made me think a lot about the future: my own personal future for once and not the ray guns and jetpacks of a sci-fi fantasy future.

Our entire life was built around New Order's continued existence. Mine and Gillian's world revolved around the band.

It was the main topic of conversation in our relationship. The main source of disagreements. We'd talked about having children, starting a family. But how could you have kids and still do everything that being in a band involves?

We'd didn't want to leave our imaginary children to be looked after by somebody else while we flounced off on tour or disappeared into a recording studio.

We'd seen it a few times when musicians had brought their children out on tour for a couple of days. The experience always seemed to me to be fraught with difficulty – there was still the staying up all night but the drinking was replaced by the dragging of reluctant infants out of cots, sticking them on planes, then dashing with them screaming straight to a gig. This didn't seem like something that would be fair to anyone; for us, for better or worse, the band had always come first.

Looking back now, I wonder what we were thinking, to be so loyal to something that was so unpredictable and chaotic.

At times I began to resent whatever it was that had brought me to this. I felt we were becoming a couple of Cinderellas. I would sink into depression and wonder what I could do with my life without New Order? The answer only depressed me more.

But the pair of us were having fun working on the music at home. So much so that, possibly infected with the property-buying frenzy that seemed to have gripped Factory at the time, we decided to up sticks and move to somewhere with a bit more space.

We gave up our two-up two-down end-of-terrace and moved into a two-hundred-year-old farmhouse near Macclesfield. It had a few outbuildings that could, with a little bit of work and a lot of imagination, be turned into a 'proper' studio.

Getting a mortgage on this edifice was difficult for it turned out there were 'structural anomalies' that suggested it might be falling down. Why were we drawn to these ruins? Did the words 'substantially reduced' and 'quick sale' still mean nothing to us?

The house was nestling on the side of a hill and had nestled there for two centuries without collapsing, but according to experts a lot of construction work would be required to ensure the nestling continued. We weren't going to let a little thing like that put us off. Gillian was definitely not for being putting off.

Les, Gillian's dad, had proved himself as an efficient if not entirely stylish constructor with bricks and mortar. He didn't see anything about our new abode that couldn't be fixed by copious amounts of concrete.

Our prospective new dwelling was the sort of place estate agents optimistically describe as having 'great potential', which turned out to mean it had neither gas nor mains water, despite being just down the road from a huge reservoir.

All the H_2O came from a spring in the garden, which went through a convoluted system of cisterns and gurgling pipes before emerging from the taps as an occasionally brownish dribble.

The estate agents were right about the place having potential. The outbuildings were much larger than the house. It came with land too: 11 acres of hillside pasture which seemed to be home to herds of militant sheep.

The perfect place for two wayward practitioners of music to set up shop. Noise would not be a problem. How could the sheep complain?

With much crossing of fingers and a little deception, we eventually managed to convince a reluctant building society that we would undertake all the necessary repairing and structural alteration, and the place was ours.

We were now technically farmers.

I practised saying, 'Get ORF my land!' and began investigating the pros and cons of shotgun ownership.

Rob, on first visiting the place, also realised that it would be a great place for a recording studio. It didn't take him long to see how it might be transformed into a budget hillside version of Real World with sheep instead of ducks.

Rob wanted New Order to buy half of it. We could have the house and the band could have the outbuildings, he suggested.

'Fuck off, Rob,' I said emphatically, for I reckoned I had enough New Order in my life without having the band moving in next door with me becoming the band's caretaker.

On learning of Rob's proposal Gillian concurred.

'You didn't say yes, did you?'

Oh ye of little faith.

Our housewarming coincided with the start of work on the second series of *Making Out*.

We'd built a studio in a partially converted barn even before we'd moved into the house itself, and started work writing for the new episodes.

The view from the studio window was stunning: rolling hills and valleys with Manchester lurking on the far horizon on clear days.

People began popping in for a visit – locals spying on what we might be up to and friends from the big city checking to see if it were true we had turned into fully fledged straw-munching yokels.

Alan Erasmus became a regular popper-inner, inspecting our ramshackle set-up and the tunes we were writing. He was probably glad to escape from the Factory office. The situation there was continuing its normal mode of haphazard business. Lurching from one crisis to the next, forever teetering on the brink.

It was Alan, however, who first came up with the suggestion that maybe Gillian and I could make an album out of our soundtrack work.

Flattered, I thought the idea was interesting, but not something that we could do immediately. There was barely enough time to do the music cues as it was, without thinking of ways to turn them into something that would work on a record.

As it turned out, this soundtrack writing would keep us very busy. The work we were doing for the BBC meant our name somehow got about. We would get to the end of one project, the phone would ring and another score would pop up. I think we were in some BBC producers' handbook of people who could be called on to knock up a tune at relatively short notice.

We even found ourselves working on some music that Michael Shamberg needed for the US TV show *America's Most Wanted*. That was a very odd experience – concocting music to accompany real-life gangland slayings in an environment where the most heinous crime imaginable was leaving a farm gate open.

The only trouble was that all of this work seemed to get credited as New Order, even though I went to some lengths to explain that we weren't actually New Order – just a couple of off-duty members who found themselves with time on their hands. Oddly this never seemed to put people off.

Compared to the rigmarole involved in being a band it really was a simple life.

Get up, walk up the hill to the studio, come up with ideas, record any that sounded promising, listen to the previous day's ideas and see if there was anything that worked with the scenes we'd been given, arrange, record, mix, go to bed. That was about it, seven days a week.

It was the only way to get anything done. Just keep plugging away, writing nine rubbish ideas and one good one. The good idea wouldn't have come about without writing the rubbish ones first.

It was all done on a Macintosh, some synths and couple of samplers. I didn't have any real drums at the farm and even if I had I didn't have the proper gear or wherewithal to successfully record them.

Nearly every day, there would be some sort of technical problem to fix and finding solutions with the limited amount of equipment we had was often challenging.

Gillian began to have piano lessons and I bought a book on song-writing. According to the book, the way New Order went about writing songs was completely wrong; apparently successful song-writing begins with a title. You couldn't just haphazardly stick one on at the end.

You learn something new every day, don't you? I decided that it was probably not a good book and stuck it on the shelf next to Bert Weedon's deceitfully titled *Play in a Day* guitar guide.

If it wasn't a music- or technical-related conundrum, there were plenty of questions about life in the middle of nowhere that needed answering.

Like why did the water stop coming out of the taps whenever we wanted a bath?

Why did the house shake whenever the heating came on?

Or who's left that dead sheep in our field?

The joys of rural life.

'What is that smell?'

The wonders of the septic tank. The house seemed to be in need of some sort of constant repair, usually a major one. As soon as one thing was fixed another crisis would arise.

At the time, it felt like being the owner of an ocean-going sieve.

It still does for that matter.

I would often find myself engrossed in writing some synthesiser nonsense only to catch a glimpse of something white and furry out of the corner of my eye.

'BAAAAH. BAAAAAAAAAAAAAH.'

The sheep, having got bored with eating grass, wanted to see where the noise was coming from and had invited themselves into the studio for a nosey.

It was all very rustic. I would leave the door open to let a bit of fresh air in and . . . It only takes one bright spark of a sheep to figure it out and the rest really do follow like . . . er, sheep.

You've never lived until you've tried herding a dozen frightened, frisky and frankly incontinent sheep from out of your prized recording studio.

'For Christ's sake, don't piss on that synth!'

'Put that floppy disk down, you baa'ing bastard.'

Previous experience at man management paid off, though. It turned out that sheep herding was actually easier than clearing the dressing room after a New Order gig.

22

THE SANDS OF MOTION

Title: THE SANDS OF DEE
Director: Michael Powell
Music: New Order
Starring: Tilda Swinton

Based on the Charles Kingsley poem, "The Sands of Dee", this short (under 10 minutes) film is to be shot in 35mm on location at the Dee Estuary outside Liverpool, as well as a recording studio in Manchester. Production is scheduled for mid-March and completion for early April.

The film will be comprised of three sections: (1) the visualization of the poem concerning a hapless young girl who, in search of her cattle, is swept out by the tides to the sea and her death, (2) the visual reading of the poem by a well known actor who hails from the Manchester area (e.g. Ben Kingsley), and (3) New Order in their studio recording the music for the poem/film.

At 84 years of age, Mr. Powell ("The Red Shoes", "Peeping Tom", "Black Narcissus") should need no introduction as one of England's finest and most prolific filmmakers. It was New Order's music which provided him with the inspiration to develop this film, and it is this unique and most unusual collaboration which will make for a major film event. New Order are known both for their music (they just reached their first-ever number one position in the British charts with their current album, "Technique") as well as their videos, through which they've worked with the likes of directors Charles Sturridge and Jonathan Demme, choreographer Phillipe Decoufle, cinematographer Henri Alekan, and artists Robert Longo, Robert Breer and William Wegman. Last year their video "True Faith" won the BPI's "Video of the Year" award.

This film is intended for theatrical release and television broadcast. It will be available as a commercial product on laser disc and will, of course, be circulated to film festivals around the world.

Producer: Michael H. Shamberg
phone: (212) 71 -175

Production company (London):   Anita Ovaland
                                 Helen Langridge Associates

Michael explains 'The Sands of Dee'

The first time I saw *A Matter of Life and Death* I thought it was the best and weirdest film I'd ever seen. The way it kept switching from technicolour to black and white; a story that largely took place in an afterlife of someone stuck between Heaven and Earth. That was exactly the stuff that appealed to me. Weird and unusual, the films of Powell and Pressburger all have an otherworldly, dreamlike quality. They have a strange atmosphere.

In the mid-eighties, after a longish spell in the celluloid wilderness, Michael Powell was undergoing a bit of a renaissance, first with the book *Arrows of Desire* about Powell and Pressburger's films as The Archers, and then the first volume of Powell's autobiography, *A Life in Movies*. Along with a *South Bank Show* TV special, the books reminded the world of Powell's genius and also the fact that he was still present in the land of the living.

Bernard also loved the films of Powell and Pressburger and, during late-night phone conversations with Michael Shamberg, the idea that the legendary director might be approached to make a New Order video got hatched.

Michael Powell was married to Thelma Schoonmaker, Martin Scorsese's editor, and in 1989 he was working in New York. Shamberg met up with Powell and asked how he felt about possibly making a film with New Order. The eighty-three-year-old was perhaps surprisingly receptive to the idea of undertaking a film/music collaboration with a band. He had an idea for a film that he'd always wanted to make. That idea was based on the poem 'The Sands of Dee' by Charles Kingsley.

The poem tells the story of a farm girl sent to bring home the cattle grazing on the Dee estuary. She gets lost in the thickening mist, becomes trapped by the tide and drowns.

That's it in a nutshell. Pretty short, eh?

Mr Powell was going to be in London in a few weeks' time and suggested that he would like to meet us and see how the thing might work.

Tony wasn't keen.

I'd brought the matter up at one of the many Haçienda crisis meetings that took place around the end of the eighties.

Tony had two problems with the film idea. Firstly, he said that there was no market for short films, and, secondly, it would be too expensive and there was no money available to fund it.

All spent on the Haçienda, Dry and the brand new and highly expensive new Factory HQ on Charles Street.

Maybe Tony thought it was just another insane New Order idea, but he had a downer on the thing from the start. Which I confess surprised me. The making of unlikely collaborations had been his big thing once upon a time.

Regardless, we arranged to meet Michael and Thelma in London at the offices of his agent.

Climbing the stairs to the reception was like stepping back in time. It felt like I was stepping into a world of British cinema that had boomed in the thirties and forties and had last seen a coat of paint in the late sixties.

Leaded windows and motes of dust caught in the sunlight, like a scene from *A Canterbury Tale*. Mr Powell awaited in his tweeds.

He may have been an old gentleman but he had lively eyes, very sharp and alert. He said he'd been listening to our music, which he liked very much, 'particularly the drums'. Honest, I'm not making it up.

'I especially enjoyed that song on the record with the flowers on it, ah yes, "Age of Consent".' This naturally delighted Hooky.

Oh fuck! It was at that point I realised it might look like we'd nicked the title of one of his films. Like we might be stalkers of some kind. He didn't let on.

'I'd like the drums to sound like that.' He really did say that. Michael Powell was my sort of guy.

We talked through the idea. He thought a day's shooting on the Dee estuary would be enough.

He'd need a helicopter, Navy pilot. 'Always use a Navy helicopter pilot, not the RAF or the Army. Navy, they're the best.' He spoke from experience.

It's a piece of advice I've never had occasion to put to the test.

Michael wanted to cast Tilda Swinton as Mary the shepherdess. He thought she'd be good at drowning. Maybe Albert Finney too, if he wasn't too busy?

I think we all took to Michael Powell. He was like someone's eccentric grandad. We agreed that Michael, Thelma and Michael Shamberg would work together on a script and scouting out locations and finance. It was a very pleasant meeting.

'Do you mind if I take a picture?' asked Hooky. Until then I hadn't figured him to be much of a Powell and Pressburger film buff.

'Not at all,' said Mr Powell, getting to his feet and preparing for his close-up as Hooky produced a small compact and framed his shot.

'Do you mind getting out of the way, mate?' the bass player asked the noted director. 'Only I think these oak panels would look really good in me new front room . . .'

Mr Powell looked slightly confused but obligingly stepped aside. I felt mortified, hoping desperately that no offence had been taken.

To be fair, they were lovely oak panels. Gentleman's club stuff.

Michael Shamberg went ahead with liaising and scripting, and working on Tilda Swinton's availability.

Towards the end of 1989 a very strange and surprising thing happened. I can't remember the exact date but I'm pretty sure it was a Friday. Bad news often arrives on a Friday. A note came from Rob in the form of a fax, that then being the main method of rapid written communication, sort of like email but with more paper. It said something like:

'As you know I have been thinking for some time about giving up my career in the music business. That day has now arrived and with immediate effect.'

For reasons best known to himself, Rob had resigned, just like that.

No ifs, no buts.

After everything we'd been through together, he'd just quit. He wasn't joking either. Mr Gretton had left the building.

This was a bit of a shock. Rob had his breakdown in 1986 but, three years later, with all that over and done and even the indefatigable revenue inquisitors apparently satisfied, Rob was throwing in the towel. Following his illness he'd resigned as director of Factory; all the arguing with Tony was bad for his health. Now maybe we were too, who can say? New Order in the late eighties wasn't the best environment for anyone's physical and mental well-being.

Whatever his reasons, he was serious, so the management of the band fell to Rebecca, Rob's assistant since 1986, and Iain Adam, the group's legal advisor.

We began having weekly meetings to weigh up what New Order should be doing. Which felt very strange when it was usually Rob who told us.

Meanwhile, unknown to us, Tony was having discussions with David Bloomfield, the England Football Association's press officer. David, having heard the music New Order had done for Granada's *Best & Marsh: The Perfect Match* TV show, wanted to know if we would do a song for the England squad. There was a World Cup coming up the following year in Italy.

Tony eventually got around to asking us what we thought of his plan.

'I think it's a great idea,' said Tony, doing his yuk-yuk-yuk seal laugh. 'The FA are really keen.' I grimly recalled every football-related tune I'd ever heard – without exception they were universally dire.

'Three words, Tony,' I said. 'World Cup Willie! It's a fucking shit idea.'

It was without doubt the worst idea I'd ever heard in my entire life. Football songs were the pits, appalling, and the least hip or rock-and-roll thing ever conceived by man. Absolutely dreadful. There had never been a halfway decent football song ever. *Ever!*

The thing turned into an argument of art (the Michael Powell film) versus commerce (the football tune). For once though, it was the band pushing for art and Tony for commerciality.

The usual compromise was reached.

The Michael Powell film could always be postponed until a later date. The World Cup, however, couldn't. So, shit idea or not, it was Tony and the FA's idea that won the day.

How do you write a decent football song then?

Is it even possible?

I did a bit of research, spoke to people who might know (well, Adrian Sherwood anyway) and the consensus was you needed something that would translate into a sort of terrace anthem.

All well and good, but how the fuck did you do that exactly? We knew we could write a good tune but what was it supposed to say?

'We're going home after the first game!' or 'Let's face it, we're hopeless' were not lyrically quite the sort of thing the FA were hoping for.

A bit of optimism was called for and, if football was at least referenced somehow, then we'd be on to a winner . . . maybe?

I watched a film about England's 1966 victory for inspiration and maybe some samples to 'borrow'.

As we hadn't been working together for a while, what with Electronic and Revenge taking up Bernard and Hooky's time, the New Order riff cupboard was a little bare. OK, it was totally bare.

To get the ball rolling, I made a cassette of a couple of ideas that Gillian and I had come up with for Janet Street-Porter's reportage 'yoof' TV show. The music had been credited to New Order anyway, so what the heck. Bernard quite liked the more melodic idea that ended up being the closing theme. So that was a start. A step in the right direction.

Coincidentally Bernard had struck up a friendship or more accurately a drinking relationship with Keith Allen who, while not filming *Making Out*, had been a regular visitor to the Haçienda. He was frequently to be found at the bar without his trousers, so they say. But you know the kind of stuff *they* come out with so . . .

Bernard had never seen *Making Out*, but apart from the Haçienda bar he knew Keith from *The Comic Strip Presents* . . . especially 'Funseekers', the major source of inspiration during our time in Ibiza.

'Why don't we ask Keith if he'd help out with the lyrics?'

Keith was sharp, funny and knew about football. The ideal man for the job, in fact.

We'd got a plan and began doing some work together at the farm. Our old rehearsal room in Cheetham Hill had been rented out to various bands since we'd last used it, so it was easier and more convenient for Bernard and Hooky to come to the country for a change. This was the first time the four of us had got together there and the studio wasn't really set up for more than two people. It was a bit rough and ready but we got something done. The sheep stayed away. The ball was rolling, as they say.

We loaded up the van and headed back to Real World in February 1990 to record what would become 'World in Motion'.

We'd got *Technique* done there and the food was good so . . . where else? The end-of-*Technique* party is still talked about in the area to this day. The stuff of legend, apparently. Mike Large, the studio manager, asked only half jokingly if we were thinking of having any more parties.

On the first day at work in Peter Gabriel's upstairs room at Real World the phone rang. It was Alan Erasmus.

'Hi Steve, just had a piece of bad news. Michael Powell's died.'

'Oh no, that's really terrible.'

'Yes, I know. Good job you didn't do the film isn't it?'

I felt sorrow, disappointment and anger, my usual three death-related emotions.

I couldn't believe it; oh yes, disbelief, that's the other one.

We'd never get to make 'The Sands of Dee' now thanks to this sodding football fuckabout.

On the plus side we wouldn't be forever known as the band that brought about the death of one of England's greatest film-makers. So it goes.

The musical side of the football song came together surprisingly quickly, with Bernard coming up with a whole new section that rounded it off really well. Keith came up with a rap section that he reckoned the England team would have a job fucking up.

This theory was road tested by a volunteer team of bad singers, me, Keith and the engineer Richard 'Dickie' Chappell standing in for the actual squad, and can be heard on the B-side of the single.

We moved to Mayfair Studios in London for a few days to finish off the backing track and Bernard's vocals, with Stephen Hague producing, before heading out to the Mill studio in Berkshire for our date with destiny, or the England squad, if they could be bothered to turn up.

For it turned out the team had about as much faith in the idea of a football anthem as I did.

The football song at that time was widely held to be a new low in that already subterranean genre of the novelty record. The majority of the England squad were holders of this view and were unsurprisingly reluctant to take part in the escapade.

The few that were mildly interested found themselves swayed by the promise of a bounty of limitless free champagne: two or three floor-to-ceiling fridges chock full of chilling Moët & Chandon, none of your rubbish. Paul Gascoigne, Peter Beardsley, Des Walker and of course John Barnes all turned up.

The day was borderline chaos verging on anarchy. Even the normally calm and unshakable Stephen Hague was showing signs of fluster. We didn't have enough words for the entire rap section for a start. But Keith Allen was a natural at the shepherding of soccer players in a recording studio, and by the time the first fridge full of fizz had been demolished some workable words and tactics had been developed.

A few takes of the assembled squad doing the chorus in unison and then, once they had warmed to the business of being in a studio, each member had a go at doing the rap with the idea we would edit together the best bits. John Barnes came out of it covered in glory, of course; Gazza's rap was funny and the rest were a bit, er, so-so – better than me, though, it has to be said.

As swiftly as they had arrived the team departed, leaving a pile of empty bottles in their wake.

I was a little taken aback by the amount of alcohol the professional footballer could consume in the course of an afternoon. They almost put us, with all our years of professional champion's league drinking, to shame.

The thing I ask myself now is: was there any actual drumming involved in the making of this record? I can remember having a go at making some loops early on in Real World but honestly the answer is no. The parts were all constructed in the sampler with sounds taken from me hitting actual drums. But nothing that you could call proper playing. The rhythm track is pretty much the same thing we'd come up with for *Reportage* in 1989.

This was the way things were in the late 1980s and early 1990s. I spent more time shifting dots about on a computer screen and auditioning different snare sounds in an Akai sampler than doing any real drumming. Although in the long run this would take less time and ultimately sound 'better', it could still be a frustrating process requiring a great deal of patience. Unlike actual drumming it was not intuitive at all. The sort of thing best done without someone looking over your shoulder saying, 'Wouldn't it be better if . . .?'

For the fact was, as I had hoped years earlier, a computer could let me create keyboard parts that I hadn't got a hope in hell of ever being able to actually play, and now *anybody* with the right software and a bit of patience could knock up convincing drum patterns that they would never be able to pull off on a drum kit. It was a great leveller and could be perceived in two ways: asset or threat.

To me and Bernard it was a definite asset. To Gillian it was neither since she wouldn't trust a computer as far as she could throw it.

She would always work with someone else – me or Stephen Hague usually – to get her ideas into the sequencer. She tended to stick to the reliable Sony cassette method as the best way to record and work her ideas out. These usually originated on a piano rather than a synth. I tried getting her interested in using an Atari as a musical tool but Gillian was too easily distracted by the machine's entertainment potential. The high dive in the 'Summer Olympiad' was a big hit, the real-time sequencer program not so much.

Although I missed playing the drums – banging a kit regularly is a great way of keeping sane and fit – it wasn't as if I was sat around doing nothing. There was plenty to keep me busy. Always some head scratching and keyboard tapping to do.

Somehow I don't think this was something that deeply concerned the members of the England World Cup squad as they left the studio. I think they were on their way to open a new branch of Topman.

The song we made together became New Order's first (and so far only) number-one single. 'World in Motion' also became part of a shift in the way football, with its bad rep for mindless hooliganism, and football songs in particular were perceived. Doing a football song, it turned out, could actually be a good thing instead of something cheesy and naff. England made it to the semis and there was a new loved-up feeling about the game.

All right I admit it, I was wrong about the song. Tony was right. It was a great thing to do and I'm very proud to have been involved in it.

Then Rob somehow unresigned himself. He didn't send a letter saying he'd reconsidered or anything. He just started ringing up and got back to doing what he'd always done. It was as if the whole quitting thing had been a dream.

I don't know which was weirder: the walking out or the walking back in again, neither with any proper explanation. Talking about things within New Order was and still is something fraught with difficulty. One of our greatest problems was our inability to successfully communicate to each other how we actually felt. It stemmed from the stupid stoic Northern man thing: that emotional displays were a sign of weakness. It had always been that way and is a sure-fire recipe for paranoia and ill will.

One of the preconceptions I'd always had about bands and their members was that they might actually be chums in real life; that they might socialise outside of their day job. I probably got that idea from watching *Help* as a youngster. I thought the bit where the Fab Four shared a house was really cool. The reality is of course very different. After being stuck on tour, or in a studio for a few months, most sensible folk will have had more than enough of each other's company.

Maybe Rob had had enough of dealing with Tony, or maybe he'd had enough of the four of us. To be honest, there were times when I wondered whether having him looking after us, the other two and our TV tunes, was such a good idea, even though we didn't need much looking after at the best, or worst, of times.

'The other two' . . . now there's an idea.

23

THE OTHER TWO

Laurel and Hardy

By the time the nineties rolled around the legal and financial wrangling at Factory seemed to be coming to a head.

After a wait of a decade Tina Simmons, by then a director, had put together figures which showed exactly how many records Joy Division and New Order had sold.

A handy bit of information to have for an independent record company trying to negotiate a deal with a larger conglomerate like London records

It suggested efficiency, reliability, a horse with four good legs.

As well as London's deal with Factory, CBS were still interested in signing New Order directly, Def America too had been mentioned. The principal attraction of these deals was the large advance they might provide. Tempting as all this seemed, in reality there was no way we could seriously consider leaving Factory. One way or another we were a little too entwined.

At last, it seemed some sort of end was in sight. The London deal with Factory was going to get done . . . or was it?

In bands there are usually 'other twos' or occasionally 'other threes'.

They didn't sign up specifically for that role.

That of pop cipher.

Thinking, 'Oh that's OK, bit of a cushy one that, won't have to do much, just stand at the back and simper.'

Not minding one bit that the man in the street/pub/on the omnibus might think, 'It's the cream that rises, the shit that sinks.'

I'm not biting my lip here. Honest, I'm not.

Or fretting over remarks occasionally overheard at gigs.

'Those two don't do much, do they? You think they'd at least make the effort to jig about a bit. Looking at the audience once in a while wouldn't go amiss either. We didn't pay our hard-earned just to be ignored.'

'I like the guitarist, though, and the one in the leather pants.'

No one likes to be ignored. You know this. I know this. The feeling that I have acquired the power of invisibility is persistent and occasionally troubling.

Take, for example, the opening night of the Haçienda, the old 'No mate, yer not coming in' scenario, of which I did see the funny side.

My failure to get into many New Order gigs on the *Low-life* tour at a time when my face was on the posters and all the AAA passes I kept losing, again, I found amusing. Why me? I wondered. And chuckled.

A bigger and more recent worry, though, was London Records' market research survey to accurately gauge the man in the street's response to and perception of the popular music quartet known as New Order. This quiz was conducted as part of their exploration into the potential involvement with Factory and New Order. Quite what was the point of the exercise, or criteria used by those carrying out the survey, was never explained.

Perhaps the methodology was akin to that used on *Family Fortunes*.

'We asked one hundred people to name a member of the band New Order. Maureen, you said Neil Tennant . . . Our Survey said . . .'

WAHHHH WAHHHHH.

The TV audience gasps in disbelief.

'I'm sorry, Maureen that's wrong. There's opportunity for the Arkright family to steal here.'

Or perhaps they used something more scientific. They never said.

Nevertheless the finding that was gleefully presented to me by the southern record company and management was conclusive: Gillian and myself had, and here I quote:

'POOR VISUAL RECALL.'

So, not just 'I think there might be more than one of them but I can't remember their actual names . . .', but also '. . . or what they actually look like other than a kind of blurred, fuzzy, semi-humanoid outline.'

The Morris/Gilbert bit of the combo seemed to cause amnesia in the man on the street.

We might as well not be there.

Hooky and Bernard, of course, were top trumps along with Tony Wilson, Keith Allen and the entire 1990 England World Cup squad.

Everyone remembered them, quite rightly too.

I'm not feeling sorry for myself and I'm not an egomaniac, even though I know that's how it looks, but to be told by the people who might one day be responsible for our future that we were potential nonentities . . . I found a little harsh. Funny though, I mean who comes up with these ideas?

So, what do you do? Who do you see to fix this particular problem? If, in fact, it is a problem at all, for it has to be said that anonymity is not without its benefits.

But there was a problem here: London Records' entire motivation was to sell records to a fickle public. London already knew that New Order could be awkward bastards with an unpredictable manager; now they had taken the time and trouble to discover that half the band had less appeal to that fickle public than a slug smoothie. And they went to the trouble of pointing that out to me.

Good job I'm not paranoid, isn't it?

The year 1990 turned out to be critical for Factory. Moving out of the Palatine Road flat to the swanky (and expensive) Charles Street office might have looked good but somewhere alarm bells should have been ringing. Tina, for a long time the voice of reason at Factory, had pointed out to Tony that things could not continue the way they were going for much longer.

Typically Tony took little or no notice, so having seen the way things were going and getting the Cassandra treatment, once more she resigned.

To commemorate the grand opening of the Charles Street office, Tony asked me and Gillian to do some music which would be given free to all attendees at the office's inaugural piss-up.

Using samples from the *Play at Home* documentary of 1982, we put together 'Loved It' – note the past tense – as a bit of a comment on the way I felt things were going.

Nobody got the joke and, in typical Factory fashion, nobody

collected the free CDs on the night either and most ended up getting binned. How hard is it to give stuff away?

Despite my misgivings about our label's future, everybody was acting as though good times really were just around the corner. Things would be just peachy once London Records stopped dragging their feet with stupid surveys and figure inspecting.

On the face of it, how could things be going badly? This was Manchester, after all.

Factory's name, catalogue and reputation were a valuable commodity and having a piece of that was something that would surely entice a major label with cash to spend. London Records, the irony of the name not lost on anyone, appeared to be the solution that would allow the shiny future of financially beleaguered Factory to become reality.

Caveat emptor. Let the buyer beware.

The question for London was what exactly would they be getting for their money? The answer to that question was, of course, somewhat vague.

They didn't want the club for a start. What would a record company want a club for? The Haçienda was by then actually doing a roaring trade with the rave scene becoming massive. Hardly a day went by without it popping up in the tabloids or the evening news. But not all the news was good. The stories were frequently tragic. There was a downside to ecstasy – a very large one – it could kill.

As if that wasn't bad enough the summer of love vibe had gone sour and the matey happy-go-lucky pill dealing had been superseded by a more sinister, gun-toting, gang-controlled system.

Weapons and violence began to insidiously creep in.

Not just into the Haçienda but the entire city. Turf wars and random shootings were becoming daily occurrences in Manchester and by June 1990 the smiley culture had been replaced by fear, heaviness and firearms.

And cocaine, of course, the music-biz drug of choice.

The London deal dragged on and on and became more and more convoluted as the potential investors realised exactly what it was they would be getting involved with.

The Haçienda was in the news for all the wrong reasons.

Alan Erasmus continued to be a frequent visitor to the farm, bringing news of how well things were going with the club and the London negotiations.

Which was usually not that well at all. The club was getting more and more violent. An armed robbery, a gangster running amok with an Uzi. The dealers had all but taken control of the club. The Police were threatening to withdraw the licence. What had begun as inclusive space was becoming anything but. It really was a very dangerous time. The only solution was to close the doors for a while at least. The crisis meetings became bleaker and bleaker. The Haçienda began to feel more and more like a millstone. More accurately, a besieged fortress down to its last bottle of water.

To escape from the desperate situation in town, I found myself thinking more and more about Alan's suggestion that we should bung together some of the music we'd done for television and put out a kind of soundtrack record. Sounded easy enough, cheap and cheerful even, and anyway, Bernard and Hooky were still otherwise engaged. So I put together a tape of our best bits to get an idea of what this record might sound like.

The main problem I found was that all the music we'd written for TV worked fine with a picture, but sounded a bit unsubstantial on their own. They needed a bit more work (this had been a recurring theme in my life since school) to make them stand up as instrumentals.

A couple of them sounded like they might work better with vocals, but how would we do that?

I'd already established myself as a terrible singer in the early days of New Order. But just to make sure things hadn't changed I had another go.

Sadly, they hadn't. I was still an appalling vocalist. I could do a convincing Iggy or Jim Morrison impression, but even then only if blind drunk, so what was the point?

Gillian wasn't keen on the idea of doing more warbling either. If we were going to go into the song-writing business we would have to find someone else to do the singing.

Now through some mysterious and convoluted process lost in the mists of time, an instrumental demo of one of our tracks came to the attention of the well-known pop singer Kim Wilde.

Kim seemed quite taken with the tune and fancied having a go at singing on it. She came up to the farm and turned out to be a completely unpretentious person. Even Rob, who turned up specially for the occasion, was quite taken with her.

Kim did some singing and everyone was happy – optimistic even. Even Tony said he was keen, but nothing much ever came of it. Most likely, my umming and aahing and poor organisational skills were to blame, yet again.

Kim Wilde's interest, however, stirred something in Gillian. A reluctant something perhaps, but the idea that she should have another go at the singing caper came up – it was Rob who was the biggest advocate of the idea – and for once the idea wasn't dismissed by Ms Gilbert.

By this time, the barn was beginning to look a bit more like a proper recording studio. I'd cleaned up the sheep shit and bought a thirty-six-channel mixing desk, a twenty-four-track tape machine and some microphones. Everything you could need to make a proper record. Gillian signed up for singing lessons and Stephen Hague paid a visit to work on a couple of ideas with her.

The biggest problem was writing lyrics. We resorted to late-night scribbling sessions, most of which turned out to be either hackneyed rubbish or total gibberish the next day. It felt a little bit like a rerun of the early days of New Order, trying to bolt some random words onto an instrumental in the hope it would miraculously turn itself into a song. Only with slightly less success.

We got some help from Jez Kerr from A Certain Ratio, and eventually it felt like we'd got enough material for a half-song/half-instrumental kind of record.

Actually, I was lying when I said the writing of lyrics was the biggest problem, for that honour must surely go to titles. We called ourselves 'The Other Two' mostly because that's what people called us anyway and it felt comically fitting. The song titles were quirkily random – and that's being kind. What were we thinking?

The kebab's arent't bad either

The first single, 'Tasty Fish', was named after a chip shop in Stockport for no obvious reason and may be the worst title of anything ever. Stephen Hague did his best to dissuade us from this folly. 'How can you expect anyone to go for a song called "Tasty Fish". It's a ridiculous title.'

In retrospect I have to admit he had a point, but we weren't being bloody-minded – we just couldn't think of anything else that wasn't equally naff or cheesy.

We'd finished mixing the first Other Two album (or thought we had) at Mayfair Studios in July 1991. The experience was enlivened every Thursday teatime when Bryan Adams, who was in the adjoining studio, would celebrate his song '(Everything I Do) I Do It for You' still being at number one. The song ended up being number one for sixteen weeks. Following any given week's *TOTP* climax he would celebrate by whooping and helping himself to the contents of the studio fridge. When after finishing a mix late in the evening and feeling in need of refreshment, I would discover to my horror that my stash of Boddingtons bitter had mysteriously disappeared.

Pop stars do this sort of thing all the time. They're noted for it.

I should have taken to surrounding my cans with mousetraps. The irony of the song being featured in the film *Robin Hood: Prince of Thieves* was not entirely lost on me.

'Tasty Fish' came out in October 1991 to some critical acclaim but sadly didn't quite match the chart success of Bryan's single. It just scraped the bottom of the top forty. It was our first record, though, so even that was pretty amazing.

By the end of the year the album, *The Other Two & You*, was finished and ready to go. Then the whole thing stalled. There were a few reasons for this.

There was the Factory/London crisis coming to yet another head for one, plus some problematical sample clearance issues. It also turned out Tony didn't much like our record or even the idea of the Other Two – too poppy, he felt. Why didn't he say something sooner?

It would have saved everyone a lot of time and money.

The general opinion was we'd be better off doing another New Order album instead.

The world had had enough of our antics for one day.

Rob and Tony pointed out to us that the main reason for Factory's current financial woes was the lack of a New Order release and the sooner that gap got filled the better. Gone were the free and easy days of releasing what we liked when we liked.

We were persuaded to put the Other Two record on hold until the rest of New Order got back from their breakaway or Factory sorted themselves out or went bust – whichever happened first.

Wimps that we are, and not wanting to hamper any prospective New Order activity, we began turning down soundtrack work, put our album on a shelf and began waiting.

If there is one thing I'd learned as I grew older, it was the simple truth that however long you think a thing will take, it will always turn out to take much, much longer. Always more, never less. Not just making music or reading books, but everything you do. Does time get shorter with age or do we slow down over time?

Whatever, the older you get the longer it takes.

I wonder why that is?

There seemed to be a competition going on between Hooky and Bernard as to whose side project would be finished last and, like most competitions of this kind, I'm still not sure who won. To fill in some time Gillian and I set about making a compilation tape of ideas that maybe we could start working on with Hooky and Bernard when they actually did finish whatever it was that they were doing.

I'd finally heard Electronic and Revenge's singles on the radio and I have to admit that there were times when I thought I'd never see or hear from either of them again.

The whole non-New Order album thing just seemed to be like one big battle between the two of them.

Hooky in theory striking a blow for real guitar music as opposed to synthesised sequenced shit he hated by using . . . the same stuff we used in New Order to do the sequenced shit. Oh well. I was expecting something more . . . Motörheady.

Part of the drive behind Electronic seemed to be Manchester's finest guitarist Johnny Marr getting into synths, and the equally fine Neil and Chris from the Pet Shop Boys came on board for some songs, the upshot being Bernard found himself in what the Rock Rulebook states must be termed a 'Supergroup'. An unfortunate prejudice that I think Bernard and Johnny largely overcame just by being . . . Bernard and Johnny.

Meanwhile in the sleepy hills of Rainow, the Devil was making yet more work for idle hands and getting fed up with the twiddling of thumbs. I began exploring the possibilities opening up in the embryonic and possibly mind-numbing world of multitrack hard-disk recording.

I was bored and had been reading too many hi-tech music magazines for my own safety.

The idea of a computer replacing the tape machine had been around for a few years by then. Stereo editing software was getting fairly widely used by the early nineties. But getting more than two tracks was a new thing. Not having yet learned that great lesson of life and computers – never under any circumstances be an early adopter – I took the plunge and invested in one of the first Pro Tools hard-disk recording and editing systems.

It promised four – count 'em – four tracks of pristine 16-bit digital audio. My twenty-four-track analogue tape machine looked pretty smug. It seemed to ask 'Why would anyone want to go back to using four tracks? It'll be back to mono next.'

And that is very true. But where Pro Tools had the edge was in the editing.

With analogue, tape editing was a destructive process and fixing a mistake was difficult, not impossible, but tricky. Digital editing, on the other hand, let you make as many mistakes as you like and no harm done. You could always revert back to where you started with a quick undo.

In fact, some of the mistakes could sound quite interesting in their own digital stu-stu-stu-stutter way.

I still had a renewed sense of optimism and hope for the future that technology would make the creation and the production of music even easier. Particularly for the less musically informed practitioner such as myself.

PART 4:

CRASH

Getting the four of us together in one room at the same time was beginning to feel like herding cats or knitting fog or some other equally pointless and thankless task. But eventually a date and time was found in everybody's diaries and Hooky and Bernard made their way to the farm to talk about how we should set about making this new New Order record.

Word soon got about. In the streets of Macclesfield total strangers would ask, 'I hear you're New Ordering again ... How's it going?' with the kind of sympathetic look that is usually reserved for those suffering from a long-term illness.

'Oh, it's going OK,' I'd reply, for in truth we had only just agreed to meet and talk about the idea of actually doing something.

'Oh good,' the questioner would smile sympathetically before adding a cheery fingers crossed. 'Good luck!'

That sort of stuff could make you apprehensive, maybe a bit uneasy.

Did they know something I didn't?

It hadn't been that long since 'World in Motion', after all, and when we did finally get together at the farm nothing much seemed to have changed.

There might have been the odd hint of being older and wiser from Hooky and Bernard, but they didn't fool me. Underneath everything was pretty much the same, for good or ill, despite the enhanced sense of competition following the side projects.

The biggest difference was we decided to carry on working at the farm instead of Cheetham Hill. The barn was kind of looking like a studio, so why not?

Bernard still had a couple of Electronic loose ends to attend to, so while he was doing that, Gillian and me would try writing some stuff with Hooky. I dished out our demo ideas cassette with a nervous 'And if there's anything on there you fancy working on . . .'

You never know?

We did end up using a couple of snippets as starters for the next record.

It felt a little strange at first, just the three of us working together with Jacko, New Order's monitor engineer who'd helped design, build and wire up the studio, but we got off to a really good start, coming up with the chords and bass line that in the parlance of the day had all the makings of a 'top tune'.

Being keen to show off my shiny new Pro Tools system, I recorded all the ideas on to my posh new Mac 2's hard drive and soon had the parts edited together into something that sounded uncannily like a song. A great song too. Better than you might expect for a first day's work following a few years' layoff. So, not wanting to push our luck, we decided to knock off early, have a drink and start fresh on Monday.

Imagine my horror when Monday rolled around and I loaded up the song file to find nothing but silence. I knew that I had recorded it all, as we'd edited it and heard it back. We'd even made a cassette. It hadn't all been a dream had it?

Thinking that this was most likely operator error on my part, I made the obligatory call to the Pro Tools tech support hotline expecting to receive reassuring words of assistance. I explained my situation – a day's work of genius going AWOL and all that.

'Did you save it?' Sean, the tech support man, asked.

Now if there's one thing I'd learned from my 'Blue Monday' cassette fiasco it was *always save everything*.

'Yes,' I said, 'of course I saved it. I don't think it's that old school-boy error.'

'Ah,' said a now sheepish-sounding Sean. 'Oh dear, that might be your problem. There's this bug in version 0.9, people keep ringing, quite upset and complaining about this minor glitch. Occasionally and it is quite rare, if you save the session, it deletes everything instead of saving it.'

'Yes, but surely it's still there somewhere, isn't it? I mean, that's the great thing about digital hard-disk recording, isn't it? It'll be on the drive somewhere.'

'You would think so, wouldn't you? But no, it's all gone, wipes everything you've recorded off your drive. No way to get it back. Sorry, we're working on a fix.'

Minor glitch?! Thanks a fucking bunch! No wonder they fucking complain.

How was I going to explain that – yet again – our first great idea had once more vanished into the ether? Trumped yet again by technology.

Not just the drums this time, but Hooky's bass and Gillian's keyboards too, everything! And all the editing. The pioneering spirit had dumped me in the shit again.

They never showed you things like that on *Tomorrow's World*.

I bet Kraftwerk never had this trouble.

No wonder the song ended up being called 'Regret'.

So we began week two by reconstructing the previous week's work from the cassette mix that we'd made. It took much longer than a day.

I could hear the DMX and the analogue twenty-four track chuckling to themselves in the corner, the smug gits.

I got a telling-off from Bernard for being too optimistic and henceforth it became band policy that *everything* had to be recorded on to the tape machine, however slight an idea it might be.

That was me told.

It became a pattern. Any new equipment that worked perfectly well for me and Gillian would go spectacularly wrong when first introduced to Hooky and Bernard.

At least we had got the ball rolling – and scored an own goal.

24

REPUBLIC OF DISCORD

In the early days at Cheetham Hill we'd all turn up at more or less the same time each morning and work together until teatime. Since the drifting-off-to-the beach regime that had been a staple of *Technique*, plus maybe the experiences of the extracurricular endeavours, things were now slightly different.

At the farm, Gillian and I were always there, obviously. Hooky liked early starts so he'd turn up in the morning and the three of us would get on with stuff until Bernard arrived in the middle of the afternoon.

There would be a bit of Factory gossip, griping and worry, and then the four of us would try to get something done. Hooky would depart at sunset, leaving us two and Bernard to carry on until late. Very slowly, we got on with coming up with ideas.

In the interest of expedience and dispute resolution, eventually it was decided we'd work with Stephen Hague again.

So, bowing to popular opinion, that another trip to Ibiza was best avoided, we went along with the suggestion that New Order would go into Real World for a couple of weeks to make a start on the new album. Then Bernard and Hooky could take a couple of weeks off, during which time we would finally, once and for all, finish off the Other Two album with Stephen Hague.

After that, Bernard and Hooky would come back and we'd get on with finishing New Order's latest. Simple, eh?

Well, the Other Two part of the plan was.

The New Order bit, however, turned out to be somewhat more complicated. A whole twisted saga of fear and loathing in which the drugs definitely didn't help.

Despite all the trials and tribulations of Factory and the Haçienda the four of us were all still more or less friends.

There was a lot of mutual bitching, of course, there always had been. It's a natural consequence of being around the same group of people for such a long time. Banter, you might say, but never any real malice. Life's too short for that, a fact brought home by Martin Hannett's premature death in April 1991. Despite Martin's earlier Factory grievances and fights with Tony, he'd made a great job of producing *Bummed* by the Happy Mondays in 1988 – Martin and the Mondays were made for each other. That record became a cornerstone of the predictably named 'Madchester' scene and gave Factory another band that sold lots of records.

Acid house and the Haçienda too were made for each other. The scene had become a national phenomenon and, to the casual observer, it looked like Factory were making a fortune.

Looks, as we've learnt, can be deceiving.

In September 1991, the London deal glacially edged a little closer to completion. Factory signed an international label deal with London.

Ultimately the idea of the wider deal was that, as Factory's existing distribution and licensing arrangements expired, territories would be added until London finally attained total world domination.

The money London paid out was, it seemed, going to sort out all of Factory's woes.

The initial advance was just shy of half a million quid. More than enough to right the ship. It would be plain sailing from now on.

It came as no surprise to discover that it was nothing of the sort.

By the time we went into the studio to record *Republic* we had no songs finished, two ideas half done and a bunch of riffs. I think it was the skimpiest start to a New Order album yet.

But Stephen Hague had delivered with 'True Faith' in a similar situation and the assumption was he would do it again on the album.

We began work in February 1992 in the big room at Real World.

The 'big room' at Real World Studios

Only recently completed, the name 'big room' really only hints at the size and grandeur of the place. It was *huge*, massive, more like a small hall than a big room. It was partially submerged in the mill pond, so swans would majestically swim past the vast expanse of glass that made up one whole side of the control room.

From the outside it looked like the building was a nuclear bunker from some sci-fi movie. It was somehow both cutting edge hi-tech and olde worlde at the same time.

Stephen Hague was going through a bit of a real ale phase at the time (this sort of thing happens once you get to a certain age; before you know it you're listening to smooth jazz and wearing slippers). In a bit of rock-and-roll self-indulgence, two large wooden barrels of Tanglefoot ale were installed in a room adjacent to the studio, just next to the two very expensive hired Sony digital tape machines.

This was an accident waiting to happen – keeping seventy-two gallons of fizzy liquid in close proximity to a couple of hundred grand's worth of extremely warm digital tape machines and all that attendant electricity wasn't the best idea in the world.

Of course, disaster struck. How could it not?

One of the kegs split as the tap was being installed and a fast-growing lake of doubtless excellent beer began to seep into the machine room. An expensive catastrophe was only averted by frantic mopping and improvised sandbags.

The familiar pub smell of stale beer never went away the whole time we were there. Not really the sort of odour you expect in a brand new state-of-the-art recording facility.

Despite this minor upset, proceedings began well enough. Bernard and Hooky left after two weeks as planned so that the never-ending Other Two album could, once and for all, finally be completed. We re-recorded a few tracks and remixed the rest in ten days of frantic late-night sessions, just about managing to finish before the wanderers returned refreshed to get on with New Order business.

We then put the Other Two album back on a shelf for another eighteen months, presumably in the hope it would mature like some fine wine or cheese.

After that, true to form, things went downhill.

Factory lurched into yet another financial crisis.

Tony and Chris, Factory's money man, along with various accountants would come down and have emergency meetings with us – bad news of impending disaster being just what you need when you're struggling to create. At one of these meetings Tony got all philosophical and proposed a Schrödinger's cat-type thought experiment.

'If there was a button that you could press that meant the Hacienda had never happened, would you press it?'

Bernard beat me to the punch: 'Where's the fucking button?'

There would be doom-laden phone calls, usually on a Friday afternoon. If the Haçienda didn't get forty grand by teatime, it would go bust and have to close for good. So how about it?

The studio wasn't getting paid. If Real World didn't get some money by the weekend we were getting kicked out. Stephen also wasn't getting paid. Rob would disappear for hours at a time trying to sort something out to placate Stephen and the studio manager.

The general vibe was: for fuck's sake, hurry up and finish this record so Factory can get a bit of cash. Which, again, was not really an incentive to inspired music making. Considering that we got into this business because we loved making music not money, it felt totally depressing and perverse.

To top it all, the writing was not going well. No surprise really. In what at first seemed a bold attempt to increase productivity, Bernard set himself up in a satellite studio in a recently built pagoda, normally Peter Gabriel's personal writing space.

Bernard would work there with Richard Chappell engineering.

When the ideas we'd come up with at the farm hit a brick wall, Bernard would come up with new more promising ideas that we would then try working on in the big room.

While Bernard carried on coming up with more parts and vocals, Gillian, not to be outdone, had another set-up going in our bedroom and started working on her own in there.

Instead of feeling like we were getting somewhere (which perhaps, we were) the whole thing felt to me like we were wading through treacle.

Everyone working on their own thing, every man and woman for themselves. Which way are the lifeboats?

The gloom would only be alleviated when the coke arrived in the evening.

Then things would take an odd, jazzy direction. Stephen would get out his accordion and do a bit of serenading but, realising the band were now mostly gurning fools, wisely decide to call it a night.

At times the whole process felt more like torture. Not the kind formerly dispensed by Martin Hannett, but really physical painful.

It's an understatement to say it was the least enjoyable album we'd ever made. That it got finished at all is more down to Stephen Hague's perseverance than our enthusiasm for the job at hand.

By the end, we were barely speaking. The worst bit for me was when, again in the interest of expedience, Stephen brought in a session player to do what little real drumming the songs required. I grinned and went along with it, of course, polite wimp that I am, but inside I felt well and truly rejected.

There seemed little point asking if I could do a triangle overdub. I put floppy disks into samplers, pushed buttons and wondered if Michael Collins felt the same way back in July 1969, when his crewmates walked on the moon.

At more or less the same time, yet another layer to the Factory crisis was unfolding. Not having learned a single thing from the New Order in Ibiza recording experience, the Happy Mondays had been dispatched to Barbados to make an album with Chris Frantz and Tina Weymouth, the rhythm section from Talking Heads.

Predictably with very similar results to our own Balearic jolly.

It is debatable which of the two sun-soaked musical debacles ran up the highest bill or involved the most mayhem and the least productivity.

Plenty of drugs consumed; not much recording done. On paper, getting two big records out (ours and the Mondays) looked like a world beater. It certainly made sense for Factory. Madchester was big, big news. In many ways a smiley dayglo version of punk.

The Mondays were the biggest band in town by then. They'd gone from being a regular New Order support band in the mid-1980s to Factory's (if not the UK's) biggest band by the start of the 1990s. The tabloids loved them.

Sean Ryder and Bez, who are both lovely, intelligent people – came across in the *Sun* and the *Mirror* as cartoon rock stars, with Tony as the scene's not-quite-straight man. Tony was billed as 'Manchester Music Mogul and Night Club Manager (whose other acts include bands like Joy Division and New Order)'. The Haçienda was the heart of early 1990s Manchester's rapidly expanding music scene, with Tony as some kind of figurehead.

The Mondays deservedly had hits. They had great songs and a great attitude to life.

The same kind of anarchic energy that Factory was built on.

They also had a dangerous appetite for hard drugs.

As we did.

The same expensive chaos that we'd relished when making *Technique* was making an ill-timed come back.

The worst possible time.

The Happy Mondays could do no wrong, and Tony's feeling was that the Mondays album would be a sure-fire winner.

But with budget rapidly disappearing, it felt like we were having to pay for Factory's misplaced optimism.

London kept talking to Factory about another buyout of some kind. But every time they talked the black hole and the confusion got bigger. Possibly the biggest shock for London was the discovery that it was Joy Division and New Order and not Factory who owned the recordings of our songs: we had a piece of paper that confirmed that fact and despite cries of foul and fix. it was genuine and legal. We'd simply forgotten it existed, that's all.

Always read the small print.

Having outstayed our welcome at Real World, we headed home, with Stephen Hague working with Bernard at his home and the rest of us fixing up bits at the farm before going back to London to mix at Rak.

It struck me that all these big-money wheelings and dealings would undoubtedly affect my future, but New Order didn't seem to be having much say in them.

Rob, as our manager, should have been looking after us, but he was also involved with Factory and the Haçienda, and could possibly be accused of wearing too many hats. Of having that terrible thing they call a conflict of interests.

Encouraged by Tom Atencio, our US manager, I took it on myself to visit a music-biz lawyer in London and asked his opinion on the situation.

It wasn't so much that I distrusted Rob – I didn't – but I felt he was in an awkward spot, one in which he was unavoidably conflicted, torn between Factory, the Haçienda and us. If the whole shebang went down, where would that leave us?

Rightly or wrongly I thought it would be good to get an independent party's take on the situation.

I am not a naturally devious person, and I found the whole experience very uncomfortable and unnatural to the point where the worry of what I was doing began to make me physically ill. After each of these depressing legal meetings, I would have to run to the sleek office's toilets for a worry-induced puke.

The upshot of the lawyer's advice was that Rob's position was compromised and we should think about 'restructuring' our relationship with both Rob and Factory. Finding out that the only sensible thing to do was to stage a musical coup didn't make me feel any better. I had done the dirty on Rob, I had betrayed him.

I first told Hooky what I'd been up to at the bar of Soho's Groucho Club – at the time we were all regulars there.

In fact, it was Hooky who first brought the subject up. He was getting worried about the situation and thought we should be getting independent advice, so it was easy to admit that I had already been talking to someone. The next step was for the four of us to meet with him and see what he had to say.

The upshot of which was that New Order would be better off doing their own deal with London or someone else, rather than getting sold as a packaged item as part of Factory. He proposed that we set up a new company, Vitalturn, which would be just the four of us (unlike Gainwest which included Rob), with which Rob would have a management contract.

Rob would still get the same money he always had and he would still be doing the same job. But the all-for-one and equal-shares-for-all democracy that had always existed would shift slightly.

Unsurprisingly, Rob was not happy with this and felt that we'd betrayed him. Which made me feel even more guilty for instigating the whole thing in the first place.

It was all a bit unpleasant for a while. Rob's pride had taken a knock but reluctantly he came round and we went ahead with the new arrangements. It was a very small technical change to our relationship but things would never be quite the same between us.

Fax machines were a big thing in the early nineties. You were nobody if you didn't have your own fax machine. The trouble with mine was that it didn't bother slicing the paper into manageable pages.

I would get home some days and find the floor carpeted with a 50-foot scroll of legalese, which would stop abruptly at the crucial point as the machine had once again run out of paper, like reading a novel with the last page missing.

Not that it would have helped, for most of it might as well have been written in Latin for all the sense it made to me.

We would then need to have yet another meeting with the lawyers to have it all translated into plain English. But all the facts, figures and jargon added up to just one thing: Factory were completely fucked and New Order could end up fucked too unless we . . . at this point it all got legalese again and I usually went back to the toilet to throw up again.

After finishing the albums – *Republic* and *The Other Two & You* – and with nerves shredded from ever-worsening Factory news, Gillian decided we needed a holiday. We'd never had a proper one and, despite not being a natural holidaymaker, for once I agreed it might be a good idea to have a nice rest. Get away from it all

We were seduced by the glossy photos of white sands and deserted beaches.

We went to Thomas Cook and booked two weeks in the Seychelles over the 1992 Christmas holidays.

My track record for successful holidaying was pretty abysmal and, you guessed it, this was not about to change.

As soon as we arrived on the tiny island of Mahé the overcast sky opened and a torrential downpour began. We hadn't even made it to our beach chalet. When realising that it might have been a grave error to allow me to do the holiday planning, Gillian burst into tears.

'I thought it was going to be sunny. Why have you brought me here?'

I decided not to answer.

Still, what's a spot of rain? It'll soon blow over, I thought optimistically. This was a tropical paradise, after all, and despite the downpour at least it was warm rain and we'd finally left all our troubles and woes at home.

After lugging the suitcases into our island chalet with its thatched roof, there was knock at the door. I answered and was confronted by a slightly confused bellboy bearing the familiar and by now dreaded large scroll of fax paper. There was no escape. London had decided the deal was finally going ahead and *had* to be completed before the end of the year without fail or the whole thing was all off. Whatever happened to nothing happening at Christmas apart from turkey and Advocaat?

Could I please give my consent to the following items? . . .

The once-in-a-lifetime 'Xmas Holiday in the Sun' became nothing more than a continuation of the Factory strife we were trying to escape. Fax after fax after fax kept getting pushed under the door, there were long-distance crackly phone calls as the wrangling reached some sort of crescendo. The latest sticking point was that, unless Gillian and I signed to London both independently and as part of New Order, the deal was off.

It had become a game of ever-moving goalposts. As soon as every-thing had been agreed, something else that was a deal breaker would pop up. (Isn't it strange how two people who London had effectively informed were non entities could break the entire deal?)

I refused to agree. This led to serial badgering:

'Are you sure?'

'Are you absolutely certain that you want to refuse?'

'Because if you do refuse terrible things will happen and your friends may end up losing their homes.'

'Take the money or open the box?' As Michael Miles used to put it.

The long-distance phone rambles were spread over the course of a few days. This was not the tropical getaway we'd been expecting; I'd have been better off at Butlin's in Minehead.

The pair of us spent all our time arguing about the should we/shouldn't we of the whole, never-ending affair.

I'm easily browbeaten at the best of times. Finally, completely sick of the whole thing dragging on and on, we relented, and our Factory deal was transplanted to London Records (90) Ltd. Rob, Bernard and Debbie Curtis signed on our behalf, and we returned to the cold drizzle of a new year with a new label. Factory – the thing, the idea, that had been part of us since the earliest days was gone; you can't beat Entropy.

A campaign of promotion was put together for the new record, including the making of a video for the first single and a rather bizarre press conference to be held in Rome, possibly to compensate for our previous general neglect of Italy.

The only question I remember from the executive summit-style press conference was:

'So . . . Ian Curtis . . . why *did* he kill himself?'

The question that never ever went away.

I began to get a little worried that Joy Division might be turning into some kind of death cult.

An eternal mystery.

The new album *Republic,* released through London, got to number one. The single 'Regret', the first and possibly only thing on the album we actually wrote together, was also a hit. This ironically ended up with us competing with Rob who'd had a hit with Sub Sub's 'Ain't No Love (Ain't No Use)' on his own solo-project record label.

Rob could always spot groups with potential.

Keeping a bit of Factory continuity, Peter Saville did the art directing for *Republic.* I went to visit him at his new office at Pentagram, where he was putting together what he described as a photo-realism type of sleeve for the album. Burning buildings juxtaposed with beach scenes – it all made perfect sense to me. As he was going through the prints of his ideas, I happened to notice the vast number of Macintosh computers dotted about the building.

'See you've got the latest Mac there, Peter,' I said. He went on to explain that the work he was doing these days was done entirely on an Apple-produced computer.

'They're great, aren't they?' I said. 'I've got a couple in the studio at home.'

He was incredulous: what on earth could I be possibly be doing with one of these machines, he wondered, much less two?

The idea that they had uses other than in the design and print world seemed to him very odd indeed.

I think he thought I was joking.

After all the hassle of making the record, it was a lot of fun doing a *Top of the Pops* special performance – special in that we were miming for a change – from the set of *Baywatch* in LA. David Hasselhoff was a lot nicer than I was expecting. He was also a lot taller. He dug a hole in the beach so he would appear a similar height to the rest of us.

So it wasn't *all* bad. Nothing ever is, really, but that time it definitely felt like it was. I was still feeling guilty about going to the lawyers; I still felt like I'd grassed Rob up. I couldn't shake off the sickly feeling of drowning in treacle. That all the work might still end up being for nothing. It had been an ordeal.

I find *Republic* very difficult to listen to objectively these days. It just reminds me of all the trouble and angst that surrounded its creation. The loose ends of the London deal, the ones that involved New Order at any rate, were concluded in February 93. Everything changed. A new company, Vitalturn Ltd, was established. The total democracy ideal we'd had since the start ended. In future Rob would be paid as a regular manager, he would no longer get a direct split of the music publishing. Bernard felt as he had done most of the work on *Republic*, he should in future receive a greater share of that publishing. The sort of deal that existed in normal bands. We agreed. We became normalised.

A great deal of time got spent programming the new songs for live performances, transferring samples and loops from DAT tapes to samplers, exporting MIDI data from the computer to the Yamaha

QX3 sequencers to produce a backing track. Not so much actual playing.

I think we only rehearsed together at Cheetham Hill once or twice before we started gigging again. Getting everyone together in the same room at the same time was becoming ever more difficult, if not well-nigh impossible.

By then I was getting completely fed up of the whole situation. It all seemed to have reached a new low. Whatever we'd done, Factory would still have been sold anyway eventually. Us making the album hadn't changed anything. IT WAS POINTLESS. It hadn't saved anything.

A happy US dressing-room scene.

We did a few festival gigs before embarking on yet another American tour. This would turn out to be the worst one yet. It was an all-time low: the opposite of fun, a job, not a party I have some videos of those gigs and no one looks as if they want to be there. You can sense the frosty atmosphere between us just by looking at the body language.

Hooky blamed Bernard for making the album sound too much like Electronic (which was a bit ridiculous, though hardly surprising as Bernard had done much of the work).

Bernard had had enough of Hooky, and the pair of them had probably had more than enough of the two of us.

The drug consumption went through the roof and just became something else to argue about. Even taking drugs had turned into a competition with Hooky. Every eight-ball became a snorting sprint to be hoovered as quickly as possible; order another and repeat. Of course I joined in.

Who wouldn't?

Someone with some sense. That's who.

Even getting out of it became a grind. The drugs didn't make anyone any happier. There was no funny side to any of this. It was just grim.

Rob, against his doctor's advice, was also consuming ridiculously vast amounts of pot. I know, who was I to talk? Pot, kettle, black.

Rob was beginning to get manic again, as bad if not worse than he'd been back in 1986, ranting and raving. All this did nothing for his health. At times, you could literally see his heart pounding through his Fred Perry T-shirt. Rob was clearly not well, but being ill and admitting it were two very different things, something we already knew. He was stubborn. Maybe he thought admitting he had a health problem was a sign of weakness.

'Just need to get fit. I used to be really fit. I did karate, you know. Might take it up again when we get home.'

Eventually it turned out that Rob had an undiagnosed thyroid problem, which had been left untreated. He'd probably had it since his incident in 1986. His self-medicating with beer, dope and mountains of butter had only made this worse.

The whole thing came to a grinding halt at Reading Festival on 29 August 1993. There was a sad panto vibe about the affair.

'They're splitting up, you know,' went the rumour

'Oh no they're not.'

'Oh yes they are.'

I had no idea or opinion on the matter either way.

Not one that counted for much any more.

Still plagued with guilt, I threw up as soon as we came offstage, got in the car with Gillian and went home.

It's easy to blame all of this on Factory and the accumulated stress but honestly by this time I think we were well and truly sick to death of each other and the whole business.

Business and money had somehow poisoned the pleasure of making music together. Following Dylan's advice, I did my best not to look back.

It was as if Frankenstein's monster had finally had its revenge on its creator.

25

POP PUPPETS

First rule of showbiz: you've got to have a gimmick

'Oh No – It's the Other Two' was one of the titles we considered for our first not really solo album. Colin Bell and the other music-biz professionals at London Records weren't impressed with the idea. They didn't get it. It's not hard to see why.

I was a little bit puzzled as to why they still wanted our record, their marketing survey having given them all they needed to know about our marketability. I would have expected them to come up with a polite excuse to shelve the whole caper permanently.

Perhaps advise us to look elsewhere? A smaller label?

But no.

'Tasty Fish' had been an almost but not quite minor hit in December 1991, but that was nearly two years ago by then. Surely, though, London must have known what they were doing. At least they seemed interested in the record, which was more than Tony had been.

The thing was, when we started turning our soundtrack snippets into 'songs' it was more of an experiment. The idea of being an actual real-life band was something that never seriously crossed our minds. Or if it did, it must have crossed very quickly indeed.

When I'd started out with Warsaw the whole enjoyment came from creating and playing music with a group of people, then playing these creations before an audience.

Although it had been frustrating at times, we enjoyed writing the music of the Other Two. But playing it live? How could that work? It wasn't that we weren't interested in the idea, but I just pressed a button and the music played itself, either on a computer or a tape machine. Not a particularly entertaining spectacle and for Gillian the whole idea of singing in public filled her with dread.

The old punk us versus the world, the 'we are the greatest so fuck you' spirit, the thing that is the spark of most neophyte bands, just wasn't there.

Neither of us were what you might call front-person material. It was yet another repeat of the nobody-wants-to-be-at-the-front-doing-the-singing routine.

Perhaps what we needed was some sort of gimmick. I've heard it can help. I thought that London, being a commercial concern, would have some suggestions along those lines. After all, pop was their business.

Things, they suggested, had move on since 1976 and to a lot of people the 'band' thing was a bit long in the tooth anyway. The rise of dance music, clubs and DJ culture had led to the phenomenon of the public appearance: artistes turning up at a club, miming to a couple of their songs, signing autographs, then drinking the night away.

Everybody was doing it, apparently. But just because it was happening elsewhere didn't make it right or even remotely cool. The idea felt a bit cabaret somehow, like going back to the pub at Leek in 1973 and playing Tony Orlando covers to bored diners.

But by 1993, even that public appearance concept was starting to wane, possibly as a reaction to its inherent naffness. And in the ever-cyclical nature of popular music, it was now loud, raucous bands from America who were taking over. Seattle began to replace Manchester as *the* happening place for exciting new music.

We were on our own, trying awkwardly to figure out what exactly we were supposed to do. Not knowing what that was meant that our interviews, when they weren't all about New Order and Joy Division anyway, were vague and half baked.

The biggest problem was that Gillian would not under any circumstances consider singing in front of an audience. I understood that and didn't blame her at all. But for London it was all a bit hard to swallow.

All this sounds like I've got a downer on the whole thing, which I really haven't. Even after all this time I still like the record. It sounds upbeat and optimistic compared to *Republic*. And the remixes – then a bit of a novelty, for us at any rate – were really good. Moby had done four versions of 'Movin' On', a *Thelma and Louise* kind of song. When talking to him about possible directions, I suggested maybe doing one which sounded like a cross between Gram Parsons-era Byrds and Kraftwerk. This ended up being called the Sawdust mix, which London thought had some commercial potential. We went to a meeting in the London boardroom and they enthused about the track, which 'with a bit more work' they believed could have all the makings of a 'smash hit'.

To which Gillian replied emphatically, 'If you think I'm going to mime on *Top of the Pops* wearing a red gingham shirt and dungarees with a pig under my arm, you've got another think coming.'

The boardroom went suddenly quiet, looks were exchanged and sighs reflexively exhaled. And that was pretty much the end of that, because that was exactly what the men were thinking. You could hear the pop bubble bursting.

The single 'Selfish' topped the US dance charts and there was talk of us going over to do some promo of some description but it never materialised.

I'm not apologising for the record, but I think, like a majority of band solo or side 'projects', there was nothing substantial behind it. It was unintentionally self-indulgent. It had no real reason to exist other than to prove to ourselves that we could do it.

We had treated the whole thing as a bit of a joke, neither of us harbouring a craving for limelight. It wasn't as if we had some bottled-up musical frustrations that couldn't be vented elsewhere.

For London, New Order was an easily sellable item with a track record and back catalogue appealing to a fair proportion of the music-buying public.

I guess they banked on a bit of that rubbing off on us. A fair assumption, you'd think. But they'd already been told we were invisible to the man in the street, imperceptible and uninteresting, and it was now becoming clear that we were not really bothered about selling ourselves anyway.

I'm not even selling it now, am I? Shouldn't I be saying that we were the best thing since sliced bread and the comparative lack of success of our record was down to someone else's failure? If only, if only if only . . .

I probably did try that textbook gripe at the time. The truth is that a spin-off, solo project or re-recording of classic tracks on a kazoo will *rarely* be as successful as the original. It's just how it is. They are a distraction that curious completist fans may buy into but they'll never beat the appeal of the real thing.

Nonetheless, London put out our single 'Selfish' and *The Other Two & You* (although I still think 'Oh No – It's the Other Two' would have been better, but what do I know?). They did pretty well, I suppose, considering there were no gigs to go with them.

We did some promo for The Other Two album – press interviews mostly – and in the process I managed to upset Bernard by saying something that got taken the wrong way.

'It was a joke,' I explained.

'Well, if it was a joke then you should have said HA HA HA afterwards so everyone would have known it was meant to be funny.'

I got given detention and was ordered to take a course in interview technique. And write 'Steve should keep his big mouth shut' a thousand times. Whoops.

Our final ties with what was left of the Factory wreckage in the form of the Haçienda, Dry and TGP 225 (the entity that owned the Haçienda building) came to an end not long after that. There was a meeting at the offices of Ernst & Young (the then accountants) opposite Manchester Town Hall some time towards the end of 1993.

Options were discussed for the future management/funding of the club and bar business in the absence of Factory. In a nutshell these were:

One, carry on as before, putting in money as and when required with the dim and distant glimmer of hope that one day everything would be repaid.

Two, stay involved but refrain from putting in any more money in the hope that at some point in the future the businesses starting making enough money to stand on their own and maybe even repay some of the 'initial investment'.

Three, get out of everything and in the process give up any hope of ever seeing any of it. Just wave bye-bye to all that cash.

I went for option number three. A bit defeatist, I know, but it was the only one that offered any certainty, however, bleak. I had long resigned myself to never getting anything. For me it was a simple case of what you never have you never miss. Gillian and I waved bye-bye.

Rob, ever the betting man, and Hooky went for option one, leaving Bernard sitting on the fence – surely that was my job? – by going for option two.

Following on from Republic, the tour and Reading, this was really just the icing on the cake, the finishing touches, the end of the road.

I have honestly no idea how much I waved goodbye to at that meeting. Every year with every book and every retelling the amount goes up and up.

I still don't care. That money made a lot of people very happy, it helped to make something that in some small way changed the way the world worked and the way people thought. That is priceless.

On the whole, I had a great time while losing it, so I mustn't grumble.

The Other Two were never going to be Two Unlimited. We were definitely never going to be Nirvana either. What people wanted most was New Order and Joy Division. London, not being fools, recognised this equally simple fact and having a fair bit of cash to recoup set about fulfilling that need.

To a major record label this generally seems to take the form of the compilation album, the greatest hits album, the remix album or, if all else fails, there's the Johnny come lately . . . the remastered original album.

All these are relatively cheap and fast to produce. Most of the expenditure and energy required comes from the marketing department, with sales projections and profit-and-loss spreadsheets being the main driver. They don't call it the music business for nothing.

It was about as far away from the ethos of the early days of Factory and New Order as it was possible to get.

'The Biggest Thing Since Sliced Bread' or 'Corpse of the Unflogged Horse' were my title choices for this latest in a series of rehashes. You've probably guessed that new compilation, released in November 1994, didn't get my vote, not that it mattered. They called it, imaginatively, *The Best of New Order*. This they followed up with *The Rest of New Order* a year later.

You really can't have too much of a good thing can you?

I am, of course, joking.

'You, fucking hypocrite,' I hear you cry, quite rightly. Yes, I took the money, and yes I did the interviews to promote the sodding things. I am guilty of rank hypocrisy in this and many other things, and saying that the label or the others made me do it is no excuse. I hold my hands up. It's a fair cop and I'm sorry.

I cannot argue with my teenage conscience's taunts of 'sell-out' and 'rip-off'. That was exactly what all this amounted to.

London, who were eventually swallowed up by Warner, wanted to maintain a bit of Factory's look and feel, a bit of their art, a mantle of Tony's integrity and Peter's gloss, but only if the price was right. There have now been somewhere between six and ten (depending on your classification) of these rejigged and reshuffled records and counting. Reselling the same Barbie doll in a slightly different costume or snazzier box.

As a music fan and record buyer, I fall for this all the time. And despite the flashy new sleeve and booklet thingy, the feeling of disappointment on finding I've just bought half a CD for the third or fourth time is something I know all too well.

It doesn't stop me from doing it, though, and I sometimes feel like

I'm keeping the record industry alive with my boxset impulse purchases alone. I love all this reissuing: I'm a particular sucker for the giant boxes stuffed with twenty-odd discs that in my heart of hearts I know I'll never listen to. But the lure of all the photos and glossy memorabilia and knick-knacks is too much. It just doesn't seem like Christmas unless I've shelled out a fortune for a lovingly compiled boxset of King Crimson, Lee Hazlewood or even Led Zep.

But when it comes to our own stuff, I wonder why the hell anybody would want something they've bought five times already, and I don't like feeling responsible for inflicting buyer's remorse on anyone. I've suffered enough myself.

I think you can tell you're turning into what is sometimes referred to as a heritage act by the number of 'best ofs' and reissues in your catalogue. If by chance you are still making new music, this state of affairs sends the message: 'They used to be really good. Just check out the old stuff.'

The worst of it for me was all the remixes. A VERY big thing in the nineties; I have never got to the end of most of them. I don't think any of us have, to be honest.

No, that's not true. The worst of it was when someone decided that '1963' needed reworking to help sell a New Order compilation. Since none of the band were speaking to me and Gillian, I only heard about it third-hand, and typically didn't think it was a good idea. I was asked if I wanted to be in the video and attend the 'launch party', but there wasn't a peep from anybody in the band.

It's still a great song with a great Hooky bass solo, but this new version of a New Order record (as opposed to just a remix) had absolutely nothing to do with me or Gillian. We hadn't moved or changed our phone number. Maybe the old invisibility was spreading.

I wasn't going to take this lying down, so to calm myself I went and bought myself a tank.

At the time, it seemed the best thing to do.

Say hello to my little friend

Almost at once, the fact I'd purchased an armoured fighting vehicle became the single most interesting thing about me. I went from being a boring nerd to a boring nerd with a tank. How rock and roll is that?

'Mad rock drummer runs amok in Cheshire countryside in a tank!' I could picture the *Evening News* headline.

My Mother raised one important point. Now I was the proud owner of 15 tonnes of green and black metal, what was I going to do with it? How on earth did I think that tank ownership was going to improve my wellbeing?

But thoughts like that are normal with a superficially useless purchase of any size. The 'Oh no what the fuck have I done?' reaction – well known from awakening from a drunken bender.

Before one of the trainspotters among you pipes up, I know it's not actually a tank. What I had purchased was in fact an Abbot FV433 Self-Propelled Gun. But it had tracks, a turret and a big gun, which makes it a tank in most people's book.

To be honest, I'd never passionately wanted to become a tank owner. I'd never considered joining the army. The brief spell I'd had in the wolf cubs had been enough. I don't know what came over me. It just sort of happened.

One morning I drove past a garage that happened to have the tracked titan parked on its forecourt. An attention grabber or publicity stunt of some kind. A very effective one as it turned out. Even Gillian's interest was piqued

'Oohh look at that!'

As though I could have failed to spot it. I performed a brisk emergency stop and slewed haphazardly on to the premises.

Parking untidily before embarking upon the practice loathed by the motor trade known as tyre (or in this case track) kicking.

I did my best to impress Gillian with my knowledge in such matters as I asked the garage's proprietor:

'Does it go?'

'Is it for sale?'

And the clincher.

'How much?'

It doesn't happen every day, I know – and being in the dangerous situation of having more money than sense, I went and bought it.

I was recapturing my Airfix model-infatuated childhood, only on a much bigger scale. This nostalgia for the halcyon days of yore had also been behind my earlier impulse buys of a life-size Dalek and a Cyberman which now protected the studio from further livestock incursions.

These sci-fi spontaneous whims were despite their fearsome appearances trouble-free white elephants and dust collectors, but the Abbot was different. Not only in size but also in the amount of work involved in repairing and keeping the thing running.

I knew very little about guns and even less about the inner

workings of engines. But I am naturally curious about things and I slowly learned the basics. I had to if I wanted to ever shift the monster.

Maybe it was a male midlife crisis. It's quite common for men of a certain age to go through a phase where they begin to enjoy hanging about in sheds, getting covered in grease and yearning for an even larger spanner and power tool collection. It is generally tolerated by the better half and Gillian was no exception, she made the resigned observation that 'at least it'll keep him out of trouble'.

Other than the side projects, all my bandmates had acquired expensive hobbies and indulged in pointless pursuits by this time: Bernard had become a yachtsman and Hooky remained fascinated by expensive cars and motorbikes, the faster the better.

My acquisition of the Abbot coincided with my giving up drugs. I'd been out of my head enough times in my life and had long passed the point where it felt even remotely enjoyable.

It began to seem like a very self-destructive pastime. I had always known it was, but when you're young and foolish you don't think anything can touch you. Since my teenage years, I had possessed a false sense of invincibility.

By most people's standards I was still young but the idea of still being a drug-addled fool at forty just seemed ridiculous.

So I just stopped.

I just woke up feeling bad too many times.

Drugs and tanks aren't generally regarded as a good mix.

I settled into exploring my mid-life crisis. I didn't know what I was doing half the time, but I wasn't going to let a thing like that stop me. It reminded me a little of starting out in music.

When I knew nothing. When everything was new, exciting and ever so slightly dangerous. Driving a tank, though, is exceedingly dangerous – you can do a LOT of damage. I speak from experience here.

Learning how the thing worked was both frustrating and very

satisfying, though probably not as satisfying as discovering that its gun had a range of ten miles, making Bernard's house an easy target. Fortunately, ammunition was quite hard to get hold of. The Army are quite picky about things like that.

The tank kept me occupied and there is a lot to be said for that. Having my mind focused on mundane practical matters such as finding the right spanner stopped me fretting about the pain of the past few years. I became almost relaxed and wondered what else I could change about myself.

Cigarettes were the hardest things for me to abandon. I could easily see myself living without drugs or much alcohol but a life without a cigarette was unimaginable. It took years of trying and failing, over and over again, before I managed to lose that particular habit.

I eventually replaced it with the habit of acquiring more military vehicles and the assorted ephemera required to maintain them.

I ended up owning four, which I thought was probably enough given that my once massive cowshed was beginning to feel a little cramped and claustrophobic.

The tanks generate a lot of interest from passing country ramblers, the occasional tank groupies (yes, they do exist) and boy scouts. They usually walk up to them and ask, 'Do they go?' when what they really mean is, 'Can I have a ride in one please, mister?'

Rob was disappointed that I had filled my shed with military machinery.

'You want to put a swimming pool in there, Steve, and a helicopter pad at the back' had always been his advice.

26

THE TIDE GOES OUT

'Ding ding' goes the iPhone next to the laptop I'm tapping away on, trying to write some words that might one day seem intelligible to someone happening to read them.

'Ding ding,' it goes again.

The message says cryptically: 'You and Gillian are celebrating nine years of friendship on Facebook.'

What? Is there a party. Do I have to buy a present or produce a cake with candles? Do I have to go somewhere and actually *do* something?

I'm not even on Facebook. Or am I? Let's see, is that me? Or someone pretending to be me?

Hang on . . . nine years . . . that's a bit of an underestimate, isn't it?

All these words floating on a computer screen. Words that supposedly represent sixty years (and counting) of an undisciplined life. I do a bit of totting up. For around 66 per cent of that time – why that's around two-thirds! – I've shared my time with just one person and yet where is she in this story? Certainly not on anything like two-thirds of the pages. Nowhere near that. And I keep on saying 'I' sometimes when surely I mean 'we'.

What can I say, that I have been overcome with egomania and I'm just forgetful? Mm, what sort of heartless person does that make me? Tony and Rob get more attention and they never made me breakfast once.

Never put up with half the shit.

What should I say then? Something cornball like, 'Gillian is my rock'?

Only for her to say, 'You think I'm a rock? Charming.'

Or perhaps 'I don't know where I'd be without her' would be better.

But that might be taken as a dig at her appalling sense of direction – her unique directional dyslexia.

So no, that wouldn't be better, would it?

Probably best not to mention how important she is at all.

After what? Forty years of being with someone, of being closer than I ever thought I'd be or like to be with anyone.

I honestly suspect that I haven't got a romantic bone in my body. This might be aligned with my inability to relax, to ever feel totally comfortable. It's not that I'm nervous – I'm too old now for nerves – just suspicious that it might all be a trap. Wary, that's the word, though what I've got to be wary about exactly I don't know. I have gone from having faith in the absurd, from being a believer in all sorts of ridiculous mumbo jumbo, to being a hardened sceptic.

Gillian did teach me how to shop. She taught me to enjoy the buying of food and the pushing of a trolley round a supermarket.

I became adept at looking only slightly embarrassed while hanging around the lipsticks and powders, shuffling my feet until asked, 'What do you think of this one?'

Then unable to think of a satisfactory answer, 'Yeah, that one.'

I'm still an awkward bastard, apparently.

Working with Gillian is frequently difficult. Her mind works in a completely different way to mine. I think I do things a linear way. More often than not it's a haphazard, roundabout way, that only makes sense to me.

It makes no sense to Gillian. Equally what makes sense to her baffles me.

At times, it's as if we are speaking two completely different languages.

The workings of a software sequencer annoy her. We end up arguing over ridiculous things. The timing and whereabouts of notes mostly.

'I don't want it to go ding like that. I want it to go ding like this . . . ding.'

The exact placing of the ding can be inflammatory, a thing of earth-shattering importance that has catastrophic consequences for humankind.

'It's just a ding,' I say.

'Yes, but it's not the way I want it to sound! I want it more . . . ding. Like it was before you messed with it.'

'It's still just a ding.'

'Yes, but it's *my* ding!'

Creating and performing music can seem like a life or death situation at times. It's very easy to lose perspective.

For music stirs strange emotions in people. You can get very possessive about something you've created, even a ding. To see it altered in some way can be distressing to the ding's originator. As if sound can actually be possessed.

If you could see us working in the studio together, and I hope to God you never have to, you would think that we were on the brink of imminent marital break-up. That plates are about to be thrown, china smashed, followed by a storming out of house and home.

It's not always like that. Everybody rows sometimes, throws their toys out of the pram over some trivial nonsense. It's being able to laugh at yourself and realise how ridiculous your behaviour actually is that's the trick.

*　　*　　*

After the demise of Factory and the release of the first *Other Two* album, Gillian and I fell back into writing music for film and TV. John Chapman, who had produced *Making Out*, called sometime in 1994. He had another series, a BBC One comedy drama called *Common as Muck* about the lives of dustbin men. It starred Edward Woodward, widely known from the US crime drama *The Equalizer* and *The Wicker Man*, Roy Hudd and Neil Dudgeon.

Knowing how John liked to work made it easy to get back into the routine of writing and scoring music again. We didn't really give any thought to the idea of making another record. As for gigs or anything else with New Order, that all seemed to be over and done with.

Thirteen years – lucky for some – that's how long mine and Gillian's lives had been entwined with the rest of New Order and all its jumble of connected activities.

Now, I spent all of my time at home, working on music and mending tanks, to the point where I was becoming a recluse. I never visited Manchester – there was no reason why I would want to really. We got the occasional fax and phone call from Rob but that was about it.

Once clear of the craziness and worry of New Order, our life became calmer if not exactly tranquil, but mostly life was sedate and angst-free. Not having to wait for anyone else to turn up. Just doing whatever, whenever we wanted.

Believing that we had probably seen the last of Bernard and Hooky, we decided to fully embrace normality, and what could be more normal than getting wed?

I reckoned we'd been engaged for long enough, so I finally asked Gillian to be my lawful wedded wife.

We set a date and on 29 April 1994 headed to the register office. This, of course, made my parents, especially my mum, very happy. Having long harboured the view that I would never make an honest woman out of Gillian, my mother delighted I was finally doing the right thing. It was (as Sly says) a family affair. I don't think there were any speeches though my dad did his best to embarrass me – he never failed in that, it's what dads do best by wheeling out some of his embarrassing stories of my childhood unsportiness and my time in his employ.

Being one half of a disorganised and indecisive couple, I somehow managed to forget to organise a honeymoon. It only took three years to get round to that.

In less time than it took me to sort out a trip to the seaside, our first daughter Matilda Florence Morris – Tilly – was born on 7 February 1996. As there seemed to be very little prospect of New Order resuming touring, or anything else that might interrupt our lives, it seemed like a good time to become parents.

I'd always liked the idea of becoming a father. At the same time I found the idea daunting and scary.

People say having children is life changing: 'you're never the same afterwards', which I took to mean 'and not in a good way'.

As well as drugs and fags, I moved on to quitting booze in an attempt to be sensible father material. Responsible or not, I was cleaning up my act: a total clean-living chap well on my way to joining the ranks of the terminally boring. Yes, I got worse.

Alcohol is a very insidious thing and it's very easy to underestimate its destructive capabilities. These days I still have a drink, but I only enjoy it up to a point. One or two is enough. The days of my getting obscenely drunk down the pub, waking up with a banging head and uncertainty about exactly what I'd said and done in the hours prior to my collapse into oblivion – those days were well and truly gone.

I'd seen drink mess up a good few lives over the years. The fact that drinking heavily is socially acceptable, popularised and encouraged in ways that drugs are not doesn't exactly help.

I can't really condemn it, though, without sounding like a total hypocrite. For I have been as stupid about abusing alcohol as anyone else and from quite a very early age too. Drinking four bottles of cooking sherry on a sunny Saturday afternoon on the top floor of a multi-storey car park should have been enough to put off most fourteen-year-olds. Not me.

The hangover was epic but what did I expect for seventy-five pence?

There was little time for either nicotine or booze anyway as our daughter seemed to be on a band-on-tour sleeping schedule from birth.

'No sleep till breakfast!'

She changed our lives for the better, though, I think it's fair to say that.

Her first words were 'Spice Girls!' and she would bounce enthusiastically to 'Wannabe' even before she could walk. A warning sign I cheerfully ignored.

I would watch *Teletubbies* with her on my knee. I wondered what psychedelic drugs were needed to come up with such outlandish programmes. It was like an acid flashback. What was wrong with the good old black-and-white *Woodentops*?

We would push Tilly's pram around town during the day and drive her around in the car seat in the evening. Each night, I would pace about with her tiny body curled up on my shoulder. All in the hope that tonight would be the night that she finally slept through until dawn. Nothing ever worked. Until one day it did.

It seems crazy to say it now but I really miss all that.

I never thought I'd say that back then.

For the one thing that parenthood seemed to bring was an even greater acceleration in time passing: a day began to feel like an hour, a week seemed to only last a day, a year was gone before I knew it. Why was that?

In the blink of an eye Tilly was running about the house singing and dancing, then the next minute she was off to school.

We carried on writing bits and pieces for telly. Our names, address and phone number were still on the 'music done quick and cheap' BBC-approved list, and we started getting requests for all sorts of odd things: a soundtrack for a genital mutilation documentary, a film about bridge building, a *That's Showbusiness Christmas* special and even theme music for Mike Read's *Pop Quiz*.

They all wanted music written by next week, if we could manage it. There was no way we could do it all and my standard reply of 'We don't usually do this sort of thing really, we're not actually professionals at it or anything' wasn't enough to put most people off. Finally I had to be straight and just say, 'Much as we'd like to do it, we're a bit snowed under at the minute. But please bear us in mind for any future projects you may be considering making,' which was a polite mouthful and only half a lie.

Sooner or later some bright spark came up with the suggestion, 'Why don't you put all your soundtrack material together on an album and we'll see if we can put it out?' Ring any bells?

This déjà-vu-ish suggestion didn't come from a record company. I have a feeling it came from someone at BBC Enterprises or something. I think they were looking to expand further into the record business. After listening to me waffle for a bit, they soon thought better of the idea and decided to stick with what they knew best.

But before you could say, 'Hang on, haven't we been here before?' we were at it again, turning our bits of TV tunes into something that might be mistaken for a song.

I'd been listening to a lot of jungle and drum and bass, so I'd got the idea of doing something that sounded a bit like Squarepusher jamming with Fairport Convention. I presume that I was still drinking at that point.

But you've got to start somewhere, even if where you actually end up is nowhere near where you intended.

This time things would be different. (Oh yeah? How many times have I heard that one?) With the idea of maybe doing something that could actually work live, we figured on getting someone else to do the singing and lyric writing. This would end up being Melanie Williams who had done the vocals on Rob's smash hit, Sub Sub's 'Ain't No Use'.

Melanie lived in Macclesfield so was in the right place and as she is a great singer as well, it was a pretty easy decision to make.

This would eventually become the first record we'd ever done that involved the traditional (by record-label standards) involvement of an A & R man in the form of the multi-talented Pete Tong, then working at London records specialising in their dance department.

The role of the A & R man was conceived early on in the evolution of recorded music. It stands for 'artist and repertoire' meaning finding people who perform music (the artist) and making sure the music and songs they perform and record are the best they can be (the repertoire). In the early days this involved hooking up performers with writers who could provide material. But from the sixties, when the Beatles and other groups began to write their own stuff, this role had become surplus to requirements. The A & R man's chief function, it seemed to me in the late seventies, was to go to gigs, watch bands, have a few free drinks and then sign the ones that got the best reviews in the music papers. They were bandwagon spotters, I suppose. An oversimplification or exaggeration perhaps but I honestly thought it worked exactly like that.

In reality, it turned out to be very handy to have an outsider's opinions on what we were doing and what we ought to be doing. An outside opinion alleviates some of the self-doubt.

Some, but not all.

There was the usual agony of lyric writing and singing, even with Melanie helping out. It was still the most difficult bit of making the record. It's always words that are hard.

No wonder singers tend to get so finicky. It makes drumming seem dead easy!!!

Despite the rest of New Order being otherwise engaged, Rob was still around and technically still our manager. He would pop in to the farm every now and then for a cheese sandwich and to check up on how things were going. But most of the time it was Rebecca, who was doing the actual work and running the office while Rob popped out to the pub for the afternoon, something he did most days despite his doctor's advice. Rob's weight kept seesawing from nearly obese to (for him) skinny.

He had a lot on his plate still, with him and Hooky, keeping the Haçienda afloat. Despite everybody's efforts, it finally went under in June 1997. I wasn't surprised but I wasn't happy about it either. All that time, effort, money and worry and it still ended in failure. By that time it had apparently managed to lose an estimated £18 million – a surprise even then but, as I have mentioned, the figure somehow still magically continues to rise.

I'm not sure exactly what I felt when Rob rang to tell me that the Haçienda had finally run out of road. I hadn't had anything to do with it for a few years by then. I'd see it mentioned in the papers and on TV occasionally. A symbol of something great that turned bad. Despite all the trouble and strife, it was very sad to see the last link to Factory come to an end.

Early in 1998, we were halfway through finishing recording what would become *Super Highways*, the second Other Two album, when Rob called with yet another of his 'I've been thinking' ideas.

He had been called by Vince Power, the promoter of the Phoenix Festival and many others. Vince made what is commonly known as 'an offer you couldn't refuse': a vast amount of money in return for New Order performing at that year's Phoenix.

'It's a lot of money, you should think about it. Decide once and for all what you want to do. I'm getting sick of people ringing up, asking about gigs, and I don't know what to tell the fuckers.'

'Well, it's not really up to me is it, Rob?' was my peevish answer.

'No, but I've been thinking,' there it was again, 'you should have a meeting and decide what it is you want to do. Have you split up or haven't you? I'm not arsed, but at least I'll know what to tell people instead of sounding like a twat.'

'Fine by me, you'd best ask the others then, hadn't you?' Still passing the buck. For some reason, I didn't want to be the one who said no, but I felt reasonably confident that someone else would.

I put the phone down, told Gillian of Rob's news and we got back to making music.

27

HERE WE GO AGAIN

One dark winter's evening early in the new year, we strapped Tilly into the car seat and headed into Manchester for the first time in God knows how long, eighteen months at least. This was Tilly's first (and possibly only) trip to Rob's office, which was now upstairs above the deserted Haçienda.

We carefully made our way up the stairs, past a pile of Haçienda posters and detritus, carrying the sleeping toddler in her car seat. It's baffling how infants can sleep in the most unlikely of situations, generally one that's nowhere near an actual bed and the most ungodly hours.

It was a chilly evening and I was wearing a new fleeced hoody. These garments were very popular in the late nineties, the height of fashion you might say. We said our hellos to Rob as Rebecca put the kettle on, before reverting to our former duty of waiting for the rest of New Order to turn up.

True to form Hooky was next to arrive, affable as ever, admiring baby Matilda and swapping stories of domestic strife.

And the last to arrive, no surprises again, was Bernard.

'Sorry I'm late,' he said, wondering about the suitability of the lighting and taking off his coat, when I noticed he was wearing exactly the same fleecy jumper as me. Not just something a bit similar, but the exact same one.

'Nice pully,' I said as he did a double-take and we both laughed. Ice broken, the years fell away. It was as though the last five years hadn't happened.

We were all ostensibly older and wiser. No longer burners of the midnight lamp, we were keepers of regular hours, followers of healthy lifestyles, no longer competitive in any way, shape or form. I was glad we could all sit in the same room for a while and just be positive about each other.

Rob relayed Vince Power's offer for us to play the Phoenix Festival in July 1998. Was there any interest in doing it or should he just tell him and any other callers to fuck off, there was no more New Order to be had?

'Well, I'm up for it, if you lot are. You know me, eh Barn?' from Hooky.

For it had always been true: for Hooky the gigs were the most important element – the roar of the crowd and rocking out was his thing. He really couldn't get enough.

Me and gigs?

I was a bit more wary. Yes, gigs are a lot of fun. I really do enjoy them and being in a band is also mostly tremendous fun, but like anything, do too much and the fun stops, it becomes a drag and resentment creeps in. Thoughts such as 'Why did I agree to do this?' and 'I'm never doing this again' rear their ugly heads and, before you know it, you turn into a miserable bastard and hate the whole thing and everyone involved. I wanted to take it in small steps, one at a time, as did Gillian. We were parents now and unsure how it would all work. If it *could* actually work. Bernard too was cautious.

We may not have been quite as gung ho for the reunion as Hooky, but everyone was still open and receptive to the idea.

At the time, Bernard was working on a third Electronic album with Johnny but, as it was just one gig, he didn't think that would be too much of a problem. But he said he had concerns about his hearing. He had fallen prey to rock and roll's most common ailment, tinnitus, and was worried about it worsening. He didn't want to be overexposed to any loud, aggressive volumes such as might come from, say, a drummer at work or an over-large bass guitar rig. I sympathised with Bernard's plight for it's the drummer who is most prone to this debilitating and frequently depressing condition. I blame my overzealous bashing of the twenty-inch crash cymbal in Warsaw.

I took my ever-pragmatic approach that any volume-related problems could be easily dealt with simply by the miracle of technology – the acqusition of yet more gear! Parenthood had made me cut down on a lot of things but I was still 'investing' in new musical gimmicks and gizmos. Roland had recently introduced a new electronic drum kit called V-Drums (the V I think stood for virtual). According to the ads it was a 'drumming revolution'. Instead of using samples, Roland used digital simulations. These they claimed sounded and played exactly like a real drum kit, but with a volume control. This sounded like just the thing to placate Bernard's tinnitus worries. Well, my part in the ear ringing at least.

The worry for me was the length of time it would take to get the songs rehearsed and programmed.

All the equipment we'd used on the *Republic* tour had been scattered between the four of us and most of it was either broken or obsolete. So we would be more or less starting from scratch. Three months I figured was just enough time, if we started quickly.

I had expected us to come away from the meeting with either a 'you must be joking, never again!!' or at best a tentative 'maybe' – the usual New Order indecision. But instead we'd pretty much agreed to the gig on the spot with the odd slight reservation.

'I don't want it all turning into a competition like last time,' was Bernard's qualification to Hooky.

'Oh no, I'm not like that any more. Older and wiser, you know. Besides, I thought it was Steve you had the problem with?'

I shrugged, Bernard shrugged and, the problem whatever it was, was forgiven and forgotten.

We agreed to do the one gig to see how it went, before we committed to anything longer-term. We had all learned that much, at least. Try to walk before you run.

Bang on cue, Tilly woke up, having had enough sleep for one night and ready to toddle round and explore Rob's office.

We began rehearsing in the barn at the farm.

I'd been using it for recording drums and vocals and the make-shift booth that I'd made out of a sun umbrella and gaffer-taped tea towels was a source of great amusement.

The new electronic kit was an immediate hit with the rest of the band. Finally, you could turn the drummer down or even off if necessary – a great step forward for mankind and the rest of the band. I paid the price of falling for the early-adopter gig again. I had high hopes for the set-up. I'd been playing electronic drums and triggering samples for two decades and figured using this new invention would just be an extension of that; of course it wasn't. It was a great thing to practise on without annoying the neighbours and it had lots of sliders to play with but I never really got on with it. I tried though, I really, really did.

The V-Drums made great and sometimes very convincing drum sounds, but setting up and playing the kit was a bit fiddly. Bits would stop working at the worst possible moment, and it didn't actually feel that much like playing a real kit. Not really. More importantly, I couldn't hide behind it as successfully as I could with the real thing. The trigger pads were tiny. It looked more like the old Sooty toy kit than anything Keith Moon or Kraftwerk would employ. A small price to pay, though, if it prevented premature front-person deafness.

While we were still finding our feet and remembering how to play together again, Bernard made the suggestion that we should try including a few Joy Division songs in the set. Over the years, we'd played the odd one or two, generally 'Love Will Tear Us Apart' or 'Atmosphere', on special occasions. Maybe we should try adding a few more like 'Heart and Soul' or maybe a jazzed-up version of 'Isolation' that Andy Robinson had worked out?

It seemed like good idea. It had been ten years after all.

We booked ourselves a warm-up gig at Manchester Apollo on 16 July, and Phoenix was on Saturday the 18th.

Then the festival, the thing that got us back together in the first place, was cancelled due to slow ticket sales. Instead, we got slotted into the line-up for the Reading Festival at the end of August.

We did the Apollo anyway: 'the New Order comeback gig' is how most people remember it. It was a Manchester affair, so not exactly a tricky crowd, but it was a genuinely good night despite my atrociously weedy pretend drum sound. Everybody seemed to love it. Even my sister Amanda made it to the gig: the first time she'd seen me and the band play. And the last, so she said.

I confess I was very surprised by how many people still wanted to see us after all that time.

We had been absent for most of the nineties and things had moved on. First grunge, then Britpop was king of the hill. In 1995, Oasis, then Manchester's number-one band, had duked it out with Blur in a 'We Are the Greatest' slag-off that harked back to the golden age of punk. Bands with amps and real drums were back leaving Fatboy Slim, the Prodigy and the Chemical Brothers to crank up the samplers, drum machines and synths.

The Reading Festival was followed by two Christmas gigs: Manchester Arena, which was awful, and Alexandra Palace, which was pretty good mainly because it was New Year's Eve. It's pretty hard to fuck up a New Year's do as most people are up for it whatever it is. I recall a particularly ramshackle encore attempt of the Hardfloor remix of 'Blue Monday' featuring Bez from the Mondays – the sort of thing that New Year's Eves are made for.

Four gigs and we were still speaking. Who would have thought it possible twelve months earlier? Not me, that's for sure.

The second Other Two album remained unfinished. It was starting to feel like a rerun of the first record. I had a theory that the way to get New Order to do anything was to start doing an Other Two album and just as it's almost, but not quite, completed, up they'll pop like bad pennies back for another go on the merry-go-round.

We weren't alone with our unfinished business, Bernard still had his Electronic album to finish so once the gigs were done we got on with completing our parked projects.

I ended up mixing most of *Super Highways* with Ash Howes in London.

We had tried taking Tilly away to a studio when we were doing some of the recording, but although she seemed to enjoy being away from home, the novelty soon wore off. So I ended up doing the final mixing sessions on my own, which felt weird.

I'd not been away from Gillian for any length of time before and I felt a bit lost and lonely. I was stuck in a series of dodgy hotels and pubs, each one dodgier than the last. The best one (and by that I mean worst) was near Kew Gardens – quite a nice area, you'd think. I had a job getting the door to my room open. It kept sticking on something. A hefty shove soon revealed the source of the problem: the toilet seat had been ripped from its customary place of residence and had been used as a somewhat unconventional doorstop. The rest of the room was similarly wrecked. The remains of what might have once been furniture were just dumped in piles of debris on a carpet of indeterminate colour and pattern. Only the sagging wallpaper was making any effort to remain in its rightful place.

In what had to be a rock-and-roll first, I inversed the usual hotel-room wrecking and set about restoring the place as best I could. It was to no avail as the more I tidied up the more damage I uncovered. In the end, I did a runner to the next place along the street. This one was advertising 'Wide Screen Sky Football' and came with an adjacent chippy and en suite bathroom.

I travelled by bus as it was the easiest way to get around London. Pete Tong would come to the studio and complain about how long the short journey from Hammersmith to Barnes had taken in a cab.

'Only ten minutes by bus on the 209, Pete.'

I think he thought I was joking.

London had high hopes for our new album. They believed that one song 'You Can Fly', had all the makings of a smash hit and even splashed out for a video.

I was not so certain myself, but supposed they must know what they were doing. Of course, the single bombed and London quickly lost interest. It is a wonder the album ever came out at all.

Pete Saville did a nice job on the sleeve, though. It's a digital rendering of a virus.

Bernard completed the third Electronic album with Johnny, and New Order reconvened back at the farm, to work on a revamp of the *Mission Impossible* theme for the film franchise's second outing.

Looking for something to sell the soundtrack album, I think, they speculated on the draw of New Order's name. But with no new 'product' out for five years, our stock in the US was pretty low. Limp Bizkit, the hot new thing then, ended up as the album's main attraction. Our offering got a polite thanks but no thanks.

Next up was a more likely prospect, an opportunity to answer the 'could we actually write a new song together again?' question. Danny Boyle was making a film of Alex Garland's novel *The Beach* and London were involved. Could we write a track for the film?

Nothing ventured, nothing gained. We agreed to give it our best shot, and came up with 'Brutal', which was included on the soundtrack, All Saint's *Pure Shores* being the track that everyone rightly remembers.

Around that time we discovered that Gillian and I were to become parents again.

'Not a brilliant piece of planning,' someone at London said upon hearing the glad-tidings, somewhat unsympathetically, I thought, to put it mildly.

Gillian was not too impressed either.

'Charming.'

One Saturday morning in May 1999, I was in the kitchen at the farm, trying to entertain Tilly. I'd decided it was time to broaden her musical horizons beyond the Spice Girls. I was not doing particularly well. So far both Can and Kraftwerk had reduced her to tears, and drum and bass just got her really annoyed.

Undeterred, I decided to forgo Van der Graaf and move on to something a little more soothing and randomly dug out Todd Rundgren's *Something/Anything*. I was looking for Roxy Music but my never wholly accurate filing system had gone to pot. We'd just got through the first verse of 'I Saw the Light' when the phone rang, unusual for that early on Saturday morning.

It was Hooky.

'Bad news, Steve, Rob's died.'

He'd had a heart attack in his sleep.

It felt like that tragic phone call of May 1980 all over again. A different kitchen but Hooky once again bearing the sad tidings.

'Why is it always you, Hooky, with the death notices?' The words left my mouth while the shock still flooded through me. They weren't funny.

There wasn't much else to say. I hit pause on the CD and the room was silent. Even Tilly in her play pen was lost for words.

The old gut-wrenching, punch in the face, shocked reaction to sudden and unexpected death.

Yes, Rob had been ill for a long, long time, truth be told. His weight had been up and down. He'd ballooned then shrunk. For the best part of the past year, Rob had employed a Chinese healer to cleanse his chi of negative energies with the laying on of hands. After many sessions the therapist admitted Rob had the worst case of bad chi he'd ever come across. He'd done his best, but the Gretton chi had him beat. He was never the healthiest or fittest man even at the best of times, but it never seemed like he was about to meet his maker any time soon. It was 15 May, three days short of the anniversary of Ian's death.

I felt gutted, speechless and numb.

It was sad and it was terrible. Rob left two children. The fact it came out of the blue like that brought back the same shocked disbelief that Ian's death had. I picked up my daughter and gave her a hug.

I could never listen to *Something/Anything* the same way again.

I have always hated funerals. There's not much to like about them really. I'd been to one in my early teens, when a friend of mine died in a car accident. His parents were atheists, and at the funeral nobody sang, nobody spoke. We, the mourners, all shuffled in and silently watched the coffin glide through the curtains, and then shuffled out again.

That was it. Nothing else.

It confused and angered me. I never wanted to go to a funeral ever again if I could avoid it.

Rob's funeral was a very different send off. A grand old-school proper church ceremony. Packed to the rafters. Rob had a lot of friends, a lot of respect. It was a good do, if any funeral can be such a thing.

Grace, our second daughter, was born on 20 October 1999. I was beginning to feel slightly outnumbered, three girls and me the only male. I got another tank to compensate for the threat to my masculinity.

Rob died, Grace was born. Life goes on. That's what they say, isn't it? I'm not sure it makes anyone feel any better.

Tilly had by then developed a catchphrase, 'I've got a good idea.' I feared a career in band management beckoned.

Tilly was full of good ideas. She wanted to change her name to Monica Tilly Spyro Bat.

Then we discovered we had two children to keep us up all night. One would wake up the other, then that would be it. Never believe anyone who says, 'Two children aren't as much trouble as one. They keep each other entertained.'

No, they don't, they keep each other awake all night.

Despite that, Grace was a much calmer child than Tilly. She always seemed to have a cold, though. From birth she always had a snotty nose. I never thought anything of it, it was part of who she was. We mentioned it to the health visitor, who didn't think much of it either. Maybe it was nothing after all.

Dad, Dad, pull us back up that hill

28

A SENSE OF LOSS

Towards the end of the 1990s I found myself feeling a bit adrift.

I had no idea of where music was going and even less idea of what I was supposed to be doing in it.

There were a lot of things I thought I could be doing, but younger, smarter folk always seemed to get there first.

I'd been listening to Squarepusher, Photek, Ed Rush and Grooverider. I found drum and bass exciting and relaxing at the same time like some kind of hyperactive, electro jazz. Great interesting music, but like the hip-hop and the multifarious dance scenes of the late nineties, it was hard to get a fix on what was behind it. Where it came from.

They certainly weren't bands. Anyone with a computer in their bedroom could knock up an incredibly sophisticated drum and bass track.

As that had been my area of speciality, I began to feel I was being programmed out of a job.

A little bit of an old gooseberry.

Maybe I should leave it to the young folks?

Before we began work on the next New Order record, our first without Rob, we had a meeting to discuss the hows, whys and wherefores, and to get a plan together.

You can't beat a good plan, although in the past we'd just followed our noses and left the planning to fate.

We were older and wiser now and more professional, was how I justified it to myself.

The plan that we came up with was that we should try and make a more guitar-based record.

More like a Joy Division record.

Ditch the keyboards and just, er, rock out.

Bernard said he'd had been listening to Nirvana. He liked what he'd heard and Hooky liked what he'd heard from Bernard.

I was not entirely convinced by this scheme but knowing that dissent would result in going round and round the houses until we ended up back where we'd started, I decided to forgo the circular motion of the indecision.

You've got to start somewhere and there is absolutely nothing wrong with Nirvana. An absolutely fantastic band if ever there was one.

I don't think that anything we came up with sounded anything vaguely like them.

To be honest, during the writing and recording of *Get Ready* my mind was elsewhere. For most of the time, I was trying unsuccessfully to sort out my father's affairs. Something that began to feel depressingly like trying to sort out the Haçienda.

Over the years, whenever I was home in Macclesfield, I would always do my best to visit my parents' house. Once a week, as a rule.

Sunday was always a good day for this as that was pretty much the only day when my dad's presence was guaranteed.

Despite this regular personal contact, my father's preferred method of communication with me remained the written word. The memo. Very much as it had been when I hung about his office pretending to work back in the 1970s.

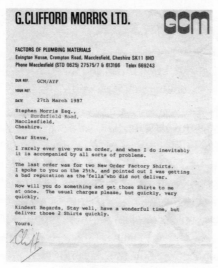

G.CLIFFORD MORRIS LTD. GCM

FACTORS OF PLUMBING MATERIALS
Evington House, Crompton Road, Macclesfield, Cheshire SK11 8HD
Phone Macclesfield (STD 0625) 27575/7 & 613166   Telex 669243

OUR REF.   GCM/AYF

YOUR REF.

DATE   27th March 1987

Stephen Morris Esq.,
. Hurdsfield Road,
Macclesfield,
Cheshire.

Dear Steve,

I rarely ever give you an order, and when I do inevitably
it is accompanied by all sorts of problems.

The last order was for two New Order Factory Shirts.
I spoke to you on the 25th, and pointed out I was getting
a bad reputation as the 'fella' who did not deliver.

Now will you do something and get those Shirts to me
at once. The usual charges please, but quickly, very
quickly.

Kindest Regards, Stay well, have a wonderful time, but
deliver those 2 Shirts quickly.

Yours,

Don't make me wait

Apart from the modern innovation of the UPVC glass conservatory that had been constructed into the back garden, my parents' house had changed little over the years.

The smell of tea tree oil, the same green carpet, same horse brasses on the pelmet, the same Royal Doulton figurines my mother had collected.

I would turn up after Sunday lunch and find the usual household division. My mother and my sister Amanda, still resident at the family home, would be in the back room watching snooker on TV; my dad in the front room having his solitary after-dinner sleep surrounded by a heap of newspapers and office paperwork.

He was not to be disturbed unnecessarily. Mum, always a great source of useful information, would bring me up to date with important things I might have missed in the world.

'You'll never guess who's died.'

I never could.

'Lynn Fogarty's husband, Jim.'

'Who?'

'You know Jim! He used to have the paper shop next to the butcher's on Chestergate.'

Still none the wiser, I would nod and say, 'Oh aye.'

'He hadn't been looking well for a while.'

'Oh dear, that's a shame.'

She would follow this with, 'Oh, what else had I meant to tell you? . . . That's it. Did you see . . . oozit . . . what's his name, Amanda?'

'Edgar.'

'That's it! Your cousin Edgar. He's been had up for assaulting a policeman. It was in the Macc paper. Drunk and disorderly!'

I'd swear I'd never heard of any of these people before in my life. Distracted by New Order, I really hadn't been paying enough attention to the complexities of the Morris family tree.

'Daft beggar. He's always sozzled.'

Eventually this bulletin on the depreciation of the town's population and the crimes committed therein would be interrupted by a plaintive cry from the next room.

'Amanda!'

'Oh heck, he's up. Best take him his cup of tea. I'll bet the other one's gone cold. Coming, Father . . .'

Which was my cue to visit the next room and check on my father's health.

'All right, Clifford?'

He would squint groggily through his spectacles trying to place me. Then it would dawn. 'Stevie, Stevie, come in, sit down. What can I do for you?'

I think he was pleased that I'd stuck with a life in music

'How's the band doing?' always his first question.

He'd had some heart problems in the early 1990s and was now partially bionic, fitted with a pacemaker. This despite always doing his utmost to keep himself fit and well.

Over the years, he'd invested in a wealth of exercise machines and a plethora of keep-fit gadgets. These had filled the void left in his bedroom by my departing drums. An exercise bike, a rowing machine, a treadmill and God knows what else made up his mini gym.

He worked out first thing every morning to a soundtrack of Duke Ellington, Ella Fitzgerald and Fats Waller before setting off on his tap-selling travels, bright and early, same as he'd always done, ever since I could remember.

'You're looking well, Clifford,' people would say. And he did look well, always bright-eyed, bushy-tailed and full of life.

He loved to work. Loved travelling and meeting people.

He loved his granddaughters' visits. Being a granddad suited him somehow.

Gradually 'I'm worried about your father' replaced my mum's weekly obituary news roundup.

'He doesn't know where he is half the time.'

I thought my mother was probably over-exaggerating a little and would go for my weekly audience with Clifford. Little by little, week after week, I began to notice what she was on about.

He began to take longer to remember who I was.

He would begin sentences then drift off into some unconnected reminiscence of something that had happened long ago.

These historic tales of times before the war, he would tell with great intricate detail. But when asked what he'd just had for lunch, less than half an hour ago, he would think hard for a moment, then look a little confused, before changing the subject with 'Ask Amanda if she'll make me a cup of tea. This one's gone cold.'

Just old age, I thought.

Clifford was in his late eighties, almost a decade older than my mum. Bound to happen to anyone that age, bit of mild memory loss, course it was.

I hoped he wasn't going senile like my maternal grandma. I'd been very young but I still remembered her getting occasionally scary and violent at times. She ended up in Parkside, Macclesfield's centre for treatment and containment of the unsound mind.

'Our mum's gone senile,' I remembered overhearing Auntie Elsie saying at the time.

It was what grown-ups did when I was a child. Something similar happened to dad's brother Uncle Johnny before cancer was declared the winner.

When the old lost their minds – lost their marbles, we kids said – they became angry and generally acted crazy and mad. That's what I thought. My father wasn't acting crazy and mad, just a bit well ... forgetful.

His business had thrived in the years since I'd left its employ. He'd started importing his own range of taps and had a couple of warehouses full of stock and a fleet of vans. The office where I used to snooze, slouch and skive between Warsaw gigs had changed beyond recognition.

But even at work my father's behaviour, always slightly eccentric, had been noted as becoming a little bit more wayward than normal.

Reports reached my mother – there wasn't much that didn't get back to my mother sooner or later.

Things were not going well.

In fact, they were going quite badly. This, my mother discovered, had been going on for a while and she was getting worried.

Something would have to be done. As the eldest son – well, the only son come to that – the responsibility would fall to me.

Our next Sunday afternoon conference began well enough.

'Dad, we're a bit worried about you.'

'Why's that then? There's nothing to be worried about, I'm fine.'

'But you're not though, are you? What's been going on at work?'

He furrowed his brow and thought for a while. 'Well, I don't know what you've heard. But I'm having a devil of a job getting any sense out of that damn accountant. I keep asking him for . . .'

He then launched into a highly complex but plausible explanation that, whatever I had heard, was tittle-tattle. He had everything under control and was constantly being let down by other people not doing their job properly. He then turned the story into some tale of his early years in the trade with his brothers.

'But Dad, you've not made any money for the past five years.'

I knew this for I had seen the books. I'd been to enough Factory crisis meetings over the years, stared at enough columns of numbers to roughly guess their meaning.

He became rattled.

'Rubbish! It's that bloody accountant, he need's seeing to. Get him on the phone now! Where's the phone? Stephen, get me the phone. Amanda, where's that tea?'

Before I knew what was happening, he offered me my old job back.

'The internet! That's what it is, Stevie! That internet! Everything's on that internet. You know why that is, don't you, Stephen? That accountant doesn't. Why don't you come and sort it out for me?'

I was flummoxed. I said I would do whatever I could to help him and I did, though whether I was any help or not is debatable.

I tried time and again to suggest that maybe he should retire or sell up and consider taking a life of leisure.

'But what would I do?' he replied forlornly. 'I've seen enough people in my time, they take retirement then drop down dead from boredom. No, not for me, never!'

My father became adept at shifting the subject from one on which his memory failed to something about which there was some recollection. And he could still string together a plausible enough excuse for any problems. He was sharp enough at this. He had been selling for decades and had the patter on automatic at times. But the reality

– the present, the who, the where and the why – were receding like an ebbtide.

At the same time, part of my trouble while getting ready for *Get Ready* was imagining life in New Order without Rob.

We hadn't always seen eye to eye, but Rob and Factory had always been there. Rob had not necessarily been doing much at times, it has to be said . . . but, he'd always been a part of who we were. In the very early days, he'd got us somewhere we'd all wanted to go.

Possibly my doubt about the return of New Order was an age thing. Another midlife crisis maybe? I'd never thought about it before, but approaching middle age in a band suddenly seemed a bit odd, unnatural somehow. Whatever happened to the auto-destructive 'hope I die before I get old'?

I'd always thought music was a young person's thing and I was beginning to feel like the oldest swinger in town. I'll admit it, I was glum. I peeped in the mirror and didn't much like the guy peeping back.

The record company and management were happy, though. A new record in the works; something to get their teeth stuck into.

As a young, enthusiastic collector of records, a band's new release had been one of the highlights of my life.

I remember the anticipation, the excitement of waiting for the latest vinyl offering to turn up at my friend Simon Shepherd's shop in Macclesfield or Virgin in Manchester. Taking it home and giving it the critical first-spin appraisal, sometimes as I read the music press reviews at the same time.

It seemed that in those days we had much longer attention spans. Time moved more slowly then, and we were easily pleased. Nobody ever considered the hiss and crackle of a vinyl LP much to moan about.

Yes, those were the days, my friend. The ones they call the good and the old.

I found myself thinking, 'Here I am finally, alive in the twenty-first century, an epoch I couldn't wait for as a child. The time when I believed I'd be living in a house on the moon or Mars, and be flitting about with the aid of a jetpack.'

What I hadn't anticipated was that I'd be carrying a camera in my pocket that doubled as a telephone or be listening to music on tiny silver discs supplied in plastic containers that disintegrated soon after opening.

No more considered evaluation of a band's latest thirty-six minutes of creativity.

No more savouring and sipping and discussions with mates.

At the beginning of the noughties (who bloody dreamed that name up then?), it was grab 'em by the balls time. If the listener wasn't hooked within the first minute of exposure to the latest work, it was game over: skip to the next track for maybe another fifteen seconds, and if there was nothing of interest there, then it was most likely a dud to be tossed aside. Never to be played again.

Maybe the only difference in the olden days was the difficulty in moving from track to track on a vinyl gramophone. Maybe not.

An age of instant gratification in every walk of life was dawning. Spinning faster and faster.

I still believe the arrival of the fast forward and skip buttons on the 1980s CD player has a lot to answer for.

The idea of the single as the album appetiser was still around but only just. The 7-inch vinyl had gone the way of the dodo, replaced by the CD single. That too was on the wane, kept breathing by the life support of hype and clever marketing gimmicks such as bonus tracks, remixes, remixes of remixes and the odd old rare classic stuck in as a lure to ageing completists.

The visual feast of a 12-inch gatefold sleeve was gone for good and that for me had always been a great part of the enjoyment of listening to music.

The ritual.

The admiring of the sleeve and the reading of the sleeve notes gone with the passage of time and the urgency of the new age.

Can't turn back the clock, though, much as many would like. There's no point whingeing.

SNAP OUT OF IT, STEPHEN!

Get on with making the album.

But everything was different this time. No Factory, no Rob.

By this time Rebecca Boulton and Andy Robinson had taken over managerial responsibility. Rebecca had been doing most of the work with Rob for the past few years anyway and was probably the only person who understood how our convoluted business affairs worked. Rebecca did a fantastic job of sorting out the chaos and turning it into something that more or less made sense.

Even to me.

What she never did was turn round to us and say, 'You know the trouble with you lot, you bunch of fuckin' idiots. If you had a brain between you, you'd be dangerous.' Which had been the usual signal for the start of one of Rob's little pep talks on our failings.

That was not Rebecca's style.

It wasn't Andy's either.

I'm not saying that was entirely a bad thing.

We weren't all totally keen of the idea of having Rebecca and Andy running our lives. Hooky felt maybe we should have given the job to someone new, maybe a proper showbiz mogul-type manager. We'd known Andy since he had been part of the road crew; Andy and Rebecca gave me some sense of family and continuity.

Gillian and Bernard agreed they were the right people for the job. Occasionally the old democracy still held.

Then there was the new label, London.

How ironic is that? If there was one thing Rob had hated most about that company, it had been the name. A band from Manchester reduced to being on a label called London.

The shame of it.

To fire the starting pistol on this new endeavour, Bernard suggested a track he'd been working on, a techno-ish house piano kind of tune.

Yes, it had been partly Bernard's idea that we should make a guitar record but nothing's ever been straightforward in this band.

I had never expected to end up in a situation where we would be working with New Order again *and* bringing up children. It was something that I'd always feared wasn't going to be easy, but at least we had the studio next door. It wasn't a long commute.

The *Republic* writing routine recommenced. Bernard would work some days, Hooky others, and once again only occasionally would the four of us get together.

Trying to arrange getting everybody in the same place at the same time sounds simple, but for some reason musicians seem to resist organisation. It flies in the face of being some kind of free-spirited rebel, I imagine.

My recent livestock-shifting experiences were again of little help.

We did get bits of things done but, like *Republic*, it was a disjointed process. In the morning I'd play the ideas that Bernard had evolved from the night before to Hooky, and he'd get annoyed that they didn't work with any of his bass bits. So he'd do some more bass bits. Then Bernard would come and do some more work on the idea and ... well, you get the idea. It got a bit awkward. Circular.

Sisyphean, if you will.

We badly needed some organisation. A producer, a referee, a coordinator.

After Bernard had taken the idea that became 'Crystal' as far as he could, we met up with Steve Osborne, whose mix of 'Brutal' had gone down well , with the idea of trying out one track with him. If that worked out, he could have the job of organising and producing the entire record.

Steve came up to the farm to work with us for a few days on the understanding that we would treat the place as though it was an actual proper residential studio. Not a crèche with a desk.

It took some imagination.

Steve and Bruno Ellingham, an engineer from Real World, spent the best part of a day just blowing the dust off the mixing desk while I explained the eccentricities and quirks of the studio's slightly unconventional and temperamental wiring. I don't think Steve was too impressed.

But the idea worked after a fashion. At least we all got together in the same room at the same time.

Steve then booked a few days in the legendary Rockfield Studios in Monmouthshire, a studio with which he was more familiar. A place with a bit of reliability and history.

Hooky and Bernard went there with him.

Gillian and myself didn't. No room at the inn; insufficient accommodation for children. Not that we would have taken Tilly and Grace anyway.

Andy Robinson put it bluntly, 'You don't have to come. I don't think Gillian would like it anyway.'

Now I may have got hold of the wrong end of the stick here. It wouldn't be the first time I'd misunderstood Andy. But I thought that was slightly odd. It felt like a brush-off. We'd stopped in some pretty rough places in the past and it couldn't be any worse than any of my *Super Highways* B & Bs.

To be fair, I suppose Andy thought he'd be saving time and money and, as long as Bernard and Hooky were happy, all would be well.

It wasn't as if I had nothing else to do.

Everyone loved what Steve Osborne did with 'Crystal', myself included, and it earned him the role of producer for the entire album.

The way we went about recording *Get Ready* was different from the way we'd worked in the past.

Steve wanted to get the drums done first.

Great!

If there is one thing I enjoy doing, it's playing the drums. But instead of us all being there at the same time this drumming was happening, it would just be me on my own with Steve and some very rough backing tracks.

I packed a Transit full of drums and synths and, with Andy at the wheel, hit the road back down to Real World. I was a regular there.

Steve lived in Bath so it was handy for him too.

I then drummed solidly, night and day, for a week.

Just me on my own, but somehow I don't think the rest of the band felt they were missing out. Not totally on my own – having two Steves in the same studio did get a bit confusing for us both.

I played along to demos we'd done, to synth loops Steve concocted and sometimes to nothing at all. It was the nearest I ever got to doing a drum solo record. We ended up with a gargantuan amount of ideas, most of which would end up getting binned. It felt great to be playing proper real drums and cymbals again instead of the tiny quiet ersatz synth kit I'd been using live.

It also felt good to be playing whatever I wanted again. Steve wanted me to experiment, do something different. Be a bit indisciplined. Bernard, as a rule, preferred it if I just stuck to something simple.

'Could you not just go boom, crack, boom, boom, crack?' He would ask.

'Yeah, I think I could,' and for a quiet life I occasionally did.

I love minimalism, but experimentation is an exciting word.

Then finally Steve Osborne, his hard disk full to breaking point with drumming, could take no more. He said thanks, he thought he had enough now, and sent me on my way.

I came away feeling a bit puzzled. Was that it?

Was I was no longer needed? I went home. Home to try and sort out my ailing father's affairs.

Amanda and I had got my father to sign a power of attorney agreement, which let us look after his precarious financial affairs. Amanda, as an accountant, had no trouble with this, but it was something I hated doing.

After Rob, it felt like yet another betrayal.

I don't think my dad liked it that much either. His health began to slowly deteriorate.

Shortly after that, my father's business went into receivership. Something he'd worked at and built up for over fifty years came to a messy, abrupt and troubled end.

I had the same sense of failure I'd had following *Republic* – it had all been for nothing.

My father went into a series of nursing homes. He kept getting kicked out for being a troublemaker.

I visited him with the kids and worried.

Each time I took Gillian down the M5 to Real World to do more work on the album, my dad's health would take a turn for the worse.

'He's not got long left,' my mother would say when I rang to check up on his condition and I would end up coming straight home again.

Understandably this began to piss off Hooky and Bernard. The room would go quiet whenever we turned up, like we had interrupted something conspiratorial.

There was a bit of an awkward atmosphere at the studio whenever we were there.

*   *   *

For a period of eighteen months my father's health and wits gradually degenerated. He became hospitalised, moved back to a nursing home, then back to hospital again.

I watched him slowly disappear. Vanish before my very eyes.

He was still living in the present mostly, but the gaps in his memory became deeper. Some days he would seem perfectly normal, other days he would just look perplexed and ask, 'And who are you?' Become confused and flustered as the recall failed.

Music, though, he never had any trouble remembering.

He rediscovered old recordings of crooner Al Bowlly from the 1920s and 1930s, remembering in great detail where and when he'd first heard them. It was as though the long-forgotten past was returning to fill the empty spaces of the present carved out by the illness.

He claimed he had been visited by his father, the disappearing George, last seen vanishing into the night around 1920-something. The villainous granddad he had told me tall tales of when I was an infant.

He now referred to him as Pa and in the present tense.

'Pa was here before,' Dad announced as though visits from the long dead were routine.

'And what did he want?' asked my mother.

'Same as he always wants, money. Always after something, that one. I sent him packing.'

All this was very strange and extremely upsetting, for somewhere in there I knew my father was still present but the world he inhabited was becoming more and more remote from mine.

He was retreating somewhere I could never go.

Dementia comes in many names and guises – Alzheimer's, Pick's, Lewy body, vascular – all similar, all vampires feeding on the soul.

In the hours before his death. I was a total stranger to him.

He was confused, afraid and alone.

Death is always a blow, even when it's expected; knowing it's coming doesn't make it easier to bear, it still stuns, knocks you off your feet.

I'd known people who had met their end suddenly, others who had long illnesses and the reaper took his time in the taking.

But somehow watching someone's personality and memory, their soul dissolve, get slowly eaten away, was the cruellest one yet.

My father's declining health and other personal issues were a large part of the backdrop in the making of *Get Ready*.

29

2001

My father died on 23 February 2001. It was the worst thing that had ever happened to me.

As things turned out the rest of 2001 didn't get any better.

The year Hal 9000 went fictionally crazy and we were all supposed be living on the moon turned into one I'd never forget for all the wrong reasons.

One week later, on 30 March 2001, the day before Mother's Day, my daughter Grace, by then a toddler, suddenly stopped toddling.

The day before, she'd been dancing at a birthday party at the village institute, the next morning she couldn't stand up.

'Probably worn out from all that jigging' was my considered medical opinion, ever hopeful. Never the doctor. Don't ever take my advice on these things.

By lunchtime there was no improvement.

I tried helping Grace back to her feet but she just kept flopping down to the floor.

Things were getting serious. We took Grace to casualty. There we saw a nurse, then a doctor, who did the traditional examining and prodding.

'You say she has been walking normally?'

'Yes, that's why we're here, this isn't normal,' Gillian replied.

He bent Grace's legs a few times and said it was probably a minor hip infection and to come back the next day if things didn't get any better.

'Told you it was all the jigging about.'

I can be a smug twat at times.

By Sunday morning things hadn't got better. They'd got worse. Grace now had a fever. She was also extremely distressed.

A Sunday morning trip to casualty, or A & E as they call it now. Still busy from the alcohol related injury influx of the night before.

The same nurse, coming off a long shift, explained to a new doctor what had happened, that Grace had just stopped walking and now had a fever and was unconsolable.

A bit more prodding and leg bending, which by now was really beginning to annoy her.

Followed by a long, tense wait.

We asked more questions.

We got no answers.

Things were getting even more serious.

An ambulance was called.

Grace was taken to Pendlebury Children's Hospital in Salford for an emergency MRI scan. We were still none the wiser as to what was going on, but we were by then extremely worried.

The nurses made three attempts to sedate Grace – the anaesthetic, instead of making her sleepy, just turned her into an angry, drunken two-year-old from hell. You've seen *The Exorcist*? It was a lot like that.

We finally got her to lie still just long enough to get her into the terrifyingly noisy MRI machine, unpleasant at the best of times even for an adult.

A sleepless night of corridor pacing.

The following day I heard two words I'd never heard before in my life.

Transverse myelitis.

Great, I thought, at least they know what it is, even if I had no idea what the hell it meant.

What it meant was Grace was paralysed from the waist down. The nerves coming down her spinal cord had been damaged, possibly by a virus – there was no way of saying for certain what the cause had been or when.

She was given a large dose of steroids, which seemed to help.

'So she'll just be on steroids for a bit and then that's it?' I asked hopefully.

'There's no way of knowing. I'm afraid we'll just have to wait and see.'

I didn't want to wait and see.

I left Gillian with Grace at the hospital and went to consult the internet, as people reflexively do when they hear of anything frightening they've never come across before.

It didn't exactly fill me with a sense of hope. According to Doctor Google, some patients recover in a few months either partially or completely, and some never recover at all.

The next day back at the hospital, Grace was scheduled to have a lumbar puncture. A large needle was inserted into the spinal cord and fluid extracted, which it was hoped would confirm the diagnosis.

Ever tried sticking a large needle into the spine of a two-year-old who refuses to be anaesthetised?

I hate needles, especially big ones. And this one was very big.

It was absolute torture. Watching Grace suffer, I felt useless.

Gillian remained with her at the hospital while I flitted back and forth to look after Tilly and theoretically myself.

I didn't do a particularly good job and found myself revisited by the ghosts of illnesses past. The first was when I attempted to reheat a thoughtfully provided steak and kidney pie. Nothing fancy, requiring a home visit from Gordon Ramsay. Just stick it in the oven and wait a bit, I thought.

It transpired that I had inherited my father's legendary cooking skills for within three hours of consuming the not particularly tasty pie, I realised I had poisoned myself with my lack of culinary knowledge.

It was Paris 1985 revisited, only without the gigs, shellfish and drugs obviously.

I was laid up in bed with a bucket for three days and, in an unforeseen role reversal, my five-year-old daughter had to look after me. Once again I had done a very thorough job of polluting my body with bacteria.

A side effect of this toxicity was I couldn't eat red meat for two years. The very thought of a morsel of beef brought on an attack of nausea like some epicurean acid flashback. At one point I took to lying through gritted teeth, 'I'm a vegetarian,' as it seemed easier than having to relive the tale of my own culinary incompetence.

After a week of torment, I had just about got over this self-inflicted misery. I'd only managed to get to the hospital to visit Grace and Gillian a couple of times before malady intervened once more.

I woke up feeling like I'd been hit by a train. I literally could not move and felt like there was some major construction work taking place behind my eyes. Perhaps my brain was being excavated?

The week before, I'd taken Tilly to a school-friend's house for a birthday party. Little did I know that this was not the regular kind of birthday party. In fact, this was a chickenpox party – where instead of a goody bag, the guests depart with a nice virus and a slice of cake. Just like the aftermath of my trip to London with Terry back in 1976, I was again covered with itchy red spots and stuck in a darkened room listening to Madonna for almost three weeks. I don't know which was worse.

I was supposed to be supporting my family, instead I was stuck in bed like a useless lummox.

I did my best to see the funny side, but I was too worried about what was happening with Grace to laugh for long.

Whichever way I looked at it, Grace faced an uncertain future. As to what that might actually mean, we'd just have to wait and see if her condition improved.

One thing was certain, though, there was no going back to how things had been.

For reasons that should have been obvious, even to the other members of New Order, Gillian and I weren't there as much as normal during the recording and mixing of *Get Ready*.

A fact that was brought home when the band went to Dublin to finish off and mix the track 'Rock the Shack' with Flood producing.

Flood (aka Mark Ellis) was another ghost from the past. I'd first met Flood at Marcus Studios in London back in 1981 when he'd been an assistant engineer on *Movement*.

Since then Flood had gone up in the world and had graduated into producing for U2, Smashing Pumpkins and Nine Inch Nails.

'Rock the Shack' was an idea that stemmed from some guitar riffing Bernard had done on a Primal Scream song, 'Shoot Speed/Kill Light' (a fabulous example of the krautrock motorik beat).

Bernard persuaded Bobby Gillespie and Andrew Innes from the Scream to repay the favour and do some reciprocal bits on 'Rock The Shack'.

None of my hours of the 'here's one I did earlier' drum-a-thon being suitable, I ended up in Ireland sticking yet more drums on.

During a break in the recording, I was cornered in a side room by Hooky and Andy Robinson and given a strong telling-off about mine and Gillian's absences during the recording and mixing of the album.

It sounded very like something along the lines of the final warning you would expect to receive from an irate boss: 'Should this behaviour continue we will have to reconsider your position in this company' – not an actual quote but you get the gist of how it felt to me.

That's what it sounded like. I was stunned.

Perhaps I should have seen it coming but ...

Not being a confrontational type, I didn't argue. Instead, I wimpily apologised and said, 'Well, I'm here now. Let's get on with it, shall we?'

'Yeah, but Gillian's not, is she?'

I couldn't argue with that.

It was then I thought I spotted some words being metaphorically etched on a nearby wall.

I started to feel lucky that I was being allowed to play on the track at all. I felt lucky that I was still in the band. I agreed to take a pay cut for the record, as did Gillian, to compensate for our tardiness.

This may have been my paranoia or Andy's people skills at work but it felt like more than that if I'm honest.

This is another of the reasons I have mixed feelings about *Get Ready*.

Later came a phone call, again from Andy, explaining how Bernard considered the guitar-manship on the new songs to be beyond the capability of our current staffing levels. The combined efforts of Bernard and Gillian and the Akai DR16 hard-disk recorder would no longer be enough. We would need an extra guitarist to do the work justice in a live setting.

I may have been getting a little touchy or oversensitive here but it sounded to me very much like he was saying 'You're wife's not good enough on the guitar, is she? We'd be doing her a favour. Saving her the pain and embarrassment.'

Gillian and I talked about where things were going. We knew that children and bands were never going to be a good mix.

When Tilly was born there seemed little chance that New Order would be doing anything in the foreseeable future. That had all gone out the window. Now there was a new album on a new label, and that would eventually mean touring and promotion, and that would mean being away from home a lot.

Leaving an ill child wasn't something that appealed to either of us.

For twenty years, New Order had been the biggest and most important thing in our world. Our lives revolved around its being. We were married to New Order long before we were married to each other. Whatever arguments we'd had, and believe me we'd had quite a few, they were all band-related.

New Order was no longer the most important thing in our lives. But the band wasn't going to stop or even pause because of that, was it?

Grace's health was more important than music, I couldn't argue with that. Gillian took the difficult decision that she was going to taking a break.

She would take care of Grace because, as my recent track record showed, I couldn't even take care of myself – a fact to which my mother had long attested.

I think Gillian found the hardest part of this to be that New Order would continue without her, right under her nose. We still rehearsed at the farm and she was always reminded of what she was missing.

Philip Cunningham landed the job as extra guitarist and now discovered this also involved playing the keyboards as well. Something I don't think he'd expected.

Phil was from Macclesfield, so he and I had all that shared Maccness: pubs, oatcakes and pies.

He had been in Marion (the biggest band to come out of Macclesfield since the Macc Lads) and had worked with Bernard and Johnny Marr in Electronic. So there was some musical continuity there apart from just geography.

Gillian would come over to rehearsals in the barn before Bernard and Hooky arrived and give Phil tips on the keyboard-playing.

I am not sure if this made Gillian feel better or worse about the situation. Schooling your replacement has to hurt, while watching everything else carry on without you.

Knowing what goes on and suspecting the worst.

Maybe the worst is 'what if I'm not even missed?' If nobody notices I'm not there or maybe, seeing it in black and white, reading the reviews and realising that it's still New Order but without me. What if they said 'They're much better now, should have ditched her years ago'?

The thought that anyone could be as disposable and replaceable as the average Bic razor does wonders for their self-esteem.

It had been Bernard who came up with the idea that we should start playing some Joy Division songs again when we reunited for the Manchester Apollo and Reading Festival gigs in 1998.

It had been over twenty years, after all. They were still great songs and if anyone should play them it should probably be us. From the *Get Ready* tour onwards, we began to routinely include Joy Division songs in the set.

I was sulkily bashing away with the electronic drum kit at gigs. I'd spend a lot of time trying to recreate the sounds from *Get Ready* with it, but it refused to sound any better no matter how much I twiddled and walloped it. In an attempt to remedy this, I took to using a real snare drum again. A great improvement, I felt.

This upset Bernard, still suffering with tinnitus, and he took to rehearsing in the control room of my studio, isolated from the rest of 'the band' and our amplified racket.

This felt a little bit strange, with us in one room and Bernard in another, his disembodied voice coming through the PA, issuing instructions to new boy Roger Lyons who was in charge of playback of the Akai hard-disk recorder and keyboard wrangling.

The old rivalry between Hooky and Bernard recommenced – good-natured banter at first, peaking in an angry dressing-room trashing and encore refusal at Barrowland in Glasgow in September 2001. I think that Hooky was keen on showing Phil Cunningham who was boss, letting him know the pecking order.

An initiation rite.

There is always going to be a pecking order in every organisation and, although we had begun life as equals – a democracy – as we headed into the twenty-first century the democratic principles began to be applied only in certain areas.

Mostly minor ones.

In almost every band that has ever existed, decisions begin democratically – when nothing matters – then slowly a situation evolves where only one or two key players start to call the shots.

Now that there were effectively only three, not four permanent members of the band, the whole dynamic changed.

For the first half-dozen of these first Gillian-less gigs, the band was a five-piece. Billy Corgan from the Smashing Pumpkins, an old friend from Chicago who had done some guest vocals on *Get Ready*'s 'Turn My Way', played even more guitar.

Gillian found it difficult watching the band continue without her. She would get upset when she came to gigs. Hooky and Bernard seemed to find Gillian turning up at gigs awkward too. A bit embarrassing somehow.

I began to feel that the wives-at-gigs embargo from 1979 was about to be reintroduced. An all-male preserve once more.

Bet you know where you were on 11 September 2001. Another J. F. Kennedy moment.

I was rehearsing at the farm with New Order when the phone rang.

'Turn the telly on. Now!'

And there it was again, another tragedy live before my eyes. Passenger planes as missiles. I don't remember that ever being mentioned in any of my sci-fi apocalypse paperbacks.

Shocking beyond words. It was one of those days when you could feel the world change for the worse.

We stopped what we were doing and watched hundreds of people die, as the twin towers fell down.

The propensity for humans to devise new and ingenious ways to kill each other is staggering. Just when you think you've seen and felt it all, along comes something even more despicable and more inhuman than the last unthinkable atrocity.

In time, you've become used to even that. I wondered what sort of a world my children would inherit. What kind of people they'd grow up to be.

The idea of flying began to terrify me. Which was unfortunate as the band had been approached to play the Big Day Out touring festival in Australia and New Zealand at the start of the following year, 2002.

The festival was promoted by Vivian Lees, a very good friend of ours who had handled all our antipodal gigs since 1982.

It was a very big offer, a lot of money.

It was also a long, long way to go. To be away from home.

I did not want to do it and I said so. Hooky and Bernard, of course, didn't agree. Rather than going for the 'you're outvoted' response, and possibly being sick of the sight of my glum face at gigs, they said, 'No problem, we'll just get another drummer.'

'Problem solved,' said management.

This failed to make me feel much better. I'd begun to suspect I was easily replaceable, but to be confronted with that reality was something completely different.

I could join Gillian on the New Order discard pile.

Stupidly, I agreed to accept this.

Quite how stupid I'd been was something that Gillian was the first to point out.

'I suppose you'll be teaching him the drum parts, won't you?' (It was a cert it was going to be a him wasn't it?) 'In the barn?'

I supposed I would.

'And sorting all the sounds out for him?'

Again Gillian was right as usual.

'Well, I think you're being daft.'

I couldn't admit that perhaps there was some truth in what she said and instead harrumphed and said that I'd think about it. I dragged this thinking on for quite a while.

Stewing on it made me realise, as if I hadn't already, just how much of an emotional wrench Gillian's abstention from music had been – to see herself being replaced so easily.

'Why don't you want to go?' she asked.

'It's too long and too far to be away from you and the kids. And I'm a bit bothered about dying in a terrible plane crash too, if I'm honest.'

'Why don't you take us with you then? On a separate plane, so should you die a terrible death I'll still be able to claim the insurance.'

She may not have actually said the last bit.

That did not seem like the perfect solution, and did nothing to ease my fear of plane-related death. But in some way it did make me feel slightly better. How shallow and selfish I am.

My conscience partially salved, I relented. And off we all went to Oz for the Big Day Out 2002.

Gillian and the girls came out for the second half of this jaunt round Australia. The experience confirmed something that the pair of us had long suspected. That young children and a touring band are mutually incompatible.

It wasn't exactly hell, but it was very complicated.

Tilly and Grace didn't enjoy it that much, apart from the day trip to see some kangaroos and koalas, and maybe bumping into Meg from the White Stripes.

It wasn't the sort of experience that anybody would have liked to carry on for much longer than a week.

The best thing about it – apart from the way my children's presence dismayed the rest of the group – was my hope that it would probably deter my offspring from considering a future in the world of showbiz.

Another Morris dream to be dashed in the years to come.

That was more or less that for 2002. There were a few more gigs (eight if you're counting), finishing in July at Old Trafford cricket ground in Manchester.

For me, it had been the weirdest, most depressing eighteen months of my life.

Maybe giving up drugs hadn't been such a good idea after all.

Struggling with tiny drum kit – look at all those wires!

30

THE TIDE COMES IN AGAIN

The more things change, the more they stay the same. That's what they say, isn't it?

Over time, the three of us and Phil began playing in the same room together (even the real drum kit was tolerated). This was the way we'd written everything in Joy Division. Back when it was the only way to write.

By 2005, though, listening back to reel-to-reel highlights while having supping a Tizer after a lengthy jam had been replaced by sitting around a Macintosh, watching waveforms moving about on a digital grid.

When we'd begun *Get Ready*, Bernard had his Nirvana concept and a demo for 'Crystal' as an idea to get us going.

This time we were starting with a blank sheet. A blank sheet that soon got filled.

Possibly overfilled.

The ideas that became the basis for *Waiting for the Sirens' Call* were the first we'd written with Phil Cunningham, and the process was very productive.

Although Phil had ended up taking Gillian's place on the keyboards at gigs, I honestly think synthesising was something he was never particularly relaxed about.

The guitar was Phil's main instrument.

He had plenty of guitars.

Phil had written plenty of songs too, with Marion, and had no shortage of ideas of his own.

Maybe it was the novelty of working with someone new that sparked this increased output of musical ideas.

Whatever it was, we became unusually prolific. We quickly amassed quite a large quantity of mostly guitar-based ideas.

Bernard, true to form, coming in the afternoon, would listen back to the rough ideas that Phil, Hooky and I had recorded that morning, select the most promising bits and take them home to tinker with, where he would also develop his own synth ideas. With Bernard tinkering on his own the three of us would then return to the churning out of more candidates for the riff bank.

The cycle continued. There came a point at which we were coming up with ideas faster than Bernard could write the words and arrange them.

Pretty soon we had a full storehouse of ideas – around twenty, far more than normal. So many, in fact, that the suggestion came up that we could do two albums.

There was also a suggestion that maybe we should slow down a little so we didn't end up with a backlog that we'd never finish. But Bernard argued that the more you write, the better you get, and maybe the next idea would be the best one yet.

He had a point.

So we carried on, thinking that the two-album idea might just work.

Seeking inspiration from what was happening in the postmodern world of electronic dance music. Bernard had asked Andy Robinson's brother Pete to compile a CD of happening dance tunes so we'd be in touch with what was hot in the by then increasingly bewildering world of EDM. Pete was young and in touch, and we were getting too old to be hanging out in clubs and discotheques. I don't think we ever actually listened to anything past the second track on Pete's lovingly compiled CD.

In a further attempt to possibly broaden our appeal, up our profile, 'expand our demographic' and, in the process, increase sales, Warners – who by this point had swallowed London Records – suggested it might be a good idea if we collaborated with some bright young things.

Still being a cynic, I suspected that idea was stick us next to someone young and good-looking so people might not notice what a bunch of ugly old fuckers we were becoming.

A recurring theme of interviews around the time of *Get Ready* was the old unanswerable chestnut, 'Why is a band from the eighties still making records in the twenty-first century?' Like we were trying to revive a flagging career or reinstate a particularly naff cult most right-thinking people had forgotten about. A feeling of creeping irrelevance.

I wondered, maybe not for the first time, whether we were beginning to be thought of as a bunch of old blokes – misfits still, but maybe not in the coolest way any more. I'd noticed that our recent gigs were attended mainly by ageing, balding men. What had happened to all the young people? Where had they all gone? Surely they couldn't have all passed on. Could they?

The first of these suggested collaborations was with Brian Higgins and his songwriting/production team Xenomania. They had produced hits for Girls Aloud, the Sugababes, Rachel Stevens and both the Minogue sisters.

Brian produced lovely shiny immaculate songs with not a hair out of place. My daughters loved them, and they were very skilfully crafted songs.

Perfect pop records, there is nothing wrong with them.

But unlikely as this pairing sounded – I am a great believer in the maxim 'Don't knock it until you've tried it' so I put my initial scepticism to one side.

Brian is a very nice man. He is very talented and brilliant at what he does. He is also a New Order fan. That usually helps a bit.

Maybe it was our bandiness that was the problem. Brian and his team were all great musicians, and they were programmers too, so they didn't need any help in that department either.

Once again I couldn't see what I was supposed to be doing.

But nothing ventured, nothing gained. Unfortunately the exercise soon became a square peg/round hole situation. A bit awkward. It didn't quite gel.

Were we supposed to write a song with them or were they writing a song for us?

We had our own way of doing things and Brian had his. The two didn't seem to mix well. Like oil and water.

For New Order, as has, I think, become abundantly clear, a producer was someone who sometimes had to act as a referee, and a scapegoat as well as an organiser. We had produced enough records on our own and knew how a studio worked well enough, so what we needed was a referee whose opinion everybody respected, someone who thought the same way as us. That was just as important as how many hits they'd worked on.

On *Sirens* we worked with Stephen Street, Jim Spencer, John Leckie, Tore Johansson, Mac Quayle, Stuart Price and (briefly) Steve Osborne again. For with old age had come not greater wisdom but greater indecision.

Obviously we didn't work with them all at the same time. That would have been crazy.

It was Stephen Street who ended up doing the bulk of the *Sirens* songs, with the others doing odd tracks here and there.

There were a lot of cooks, there was a lot of broth. Things got spilt. We had a lot of ideas and Bernard particularly wanted to finish them all rather than prioritising them into an A list, a B list and maybe even a C list.

The trouble was that, unlike the case of the infinite number of monkeys banging an infinite number of typewriters in their simian quest to replicate the complete works of Shakespeare – we didn't have an infinite amount of time.

So, as an incentive to get the album finished, the record company offered some sort of productivity bonus if we got it all done in time for Christmas. Christmas being widely accepted as a good time to finish anything from wars to opening advent calendars. It all stops for Santa.

I have to confess that as time went on I began to get even more worried and confused about exactly what it was the record company expected of us.

Maybe there was some point to Warners getting us to hook up with someone with yoof appeal, with luck some of that teen effervescent sparkle would rub off on us. So that we, rightly or wrongly, would seem to be forward-thinking. But just in case, people needed reminding of how good New Order used to be in the past. The label proposed doing yet another compilation album as well, just to remind the world how relevant New Order actually were. This wasn't purely to make yet more money out of the back catalogue they had bought when they took over London. Surely?

I think you can guess my reaction to that.

It was no. Nada, no way José!

And I think you can guess what happened next.

I was outvoted.

And so the compilation album evocatively titled *Singles* came out in 2005, the very same year that *Sirens* was released.

Meanwhile, Warners' continued persistence with their collaboration idea culminated in us doing a track, 'Jetstream', with Ana Matronic from the Scissor Sisters.

A stab at a poptastic hit.

I'd come up with the basic rhythm and sequencer track as a bit of a joke which for some reason got taken seriously.

Oh well, it can happen. People take me seriously when I'm joking. The trouble is they often laugh when I'm being deadly serious.

Ana was good fun and it turned out another big New Order fan, but I couldn't help thinking that we were a bit of an odd pairing. I suspect the rest of the world had a similar view. 'Krafty', the album's first single, which was written and performed just by New Order, had been a top-ten hit. 'Jetstream', the co-written and co-performed poptastic follow-up, only reached number 20.

I can't really blame the label for trying.

These were tough times for the majors and things would only get worse.

The new-fangled pesky Napster downloads were a big problem for them and releases getting 'leaked' was a regular occurrence. The infernal digital genie was well and truly out of the bottle, causing trouble in many unforeseen, money-leeching ways.

This new century was no time to be a luddite or an old fucker. Adapt or die so again I adapted. I moved on from drum and bass and found . . . that bands were back.

But not rawk bands, and this wasn't a grunge revival. I mean bands like us!

I discovered hip young bands who had been inspired by New Order. People like Hot Chip and LCD Soundsystem were mixing electronica and guitars in the same way we had been doing years before. They were pissing about with drum machines and old analogue synths.

We suddenly began getting hailed as pioneers.

I have to hold my hands up here and admit that some of this new-band discovering was down to the young people in mine and Gillian's lives. My nieces and my children would pass on information about this new music in exchange for me not playing 'Jollity Farm' by the Bonzo Dog Doo-Dah Band in the car.

Plus they introduced me to the fantastic MIA. Respect!

The point that I'm haphazardly hoping to make here is that by trying to team us up with shiny, hip, poptastic hitmakers, I felt that the record company was in danger of making us look uncool. A bit needy.

The songs we were writing were good, there was certainly no lack of ideas. But I still got the feeling that Warners didn't quite know what to do with us. Were we 'Rock' or were we 'Dance'? Both really. What we were was New Order and we were respected and that counts for a lot.

But that respect wasn't always shown in a way that I really warmed to.

We began to be nominated for various awards. The ones with elderly statesman-like titles: 'Lifetime Achievement Award', that sort of thing. These seemed to suggest that perhaps our life might be reaching its useful end.

I came to think of them as 'Fuck Off and Die' awards. 'They used to be really good, you know' sort of things. I'm not really an awards ceremony sort of person. I've tried often enough. God knows I've tried.

I've gone to them, watched unholy amounts of booze being consumed, and I have to admit occasionally almost enjoyed the experience.

But what does it all actually mean? Search me. Sorry if I sound ungrateful. They reminded me of a music-biz version of an old masonic dinner.

While recording the songs for *Sirens*, we worked with Stephen Street in Bath (again), this time using the actress Jane Seymour's delightful Tudor manor as a studio.

Jane's picture was in every room and her eyes seemed to follow you around. It was the ideal setting for a murder mystery weekend.

Very *Scooby Doo*.

The place had all the trappings of the traditional haunted house, creaky floors, fluttery bats roosting in canopies of Tudor four-poster beds and the obligatory spectral canine.

My room was reputed to be the most haunted – an illegimate offspring reputedly roasted on the ancient fireplace. But, despite the fifteenth-century baby's crib that occasionally rocked by itself, the spirits didn't trouble me much. The scratching coming from behind the oak-panel walls was probably just rats, I speculated hopefully.

No, my rest was rarely disturbed by Tudor wraiths and phantoms complaining about our lack of lutes and crumhorns.

It was mostly disturbed by Hooky bashing seven shades of shit out of a large plastic simulacrum with glowing eyes called a Slam Man: a state-of-the-art punching dummy that was 'a must have for every combat sports enthusiast'. Or pissed off bass player.

Slam Man was a vital part of Hooky's keep-fit-in-the-studio regime. He would get his battering at first light every day. He never complained, but I did. From the first ker-thwack of the one-sided punch-up, any prospect of further slumber would vanish, so I would tiptoe down the creaking backstairs to renew my acquaintance with Mr Kellogg's finest produce.

I would then head into Bath for the papers and a mooch round HMV, Fopp and the city's toyshops, where I was under orders to acquire Bratz dolls to satiate Grace's newfound obsession. Towards the end of our tenure, the toyshop staff were beginning to get a little suspicious of my daily visits.

We would end up completing eleven tracks for the album, leaving seven that, the plan was, we would finish off at a later date to form the basis of our next record.

Towards the end of the recording the old conflicts between Bernard and Hooky re-emerged. They had never really entirely submerged and probably had their origins in some unforgiven slight from a 1970s playground spat in Salford. Or deep-rooted misgivings over the result of the New Order singing competition.

By then we'd moved on from the spooky Seymour manor and were nearby, back on the familiar ground of Real World.

The clock was ticking. Christmas had appeared on the distant horizon and there was what seemed like a mountain to climb before anything could be considered even half finished.

The window of the previously mentioned productivity bonus – remember that? – was closing. Andy was beginning to fret that we might miss out on the promised bounty.

While Hooky and I were in the cavernous big room at Real World, awaiting Bernard's arrival, Andy decided that this would be a good time to vent his fretting. How he went about it was probably not in the best manner.

For Andy's proposed solution to the likely temporal overshoot was to push the button marked 'Danger Do Not Press'.

'So why don't we just let Bernard get on and finish it?' or words to that effect.

Another open invitation to grab the stick at the wrong end.

For Andy's words unfortunately could be easily translated as 'Fuck your twiddly bits and any time-wasting riffs you may be planning.'

Possibly erroneously, but this was nonetheless how it went down.

Hooky was furious, firstly with Andy, but mostly with the missing Bernard for it was he whom Hooky primarily perceived to be behind this fucked-up scheme.

'Has he put you up to this!?'

'If you want me to do that, then fuck you! That's it, I'm off.' He meant emphatically and permanently.

Andy, to be fair, realised his faux pas and began back-pedalling.

'No, that's not what I meant.'

It took much apologetic grovelling from Andy and denials from Bernard that he even had any knowledge of this ill-considered whim of an idea before any sense of calm was restored.

But the damage was done. The ill will and mistrust it caused never left.

It was during mixing when this became particularly evident. When Hooky felt some part was too quiet, Bernard would disagree and the matter would fester until an independent arbitrator could be found.

There was nothing unusual in this. All part of the trials and tribulations of making a record. This time, however, the nit-picking reached fever pitch. One of the perils of co-producing is that no one is sure exactly who is in charge.

'I think it should be blacker.'

'I think it would be better whiter.'

'Louder.'

'Quieter.'

The rancour of working with Hannett was nothing compared to this.

Like repelling poles it went on and on with no point of stasis.

I don't know what Phil made of all this. He had worked with Bernard for Electronic, but this was his first experience of seeing us all working in a studio. Pointless, petty disputes always arise in bands when they've been doing anything for too long, stuck together in close proximity, but this was beyond the usual.

Despite the tension, we managed to get all the tracks down in time for Christmas. Then at the eleventh hour, Bernard had second thoughts about the drums on four of these. This is nothing unusual. Bernard can be difficult to please at times. So while everybody else got off home for turkey, I got drummer detention and redid my parts with Cenzo Townshend, Stephen Street's engineer. You would be very hard pressed to tell the difference between the different versions, so I made a deliberate mistake or subtle alteration, as I like to call it, in the first couple of bars of each so at least I'd be able to recognise them.

Rock-and-roll life is a haven for childish and immature behaviour and New Order was no exception

It was Phil who said something that I'd been blithely oblivious to for the previous thirty years. Phil, who despite playing with us for four years still had the dubious honour of being thought of as the 'new boy'. But then, I was still technically on probation since my Warsaw audition in 1977.

It was following a New Order gig. Everyone was happy, nothing had broken down and Phil was in a celebratory mood.

'Wahay,' he exclaimed in the grand tradition of the late great Eric Morecambe, and sent a chair clattering over in the equally grand auto-destructive rock-and-roll tradition of the Who. A few drinks got spilled and I, being a sober and at the time professional miserable bastard, remarked, 'Steady on, Phil. I mean, grow up!'

To which he replied, 'But that's why I got into bands in the first place. So I wouldn't have to grow up. Everybody does, don't they? Didn't you? Wahay!' And over tumbled another item of furniture.

I had to think for a minute.

Did I? I'd always thought I wanted to get to the future as quickly as possible, which logically meant maturing. The possibility that perhaps I might subconsciously have wanted to subvert my transition into becoming a grown-up was one to which I'd never considered.

Now Phil came to mention it, I had to admit he did have point.

I was engaged in an escapist pursuit. Somewhere along the line, I'd forgotten that I always had been.

Even as a kid my interests had been somehow involved in the

business of running away, which continued through the teenage angst of upsetting the grown-up apple cart of respectability and conformist crap. Now here I was, hurtling headlong into my fifties. The party was becoming a job.

You can't stay a child all your life or you'll end up becoming a laughing stock. I remembered when New Order first played Glastonbury Festival 1981, in a corrugated metal pyramid cowshed built in a muddy field. This was before it became an annual event embraced by the nation, before the idea of 'glamping' and a weekend of sun- or mud-soaked frolicking in Somerset turned into the biggest live music event in the world.

Never trust a clown

Back then, I was reminiscing with Phil (Old Schoolfriend Phil, not Drummer Phil or New Order Guitarist Phil) and a fully made-up clown about the good old days of the seventies.

Phil asked me, 'Do you reckon you'll still be doing this in twenty years' time, Steve?'

'What, when I'm an old git? No fuckin' way. I don't want to end up like Mick Jagger.'

I didn't have to think about it. It was impossible that such a thing could remotely come to pass.

The clown bummed a cigarette and a light, nodded as if in agreement, then waddled off as fast as his oversized feet could carry him, still clutching my lighter. I wonder where he is now, the red-nosed thieving bastard?

Here I was over twenty years later, still in the racket, and ending up like Mick Jagger no longer seemed such a terrible fate.

I guess I'd gone soft or something. I had become a man with responsibilities and maybe that was the thing that being in a rock band was supposed to insulate against.

For what was perpetual childhood if not a life without responsibilities? Where there was always someone to clean up the mess, collect the toys from the floor and carefully replace them in the pram? Growing old while still playing what I'd thought was a young man's game left me with the uneasy feeling that I was in danger of overstaying my welcome.

Bernard and Hooky didn't seem to share my misgivings. I don't think we ever discussed the process of our longevity other than comparing age-related health complaints.

With *Waiting for the Sirens' Call* completed, all we had to do was play some gigs and watch Warners conjure up yet another compilation album to place in Santa's sack.

Nothing new there then.

Perhaps I should stop moaning about the compilation thing. After all, over the course of the previous decade I had begun to get the idea that the longer things went on, the greater the appeal of the past. Nostalgia began to exert an emotional pull greater than some imaginary utopian future.

It is probably no coincidence that around the same time (mid-1990s to early 2000s) I was staggered to notice upon scrutinising the back pages of Q magazine (it's amazing what you'll read when a session starts to drag) that just about every band that had ever existed was dragging its weary, creaking bones out on to the road for a reunion tour of some sort. This typically took the flavour of something like 'The D*******d perform their seminal classic second album *Some Crazy Shit* live and in its entirety for the first time ever!'

No beating about the bush there. You knew exactly what you would be getting even before the first 'one two, waaahn TWOOO' of the newly reanimated band's soundcheck.

Bands used to die, or they'd grow old and that used to be the same thing: rock used to be the preserve of youth. Not now. It's become a respectable profession and old men can make a respectable living at it. Wrinkles, grey hair and baldness are no longer a barrier to thriving in a profession that was once the sole preserve of the young and beautiful.

File-sharing among the young meant that record companies now needed to squeeze every last drop out of their back-catalogue assets, and resell the old songs to the same old fans who still wanted to see *Some Crazy Shit* live and were still willing to repeatedly pay for music. And when you're dealing with a band that only puts an album out every five years, which I reckon is New Order's batting average, a record company has to scrabble around to make ends meet in the meantime. So, OK, I'll stop moaning about the New Order compilations, but that doesn't mean I have to agree with it.

Shortly before his death Rob had the idea that if we must do a compilation, we might as well include *everything* we'd ever done in one massive package. It was to be called 'Recycle'. London had initially been quite taken with the idea, until they realised what a colossal undertaking this would be. More importantly, how much it would actually cost to produce. Peter Saville elaborated on the concept with the suggestion that we should treat the thing as an art piece. Produce an extremely limited number, say less than ten, to be auctioned off at Sotheby's. Neither of these ideas came to fruition.

The millennium was the beginning of the end for many long-standing rock traditions. Making a full-blown record on a laptop had become a reality, and the big recording studios began closing their doors faster than pubs after the smoking ban. By the mid-2000s Strawberry, Advision, the Townhouse and Olympic – all hallowed ground, and all rooms that we had recorded and mixed in – had become extinct.

Meanwhile, Apple launched the iPod in 2001 along with the iTunes store. The glorious 12-inch artwork I grew up with was shrunk to the size of a postage stamp. Ye gods! Whatever next? A telephone that makes movies?

In the same way that the spinning disc of the Victrola brought an end to the family singsong round the piano, so streaming and downloads seemingly killed off music you could have and hold.

Well, not quite. For every action there's an equal and opposite reaction. The twelve-inch platter has in the twenty-first century gone from strength to strength, even if it remains a marginal part of the industry. Pressing plants that at one time were down to single figures are opening up again and business is booming. The queue to get a record pressed gets longer every day.

Is this just a fad? Possibly, but as long as the vinyl album and its glorious artwork offer something that intangible digital media doesn't, it's got a pretty good chance. After all, there's a feeling of integrity about vinyl.

Begging the question, who the fuck wants to buy a compilation on vinyl?

Sorry, I just can't stop.

31

LOST IN TRANSLATION

Tokyo, July 2005.

We're meeting in the bar at seven thirty.

I put down the book and look at the clock.

Quarter to.

My room has been tidied up since I scuttled out at first light for breakfast, and the ever-efficient Japanese maids have opened the curtains, exposing the canyons between buildings far, far below. This means I must steel myself and, with my back to the window trying not to peek at the dizzying view, fiddle with the cords that will obliterate the Tokyo skyline from my sight and restore some sense of calm. Then make my way to the bar for this 'meeting'.

I can't help getting the feeling that this is not the best of ideas. The meeting I mean – not the going to the bar.

One piece of advice that I garnered from my father is that there is a time and a place for everything.

This is neither.

Fuji is the last gig we've got for a while. For the most part, the gigs since we finished making *Sirens* got off to a good start but the mood has changed. I think that whatever it is will blow over after a break. Hooky is annoyed with something, it's pretty obvious to everyone, not least Andy and Rebecca. Why not wait until we get home to talk about it?

Hooky is adamant, he wants to have a meeting to do . . . what?

State his case.

Air his grievances.

Vent his spleen.

Put his cards on the table.

Let everyone know exactly what he thinks is wrong with the band and the direction in which it is going.

This is the best job in the world.

I know I've moaned more than I should, but the truth is making music is unbeatable. I have been incredibly lucky, really I have. I'm staying in a luxury five-star hotel in Japan. Not exactly kipping in the back of a freezing Transit, is it? Despite the tragedies and all the ups and downs over the years, it's been a fantastic life.

Sometimes it's very easy to forget that.

Maybe it's boredom and frustration that brings it on. Some sort of diva-esque cry for more attention. Something that even the most normal folks can fall prone to when feeling a little tired and emotional. If the situation is right, the stars incorrectly aligned or the beer a tad too warm.

I've heard it all before.

I've even said most of it before myself. When I was younger I'd usually have another solitary drink or six to anaesthetise the soul and eventually on regaining consciousness all would be well again. Or at least I would have forgotten what it was that got me so wound up. I'm older now, not necessarily wiser, but slightly more responsible, and I know that drink and drugs caused half the trouble that I took drink and drugs to get away from. Neat little circle, that.

After going a little overboard in that department during the making of *Sirens*, Hooky was now a drug- and alcohol-free zone. He wasn't happy, but drink and drugs definitely weren't to blame.

This time around something was different. There had been an exponential increase in the grievances, the complaints and general annoyances, I have to say in fairness . . .

That's always been a problem – my attempts at fairness. Trying to see both sides. I usually end up in more trouble, accused of sitting on the fence. Of having no opinion of consequence. But I don't want to pick a side.

On the frequent post-gig car journeys we had shared, I listened to Hooky. I had no choice. Captive audience. I tried to understand his problems. See his point. He didn't like Rebecca and Andy's management style. He didn't like Bernard always getting his own way. There were many things he didn't like . . .

I would nod in what I hoped was a sage fashion and sympathetically say, 'Yeah, I know what you mean.'

This may have been taken as encouragement, but to disagree would have been more likely to invite confrontation anyway. You know I hate confrontation, don't you? Rarely seems to solve anything. If I'd had more gumption I might have said, 'OK then, what's the solution? What is it that's going to bring an end to all this misery? What is it that will make you happy?'

We can all think of the right thing to say after the event.

Bernard had been delighted on our arrival at the Tokyo hotel to discover that the reception desk was situated on the forty-first floor. A fact he sportingly pointed out to me several times on the ear-popping ascent to collect the room keys. As if his piss-taking would in some way assuage my completely irrational altitude-induced fear.

In accordance with popular hotel construction techniques, the rest of the hostelry resided at even greater heights.

This meant there was never any danger of forgetting that the planet's surface was distressingly far below. The architect had skilfully used copious amounts of glass in the building's construction to remind guests of this fact.

On a clear day you can see Mount Fuji. I spent most of my stay with my eyes firmly focused on the carpet. Hoping vainly to spot a crumb.

The charming and impeccably dressed restaurant staff would consider it a dereliction of their duty if any would-be diner was not seated within nose-touching distance of one of those floor-to-ceiling windows.

'How about over there, a bit closer to the lifts?' I mumbled.

This was not a phrase that was widely understood. And so, not wishing to cause offence, I would end up seated inches from the window and the clouds below. I let the waves of nausea ebb and flow while at the same time doing my best to ignore that the whole edifice was gently swaying.

The Park Hyatt hotel on the other hand relishes it's lofty height, my principal phobia. Like Superman's kryptonite aversion, I fear building-related altitude. It distresses me to the point of sickness.

The meeting is due to take place between 7 and 8 p.m., about half seven in my book, in the Park Hyatt's famous New York Bar, a major location in *Lost in Translation*. This, as you might expect, is situated at the pinnacle of this magnificent edifice. It's a venue I am not particularly looking forward to visiting. The prospect fills me with dread.

I go to the bar at seven thirty and I stick it as long as I can bear. About fifteen minutes (ten of which are spent trying to move from the safety of the lift to the bar) before the vertigo gets the better of me. I come over all queasy and seasick. I have attended many band meetings as a regular in the past and I think I know how things are going to go at this one. The chances of anything actually getting resolved are about as likely as Godzilla himself popping up on the far horizon for a pre-prandial snack; I cry off, throw a sicky, make my excuses and leave for safety, lower levels and firmer ground.

This, it will emerge, was a mistake.

At breakfast the next morning, sitting as close to the window as humanly possible, the meeting's instigator, Hooky, waved me over.

Reluctantly and with eyes firmly fixed once more on the carpet I tiptoed towards him.

'Well,' he said conspiratorially, 'I fucking told him!'

'Told him what?'

'Told him what I fucking thought of him!'

Oh good, I thought. Now, after a period of awkwardness and sniping, perhaps we can move on.

'Yeah, I told the fucking fucker what I thought of him!'

A little harsh, I thought, to put it mildly.

'And how did he take it?' adopting my best psychotherapist's tone.

'Well, the fucking fucker . . .'

Oh dear.

It had not gone well but Hooky felt that a great victory had been gained. Over what and to what end was never said.

*   *   *

It wasn't as if any of my previous attempts to resolve conflict had gone well. I had tried many times in my life to break up fights and, without fail, I ended up the one getting battered.

Hello fire, meet petrol, you'll get on like a . . .

Time to cross diplomat and UN peace envoy off the possible alternative career list.

There is a school of thought that says it's always best to get things off your chest. Let troubles fester and they only get worse. Better to clear the air and move on. Perhaps it did very slightly and very briefly.

People never really change, certain aspects alter maybe, but fundamentally the leopard is stuck with its spots. As long as you can accept that, all is well. If, after living with those spots for a couple of decades, something offensive and intolerable emerges then you've got a problem.

To Hooky, everything was Bernard's fault. All of it. If it wasn't for Bernard and Gillian, New Order could have been as big as U2 was a gripe from the good old days. Who really wanted to be as big as U2 anyway? As if life was just one big competition, whoever dies with the most toys wins?

Nobody's perfect, we all have our faults, and Bernard as lead singer and the band's biggest musical contributor had his fair share. But as long as things were going well, what was the big problem? Pride? Yes, Bernard did things that annoyed me, Hooky too come to that, and Phil, Andy and Rebecca. I'm sure I annoyed them too at times. There were things about the band generally that I didn't agree with, but we were still theoretically a democracy, maybe not the same democracy we had been in Joy Division or even the early days of New Order, but similar principles applied.

Ahead lay a three-month break, surely enough time for things to return to a normality of some sort. If anything in any band can ever be called normal.

*   *   *

We had twenty-three more gigs after the post-Fuji break. Two of them were all Joy Division sets – one a tribute for the late great and completely irreplaceable DJ John Peel in London. The part John played in the development of Joy Division and many other bands can never be underestimated.

The other all Joy Division show was in Manchester for the Manchester Versus Cancer charity. The rest were in the UK or Europe, topped off with a short South American tour in November 2006.

There's a DVD of the Glasgow shows that I helped put together. I find it a bit of an awkward thing to watch these days. There's some very odd alpha-male body language going on. Not all of it could be blamed on Hooky's bad back. I put the bonus DVD together from the pile of unlabelled VHS tapes, recordings of gigs I'd collected over the years as a budding video enthusiast. These tapes I like to think of as my archive, though most people refer to them as Stephen's pile of old shit.

I have some unusually vivid recollections of these gigs, particularly the one at the Manchester Apollo on 14 November 2005.

Towards the end of our first number, 'Ceremony', something went wrong. A sudden intense shock of sharp pain.

I felt as though I had been stabbed in the groin area. Somewhat taken aback by this, I instinctively stopped playing, as you would, to see if I'd been shot and was sitting in a pool of blood.

This prompted Bernard to comment as the song ground to a stop, 'Nice bit of improvising from Steve there.'

You fucking sarcastic twat! I thought. All the cock-ups you've made over the years – have I ever moaned? Bastard!

I spent the rest of the set trying to attract the attention of somebody – a roadie perhaps, preferably one with a medical background, anybody – but all eyes were fixed on the main men, Hooky and Bernard. Even Phil's attention was elsewhere.

Whenever my attempts at mouthing the words 'Doctor!' and 'Help!' did manage to catch someone's eye, they were met by a cheeky wink and a thumbs up from the crew. Just Steve's little joke. Ha fucking ha. I got to the end of the set in a state of extreme pain and hobbled off. The pain didn't leave, only festered.

It took several visits to the GP to get an answer to what might be the cause of this. I had, as my father would have put it, done myself a mischief. The old inguinal hernia, a sportsman's injury – scourge of the professional weightlifter.

How the hell had I, a natural shirker, managed to get one of those?

I was in agony for the next eighteen months, hobbling about and feeling miserable. Even more of an old git than normal, I had to wait until I had enough time off to find a surgeon to patch me up.

'I'm afraid it was pretty bad, much worse than I expected,' was his post-op summary. I could have told him that.

I began working with Gillian writing music for TV again during the summer break from touring. John Chapman was working on a series called *Goldplated*, a story of the post-millennial champagne-glugging Cheshire set. We were handy, well acquainted with the subject matter and so got the job. It felt a bit alien at first, just the two of us alone in the studio again. Nearly ten years had passed since we'd written anything together and much had changed. But not that much. We were soon back to bickering over cello sounds as if time had stood still.

Then the New Order tour resumed, and I returned to a world of more serious bickering or, worse, angry silences.

The Civic Hall at Wolverhampton was the scene of many epic wrestling 'matches' of the 1960s and 1970s, watched by the nation's kids and grannies on flickering black-and-white TVs as part of ITV's

Saturday afternoon sports ritual, *World of Sport*. Perhaps the most famous bout was the one culminating in the hotly anticipated unmasking of the superstar himself, the great enigmatic masked wrestler that was Kendo Nagasaki, in 1978.

The venue is circumnavigated by a one-way system, which means that any vehicle parked at the rear would have to perform a circuit of the building to get on the highway home. If the show was a sell-out, it could result in severe traffic congestion in front of this auspicious building. On this particular night in October 2006, this chaos was compounded by the fact that there were two gigs on that night. By an uncanny coincidence, the heroes of my youth, Hawkwind, were playing downstairs. It's a small world.

Having no inclination to hang about after the show for the enforced drinking and post-mortem of the night's sonic dissatisfaction, I decided to head home early and found myself stuck behind Hooky's Range Rover in the stationary after-show traffic jam.

It wasn't long before a large group of fans spotted the Hookmobile with its personalised registration and began tapping on his windows. This alerted others and in a short while a queue formed. A small posse broke off and began tapping anxiously on my window. I dutifully wound it down, expecting a polite 'All right, Steve, any chance of an autograph?'

What I got was 'Oi mate! Ya got a fuckin' pen?'

I rifled my pockets and had a look in the little box between the front seats. Nice collection of small change and an assortment of Happy Meal toys – but not even a pencil could I find.

'Er, no, very sorry, not got one.'

This was not the answer the music lover was looking for.

'Oh you fucking cunt! You bastard. Do you know who it is in that fucking car in front? It's only Peter Fucking Hook! PETER FUCKING HOOK! Fuck off, ya useless bastard. Tosser! Nah, Trev, this twat's not got one either,' as he banged in fury on my car roof.

Poor visual recall made manifest!

Unrecognised by the over-enthusiastic fans, I wondered if the legendary masked wrestler had ever suffered this experience and in a fit of pique decided to take drastic action.

I thought about joining the ranks of masked drummers like Thundersticks from Samson or that bloke from Slipknot. Maybe if I changed my car reg to STEVE1 and got a fuzzy-felt drum kit to hang from my rear-view mirror? Well, I thought it was funny. I chuckled all the way home.

The gigs ground to an end with a six-date South American tour, during the course of which Hooky's bass cab bore the nightly sprayed-on messages of:

Mister Horse
Two Little Boys
Formed a Band
It Fell Apart
The End

After the final show in Buenos Aires, Hooky and I were asked by a journalist what New Order would be doing next.

I replied that as Christmas was around the corner we would probably be having some turkey and time off.

'You have no plans?'

'Only Christmas dinner.'

Which the *Página*/12 journalist translated as 'we're splitting up'.

Funny how these things happen.

32

CONTROL

Writing about music has occasionally been likened to dancing about architecture. It's such a good quote that nobody's quite sure who said it in the first place. But if it's true (and I'm not sure that it is 100 per cent) then where does that leave making a film about music? Specifically a film about the life of a non-fictional musician and his life?

That Hollywood's first (almost) talking picture, *The Jazz Singer*, used a fictional tale of the good ole rags-to-riches story of a singer's triumph against the odds set some kind of precedent. The story of the struggling artiste was a proven winner at the box office. Today the film seems a little bit dodgy in places and it's hard to see what all of the fuss was about. But mixing music and movies was a winning combination.

I remember watching *The Glenn Miller Story* as a kid and loved the depiction of the 1930s swing band touring America on a train, Glenn and the boys having a jolly old singsong after the show in the dining car. A string of performances flashed by, time's passing represented by the clever device of dates fluttering away from a calendar. I did wonder how they got the piano in there.

Everybody had such a wonderful time apart from in the sad bits, of course, when they didn't.

As a youngster I knew very little of Glenn apart from he had some catchy tunes and met a mysterious end. Easy to the fill the blanks with life, love, struggle, failure, success, death – isn't that the formula for many a hit movie? Hang on, was that *The Glen Miller Story*? Or was it *The Benny Goodman Story*? Or am I getting it mixed up with Duke Ellington? So many bands, so many films, so many trains. They all rolled into one.

Either way a musical biopic could be a winner on a number of levels. If the music was good, all the better.

There's obviously more than a hint of nostalgia about Glenn's story and that's always a plus – the good old days, the ones you never actually knew and could never visit.

I'd never been a fan of modern rock biopics, though. I remember Oliver Stone's *The Doors* film and sometimes I wish I didn't. It put me off Jim Morrison for a long time. I'd been a fan since the seventies and despite the common Doors aficionado's doubts about the merits of *The Soft Parade*, I still played the records. But that film did nothing for me.

What happens then when you become the subject matter?

Your life as entertainment?

I suppose I've probably got to make an exception for the biopics in which I'm depicted in some way.

I've had minor roles in a couple of films. Not actually me, you understand, but someone pretending to be me.

In one, I actually managed to string a coherent sentence together. Gillian only got a giggle, so I shouldn't complain.

But if hearing the sound of your recorded voice for the first time is odd, seeing someone pretending to be you on screen is positively surreal. Not just one, but two films and I'm still alive to moan about them.

That must be some kind of achievement in itself.

I remember sitting in the Bull's Head in 1980s Macclesfield, not long after Ian's death. Gloomily stewing over a pint of bitter shandy and being existentially pretentious.

'One day, they'll be here with their bloody cameras wanting to make a film of the whole sorry shebang.' Luckily no one was paying much attention. 'Well, when they do, they can fuck off, I'm not having anything to do with it.'

There I was, a young man of principles being boring and tedious again.

The Joy Division film was something Rob Gretton predicted too, though he saw it in a positive light – a good thing.

'It's going to be big, you know, the Joy Division film. Someone's going to make one, bet ya, it's going to be fucking mega,' he'd say in some smoky dressing room in the mid-eighties. We all laughed, lit up, and carried on drinking.

'Yeah Rob, right, how much?' someone said.

'The Joy Division revival an' all, that's going to be fucking huge! Bet ya a tenner.'

He never collected on that one.

Two films and Rob is probably the best thing in both of them. Larger than life even in death.

The Factory story reimagined almost as a knockabout comedy romp was the first: 2002's *24 Hour Party People* with Steve Coogan doing a heroic Partridge-based Tony Wilson impression. It took a few goes before I could enjoy that one.

I like Gillian and her sister Julie's totally unnoticed and unplanned cameo at the end of the film, in that blink-and-you'll-miss-it final frame.

I'm not with them. I got the babysitting that night instead. It was probably for the best. Over half of Manchester's many musicians are in there somewhere making cameos and one less drummer is neither here nor there.

The supposedly Gillian-less New Order contributed a new track as a unique selling point on the soundtrack CD: the Chemical Brothers' mix of *Get Ready* leftover 'Here to Stay'. In fact, the music for both that song and its B-side 'Player in the League' features Gillian lurking spectrally in the background as they were recorded in 2000–1. The single charted and in the now customary process triggered a *TOTP* mime-a-thon. Revisiting it now, I've got to say there was a notable lack of conviction on the part of the drummer on that TV performance. Sorry, like most gigs of that era my mind was elsewhere.

One of the side effects of 24 *Hour Party People* was that of exponentially increasing the spread of the Factory mythology, or as Tony allegedly says, 'Given the choice between fact or myth – print the myth.'

Or something like that.

In one scene in the film, I am depicted playing the drums on the studio roof, abandoned and alone while the rest of the band fuck off home. It is very funny. I laugh every time I see it. It's become the source of the one question I always get asked, well the one after the one about Ian's death:

'Did you really play the drums on the roof of the studio?' or 'Why did Martin make you play on the roof?'

'Do I honestly look that stupid?' has become my stock reply. I'm not a complete idiot (OK, I am sometimes, but we'll keep that between ourselves . . .). It never actually happened. You may have noticed, I'm scared of heights, for a start. Plus drums generally don't sound that good outdoors. It is a good story, though, and in one brief scene it manages to sum up what working with Martin Hannett could actually be like, leaving you feeling neglected and knowing that all your work was pointless. I wonder which is the funniest: the reality that I would just carry on drumming even though nobody was actually listening, or the bizarre fiction of somebody ardently bashing drums on a roof at night?

Following on from the knockabout yarn of a record company going bust with hilarious consequences came 2007's *Control*, based on Debbie Curtis's book of her life with Ian.

It was a totally different prospect. Directed by our friend Anton Corbijn it is appropriately shot in black and white, which gives it the feel of a bleak, northern, angry-young-man drama from the sixties.

It gives Macclesfield an atmosphere and a sense of poetry that it's never managed to manifest in real life.

When Anton was shooting the scenes outside Ian's house on Barton Street, I received a number of confused calls from my Auntie Elsie wanting to know what was going on and 'would they be finished soon, only they've blocked off me way to the doctors'. I said I'd have a word.

It made the front page of the local paper.

Control is a very difficult film for me to watch. It was hard the first time and it never gets any easier.

Not that it's a bad movie – on the contrary, it's very good. Anton did a fantastic job of translating Ian's life into a film. The way the actors – the screen band – learned to play the songs, rather than just miming, worked brilliantly. The fact that they get better as the film goes on is a nice touch.

During the on again/off again period of the film's development we had meetings with Orian Williams, one of the producers. I think he wanted to keep us informed and involved in some way although we were always kind of involved whether we liked it or not.

We aren't much cop at acting, and neither are we film-makers, but there was an unspoken assumption that we might do music of some kind for the film – we could do that at least. Hooky came up with the suggestion that we could call ourselves Joy Division again. I have to say that I thought it was one of the worst ideas I'd ever heard, and I've had some stinkers myself in my time. But names aside, there was an anticipation or expectation there: that we would do *something*.

There ended up being a peculiar symmetry about it, this being the last music the three survivors would do together.

If you could call it together.

Who would have thought something so simple could end up being so divisive? Anton had worked out which bits of the film might need some original music and he passed these three clips on to Bernard with a request for him to put together some ideas for something ambient. Which, of course, Bernard did.

Unfortunately nobody told Hooky about this – I can't think why as he was bound to hear about it sooner or later. On finding out, he got rather upset and annoyed, mainly with Anton for apparently cutting him out. All right, he got *really* upset and annoyed. So the whole thing once more turned into an eggshell exercise in diplomacy.

To try and defuse this situation, Anton and Hooky came to the farm to record some bass on Bernard's finished synth and piano ideas. I don't think anybody particularly wanted any drums on the tracks, but as I was sat there, recording and editing, a suggestion that I might do something came up. Just in case I too got a bit shirty about being neglected.

I really wanted to add some foetal monitor sounds – the spooky sound of an unborn child's heartbeat – but having neither an ultrasound machine nor expectant mother to hand, the less radical tapping noise won out. I'm not sure my itchy-scratchy percussion parts added anything at all, to be honest. A bit superfluous.

In fact, if anything the percussion made them worse.

Though Hooky's relationship with Bernard was at an all-time low, he still remained friendly with me. I did a radio show with him sometime around Christmas 2006. We did our best to be amicable towards each other. Falling out would get us nowhere.

I was more than a little surprised when, shortly before the premiere of *Control* at the Cannes film festival, I received a call from a journalist at the *Manchester Evening News*. She was after a quote on the New Order split.

'What New Order Split?' I asked. 'That's news to me.' Which, despite the Argentinian journalist's earlier attempts at making a story out of nothing, it was.

'Well, according to Peter Hook, New Order are splitting up. Do you have anything to say about it?' continued the fishing.

'Well, we're about to finish off another album.'

Which wasn't really what she was looking for.

The story was in that night's edition of the *Manchester Evening News.*

New Order, Manchester's pride and joy, may well have split up. Peter Hook, the band's legendary bassist, told a radio station that he was no longer working with Bernard Sumner.

According to NME.com, speaking about his involvement in Perry Farrell's Satellite Party, Peter Hook told Xfm that the band have broken up.

He said: 'I spoke to Perry, and he asked me to play bass, as he'd heard about New Order splitting up. Well yeah, me and Bernard (Sumner) aren't working together.'

On the split, he added: 'Bernard went off for a break with Electronic, but that was different. But it's like the boy who cried wolf this time.'

The band formed in 1980, following the suicide of Ian Curtis and the disintegration of Joy Division.

Over the next decade the band invented British dance music and became heroes to a generation.

The story of their lives is also shared by Tony Wilson and Factory Records.

The band eventually bankrolled the Haçienda, Manchester's infamous nightclub.

These were heady days, when New Order and Wilson seemed to rule the world. This period of time was famously re-imagined in Michael Winterbottom's acclaimed 2002 flick *24 Hour Party People.*

While New Order entered into the folklore of the city some time ago, they will be remembered firstly for their music.

Albums like *Low-life, Power, Corruption and Lies* and *Technique* contribute to what is a magnificent body of work.

While a clutch of young pretenders like The Killers clearly

walk in their shadow, New Order will be remembered for their originality and generation-defining brilliance.

This was not exactly what I was expecting to read, an obituary almost, but I do like the generation-defining brilliance bit. Oh, and the bet hedging 'may well have'.

Of course, you are probably aware that New Order did not split up for good and Gillian, if not Hooky, would miraculously return to the fold, but for a few years after that article was printed, it really was the end of New Order.

18 May 2007.
Twenty-seven years on from Ian's suicide I found myself in the sunny south of France, a world away from Barton Street, West Park and what was left of Macclesfield's pubs and clubs.

The *Control* premiere at Cannes was a frosty affair between us.

AWKWARD!

If the body language in the *Live in Glasgow* DVD is awkward, the photos from Cannes depict a new low in band relations. Following the *Evening News* revelation, Bernard was understandably furious. I wasn't exactly happy with the way things had turned out either.

At the fancy film-biz soirée after the film's screening, Gillian, who'd come along for moral support, was impressed. Video footage of Joy Division playing at the Plan K in 1979 was projected on a huge screen. Someone said, 'Ian would have loved it.' But actually I suspect he would have hated the whole affair.

The funny thing was that, had Joy Division turned up at the same sort of event back in 1979, we'd have been swiftly shown the door. That's if we could have blagged our way in. Now we were the toast of the town.

What was left of us.

Later that year, as a sort of companion piece to *Control*, the documentary *Joy Division* was released. Directed by Grant Gee, produced by Tom Atencio and brilliantly written and put together by Jon Savage, it told the story of Joy Division in the words of the people who were there at the time, including Annik Honoré and, especially poignantly, Tony Wilson, without whom everything would have been very different.

Tony died shortly after the film was completed.

33

FRACTURED MUSIC

18 June 2007.

A month after the Cannes screening, Joy Division were being feted yet again. This time we'd been nominated for another award, *Mojo* magazine's Outstanding Contribution award. I say 'we' but by this time it seemed like the band that was being celebrated was not the same one I remembered. As if the story being told had all happened to somebody else and I was a stand-in or fake of some kind.

We'd all been invited but only me and Hooky ended up going.

I quite fancied the line-up at this one: Alice Cooper, the Stooges, Suicide, Jac Holzman and the Only Ones seemed a better offering than most awards nominations. Well, to an old git like me it did. If there was one shindig I should never have attended, however, it would be this one.

A couple of nights before, Gillian had discovered a lump on her breast. I offered my usual optimistic and completely unreliable medical opinion that it was most likely nothing but, better safe than sorry, get it checked out.

It wasn't nothing.

Half an hour after receiving the award I got a call from Gillian.

'It's cancer.'

The words nobody should ever have to hear.

That blood-freezing word. The bogeyman of the modern world.

Joy Division's Outstanding Contribution to music was suddenly insignificant. What the fuck was I doing here anyway? Collecting a bit of plastic to sit on somebody's mantelpiece, a bit of well done lads bonhomie and polite back-slapping. All at once I felt sick, selfish and stupid. An inconsiderate fool.

Nobody said the words 'You think more of that band than you do of me' but I heard them just the same.

What had I been thinking? Really, what was more important – a band or my wife and kids? Life suddenly seemed very precious and very short.

You know what *they* say: 'It certainly put things into perspective.'

Well, this time for once, they were right.

From now on, I would concentrate on what really mattered. And that wasn't being in a band.

After losing my Dad and going through Grace's illness this was the worst thing yet. I had no idea what to do, what to say. I felt pathetic.

I clung to my sense of optimism although it hadn't done me much good so far, but the alternative was too painful to consider, all I could do was believe and hope and trust in something beyond my comprehension.

And wish it was me instead.

There was no way of avoiding that first thought – as a kid growing up – cancer was synonymous with death.

Then scouring the internet and asking questions, learning new words like lobular and ductal, about stages one to four and survival statistics over five years. It's almost too much to take in, when all you want is a straight answer to the question 'what are the chances?'

Gillian had surgery to remove the lump and lymph nodes. She was attached to a thing that looked like a jam jar to drain out the fluid. On one surreal afternoon I remember we snuck out of hospital for a couple of hours for a Japanese meal. We were trying to act normal, wondering where we could hide the tubes and stuff without alarming the waitress or knife-juggling teppanyaki chef. I think we got away with it, despite the cannula sticking out of Gillian's hand.

The next nine months were scary and gruelling. A rollercoaster of ups and downs. As anyone who's been through it will tell you, radiation and chemotherapy are not fun. But mostly they do work.

Gillian's last chemo was on New Year's Eve, 2007. A year we were both glad to see the back of. Now, we could try and get on with living again.

While Gillian was at the Christie in Didsbury, Tony was in the same hospital.

At the time we didn't know, had no idea, being so wrapped up in what we were going through. Only when we'd heard of his death did we realise how close he'd been.

The Christie is only a couple of hundred yards away from Alan's Palatine Road flat, which had been Factory's office when we were all young, optimistic and full of ideas. Tony's old house with the video bunker was just across the road – more of life's surprising symmetries.

Growing old means going to an ever-increasing number of funerals. It's life's brutal way of reminding us that we are all running out of road. The gathering of a circle that gets smaller with each passing year, until there is no one left to remember what really happened.

But what you really want to know is what happened with New Order? Same thing that happens all the time with people. They fall out. There is always the expectation that, as you grow older, you grow wiser, you grow up. Maybe in some respects you do. Maybe in many more respects you don't.

Hooky and Bernard had known each other since they were boys at school, so by 2007 that was what – over forty years?

A long time.

I'd known them both for the best part of that. Chances are, you're bound to have a few differences in forty years. Little personal tics that used to be only mildly annoying or even laughable at times become a source of major grievance and even anger.

Bernard could not stand the way Hooky ate his crisps. He also had the problem with my manner of food consumption. Also too noisy apparently.

Hooky didn't think that Gillian contributed anything to the band, so probably didn't think she actually ever was in the band properly.

Hooky felt Bernard spent too much time faffing about in the studio with synths when we should have been playing live.

I thought the pair of them could be a right pain in the arse at times about most things, and they both probably felt the same about me.

Gillian didn't like Hooky's apparent sexism.

Hooky didn't like Bernard always getting his own way.

And so on and so on. The list of gripes was endless. I know that it used to drive Rob up the wall towards the end, ground him down, and it can't have been easy for Rebecca and Andy.

The frequently thankless task of band management has much in common with cat herding when it comes to frustration and complication. The thing is, you put up with the complaints and tribulations because at the end of the day they're relatively minor compared to the good things.

Being in a band and being able to make a living out of doing something creative is a very good thing, I think you'll agree.

We've all had our moments, our tantrums, our 'That's fucking it! I am never ever doing this ever again!' episodes of pique, usually accompanied by a feeling of a head being repeatedly rammed against a brick wall.

So I take break, count to ten, sleep on it, whatever, and eventually forget what it was that got me so fucking wound up in the first place . . . until the next time. It's the same as any job.

As long as the good outweighs the bad, as long as you can keep your ego under control and are prepared to compromise, then it isn't a problem. But sooner or later . . . somebody isn't able to do that.

And maybe that was Hooky. As I have said, I understood his problems. Yes, working with Bernard could be annoying at times, he can be a right fucking pain, anyone can. In essence, the problems were old, but the degree of animosity was new.

None of this had much to do with music – apart from Hooky's long-held suspicion that synths and sequencers debased the purity of what he felt were our origins. There was no criticism of anybody's musicianship at all. Nor were there many complaints about Bernard's songwriting, apart from the aforementioned use of digital devilry. The problems lay in the differences between us as people.

That was the real basis.

It didn't take much to work that out. After all, Hooky made it clear with his statement on his bass cabs on the South American tour: 'Two Little Boys/Formed a Band/It Fell Apart/The End'. Very dramatic. (I'd often thought of selling advertising space on my bass drum, but I could never find a product with a short enough name.) But there it was: a matter between the two of them.

The exuberance of youth!

For at the start of the affair, when we are fresh and young, that's when the tearing down of the wall has the most appeal, when the demolition men have the least to lose – usually nothing. All for one, and one for all. In our case, in the early days, the democracy and not just the management was a major force in shifting the whole band edifice.

As we age we attract responsibilities – everyone does and

musicians are no exception. The appeal, the revolutionary zeal, palls and the lure of the apparent security offered by the standard rules of rock and roll takes hold. You want to be the leader. By then, you've probably developed enough petty grievances against the other members of the dysfunctional band family that thoughts of scuttling the vessel are happening on at least a monthly basis.

What to do?

When you can't see the wood for all the stuff that looks like wood. Take an axe and wildly swing at all of it?

The truth is that it's physically and mentally impossible to keep doing the same thing over and over to infinity. You cannot keep churning out music and going on ever-expanding tours ad infinitum. Why? People will get sick and tired of you for a start, and you'll get sick and tired of each other.

Why not take break? Go fishing, take up yoga, gardening or tank driving. To survive, go on holiday (this is rich coming from a self-confessed holiday hater!). Not everyone will agree with that decision or its timing, but for the greater good . . . A break must be taken, just for a bit of a rest, some fresh air. Perhaps have a trial separation rather than a divorce, and everything will be OK.

We did that a couple of times, took a break from New Ordering, did other things. Most of these other things were musical tasks, so not quite the break it could have been, but, hey, spilt milk. A break couldn't make things worse, could it? We took breaks in 1989–93 and 1998–2001 for various reasons, but what was behind the reasons never really went away. Maybe therapy would have been a better bet. But I don't think that, by 2006, even that would have helped.

But what do you do if you are absolutely convinced that this is no longer what you want and there's been some dreadful irreconcilable breakdown? Do you gather your workmates together and explain that, after all the years of forced camaraderie, of fun, excitement, frolics and tears, being in the band is no longer for you? Do you bid your former bandmates a fond adieu and wish them well in their future musical endeavours?

Or do you say, 'Listen, lads (no need to bother with the girl as I never thought she was in the band anyway) – it's over. I'm through with this band lark. And if I'm not doing it any more, then you bunch of washed-up has-beens aren't either! Without me you're nothing. NOTHING!'

If only there was a book of rock-and-roll etiquette, a *Haynes Manual for Leaving a Band in an Amicable Manner* or something. Band disagreements are frequently best described as 'acrimonious' or 'messy' in much the same way as divorces are. There are definitely similarities. The word 'amicable' is very rarely to be seen and, when it is, it is generally hissed through the gritted teeth of a press release.

Members leave bands all the time, members get sacked from bands all the time – quite frequently drummers, but that's beside the point. Bands occasionally fracture in two (there are, I think, two bands called Faust, both containing ex-members of the original band also called Faust).

Splitting up a band can be even more complicated than divorce.

Nobody wins. It's madness to think that anybody does.

The songs remain unsullied by their feuding creators. They still get played. They still sell, they still make money. They still bring pleasure and have meaning. And so the grievances become monetary or matters of pride; legacy, it turns out, is a commercial reckoning. Meanwhile, as the music still exists, to the outside world there remains a perceived relationship between people who, at best, are no longer on each other's Christmas card list. And, at worst, consider each other party to some legal and/or psychological warfare. The former band members still have to deal with each other at some level, usually through a lawyer.

Bearing all this in mind I did my best to encourage my children to consider a career in psychology or the legal profession if they wanted to get into the music business. Of course, I failed in that one too.

There have been times over the years when I have hated everyone and everything involved in the New Order/Factory saga. More times than I can count, I've said to myself and others – Gillian mostly – 'That's it! I cannot stand any more of this shit. XXX is driving me insane.' I have found myself wallowing in various other forms of bitching common to the music game – too numerous to mention, and you've heard them all before.

Ultimately, though, when I weigh things up in the cold light of day the scales of pleasure and pain tip ever so slightly to the fun side. If the thrill factor exceeds the grief by even a whisker, it's still worth doing.

If there is only a deficit in the enjoyment column and nothing but a pain and anguish dividend, it's probably time to quit, move on and open a funfair.

For a band that once eschewed T-shirts in favour of tiny badges as their main method of merchandising, Joy Division in the twenty-first century have become an example of cultural iconography. The *Unknown Pleasures* cover is shorthand for a state of mind, and is available on jackets, T-shirts, dresses, shoes, knickers, hats, duvet covers, socks ... The list is mind-boggling and summed up in song by Half Man Half Biscuit's 'Joy Division Oven Gloves'.

You could be forgiven for thinking that I and the surviving members of Joy Division lie awake at night, thinking of new and devious ways to get the band immortalised on an ever-expanding range of bizarre artefacts. I don't, by the way. I do wonder who exactly does come up with these peculiar items. I have to acknowledge that I do get paid for some of them, so I shouldn't gripe that much. It is creepy and bewildering though.

Quite how this has come to be mystifies me at times. That

something I was part of for an all too brief period at the end of the 1970s has become something far bigger than any of us could have hoped or dreamed of at the time. That the *idea* of Joy Division is something that today transcends the music we produced is something that I find both humbling and absolutely staggering at the same time.

Nothing lasts forever. Energy runs out. We all decay and die. But ideas, although mutable, do persist, and whatever you may say or think about some of ours now, they were good at the time.

The music being the best of them.

I still believe that music is magical. That it can do things that appear impossible. That a sound can make you involuntarily weep, can make you move your feet, can make you cheer. That's pretty magical, isn't it?

'Is that it? I was expecting something . . . More. A bit of a punch up or a courtroom-drama showdown, perhaps.

Well, honestly, there are more endings to this story than a jumbo-sized can of worms, so no this isn't the end. Eventually Gillian came back and the band that raised itself from the ashes of Joy Division raised itself from the ashes of New Order. But the hows and the whys, that's a whole other book. Maybe one day . . .

PLAYLIST

Since this is book mostly about music, I thought it would be handy to include some – so you might get some idea of what I'm waffling on about. Since everyone enjoyed the Spotify playlist I made for the last book, I thought I'd have a go at making another one. At times I wished I hadn't, for in the process of revisiting some of my eighties purchases, I found many things that should really have remained hidden in the cupboard of bad taste.

I also found myself fretting that maybe I only really enjoyed music from the early seventies – 1974 to be specific.

Music from a pre digital/video-game era seemed to me much more diverse and interesting somehow. And maybe my taste just got a bit wayward in the eighties. (This was another worrying thought for I remember it all sounded great at the time.)

Still, the 1990s and 2000s could be included by bending the rules slightly, so surely it wasn't going to be too difficult? I did my best but ultimately a few songs that 'technically fell outside my intended timeframe' slipped through the net.

So, before you say: '"Nite flights", "Supernature", "Dream Baby Dream" and "The Belldog" are all from the wrong era and so shouldn't really have been included here. What were you thinking, Morris?'

'Too much four on the floor!!!'

'Some of these tracks only came out last week!!!'

'Wot? No Steely Dan... Shame on you.'

I hold my hands up and say, 'It's a fair cop'. I'm sorry. I really am. I broke all of my self-imposed rules of compilation. I did my best, but some songs from the seventies just refused to budge. On the plus side there are more than last time. Is that a plus? I hope so.

I find it best listened to with the Spotify shuffle switch on. Some of the algorithm's selections can be a little wayward but mostly they are genius.

So here it is for your Spotify listening pleasure: https://lnk.to/FastForward Enjoy.

The Walker Brothers, 'Nite Flights'
Warren ft. Nate Dogg, 'Regulate'
Black Devil Disco Club, '"H" Friend'
Sigue Sigue Sputnik, 'Love Missile F1-11'
Cabaret Voltaire, 'Sensoria (7" Version)'
Grace Jones, 'Pull Up to the Bumper'
Lloyd Cole and the Commotions, 'Rattlesnakes'
Marcel King, 'Reach for Love'
Echo and the Bunnymen, 'Bring on the Dancing Horses'
The Kinks, 'Celluloid Heroes'
The Jesus and Mary Chain, 'Just Like Honey'
Hashim, 'Al-Naafiysh (The Soul)'
Fujiya & Miyagi, 'Swoon'
Liaisons Dangereuses, 'Los Niños del Parque'
Klein & M.B.O., 'Dirty Talk'
Grandmaster Flash & the Furious Five, 'The Adventures of Grandmaster Flash on the Wheels of Steel (Extended Mix)'
Patrick Cowley ft. Sylvester, 'Do You Wanna Funk?'
The Chemical Brothers, 'Hey Boy Hey Girl'
The Cure, 'Inbetween Days'
The Leather Nun, 'Pink House'
Malcolm McLaren, 'Madam Butterfly (Un Bel Di Vedremo)'
Fun Boy Three, 'Our Lips Are Sealed'
A Guy Called Gerald, 'Voodoo Ray'
Mogwai, 'Tracy'
Prince, 'Sign 'O' the Times'
Mr Fingers, 'Can You Feel It'
Factory Floor, 'Fall Back'
David Bowie, 'Lazarus'
Trent Reznor & Atticus Ross, 'Nun with a Motherf*&*ing Gun'

Secret Machines, 'Nowhere Again'

Ennio Morricone, 'For a Few Dollars More: Watch Chimes (Carillion's Theme)'

Kate Bush, 'Hounds of Love'

Peter Hammill, 'Ophelia'

Robert Wyatt, 'Shipbuilding (1998 Remaster)'

Afrika Bambaataa & the Soulsonic Force, 'Planet Rock'

Sharon Redd, 'Beat the Street (Mastermix)'

Elkin & Nelson, 'Jibaro (Enrolle)'

Hot Chip, 'No Fit State'

The Flaming Lips, 'Do You Realize??'

Neil Young, 'Misfits'

Belly, 'Feed the Tree'

Material with Nona Hendryx, 'Busting Out'

Big Audio Dynamite, 'E=MC2'

The BPA, Fatboy Slim & Iggy Pop, 'He's Frank – Slight Return'

Ultra Vivid Scene, 'Staring at the Sun'

ABC, 'All of My Heart'

Shannon, 'Let the Music Play'

Wire, 'Kidney Bingos'

LCD Soundsystem, 'All My Friends'

Spiritualized, 'Run'

S'Express, 'Theme from S-Express'

A Certain Ratio, 'Flight'

Pet Shop Boys, 'Left to My Own Devices (2001 Remaster)'

DJ Shadow, 'Building Steam with a Grain of Salt'

Kraftwerk, 'Computer World (2009 Remaster)'

Max Richter, 'The Leftovers (Main Title Theme)'

Frank Sidebottom, 'Timperley Blues'

Tom Tom Club, 'Genius of Love'

The Smiths, 'There Is a Light That Never Goes Out (2011 Remaster)'

Johnny Cash, 'Hurt'

Cerrone, 'Supernature'

Mory Kante, 'Yeke Yeke (Short Mix)'

DAF, 'Der Mussolini (1998 Remastered)'

The Meters, 'Hey Pocky A-Way (Remastered Version)'

The Fall, 'Shoulder Pads #1'

New Order, 'Murder'
Delta 5, 'Mind Your Own Business'
Donna Summer, 'Our Love'
Jack Ruby, 'Global Torrents'
The Primitives, 'Crash'
William Onyeabor, 'This Kind of World'
A Girl Called Eddy, 'Tears All Over Town'
Daniel Johnston, 'Devil Town'
Martha and the Muffins, 'Echo Beach'
The Monochrome Set, 'Alphaville'
Saint Etienne, 'You're in a Bad Way'
Roy Budd, 'Main Theme (Carter Takes a Train)'
Eno Moebius Roedelius, 'The Belldog'
Sniff 'n' the Tears, 'Driver's Seat'
Suicide, 'Dream Baby Dream'
Beyond The Wizards Sleeve, 'Creation'
M.I.A., 'Boyz'
Soft Cell, 'Memorabilia (Non-stop Ecstatic Dancing Version)'
Half Man Half Biscuit, 'Joy Division Oven Gloves'
The Human League, 'Being Boiled (Fast Version)'
The Unknown Cases, 'Masimba Bele'
Junior Byron, 'Dance to the Music'
British Sea Power, 'No Lucifer'
Jamie T, 'Sticks 'n' Stones'
Moebius & Plank, 'Conditionierer'